CURRENT PERSPECTIVES
ON AGING AND
THE LIFE CYCLE

Volume 1 • 1985

WORK, RETIREMENT,
AND SOCIAL POLICY

CURRENT PERSPECTIVES ON AGING AND THE LIFE CYCLE

A Research Annual

WORK, RETIREMENT AND SOCIAL POLICY

Editor: ZENA SMITH BLAU
Department of Sociology
University of Houston

VOLUME 1 • 1985

 JAI PRESS INC.

Greenwich, Connecticut   *London, England*

Copyright © 1985 by JAI PRESS INC.
36 Sherwood Place
Greenwich, Connecticut 06830

JAI PRESS INC.
3 Henrietta Street
London WC2E 8LU
England

All rights reserved. No part of this publication may be reproduced, stored on a retrieval system, or transmitted in any form or by any means, electronic, mechanical, photocopying, filming, recording, or otherwise without prior permission in writing from the publisher.

ISBN: 0-89232-296-9

Manufactured in the United States of America

CONTENTS

LIST OF CONTRIBUTORS	vii
PREFACE *Zena Smith Blau*	ix
INTRODUCTION *Zena Smith Blau*	xi
PARENTAL INFLUENCES ON THE TIMING OF EARLY LIFE TRANSITIONS *Dennis P. Hogan*	1
PROCESSES OF ACHIEVEMENT IN THE TRANSITION TO ADULTHOOD *Geoffrey Maruyama, Michael D. Finch and Jeylan T. Mortimer*	61
AGE, COHORT, AND REPORTED JOB SATISFACTION IN THE UNITED STATES *Norval D. Glenn and Charles N. Weaver*	89
OCCUPATIONAL STRUCTURE AND RETIREMENT *Melissa A. Hardy*	111
PLANNED AND ACTUAL RETIREMENT: AN EMPIRICAL ANALYSIS *Richard V. Burkhauser and Joseph P. Quinn*	147
NONMARRIED WOMEN APPROACHING RETIREMENT: WHO ARE THEY AND WHEN DO THEY RETIRE? *Gayle Thompson Rogers*	169

WORK AND RETIREMENT AMONG THE BLACK
ELDERLY
   James S. Jackson and Rose C. Gibson   193

VARIATION IN SELECTED FORMS OF LEISURE
ACTIVITY AMONG ELDERLY MALES
   Herbert S. Parnes and Lawrence Less   223

DETERMINANTS OF LABOR FORCE
PARTICIPATION RATES OF AGED MALES IN
DEVELOPED AND DEVELOPING NATIONS,
1965–1975
   Fred C. Pampel   243

SOCIAL SECURITY-TYPE RETIREMENT POLICIES:
A CROSS-NATIONAL STUDY
   Robert C. Atchley   275

CHINESE RETIREMENT: POLICY AND PRACTICE
   Deborah Davis-Friedmann   295

THE VANISHING BABUSHKA: A ROLELESS
ROLE FOR THE OLDER SOVIET WOMEN?
   Stephen Sternheimer   315

EMPLOYMENT POLICY AND OLDER
AMERICANS: A FRAMEWORK AND ANALYSIS
   Stephen H. Sandell   335

INDEX   355

LIST OF CONTRIBUTORS

Robert C. Atchley   Scripps Foundation Gerontology Center, Miami University, Oxford, Ohio

Richard V. Burkhauser   Institute for Public Policy Studies and Department of Economics, Vanderbilt University

Deborah Davis-Friedman   Department of Sociology, Yale University

Michael D. Finch   Department of Sociology, University of Minnesota

Rose C. Gibson   Institute of Gerontology, University of Michigan

Norval D. Glenn   Department of Sociology, University of Texas at Austin

Melissa A. Hardy   Department of Sociology, Florida State University

Dennis P. Hogan   Population Research Center, Department of Sociology, University of Chicago

James S. Jackson   Institute for Social Research, University of Michigan

Lawrence Less   Center for Human Resources Psychology, University of Minnesota

Geoffrey Maruyama	Department of Educational Psychology, University of Minnesota
Jeylan T. Mortimer	Department of Sociology, University of Minnesota
Fred C. Pampel	Department of Sociology, Iowa State University
Herbert S. Parnes	Center for Human Resources Research, Ohio State University
Joseph P. Quinn	Department of Economics, Boston College
Gayle Thompson Rogers	Formerly Social Security Administration, Department of Health and Human Services
Stephen H. Sandell	National Commission for Employment Policy, Washington, D.C.
Stephen Sternheimer	Central Intelligence Agency, Columbia, Maryland
Charles N. Weaver	Department of Management, St. Mary's University, San Antonio, Texas

PREFACE

This volume is the first in an ongoing series that I have titled *Current Perspectives on Aging and the Life Cycle*. The series is intended to serve as a forum for the publication of new work on aging viewed in a life cycle perspective. According to this view aging is a multifaceted and continuous process that extends from birth to death. At the societal level age is a basis for the allocation of institutional roles and the life cycle is partitioned into a succession of stages that pattern the timing of entry, the duration of performance, and timing of exit from such roles. In societies and historical epochs in which the typical life span is short the duration of each stage of life is shorter and less differentiated than in contemporary industrial societies in which life expectancy has increased dramatically and the stages of life correspondingly have become more differentiated. Thus adolescence and old age have both emerged as distinctive life stages in the twentieth century, due in part to age based social policies in industrial nations designed to defer the entry of young people and to hasten the exit of older people from the full-time labor force.

The widening recognition that individual aging must be viewed in a broader social and temporal context is one of the important developments that has taken place in the social sciences over the past few decades. People are members of cohorts by virtue of the timing of their birth. In rapidly changing societies the size, composition and other properties of successive cohorts vary. Advances in knowledge and technology, changes in the occupational structure and in educational levels, significant historical events such as war or depression, and social policy innovations interact in myriad ways to produce differences in the distribution of economic and social resources, and changes in expectations, beliefs and behavior among people of similar age in successive birth cohorts. The extent of such changes is constrained by existing social institutions but may also precipitate changes in their forms and functions.

The recognition that the aging process is conditioned by broader social and historical contexts constrains scholars in various disciplines to take a new look at old generalizations about age strata and to reconsider the extent to which observed differences are products of aging per se or of specific properties of cohorts or of specifiable historical events.

My hope in launching this new series is to bring together the work of scholars from various disciplines and from various nations who share an interest in the life cycle or life course perspective. Theory and research, macro and micro, qualitative and quantitative, historical and contemporary, comparative approaches and case studies will be welcome. The series will also provide an opportunity for interested scholars not merely to author chapters but also to serve as editors or co-editors of future volumes organized around broad themes or issues relevant to aging and the life cycle.

Zena Smith Blau
Series Editor

INTRODUCTION:
WORK, RETIREMENT AND SOCIAL POLICY

The far reaching significance of work in defining and shaping adulthood was eloquently summed up by Robert and Helen Lynd, (1937:7) more than fifty years ago:

> One's job is the watershed down which the rest of one's life tends to flow in Middletown. Who one is, whom one knows, how one lives, what one aspires to be—these and many other urgent realities of living are patterned . . . by what one does to get a living and the amount of living this allows one to buy.

The Lynds were the first sociologists, to my knowledge, to call attention to the changing age and sex composition of the American work force already evident during the 1920s and to predict (correctly, it turns out) that these changes constituted the beginning of a trend that would accelerate in future decades.

Age increasingly has become an instrument of public policy, corporate practice, and union pressure to control the timing of entry into and exit from the regular labor force in the United States.

As societies industrialize, the place of work in the human life cycle undergoes profound changes and conceptions of the stages of life become more differentiated. Thus, adolescence and old age as distinct stages of life are each creations of modernity. Mechanization and automation lead to surpluses of human labor and political strategies are developed and deployed to regulate and control unemployment.

The span of ages during which men in particular are expected to engage in fulltime work narrows and tends to coincide with the ages during which they usually marry and rear children. Full time, year round jobs in the core industrial-corporate sector of the economy increasingly have become the preserve of men and women between the ages of twenty and fifty.

A detailed examination of the ways in which public policies, corporate practices and union pressures have interacted to raise the ages at which young people normally enter the regular work force is beyond the scope of the present discussion. It goes without saying that the long term secular trend in the United States toward extending the years of required and expected full time school attendance is the basic factor that has operated to delay the timing of entry into the regular work force. Legislation that prohibited child labor in the industrial sector which began to be enacted by some states around the turn of the century marked the onset of this trend and a mosaic of educational policies and other types of governmental regulations to discourage firms from hiring minors that developed in ensuing decades further promoted it.

The massive immigration into the United States between 1880 and 1920 and the large migration of young adults from rural to urban industrial centers in the 1920s provided an ample supply of young adult workers. The problem of teenage unemployment and rising unemployment rates and job insecurity among blue collar workers over age forty first surfaced during that decade of prosperity. Faced with the choice between enforced idleness or prolonging their years of schooling, rising proportions of teenagers completed high school and went on to college, more so those from middle class families but also some from working class families who did well in school (Lynd and Lynd, 1937:48).

The massive unemployment during the great Depression affected all age groups and the Roosevelt administration in an unprecedentedly short period of time initiated and gained ratification by congress of numerous measures designed to reduce joblessness in the country. Included in the National Recovery Administration Act of 1933, for example, was a provision prohibiting employment of children under 18 in manufacturing and mining. Other provisions set a minimum wage and maximum hours of employment for all employees. The NRA was declared unconstitutional by the Supreme Court in 1935 but the above provisions were incorporated into the Fair Labor Standards Act of 1938 and declared constitutional by the court (Redford, 1965:287). As the rehiring of workers began it became evident that large manufacturing firms gave preference to workers in their twenties and thirties who had the strength and endurance to keep up with the fast pace of machine production (Lynd and Lynd, 1937:52). In 1935 over half of American men 65 and older remained unemployed.

It was in this context that the Social Security Act was enacted fifty years ago. It was a wide ranging piece of legislation that first and foremost established an old age insurance system (OAI) to provide a modicum of economic security for workers beginning at age 65 (which was expanded in 1939 to provide benefits to

Introduction xiii

workers' survivors-spouses and dependent children until age 18) to be financed by payroll taxes paid by employers and employees over their working years, and administered by the federal government. Other features of the act that had an age component were the initiation of two means tested programs—Old Age Assistance (OAA) for people 65 or older and Aid to Dependent Children up to age eighteen (AFDC) to be financed by the federal government and administered by the states.

Manifestly, the legislation was designed to provide some economic security for workers when they reached an arbitrarily fixed age, but the heavy penalty placed on beneficiaries who had earnings beyond a minimal amount until age 72 (at a time when average life expectancy was about 63) was clearly designed to discourage older workers from remaining in the regular labor force and thereby to create jobs for younger age groups at a time when a quarter of the labor force was unemployed.

Since its inception the Social Security Program has commanded unwavering support from the large majority of Americans regardless of their age because it provides some protection not only to the elderly and their dependents in the form of entitlement to benefits but also because the institutionalization of retirement as a distinct stage of life has served to largely remove a growing segment of the population from the regular labor force and thereby serves to protect the work tenure of the younger generation, who after all are the children and grandchildren of the elderly.

Nevertheless, for the cohorts of men born in the latter part of the nineteenth century, retirement introduced a sharp discontinuity into their lives. Among them the work ethic was strong and their identity and self-esteem was closely bound up not merely with the work they did but also with *earning* a living. Thus, the Lynds (1937:50,54) looking back at the status of older men in the 1920s observed that:

> Middletown men on all income levels work at something until death or infirmity takes the decision to work or not to work out of their hands . . . an able bodied male who is "idle" loses caste in this culture.

My early research based on surveys of older people in the late 1940s and early 1950s revealed that among these early cohorts of men retirement had more isolating and demoralizing effects than widowhood or widowerhood, the other role exit that becomes typical in old age, and that these effects were most pronounced among working class men. That it was not age per se but retirement that produced these effects became clear when men of similar age who were still employed were compared with the retired (Blau, 1973).

Scholars whose research is based on more recent cohorts of older retired men do not find such negative effects to be prevalent and some dismiss findings such as mine as "myths." Such investigators fail to appreciate the importance of cohort and period effects. The meaning and effects of retirement early in its institutionalization differ considerably from its impact since it has become the normative status among older people. Indeed, my early findings would predict that this would be the case. For, they indicated that the effects of retirement on older people's social life was conditioned by its prevalence among a person's age, sex, and social class peers. In social contexts where it was relatively rare, retirement had isolating effects but these tended to disappear and even become reversed in those contexts in which it was prevalent (Blau, 1961) as it is by now among people in their sixties and older.

The rapidity with which the transition from work to retirement has become normative not simply at age 65 but increasingly since the 1960s at age 62 and even earlier in some industries and occupations, I believe, cannot be understood without taking into account the impact that the baby-boom phenomenon has had on public policy, corporate practices, and union power over the past thirty years.

In 1940 when the first social security benefits began to be paid out, the proportion of workers covered was very small and the benefits low. The bulk of unemployed workers 65 and over had to turn to Old Age Assistance, a means tested program for subsistence or to financial assistance from children both of which were demeaning, and for many, demoralizing experiences. The outbreak of World War II and the entry of this country into the war in 1941 revived the economy and created a sharp rise in the demand for workers to replace the millions of young men in the armed forces, which proved to be a boon for older people, for women and for minority groups generally. In 1942 for the first time since the onset of the depression, a bare majority of men 65+ were in the regular labor force. Since the end of World War II and the return of men and women to civilian status, the labor force participation rates of older people have steadily fallen and currently less than one fifth and about one tenth of men and women, respectively, are regularly employed.

In 1950 only about one quarter of workers were covered by Social Security. Coverage of workers was greatly extended over the ensuing decades so that presently nearly all workers enjoy coverage under the system.

The explosive rise in birth rates in the United States that began in 1946, peaked in 1957 and subsided in the early part of the 1960s created pressure for new initiatives to encourage retirement at ages earlier than sixty five and thereby improve the employment prospects of the incoming masses of young workers.

Amendments to the Social Security Act which extended the retirement option at age 62 with actuarily reduced benefits to women in 1956 and to men in 1962, and the considerable expansion of pension systems in the private and public sectors during the 1950s and 1960s, precipitated the mounting trend toward early retirement that continues unabated. Long overdue increases in Social Security benefits legislated in 1968 and the indexing of benefits to keep pace with the rising cost of living enacted in the early Seventies further contributed to the rise in retirement rates among workers 60 and over. A significant effect of the above developments has been a marked decline of poverty rates among people 65 and over for the past two decades.

The foregoing analysis of the structural forces that have led to the institutionalization of retirement as a normative and even desirable status in later adulthood lends empirical support to a generalization that Howard Becker (1968:156) advanced nearly two decades ago:

> A structural explanation of personal change has important implications for attempts to deliberately mold human behavior. In particular, it suggests that we need not try to develop deep and lasting interests, be they values or personality traits, in order to produce the behavior we want. It is enough to create situations which will coerce people into behaving as we want them to and then to create the conditions under which other rewards will become linked to continue this behavior.

The enactment of the Age Discrimination in Employment Act (ADEA) in 1967 marks an important turning point in public policy with respect to the issue of age and employment. The timing of the enactment of this legislation coincided with the entry into the work force of large numbers of young people better educated than previous birth cohorts. The rise in unemployment rates among workers in their forties and fifties at all occupational levels made it evident that age discrimination had become a significant threat to the job security and re-employment prospects of the very same cohorts, which since the end of World War II had been the first beneficiaries of retirement policies to encourage retirement of workers at an arbitrarily fixed age. Because entitlement to monetary benefits was linked to retirement such policies were not viewed as discriminatory but as simply a matter of bureaucratic convenience and "fairness."

The new legislation afforded protection to workers between the ages of 40 and 65 with respect to hiring, firing and promotion, and placed the burden of proof on employers charged with age discrimination to demonstrate that age bears a significant relationship to job performance.

One strategy that has developed to escape litigation under this law is exemplified by the 1970 agreement between the auto industry and the united automobile workers which offered the retirement option with pension benefits to employees after thirty years of service, following the model of the armed forces that has for long allowed retirement with a pension after twenty years of service. Large Corporations and Universities increasingly use some combination of age and years of service as a basis for entitlement to a pension to encourage early retirement of workers.

The amendments to ADEA enacted by Congress in 1978 which extended protection against mandatory retirement to workers under age seventy, and continuing efforts to prohibit mandatory retirement solely on the basis of age altogether signaled awareness among policy makers and the public generally that age is a poor predictor of job performance and that abridgement of the right to work beyond a fixed age constitutes as much a violation of the civil rights of individuals as does inequalities in work opportunities based on sex, creed or color. And furthermore it signified that Americans by now understand that such discrimination will prove increasingly costly to the population generally as the proportion of elderly rises in the next century.

However, it is questionable whether this legislation and current or projected modifications of Social Security penalties on earnings will serve to significantly stem, much less reverse, the trend toward early retirement, at least during the remaining years of this century. For it is unlikely that the policies and practices on the part of management and labor that encourage or force early retirement will change much in the present context of spreading automation in industry and agriculture that has been pushing up unemployment rates in the country.

This lack of congruence between public policy and corporate/union policies may well diminish if the projected shortage of workers actually materializes in the early decades of the next century and firms would be constrained to provide incentives to aging workers to *delay* retirement instead of following their present strategy. Merely raising the age at which eligibility for full Social Security benefits begins and imposing heavier penalties for early retirement in the next century will operate to principally penalize workers at lower occupational levels who are wholly dependent on social security income without necessarily deterring more affluent baby boomers with sufficient accumulated assets and pension wealth from following the existing pattern of early retirement. Indeed, efforts are already under way in Congress to rescind these recently enacted provisions.

It is not too early to begin to formulate a coherent set of policies aimed at extending educational, re-training and employment opportunities for aging and older people who want to continue to work or to return to work.

Several recent studies reveal that approximately a third of retired people want to work at least part-time (Harris et al., 1975; Blau et al., 1983). A smaller proportion, more often early retirees, resume work and those who do so exhibit markedly greater well-being than those who want to work but are not working, either because they cannot find jobs or believe that employers will not hire older people. Some employers' attitudes toward hiring older workers appear to be growing more favorable, at least in small firms and businesses. Employment agencies that help to place retired workers are multiplying around the country. If these trends continue it seems likely that increasing proportions of healthy elderly will choose to work longer and the timing of the work to retirement transition may become less patterned by age and more patterned by motivation and competence. Then, reality will become more congruent with the view overwhelmingly endorsed in surveys of American adults over the past decade that:

> Nobody should be forced to retire because of age if he/she wants to continue working and is still able to do a good job (Harris et al., 1975:213).

Introduction

****

I turn now to a brief overview of the thirteen papers that appear in this volume and of the issues they address.

The first two papers focus on the adolescent to adult transition and in several ways extend our understanding of early influences that mediate the relationship between family socioeconomic status of high school students and their subsequent educational and occupational attainment, each of which, needless to say, has far reaching consequences for the course of their future lives. Dennis Hogan's research, based on a nation wide cross-sectional sample of high school sophomores and seniors and their parents carried out in 1980, examines selected determinants of adolescents' expected timing of completion of education, full time entry into the labor force, independent residence, marriage, and parenthood. He shows that the expected timing of each transition is influenced by "normative patterns" associated with race, social class, and gender, but is also influenced by parents aspirations and expectations, and by adolescents' own educational and occupational aspirations.

A direct association is observed between parents' and their children's expected timing with respect to each of the transitions to adult status, although the magnitude of their influence varies according to the type of transition under consideration.

The pattern of findings that emerges from his analysis leads Hogan to conclude that the higher aspirations and expectations that higher status parents typically exhibit leads them to engage in active career socialization of their children so that by the time the latter reach high school they perceive the *connections* between their educational and occupational plans, on the one hand, and marriage and parenthood, on the other, resulting in a readiness to delay the timing of these two transitions and thereby to prolong the period of adolescence for a period of years, but generally not beyond their later twenties or early thirties, which is also consistent with their parents' expectations.

The chapter by Maruyama, Finch and Mortimer is based on a longitudinal study of white males who were interviewed over the high school years beginning in 1966 and were followed up five years after high school graduation in 1974. Their research complements that of Hogan insofar as the *actual* educational, occupational attainment and earnings constitute the dependent variables in their analysis and thus permit a test of how predictive high school seniors' aspirations are, at least over the short term.

Their analysis confirms that a substantial association exists between family socioeconomic status and students' ability when they enter high school. However, during the high school years, ability proves to be the key determinant of academic self concept and school grades.

The importance of these two variables and their dynamic interplay in shaping students' aspirations over the high school years is the major finding of the study. Also important is the finding that family background exerts a considerable influence on students aspirations in high school and a weaker but still significant net influence on their educational attainment five years after graduation.

Both studies extend our knowledge about the processes by which intergenerational continuities in socioeconomic status are maintained and each of them demonstrates the value of a life cycle perspective in the study of the status attainment process. Hogan's evidence that parental aspirations and expectations do have an important influence on their adolescent children's plans, and his proposition that parents with high aspirations pursue a different strategy of socializing their children than other parents deserves further exploration. Implicit in his discussion, I believe, is that such implementing strategies begin prior to adolescence.

My own research on black and white elementary school children (Blau, 1981) provides evidence that maternal aspirations do indeed influence their strategies of socialization and that these two variables are important independent determinants of intellectual competence of children early in their school career, and largely account for the substantial association between family socio-economic status and ability reported by Maruyama, Finch, and Mortimer. Their evidence that ability rather than family background is the key determinant of the interplay between academic self-concept and grades that shapes the educational aspirations of students over the high school years also suggests that the study of the status attainment process should begin earlier in the life cycle when patterned group differences in school competence are first observed and children's academic self concept is first formed.

The paper by Glenn and Weaver examines the effects of age and cohort membership on job satisfaction. A positive relationship between age and job satisfaction has repeatedly been reported in the survey research literature. They question whether such findings indicate that workers become more satisfied with their jobs as they grow older and hypothesize, instead, that they reflect cohort differences in attitudes toward work. Their analysis, based on national surveys conducted over the decade from 1972 to 1982, provides evidence for the proposition that there has been a long term intercohort tendency toward lessening job satisfaction among the successive birth cohorts represented in their sample and that this appears to be most pronounced among the post-War II birth cohorts. They do not rule out the possibility of age effects on job satisfaction as well but the pattern of findings that emerges from their analysis leads them to the conclusion that the cohort effect is the strongest of the two.

The three chapters that follow focus on the transition from work to retirement and are based on longitudinal studies of workers approaching retirement in the later 1960s who were followed over the next decade.

Hardy compares retirement patterns among occupational groups and identifies three variables that consistently increase the likelihood of retirement across blue collar and white collar occupational categories—health limitations, compulsory retirement with pension entitlement, and age eligibility for social security benefits. Age category variables prove to be particularly important in retirement estimations. Because they govern sources of retirement income there is a relatively narrow range of ages at which retirement typically occurs—prior to age 62, 62 to 64, or later. Once age categories are controlled, retirement rates are generally higher for blue collar and clerical workers than for those in higher white collar occupations.

Burkhauser and Quinn focus on the *relationship* between workers' retirement *plans* in 1969 and the timing of their *actual* retirement. Their analysis reveals that slightly over half of 1969 predictions were wrong: workers were three times more likely to retire earlier than later, 38% retired "on time," and only 7% were "on schedule" (those who had yet reached expected retirement age or who "never" expected to retire). Interestingly, a large minority of men who never planned to retire actually retired over the decade, which testifies to the powerful pressures to retire that structural factors exert on older workers regardless of their personal inclinations.

Workers subject to a mandatory retirement age or who have pension coverage are considerably more likely to retire on time. Poor health at the time of the prediction or subsequently, and high social security or pension wealth each promotes earlier than planned retirement whereas consistently good health and high potential earnings each increase the likelihood of later than planned retirement.

The focus of Roger's chapter is on non-married women in the same birth cohort as the men in the Burkhauser and Quinn analysis. She documents the marked differences that exist between older women and men in that cohort with respect to marital status, occupational distribution, and sources and levels of retirement income. On all comparisons, needless to say, women prove to be disadvantaged relative to their male age peers. However, with respect to the timing of retirement the patterns of non-married women and men are largely similar. The majority of both sexes retired before 65, few delayed retirement until age 68, but women were somewhat more likely than men to retire at age 62.

In general the timing of retirement was related to employment status of people at the time they became eligible for social security benefits. A very large majority of both sexes who were not employed took benefits at age 62. Among those who were employed just prior to the time of eligibility, the lowest earners were considerably more likely than higher earners to retire at 62, which is similar to the finding by Burkhauser and Quinn (which, they note, was unexpected). Rogers provides an explanation, namely that the progressive nature of the Social Security computation results in a higher replacement ratio of earnings for low than for high earners. Thus, workers earning less than the earnings test limit can continue to work without prejudice and have the greatest incentive to apply for social security benefits at the earliest possible age.

The focus of the chapter by Jackson and Gibson is on black men and women aged 55 or older who were part of the National Survey of Black Americans carried out in 1979–1980. They identify and compare three groups of black people—working retired and non-retired. The latter work less than twenty hours a week if they work at all, but do not *define* themselves as retired. They differ markedly from the retired on a host of variables. They are largely rural or small town, low income Southern women; nearly half are under age 62, and therefore, are not yet eligible for Social Security benefits or Supplemental Security Income (SSI). They have limited education, irregular work histories in marginal occupations, and more report income from welfare programs than the retired elderly.

In contrast to the non-retired, a large majority of the retired are over age 65 and fewer of them are women. More often than not they reside in large urban communities in the South, have had more schooling and their occupational distribution is more similar to that of the working elderly. They have had more regular work histories, considerably more receive social security benefits and other forms of retirement income, and report fewer health limitations than the non-retired.

The most interesting finding of the study is that the retired elderly score higher on all measures of personal efficiency and well being than either the working or non-retired groups. This suggests that the more stable and secure income that retirement affords the present cohorts of elderly blacks lends greater predictability to their daily lives than was available to them during their working years, and thus enhances their feelings of personal efficiency and well being.

The chapter by Parnes and Less, based on data from the National Longitudinal Surveys of Labor Market Experience, first compares patterns of leisure activity among black and white retired men aged 57 to 71 in 1978, and then examines the effect of variations in leisure activity on their life satisfaction two years later.

Retirement, they found, increases the amount of time devoted to leisure activities among white but not among black men, at least with respect to the six activities measured. Black retired men engaged less than their white counterparts in all activities. Among employed men the racial differences are less pronounced (except with respect to reading).

Occupational level and income are positively related to the extent of leisure activity among both retired and employed men. A strong and consistent positive relationship was found among both groups between the extent of leisure activities in 1978 and the general levels of life satisfaction exhibited in 1980, and that pattern was sustained even when multiple demographic and attitudinal variables were controlled.

The results of the study, particularly of the multivariate analyses based on a large, nationally representative sample of men provide further confirmation that leisure activities significantly enhance the level of life satisfaction among aging men before and after retirement and lend further support to the proposition that

Introduction   xxi

the type of occupational tasks people perform influences the nature and extent of their leisure activities during their working years and after retirement.

****

The next two papers employ cross national data to compare the effects of economic development and population aging on labor force participation rates of older men, on the one hand, and on national retirement policies, on the other.

Pampel uses aggregate cross-sectional and longitudinal data from a large sample of nations to test, more rigorously than has previously been done, the relationship between industrialization and declining labor force participation rates of older men. His model compares the effects of economic development variables and three additional groups of variables that could influence labor force participation rates.

The results of his multivariate analyses strongly reaffirm industrialization theory. The percentage of the male labor force engaged in agriculture proves to be the strongest positive predictor, and the old age dependency ratio the strongest negative predictor of older males' labor force participation. Three additional variables have small but significant effects on government revenues (as a ratio of GNP), eligibility for early pension benefits, and the number of years since the pension programs first began lead to reduced labor force participation.

Pampel concludes among other things, that levels of labor force participation may be difficult to manipulate with social policy variables at different stages of industrialization. Industrializing nations may have difficulty encouraging retirement whereas industrialized nations may have difficulty discouraging retirement.

The current debate over Social Security policies in the United States prompted Atchley to carry out a cross-national study of retirement pension systems in ninety-eight nations, including the United States. A series of multivariate analyses reveal that national retirement policies generally are closely linked either to the degree of economic development or to the extent of population aging or to both variables. Each variable leads to increases in the proportion of the population covered by retirement systems, length of service requirements, provision of benefits for dependents, to the incidence of funding from general revenues and to a decreased incidence of retirement tests. Increases in the minimum retirement age and in pension replacement rates are influenced more by population aging than by GNP levels.

His multivariate analysis of labor force participation rates of people 65 and over shows, consistent with Pampel's findings, that the proportion of the population engaged in agriculture and population aging together have powerful effects whereas selected retirement policy variables only slightly improve the prediction of labor force participation rates in highly industrialized societies.

Atchley concludes that highly industrialized societies, including the United

States, use retirement to control levels of unemployment. Thus, a basic issue in the debate over present and future social security policies in the United States is one of equity—should the burden of rising costs be borne by the nation, which is the principle beneficiency of unemployment control, or primarily by present and future cohorts of older Americans?

The next two papers are essentially case studies that provide new insights into retirement trends and issues in the two largest nations in the Communist bloc. While China and Russia share a similar economic and political philosophy they are at different stages of economic development and are also in different phases of the demographic transition. China is presently vigorously pursuing an anti-natalist policy throughout the nation and a policy of encouraging retirement in the urban sector as a means of unemployment control, whereas the Soviet Union, facing the prospect of labor shortages, has reverted to a pro-natalist policy and to one of encouraging older people to prolong their labor force participation. Thus, despite the number of differences in their political and economic systems, the Soviet Union and the United States are presently moving in a similar direction with respect to their retirement policies.

Davis-Friedmann's paper provides an intriguing account of the development of retirement policies and practices since the establishment of the People's Republic of China which helps to explain why population aging has not produced the same pattern of steady increases in old age pensions observed in other socialist and non-socialist nations. Although the Chinese government established a national pension system shortly after the revolution, coverage has remained limited largely to the minority of the labor force located in the urban state and industrial sector. Even in the latter, however, ideological shifts during the Maoist regime operated to depress retirement rates during a period where rising rates would normally have occurred which would have helped the nation cope with the labor surplus engendered by the urban baby boom between 1952–64. Instead, the radical leadership carried out a massive relocation of urban teenage youth to rural areas ostensibly to upgrade knowledge and skills there and thereby to reduce inequalities between the two sectors. Open acknowledgment of urban unemployment as a problem and measures to encourage retirement in the urban sector began only after the demise of the Maoist regime as part of a massive series of reforms of the economy initiated under Deng Xiao-ping. The large majority of elderly Chinese, however, who are located in the rural sector must continue to rely on the support of sons, but retirement in agricultural occupations is a gradual process and the elderly continue to perform necessary services for their adult children and grandchildren and thus intergenerational stability of the family has been strengthened. This does not appear to be the case in the Soviet Union.

Sternheimer discusses the impact of modernization on the function and status of older women in the Soviet Union. His chapter focuses on the work versus

Introduction xxiii

retirement decision and on its relationship to the grandmother role, a role that has traditionally been extolled in Russia, but one that appears to have become less attractive to older women and less widespread in contemporary Russia than has been commonly assumed. Despite the political, ideological, and structural differences between the Soviet Union and the United States, the impact of modernization on the status and functions of older women appears to be much the same. Soviet policy which had encouraged retirement between 1956 and mid-1960s was reversed as the country faced an impending labor shortage among younger age groups. Despite various incentives designed to encourage old age pensioners to remain in the work force, preference for retirement has continued to rise over the past two decades among both sexes. However, a higher proportion of pension age women than of men choose the retirement option and a similar pattern of sex differences occurs among pre-pension aged with respect to the expected timing of retirement. The minority of female old age pensioners who continue to work do so largely because of material necessity. The earnings of women in Russia have historically been lower than those of men and their income disadvantage rises relative to men with age and probable widowhood. Nevertheless, a majority of older Soviet women choose retirement and exhibit markedly less inclination than their male counterparts to continue working or to return to the work force after retirement.

Sternheimer's evidence suggests that most women pensioners value the increased leisure that retirement offers them and for the most part do not link retirement with caring for grandchildren or helping with household work. There has been a continuing decline in multi-generational households in the USSR, and the preference for living apart from children appears to be growing among old age pensioners and a similar preference with respect to their parents appears to be widespread among the younger generations.

Sternheimer concludes that while many older Soviet women are still thrust into the babushka role it is not a role that they cherish or look forward to performing after retirement. However, given the high labor force participation rates of women with young children, insufficient child care facilities, and the current natalist policy of the Soviet government, some Russian gerontologists have begun to explore ways to restore the legitimacy of the grandmother role and to make the care of grandchildren a normative activity among retired women.

The concluding chapter by Sandell focuses on the employment problems of older Americans, and on the prospects for better utilizing their productive capacity in future decades. He predicts that the labor problems of older workers 45 and older will assume greater urgency and will need to be addressed within the context of a national employment policy. Both the population and the labor force are aging and these trends will accelerate after the turn of the century. Structural changes in the economy will increase the need to develop personnel practices and government policies to improve the utilization of the productive capacities of aging workers and thereby prolong their labor force participation.

He identifies the key federal policies and programs that currently affect the work and retirement patterns of older workers—employment and training programs, income security policies, and government regulations that directly or indirectly affect the labor market. He provides illustrations of the ways in which such policies and programs interact with each other and with the hiring decisions of firms and the employment decisions of older Americans. He concludes that because policies interact with each other and with the hiring decisions of firms and employment decisions of older Americans, they must be analysed within a comprehensive framework and evaluated in terms of "efficiency, equity and civil rights issues."

Zena Smith Blau
Editor

REFERENCES

Becker, Howard S.
    1968   "Personal change in adult life." Pp. 148–156 in Bernice L. Neugarten (ed.), Middle Age and Aging: A Reader in Social Psychology. Chicago: University of Chicago Press.

Blau, Zena Smith
    1961   "Structural constraints on friendships in old age." American Sociological Review 26: 429–39.
    1973   Old Age in a Changing Society. New York: Franklin Watts.

Blau, Zena Smith, George T. Oser, and Richard C. Stephens
    1983   "Older workers: current status and future prospects." Pp. 101–124 in Ida Harper Simpson and Richard L. Simpson (eds.), Research in the Sociology of Work, Vol. 2, Peripheral Workers. Greenwich, Connecticut: JAI Press.

Lynd, Robert S. and Helen Merrell Lynd
    1937   Middletown in Transition: A Study in Cultural Conflicts. New York: Harcourt Brace.

Harris, Louis and Associates
    1975   The Myth and the Reality of Aging in America: A Study for the National Council on the Aging, Washington, D.C.

Redford, Emmette S.
    1965   American Government and the Economy. New York: MacMillan.

PARENTAL INFLUENCES ON THE TIMING OF EARLY LIFE TRANSITIONS

Dennis P. Hogan

ABSTRACT

Research on the socioeconomic attainment process has documented intergenerational continuities in the level of schooling obtained, in rates of labor force participation (among women), and in occupational and earning attainments. Intergenerational continuities in the timing of first marriage and first childbirth have also been observed. While considerable research attention has been devoted to the role of parents in the development of their children's aspirations for socioeconomic achievements, relatively little is known about the ways in which adolescents formulate plans for the timing of early life transitions. This paper considers the effects of normative subgroup affiliations, the proximate social influences of parents, and the educational and occupational aspirations of teenagers on the formation of adolescent expectations about the timing of early life transitions. Data for the study are drawn from a 1980 national sample survey of 6,564 high school sophomores and seniors and their parents.

I. INTRODUCTION

A. Adolescence in America

In many traditional societies the appropriate behaviors of members of age strata are precisely specified by normative regulations. In such societies the timing of departure from one age stratum and entrance into another (cohort succession) is strictly regulated through formal rites of passage. In some traditional societies young persons become adults with other members of their age set whereas in other societies the rites of passage are undergone individually rather than as part of a group. In either case, the timing of transitions among age strata are carefully regulated by the society (Riley, 1976; Foner and Kertzer, 1978).

As societies modernize, the emerging industrial enterprises require highly skilled laborers. This labor need conventionally has been met by expanding the education and training of young persons. The labor force skills are upgraded as the more educated cohorts replace older, less educated cohorts (Katz and Davey, 1978; Kaestle and Vinovskis, 1978; Ryder, 1965). The expansion of the system of formal education prolongs the period of youth while simultaneously shifting many of the socialization functions of the family to the schools (Kett, 1977; Friedenberg, 1963). The age-graded structure of schools increase peer group contacts and decrease the contacts of young persons with other age groups (Coleman, 1961, 1980). Taken together these shifts in the typical life experiences of young persons have resulted in the emergence of a socially recognized age stratum called adolescence (Kett, 1977; Elder, 1980).

The emergence of adolescence as a period which separates youth from adulthood was not accompanied by the development of formal rites of passage through which a child becomes an adolescent or an adolescent becomes an adult. Instead, the transition from one age stratum to another occurs through the adoption of roles and characteristics appropriate to the new age stratum and the abandonment of behaviors associated with the younger age stratum. These changes are sometimes developmental as with physical maturation (Petersen and Taylor, 1980; Garn, 1980), cognitive growth (Wohlwill, 1980; Horn and Donaldson, 1980), and belief and value systems (Feather, 1980; Hoffman, 1980). Other changes represent transitions between discrete, readily defined social statuses. These include the completion of formal education (which marks the terminus of formal socialization and training by the society), the achievement of financial independence from the family of origin (ordinarily achieved through paid employment, but also attained through marriage to a working spouse), the achievement of residential independence from the family of origin (which removes the adolescent from the daily supervision to which he or she is subject in the parental home), and formation of a family of procreation through marriage and/or childbirth.

The maturational aspects of achieving adulthood depend on the pace of physical and physiological development, which are not subject to ready manipulation by the adolescent or society (Garn, 1980; Peterson and Taylor, 1980). While the pace of cognitive development is undoubtedly affected by social contexts and individual experiences which are subject to manipulation, cognitive development is not directly subject to change by the adolescent, the family of origin, or schools (Wohlwill, 1980). Thus the maturational aspects of development have remained largely nonvolitional. The demographic transitions, on the other hand, are subject to social and individual control as discussed below.

B. Defining Adulthood

Recent innovations in the study of human development have led to the recognition that physical and cognitive development continue throughout the lifetime rather than culminating in the stabilization of characteristics in early adulthood (Featherman, 1982). This recognition has drawn attention to the difficulty of defining adulthood (as a discrete state) from developmental data and a growing dissatisfaction with theories of development which rely on discrete stages. Thus, there is no general agreement at what point an adolescent becomes an adult in the developmental sense, even though it is clear that these developmental processes are strongly age-graded. Rather, the social recognition that a young person has become an adult (in the developmental sense) occurs at an indeterminant point in time when the family, peers, and significant others recognize that a young person has reached adult status and is behaving as an adult.

The demographic transitions, on the other hand, are easily recognizable. The intimates of a young person know whether he or she is a student, is working, is living in the parental home or in an independent residence, is married or single, and whether he or she is a parent. Indeed, in thinking about initial conversations with young persons who are in the later teens or early twenties, their statuses in these regards are a usual topic of discussion. Knowledge about these five statuses permits members of the society to characterize young persons as adolescents or as adults.

Of course, these statuses do not provide a perfect guide to whether a young person has achieved adulthood. Although virtually all members of a birth cohort eventually terminate their formal education and live apart from their parents, some persons never marry and some never become parents. In these cases, as well as in the case of extended graduate or professional education, it is clear that a young person initially is recognized as an adult on the basis of developmental criteria. Because such developmental criteria are not directly ascertainable, chronological age often indicates the achievement of adulthood in the absence of completed demographic transitions. Although it is unclear at exactly what point in the life course chronological age rather than demographic statuses becomes the criterion for adult status, it is probably no later than age 25 or 26.

It also seems likely that members of the society anticipate that most, if not all, of the demographic transitions ultimately will occur even though the transitions may occur relatively late in the life course. For example, it is anticipated that a person who is a graduate student at age 25 will ultimately complete formal schooling. In the United States a person ordinarily is not thought to be a lifelong spinster or bachelor simply because marriage has not occurred by the midtwenties. Thus, even when developmental criteria (as indexed by chronological age) are the basis for characterizing someone as an adult, there is an implicit assumption that most, if not all, of the demographic statuses characteristic of adults eventually will be achieved.

C. Societal Expectations

Members of American society expect an association between demographic statuses (and transitions between statuses) and chronological age (Neugarten et al., 1965; Neugarten and Datan, 1973; Modell, 1980; Fallo-Mitchell and Ryff, 1982). It is this expected association that leads to the observation that a transition may occur on time, early, or late. To the extent that such values determine behaviors there will be an observable age grading in the timing of each transition (Featherman and Hogan, 1981).

Adolescents presumably attempt to adhere to these societal expectations about the appropriate linkages between developmental (chronological) age and demographic statuses (Neugarten and Datan, 1973). Peer pressures for conformity will reinforce these tendencies because as an individual ages chronologically, increasing proportions of the peer group will have assumed adult demographic statuses. As a young person observes the peer group it will become clear that prolonged delays in the demographic transitions will leave one "behind" the peer group and out of step with societal expectations about the appropriate timing of the youth-to-adult transitions. Thus, as an adolescent ages, it is probable that he or she will become more and more impatient to achieve the demographic statuses which mark adulthood, at least up to that point in the life course at which chronological age overrides demographic statuses in the recognition of adulthood. This positive time dependence also has a physiological basis insofar as physical maturation and cognitive development are age-graded, with a positive association between chronological age and the rate of attainment of particular maturational levels up to the age at which most of the population has achieved that developmental level (Garn, 1980; Wohlwill, 1980).

Thus, most young persons achieve adulthood through the simultaneous processes of physical and cognitive maturation and demographic transitions which mark the assumption of adult behaviors. These aspects of growing up are strongly age-graded, and there probably are societal expectations that the achievement of adulthood will be completed by a certain chronological age, perhaps the midtwenties. The observation of peers making these transitions as well as the age-graded nature of the other maturational processes being experienced by the individual create an environment in which the adolescent becomes increasingly eager to complete school, become economically and residentially independent of the family of origin, and form a family of procreation.

D. Social Differentials

Adolescents are not able to achieve adulthood through the acceleration of the developmental aspects of maturation because these are relatively outside of their control. The demographic transitions, in contrast, are subject to individual volition. The achievement of adult demographic statuses virtually guarantees societal recognition of adulthood. Therefore, to the extent that individuals and their families directly influence the timing of the transition from adolescence to adulthood, the effects will be on the timing of the demographic transitions which mark the passage to adulthood.

Indeed, research has shown that such intracohort variables as race, social class, family structure, academic achievement, and educational attainments have impacts on the timing of school completion, independent residence, and marriage (Mare, 1979; Marini, 1978, 1982; Featherman and Carter, 1976; Kobrin and Goldscheider, 1978; Hogan 1978a,b, 1981). The timing of the early life transitions also are responsive to environmental contingencies (such as employment rates, wage rates, military service obligations) which vary on an intercohort basis (Duncan, 1965; Ryder, 1969; Hogan, 1981). The life span perspective on human development hypothesizes that the effects of period events on behavior differ among cohorts and among persons with different life course histories within cohorts (Elder, 1974, 1978, 1980; Riley, 1976; Featherman, 1982). Although more research is needed, this hypothesis has been supported by empirical research (Elder and Liker, 1982; Elder and Rockwell, 1979; Moen et al., 1981).

An abundance of research also has demonstrated that young people develop educational and occupational aspirations which affect their later attainments (Sewell et al., 1969; Sewell and Hauser, 1975, 1980; Spenner and Featherman, 1978). The socioeconomic success of adolescents in their later life course depends on the timing of their early life transitions as well as on the resources which aid career achievements and the opportunity structures within which those attainments take place (Blau and Duncan, 1967; Duncan et al., 1972; Featherman and Hauser, 1978; Featherman, 1980). For example, controlling for social environmental factors, an early age at first marriage and early age at first childbirth are detrimental to occupational and earnings attainment in the early and middle career (Duncan et al., 1972; Card and Wise, 1978; Moore et al., 1978; Hofferth and Moore, 1979; Hogan, 1981). A relatively late completion of a given level of schooling (due to interruptions in educational enrollment) depresses career achievements (Featherman and Carter, 1976). Prospects for career success therefore are enhanced when the early life transitions occur at suitable ages. Furthermore, both adolescents and adults seem to recognize the connections between the timing of early life transitions and career success (Tittle, 1981; Haggstrom et al., 1981). These observations are the bases for the hypothesis that adolescents will attempt to time their early life transitions in ways that are consistent with career success.

Teenagers encounter situations in their daily lives which call for decisions about the timing of these demographic transitions. As the teenager reaches physical maturity, decisions must be made about sexual behavior and the potential reproductive consequences of those behaviors (Miller and Simon, 1980). Students who have passed the mandatory school enrollment age must make decisions about how much schooling is desirable and the timetable for that schooling. This becomes an especially crucial issue as students near the completion of high school and make decisions about post–high school education. Adolescents are constantly confronted with the qeustion of what they will do and where they will live after earning their diploma.

These daily decisions are made in the context of the entire life course. The adolescents' decisions are influenced by their attitudes and values regarding career and family achievements. Social classes differ in the values placed on educational attainment (Sewell and Shah, 1968; Sewell, 1971), and ethnic groups evaluate schooling differently (Featherman, 1971; Kobrin and Goldscheider, 1978). Orientations about the appropriate timing of marriage and parenthood as well as the perceived importance of being married at the time of first childbirth differ among ethnic groups and perhaps among social classes (Hollingshead, 1949; Stack, 1975; Otto, 1977; Hogan and Kitagawa, 1983). Certainly there are large differences in the values placed on career and familial achievements for males and females, and the linkages between career achievements and family statuses are viewed as stronger among women (Sewell, 1971; Marini and Greenberger, 1978a,b; Marini, 1978; Tittle, 1981; Miller and Garrison, 1982). Finally, preferred ages for marriage and childbirth differ by sex (Modell, 1980; Otto, 1977). These subcultural differences in value orientations provide a normative context in which adolescents decide the timing of their demographic transitions.

E. Parental Influences

There are intergenerational links in the actual timing of the developmental and demographic changes which indicate the transition to adulthood. Garn (1980) reviews evidence that the pace of physical maturation among children is positively associated with the rate at which their parents matured. The timing of the completion of schooling is largely dependent on the level of education obtained, so that the intergenerational linkages in educational attainments presumably produce positive associations between parents and children in the timing of school completion. Young persons' timing of marriage and first childbirth tend to resemble that of their parents, and intergenerational continuities in the likelihood of the first marriage ending in separation or divorce have been observed (Zelnik et al., Ford, 1982; Otto, 1977).

Research on the intergenerational continuities in educational, occupational, and income attainments has shown that the observed associations principally are due to the influence of parents on the educational attainments of their children (Blau and Duncan, 1967; Duncan et al., 1972; Featherman and Hauser, 1978). The educational and occupational aspirations of parents for their children and the encouragement they provide to them are major sources of this influence (Sewell and Shah, 1968; Sewell and Hauser, 1975).

Schools, parents, and peers offer advice and counsel about the day-to-day decisions that determine transitions between demographic states. While schools probably provide fairly limited advice about decisions that do not impact directly on educational attainments (e.g., decisions about residence, work, or marriage), parents are positioned to provide advice about the timing of each of the major early life transitions. In part, this advice will reflect the views of the subcultures (e.g., class, ethnic group) with which the parents identify. Consequently, parents act as conduits who socialize their children with values held by the particular subculture. Parents also vary in the aspirations they hold for the socioeconomic achievements of their children, controlling for social class and ethnicity. These parental aspirations undoubtedly affect the guidance parents provide to their children about the appropriate timing of early life events. Finally, parents may have personal preferences about the best times for their children to make each of the demographic transitions based on their own life course experiences and the observation of the behaviors of other young people becoming adult. Thus, in addition to acting as conduits for subcultural effects, parents are proximate socializing agents who influence the plans of adolescents for their youth-to-adult transitions, producing intergenerational continuities in the timing of early life transitions (Bengston and Black, 1973).

Despite the success social scientists have had in explaining the intergenerational connections between the attainments of parents and their children, part of the association remains unexplained, seeming to result from the "direct" inheritance of parental statuses. These unexplained connections probably result at least in part from intergenerational continuities in the timing of early life demographic transitions. Parents vary in their views about the timing of early life transitions as the result of subcultural identities and personal biography. Value differences among parents about the timing of early life transitions are reflected in the socialization of children by their parents. These socialization influences affect adolescent transition plans and behaviors. These behaviors, in turn, impact on socioeconomic achievements in the later life course. Thus, research about the parental influences on adolescent plans for the timing of youth-to-adult transitions may provide evidence that will expand our understanding of intergenerational continuities in socioeconomic attainments.

F. Educational and Career Achievements

Research on behavioral differences in the timing of life events has documented the premier position of educational attainments in influencing the timing of most early life transitions (Hogan, 1978a,b, 1981; Marini, 1978, 1982). Cultural subgroups and parents influence the later occupational and earnings attainments of their children through education. Parental advice about the timing of early life events presumably is designed to enhance their children's prospects for educational and career achievements. These observations suggest that much of the influence of parents on the youth-to-adult transition plans of their children will be mediated by the educational plans of the children.

Since the educational and career plans of adolescents are not determined fully by family background, they also will have independent influences on the expected timing of youth-to-adult transitions in addition to their role as intermediating variables. For example, a young person planning a professional occupation may anticipate an especially late age at first job because such a high-level occupation could not ordinarily be entered prior to completing advanced edcuation. The effects of educational and career plans on the expected timing of early life transitions also are likely to differ by sex. Males have considerably more leverage than females to combine spouse and parenting roles with school enrollment and/or career commitments. Although women do combine childcare responsibilities with school enrollment (Davis and Bumpass, 1976) and employment (Sweet, 1973), the difficulties entailed by such arrangements often result in life course patterns in which women either attempt to get their education completed and become established in their occupations before forming a family of procreation (a common pattern among the upper strata) or delay the completion of advanced schooling and/or career entry (Moen, 1982).

G. The Planning Process

Thus far this discussion has focused on the reasons for hypothesizing that plans about the timing of youth-to-adult transitions depend on (1) normative considerations rooted in subcultural affiliations, (2) parental influences, and (3) rational planning considerations entailed in adolescent aspirations for educational and career attainments. This suggests a fairly static view of the planning process. In reality adolescent plans for the future are constantly evolving in response to the life course experiences up to that point and the changing contingencies associated with their nonfamilial social environments.

As parents and school counselors observe the cognitive development of an adolescent, their views on the educational potential of the adolescent may be revised upward or downward. Teenagers who display unexpected academic success may increase their educational goals in response to an enhanced self-evaluation of academic ability and as a result of encouragement by parents and significant others. Evolving social conditions may modify the perceptions of adolescents, parents, and significant others about the cost of a college education and its potential returns. Such changes could result in a revision of educational aspirations. Views on the appropriate timing of marriage and childbirth have changed in response to evolving societal changes in these behaviors (Modell, 1980). However, current plans also will be influenced by previous circumstances and the plans formulated in response to those circumstances [see Glenn (1980) for a discussion of continuities in beliefs, attitudes, and values].

A likely scenario is that the adolescent formulates initial educational and career plans, and ideas about the timing of youth-to-adult transitions, based on normative considerations arising from subcultural affiliations, the proximate influence of parents, and immediate social circumstances. These initial ideas are discussed with parents, peers, and school counselors in the context of making daily decisions that will impact on the later life course. These significant others urge modifications in educational or career plans if the initial aspirations of the adolescent are inconsistent with their perceptions of the adolescent's abilities. Feedback from these significant others also may result in revised plans for the timing of early life events as the adolescent's initial plans are criticized as producing transitions that are too early or too late, or as being inconsistent with educational and occupational aspirations.

H. Uncertainties in Planning

If adolescents' plans for adulthood are continually evolving in response to present circumstances and previous life history, the unpredictability of future events means that such plans are tentative. Also, the timing of early life transitions frequently involves finding a cooperating party and stochastically distributed waiting times. (For example, an employer must be found if one is to begin work at a job paying a wage or salary, and a partner of the opposite sex is necessary in order to marry and become a parent. The waiting time for pregnancy among couples attempting to have a child depends on physiological factors and cannot be precisely planned.) Thus, adolescents' plans for adulthood, as observed at any particular moment, are more in the nature of anticipations, or expectations, than precise intentions. These anticipations may reflect ideas about future life course circumstances, with these ideas representing an amalgam of a continuation of current circumstances and projections of future changes based on perceptions of recent changes. It does not seem at all likely that adolescents anticipate radically altered social environments, normative changes, or parental influences in formulating their plans for adulthood insofar as such radical changes are largely unpredictable.

Adolescents display considerable confidence in their ability to plan for the future and in the efficacy of such planning (tabulations not shown). Only 19.7 percent of American high school sophomores and seniors believe that their life is subject to unpredictable and uncontrollable circumstances (an external locus of control). Fully 80 percent of the high school students believe that they exert considerable control over their own lives, and that plans usually work out (an internal locus of control).

An external locus of control is associated with a relatively early expected age at school completion (due mainly to lower educational aspirations) and a somewhat late age at establishment of an independent residence. An external locus of control also is associated with an increased likelihood of expecting to have an illegitimate first birth as well as continued residence in the parental home after marriage and childbirth. These differences reflect a lack of confidence that the transition to adulthood will occur in a fairly orderly (conventional) fashion without substantial and prolonged dependence on their parents. In other words, youths who believe that they will have little control over the contingencies affecting their future behaviors expect to rely somewhat more extensively on their parental families for assistance in the youth-to-adult transitions, but they do not avoid developing expectations about those transitions. In fact, the effects of sex, ethnicity, social class, and career aspirations on adolescents' plans regarding the timing of their early life events do not differ among persons with an external rather than internal locus of control.

I. Analyzing the Planning Process

Longitudinal data are required to trace the development of adolescent plans for adulthood and identify the effects of those plans on subsequent behaviors. Data on several birth cohorts would be required to evaluate the impact of social conditions on the plans for adulthood, and longitudinal data on the cohorts would be essential to understand how changing social conditions cause different responses on an intercohort basis. Such data are not available currently. Indeed, unless we can develop our knowledge more fully about the ways in which adolescents plan the transition to adulthood, we cannot sensibly determine the kinds of data necessary for a complete understanding of this dynamic process. Fortunately, as Sewell and his associates have convincingly demonstrated in their initial studies of the early educational and occupational attainment processes, a great many of the crucial issues about the formation of adolescent plans for the future can be addressed with cross-sectional data from a single cohort of adolescents.

In this paper, I report analyses of cross-sectional data collected from a national sample of high school sophomores and seniors. Matched data are also available for one parent of each of the students. These analyses identify the way in which adolescent plans for the timing of school completion, labor force entry, independent residence, marriage, and parenthood are determined by (1) normative considerations associated with social class, race, and gender; (2) the proximate social influences of parents; and (3) rational considerations implied by the educational and occupational aspirations of adolescents. The models estimated are designed to determine the dynamics of the process insofar as theoretically based causal orderings of the variables permit the statistical identification of total, direct, and indirect effects.

II. DATA

A. High School and Beyond Survey

The data for this analysis were drawn from the first (Spring 1980) wave of the National Center for Educational Statistics (NCES) study "High School and Beyond," a longitudinal study of U.S. high school seniors and sophomores. The study respondents were a nationally representative sample of 58,728 high school sophomores and seniors in 1,016 high schools. The response rate for the survey was 84 percent. A representative subsample of 7,201 students from 312 schools were selected for inclusion in a supplementary parent survey. Student respondents to High School and Beyond had been asked to provide "your parent's or guardian's name, address, and telephone number." Space was provided on the questionnaire for one parent's name. Students were not instructed which parent to name should both parents be present in the home. If only one parent or guardian was named, the parent survey questionnaire was sent to that parent. If the student reported both a male and a female parent, a letter was sent addressed to the female parent. The data from parents were collected in Fall 1980 through a combination of mailed-out questionnaires, telephone interviews, and personal interviews. A total of 6,564 parents responded to the survey for a completion rate of 91.2 percent. In combination with the student response rates, the overall completion rate for sophomores and seniors and their parents was 76.6 percent.

This analysis of parental influences on the timing of early life transitions is restricted to students whose father or mother responded to the parent survey. The 5.2 percent of the respondents living with another relative or guardian are excluded from the analysis in order to avoid the complexities that would arise if the influence of guardians on transition plans or adolescents differs from the influence of parents.

The nonrandom method of selecting the parent respondent resulted in a matched parent–student file in which 62.9 percent of the parent respondents were mothers. It is possible that the method of selecting the parent respondent and sex-based differences in parental response rates introduce biases in the survey (in terms of ethnicity, social class origins, and so on). In order to control for this possibility, a variable indicating sex of the parent respondent is included in the statistical models.

The High School and Beyond Survey oversampled schools with high proportions of Hispanics, Catholic schools with high proportions of black students, non-Catholic private schools, public alternative schools, and private schools with high-achieving students. Because this analysis does not separate out these oversampled strata, the strata are downweighted to their proper population weights, so that the weighted sample is representative of high school seniors and sophomores and their parents in the United States and in each of the nine census subregions.

B. Information Collected

The High School and Beyond Survey collected a variety of information from the student respondents concerning their demographic characteristics, social origins, school experiences, and aspirations for the future. Most important for the analysis, the student respondents were asked, "At what age do you expect to . . . (a) get married? (b) have your first child? (c) start your first regular (not summer) job? (d) live in your own home or apartment? and (e) finish your full-time education?" Students were given precoded responses permitting them to specify ages "under 18, 18, 19, 20, 21, . . . 27, 28, 29, 30 or more" or to indicate "don't expect to do this" or "have already done this." The parents questionnaire focused largely on the financial aspects of higher education, but did obtain basic demographic and socioeconomic data on the parents and their families. In addition, parents were asked, "At what age to you expect (name) to . . . (a) get married? (b) have his/her first child? (c) start his/her first regular (not temporary) job? (d) live in his/her own home or apartment? and (e) finish his/her education?" Precoded response categories identical to those of the student respondents were used.

C. Defining Control Variables

1. Specifying Sex Differentials

As indicated in the introduction, the process by which adolescents plan for adulthood differs between males and females. Females in the United States are younger at marriage and first childbirth than males. It is likely that these typical differences in behavior partly result from normative considerations about sex roles. In addition, because the role difficulties involved in simultaneously being a parent and having a career are much greater for females, it is likely that higher educational and occupational aspirations (rational planning considerations) may produce substantial delays in family formation among females, but only moderate delays among males. Consequently, the models reported here are separately estimated for male and female students in order to capture sexual differences in the effects these independent variables on the youth-to-adulthood transition plans of adolescents.

It would, of course, be possible to take one additional analytic step to determine whether the proximate social influences of mothers or of fathers are stronger in the formation of the transition plans of their sons and daughters. While this is an important research issue, it is not addressed in this paper due to a desire to minimize the intricacies in what already is a complex analysis.

2. Specifying School Class Cohort Differentials

Adolescent expectations for adulthood may vary between sophomores and seniors for several reasons. The population of high school students does not represent the entire population of adolescents since not all school-age persons in fact are enrolled in school. While this problem is not severe among sophomores, the high school seniors represent "survivors" of the school-leaving process. Adolescents who terminate their formal schooling to enter the labor force and/or to have a child are not represented by a sample of high school seniors. This suggests that, to the extent some adolescents accurately anticipate dropping out of high school, sophomores will on average expect an earlier age at school completion than seniors.

Seniors and sophomores also may differ in their plans for adulthood due to maturational (developmental) differences. Sophomores may hold unrealistic ideas about their academic abilities and revise their educational plans upward or downward as they mature. The anticipations about adulthood among sophomores may be more heavily influenced by normative considerations about the desirability of an early transition to adulthood, whereas the seniors' plans for adulthood reflect delays associated with anticipations of prolonged school enrollment and occupational success.

Finally, high school sophomores and seniors are from different birth cohorts and their transition plans may be influenced by unmeasured variables distinguishing the cohorts. For example, adjacent birth cohorts (such as those of 1945 and 1947) sometimes differ substantially in size, military service obligations and the like. The most obvious such intercohort difference in this case is that financial aid for college enrollment was more plentiful for the 1980 seniors (who were the entering college class of Fall 1980) than for the 1980 sophomores (who were the entering college class of Fall 1982). However, it seems unlikely that the sophomores anticipated this change in formulating their expectations about the timing of the youth-to-adult transitions in Spring of 1980. In any case, the models estimated include a variable indicating grade in school to measure these potential differences between sophomores and seniors, and to control for any biases arising therefrom.

D. Defining Independent Variables

Theoretical considerations dictate that the models of plans for the timing of youth-to-adult transitions include variables indexing normative considerations rooted in subcultural identities, proximate parental influences, and adolescent educational and career aspirations. I selected variables from the Student and Parent components of the High School and Beyond Survey which could be used to represent these concepts adequately and had limited rates of nonresponse. I then produced survival table estimates of the expected timing of each of the five transitions for the various response categories of each variable to determine whether a particular independent variable in fact was related to some aspect of the planning process, and the character of that relationship. This information was used to decide on appropriate categorizations of the variables and the assignment of respondents with missing data on an independent variable. Finally, the expected age-specific rates calculated for each transition were examined to confirm that the assumption of the statistical model that these processes are characterized by positive time dependency (up to age 25) is valid.

In defining variables for inclusion in the multivariate models I decided to use independent variables that are categorical rather than interval level of measurement. This decision was based on heuristic as well as practical considerations. The use of categorical independent variables in the continuous-time semi-Markov models that are estimated produces a set of results that more closely parallel standard demographic analyses of intergroup differentials in age-specific rates of events. Detailed cross-tabulations and survival tables indicated that the association between more refined measures of the independent variables and the anticipated transition rates do not differ substantially in direction and magnitude from associations observed with the cruder categorizations used in this analysis.

As described below, a sizable minority of parents reported no opinion about the ages at which they expected their child to achieve the various youth-to-adult transitions. By using an ordinal measure of the parent's expectation about the timing of a transition, a category signifying "no opinion" could be included in the analysis. Finally, a categorical measure was preferable to index the combined labor force participation and occupational aspirations of parents and their children.

1. Measures of Subcultural Identity

Based on these considerations, variables measuring four aspects of subcultural identity are included in the analysis. The first variable distinguishes blacks and whites. Research documents that blacks have higher rates of first birth and lower rates of first marriage than whites (Zelnik et al., 1981; Zelnik and Kantner, 1978, 1980; Kitagawa, 1981; Cherlin, 1981). These racial differentials in behavior in part appear to result from different normative evaluations of marriage, childbearing, and illegitimacy among blacks and whites (Stack, 1975; Tanner, 1974). There is no evidence that blacks and whites continue to differ substantially in the timing of school completion, first job, or independent residence, although historical differences in educational attainment were associated with somewhat earlier transitions among blacks (Featherman, Hogan and Sørensen, 1984). The 10 percent of the respondents who reported another race (Asian, American Indian, or other) or did not provide race information are excluded from this analysis in order to clarify the contrast between blacks and whites.

As discussed above, there is substantial evidence that the timing of youth-to-adult transitions varies substantially by social class, with middle and upper class origin children having later ages at school completion, first job, and family formation. It is hypothesized that most of the social class differentials in early life transition plans are due to the lower educational aspirations of working class parents and their children. This analysis distinguishes blue collar from white collar social class origins based on information about the father's occupation. In cases where the father is not present in the home or father's occupation is not reported, maternal occupation is used to assign social class. The small number of respondents (9.7 percent) for whom social class information was missing were assigned blue collar origins based on the examination of survival tables of social class differences in transition plans.

I have hypothesized that educational aspiration is a key variable determining the anticipations of adolescents about the timing of youth-to-adult transitions. Research on educational attainment has demonstrated that the educational level of parents has an important impact on the educational plans and attainments of their children, controlling for the occupational standing of the head of the household (Blau and Duncan, 1967; Sewell and Hauser, 1975; Featherman and Hauser, 1978). Therefore, the models estimated for this paper include a variable indexing the educational level (high school diploma or less, trade or vocational school or some college, and college bachelor's degree or above) of the parent who responded to the parent survey. The 0.8 percent of parents for whom education information was missing were combined with parents having a high school diploma or less based on preliminary data analysis.

As argued in the introduction, plans about the timing of early life transitions among females probably are more responsive to educational and occupational aspirations than is the case for males. Recent emphasis on educational attainments for the career preparation of daughters are associated with a nontraditional (liberated) view of female roles. Whereas traditional views of female roles are associated with relatively low educational aspirations, an early age at school completion, and early family formation among women, liberated views of female roles provide a normative justification for delaying school completion and family formation in the pursuit of higher education and career achievements. For this paper, normative prescriptions about female roles are measured by the parents' responses (agree strongly, agree, disagree, disagree strongly) to three statements: (1) "A working mother of preschool children can be just as good a mother as the woman who doesn't work"; (2) "It is much better for everyone concerned if the man is the achiever outside of the home and the woman takes care of the home and family"; and (3) "Women are much happier if they stay at home and take care of their children." A scale was constructed by summing the Likert-coded responses to these items. Based on preliminary tabulations, the detailed scale was dichotomized to distinguish parents with traditional views from those with liberated views of female roles. The 3.3 percent of the respondents missing data on one or more of these female roles questions were classified as having liberated views based on the preliminary tabulations.

2. Measures of Parental Influences

As socialization agents, parents mediate the effects of subcultural normative considerations on the adolescents' plans for adulthood. The critical role of parents in the formation of their children's educational and occupational aspirations was reviewed earlier. These aspirations will affect the parents' timetables of the appropriate ages for the youth-to-adult transitions. These parental timetables also are based on the normative considerations of parents as formed by their subcultural identities and modified by their personal experiences and observations. Therefore, this analysis includes three measures of the proximate social influences of parents: the parent's educational aspiration and occupational aspiration for the child, and the parent's own anticipation of the timing of each transition by the child.

The educational aspiration of parents for their children is measured by a three-category variable which distinguishes less than a college degree, a college bachelor's degree, and an advanced graduate or professional degree. Previous research has shown that the actual timing of early life transitions does not differ greatly by educational level among those persons with less than a college degree (Hogan, 1981). The prolongation of school enrollment associated with a bachelor's degree and, in particular, the extended enrollment of graduate and professional degree-seeking students have major delaying effects on the timing of the youth-to-adulthood transitions.

The aspiration of parents for their children's occupational attainments at age 30 distinguish a preference for labor force participation and for type of occupation. Parents indicating the homemaker, not working, and don't know responses are grouped together into a no-paid occupation category. The status level of the occupation named by other parents is classified into four broad occupational levels: (1) blue collar (farmer, laborer, military service, operative, protective service, service); (2) skilled crafts and lower white collar (craftsperson, clerical, secretarial, sales, and technical); (3) lower level professional (e.g., accountant, registered nurse, librarian, social worker, elementary or secondary school teacher, and proprietor); and (4) higher level professional (e.g., dentist, physician, lawyer, scientist, college teacher, and manager or administrator).

These occupational levels are somewhat crude in that only four occupational levels are distinguished. Preliminary tabulations indicated that a finer categorization of the occupational aspirations variable would not add significantly to this analysis of the formation of early life transition plans. This occupational classification departs from conventional practices by combining skilled crafts and lower white-collar professionals, and by distinguishing lower status from higher status professionals. The former decision was based on the comparable educational requirements for people now entering the crafts and lower white-collar occupations, and the similar impacts of the two types of occupations on transition plans. The distinction between lower level and higher level professional was based on the differing educational requirements of the two types of occupations and the recognition that women traditionally are more likely to enter the lower level professions than the higher level professions. It is hypothesized that parents aspiring to a higher level professional occupation for their daughter will hold nontraditional sex role views and are especially likely to expect their daughters to delay family formation as a way of facilitating their unconventional career attainments.

The parental timetables for their children's youth-to-adult transitions are based on the questions parents were asked about the expected age at which their child (the student respondent) would experience each of the early life transitions (described above). The model of the planning process for each transition includes a variable indicating the parent's anticipation of the age at which that transition will occur. Five response categories are distinguished: age 19 or earlier (including those who have already done the transition); 20–22; 23–25; 26 or later (including those parents who expect that their child will not do the transition); and those parents answering "don't know" or not answering the question. If all parents had expressed an age response to these transition questions it would have been preferable to maintain an interval level (single year of age) metric for this variable. However, some parents did not expect their child to experience a transition (ranging from 0 percent for school completion to 2 percent for having a child), and many others did not express an age expectation (fewer than 10 percent for the school completion and first job transitions, 15 percent for independent residence, 21 percent for marriage, and 26 percent for having a child). The use of age range categories for the responses to these questions permits the inclusion in the analyses of those parents giving nonnumeric answers.

In general, I anticipate that children of parents expecting an early transition will plan a relatively early transition (i.e., expect a higher age-specific rate of transition). Parents who are unable to express an opinion on these questions presumably provide less guidance to their children about the appropriate timing of these demographic events. I expect that this lack of guidance will result in "off-time" transition plans among the adolescents. Because schools provide some guidance about education and career planning the effect of parental guidance may be less important for these transitions than for the planning of family formation.

3. Measures of Rational Planning Considerations

Finally, it is hypothesized that the rational planning considerations arising from an adolescent's educational and career goals are important in the formation of plans for the timing of the youth-to-adult transitions. Specifically, the literature reviewed above leads to the hypothesis that students planning advanced levels of education will delay the demographic transitions which mark adulthood. Professional careers (whether high or low status) are difficult to begin until formal schooling is completed and a degree is in hand. Other occupations can begin prior to the attainment of credentials. In fact, high school students sometimes begin blue-collar, secretarial, or clerical jobs while still in school and plan to assume these jobs full time after earning the diploma (Lewin-Epstein, 1980). Thus, even controlling for educational attainment, youths planning professional occupations are expected to delay the beginning of work. Childbearing, and perhaps marriage, is likely to be delayed to facilitate career entry into a professional job, especially among females. It is hypothesized that the educational and career aspirations of adolescents mediate much of the impact of normative consideration and parental influences on plans about the timing of youth-to-adult transitions. The educational and occupational aspirations of students are defined using procedures identical to those for the parental aspirations variables.

4. The Dependent Variables

The five dependent variables for these models are the adolescent's expectations regarding the timing of school completion, beginning of regular employment, establishment of independent residence, marriage, and birth of a first child. Each of these transitions represent a movement between discrete demographic states (e.g., single to married). Movements between these states are of interest, as are differences in the rate of state-to-state transitions among persons within the population (i.e., heterogeneity).

There are a variety of ways to examine such transitions as they actually occur and these techniques are also applicable in studies of the desired or expected timing of transitions. Two which have been popular in studies of early life transitions have been (1) to calculate the percentage undergoing a transition by a particular age and to measure differences in this percentage among groups (Modell et al., 1976; Zelnik et al., 1982) and (2) to calculate the waiting time until the transition occurs (in this analysis, age at transition) and differences in mean waiting times among groups (Bayer, 1969; Marini, 1978, 1982; Hogan, 1978a; Zelnik et al., 1982).

The first of these techniques (applied to analysis of actual behaviors) uses only the cross-sectional information obtained in the event history data on dates of transitions. The analysis of differences in states in cross-section provide unbiased estimates of differences in underlying transition rates only when the transition process is in equilibrium (Tuma et al., 1979). While this difficulty is not an important consideration in a study of anticipated behaviors in which all respondents project their behaviors, it is awkward to model the effects of multiple independent variables on transition rates using logit dependent variables when data on the exact expected age at transition are sometimes unavailable. As described below, it is simpler to consider the effects of the multiple independent variables on the instantaneous transition rate.

The second technique (analysis of waiting times) produces biased estimates when observation (in the case of actual behaviors, a survey interview) is terminated at any arbitrary point in relation to the transition process (Sørensen, 1980). The biases inherent in severe right censoring cannot be overcome in the analysis of waiting times but can be handled with a properly specified continuous-time semi-Markov model. In this analysis of expected behaviors there are two types of problems resembling censorship. One is the upper-bound cutoff on age at transition, with any person expecting a transition at age 30 or older providing a common response (''30 or more'') which does not provide an exact age for analysis of mean age at the transition. The second problem is that some young people (1.5 percent in the case of first job up to 10.1 percent in the case of parenthood) do not expect to undergo a transition. Any analysis which excludes these individuals in order to examine mean expected ages at transition would be subject to potentially serious biases resembling those associated with right censoring. Analyses of the instantaneous transition rate are able to avoid these censoring problems.

III. MODELING TRANSITION EXPECTATIONS

In this paper I measure the effects of normative considerations, parental influences, and educational and occupational plans on the processes of completing school, beginning work, establishing an independent residence, marriage, and parenthood by means of continuous-time semi-Markov models. These models estimate the instantaneous rate of a transition from the origin state j (e.g., being single) to the destination state k (married) at time t as a log linear function of the v independent variables of interest (x_i) and duration in origin state j (equal to t):

$$\ln r_{jk}(t) = b_0 + b_1x_1 + b_2x_2 + \cdots + b_vx_v + zt \quad (1)$$

or, equivalently,

$$r_{jk}(t) = e^{b_0} \cdot e^{b_1x_1} \cdot e^{b_2x_2} \cdots \cdots e^{b_vx_v} \cdot e^{zt} \quad (2)$$

The coefficients of the variables in the model (the b_i's and z) are estimated by the method of maximum likelihood. This method provides a likelihood-ratio χ^2

statistic to test the statistical significance of sets of variables, as well as the standard errors of the coefficients to test the statistical significance of a particular variable. (See Tuma et al., 1979 and Tuma, 1979 for formal expositions on this type of model. For a very useful didactic exposition on the reasons for using such a model and its properties see Sørensen, 1980. Applications of this model to the timing of life events are found in Hannan et al., 1977 and Sandefur and Scott, 1981.)

This model uses the full amount of information available in the expected age-at-transition questions. The instantaneous rate that is analyzed in this model determines both the percentage of teenagers expecting to experience a transition by a given age and the average waiting time until (i.e., expected age at) the transition (Tuma et al., 1979; Tuma, 1979). The analysis of instantaneous rates of anticipated transitions therefore does not sacrifice information produced by these other types of analyses.

The maximum likelihood procedure developed by Tuma and her associates has desirable asymptotic properties (i.e., consistency, asymptotic normality) that remain quite good in small samples. The technique works well even in instances when completed transition times are not available for many observations (Tuma and Hannan, 1979; Tuma, 1982). This contrasts with the serious problems censoring can produce for the satisfactory estimation of rates using other (moment) estimation techniques.

A. Censored Data

The number of adolescents who cannot be assigned an age at transition because they expect to undergo the transition at age 30 or older or do not expect to experience this transition is greatest for the parenthood transition (15.7 percent). While this level of censoring is sufficient in itself to require the use of this type of semi-Markov model, another theoretical consideration also is important. As discussed above, the timing of these demographic transitions is indicative of achieved adult statuses. As such it acts as a readily observable, as well as manipulatable, marker of adulthood. Developmental criteria, which are not as easily ascertained and not readily manipulatable, also are involved in the definition of adulthood. Chronological age (as an index of developmental age or maturity) thus defines adulthood in combination with the demographic statuses. I have argued that an American is defined as an adult on the basis of the demographic statuses during the later teens and early twenties, but that by age 25 or 26, at the latest, chronological age becomes the sole criterion for adulthood. This theoretical argument is operationalized in the statistical model estimated here by measuring the rates at which young persons expect to make each youth-to-adult transition from age at the date of interview up to age 25. The effects of normative considerations, parental influences, and rational planning considerations on these rates are measured. Any person not completing a transition by age 25 is treated as censored at age 26. In other words, the rate of each transition up to age 25 is treated as an important indicator of the achievement of adult status, but all persons are regarded as becoming adults on the basis of chronological age at 26 years. While it is assumed that many of the young persons who have not made a transition by age 26 will eventually make that transition, this is treated as an irrelevant consideration in the definition of that person as an adult. The proportions of the total population of each sex treated as censored with these procedures is less than 5 percent for the completion of formal education, first job, and independent transitions. Among females, 15 percent are treated as censored on the first marriage transition and 39 percent are censored on the parenthood transition. The percentages of males censored on these transitions are 26 and 49 percent, respectively.

B. Duration Dependence

Besides the theoretical arguments advanced earlier, an inspection of the expected age-specific rates for each transition provided support for the decision to terminate observation at age 26 (tabulations not shown). The expected age-specific rates of the school, job, and residence transitions increased fairly regularly for each sex until age 22 and remained at a high level until age 25, declining precipitously thereafter. For both sexes, expected rates of first marriage increased steadily until age 25, declining thereafter. The expected rates of first childbirth increased steadily, but at a somewhat slow rate, until age 25 and remained roughly level until age 27, declining thereafter. The positive duration (age) dependence characteristic of these transition plans up to age 25 are consistent with the theoretical argument that the adolescent increasingly will be impatient to achieve the demographic statuses which mark adulthood, up to that point in the life course at which chronological age overrides demographic statuses in the recognition of adulthood.

By examining the expected rate of transitions up to age 25 the nature of the duration dependence is properly specified with the continuous-time semi-Markov models estimated here. This estimation technique provides maximum likelihood estimation of the complete rate function, including the duration dependence. Partial likelihood estimation techniques partial out the duration dependence in the rate, treating it as an unspecified error term (Tuma, 1982). Since there are substantive reasons to expect positive age dependence in these transitions and to be interested in its relative magnitude among the transitions, it is preferable to model the nonstationarity directly rather than utilize a partial likelihood estimation procedure. With binary outcomes transition rates are identical to hazard rates. Thus, partial and maximum likelihood methods should provide the same results in terms of heterogeneity in the rate if the duration dependence is correctly specified in the maximum likelihood model or if there is no time dependency, even with extensive right censoring (Tuma, 1982).

C. Survival Table Analysis

The survival table approach frequently utilized by demographers (Gross and Clark, 1975; Potter, 1977; McCarthy, 1978) utilizes the full event history data and resolves biases due to censoring. As discussed above, I used such survival table procedures to decide on appropriate definitions for the independent variables and to test the assumptions of the multivariate continuous-time semi-Markov model estimated here. However, the survival table approach is quite cumbersome for multivariate causal analysis and has the disadvantage of requiring a very large number of cases (Menken et al., 1981; Teachman, 1982).

D. Interpreting the Results

The results of the analysis are reported in part a (females) and part b (males) of Tables 1–5. The entries in the tables are the estimated multipliers of the expected transition rates, that is, $e^{(b_i)}$ and $e^{(zt)}$, where $t = 1$. In this paper the $e^{(b_i)}$'s are coefficients of dummy variables. Categories of the variables excluded from the model are shown in the tables with coefficients of 1.00. These variable categories by definition have no effect on the expected rate of transition estimated from the intercept and $e^{(zt)}$ parameters. These categories provide the baseline against which the effects of other characteristics are compared. Characteristics that increase the rate of the transition relative to the rate of those in the criterion category have multipliers greater than 1.00; those that decrease the rate have multipliers less than 1.00. Because the $e^{(b_i)}$'s in this paper are coefficients of dummy variables, $e^{(b_i)}$ is the estimated ratio of the rate of individuals with that characteristic to the rate of those individuals in the criterion category, when all other variables in the model and the time dependency are controlled (see Hannan et al., 1977). The statistical significance of the effect of a particular characteristic relative to the criterion category is determined by reference to an F test which compares the magnitude of the coefficient to its standard error. Statistically significant coefficients ($p < .05$) are signified in the table by an asterisk next to the coefficient. The χ^2 test reported at the bottom of the table measures the statistical significance of the improvement in fit due to the additional variables included in that model compared with the previous model.

IV. ANALYSIS RESULTS

A. Duration Dependence

As hypothesized, there is statistically significant positive duration dependence (nonstationarity) in the transition plans of both males and females (see model 1 in each of the tables). For example, model 1 of Table 1a shows that there is a statistically significant improvement in fit ($\chi^2 = 843.6$ with 1 degree of freedom) in a model predicting the expected rate of school completion when the dependence of rate of school completion on duration in the origin state (in this case, age in years beginning with the sixteenth birthday) is taken into account. Evaluating this effect at $t = 1$ (age 17), the model estimates a 27 percent increase in the anticipated rate of school completion over the anticipated rate at age 16. The magnitude of this positive duration dependence is relatively small for first job plans. The positive duration dependence is much larger for age at school completion and independent residence, and largest for marriage and childbirth.

These results suggest that adolescents are subject to increasing impatience to achieve adult demographic status as they age chronologically. This impatience is greatest for those transitions which are the manifestations of biological development (i.e., marriage and childbearing as social responses to biological drives to be sexually active and reproduce). Peer pressure may be important in producing these differentials. At age 16 a single person is in a typical marriage status for members of his or her birth cohort. As the person ages, peers are increasingly likely to be married and fewer fellow members of the cohort are in the single state. At the same time that being single is becoming more rare, potential mates will also become relatively rare (since persons of the opposite sex from the same or adjacent cohorts are also marrying and withdrawing from the marriage market). Biological factors and a desire to be like one's peers coupled with the fear that the future ability to make the transition gets poorer as one ages would produce the stronger pattern of positive duration dependence observed for the marriage and childbearing transitions. Biological needs and market considerations do not apply (at least in any obvious ways) to plans for completing school, beginning work, or living apart from the parental family, producing the weaker patterns of age-grading observed for those transitions.

The magnitude of age-grading of transitions differs between males and females, with a stronger age-grading observed for the expected rates of marriage and childbearing among the males. It may be that females, among whom the role conflicts between advanced education and a career and family roles are stronger, expect to have two options available to them. Some women, aspiring to more traditional family achievements with minimal career goals, will anticipate an early marriage, whereas other females with high educational and career aspirations expect to postpone marriage and childbearing until their later twenties or early thirties, long after they have achieved recognition as adults. This hypothesis receives support from the increased duration dependence that is observed when controls are introduced for the educational and occupational plans of the parents and the adolescents. (Similar though smaller increases also are observed among males, indicating that they, too, may be characterized by these different strategies.) In any event, the increases in duration dependence observed when the

Table 1a. Effects of Variables on the Expected Rate of School Completion: Females

Independent Variables	Model 1	2	3	4	5	6	7	8
Duration	1.27**	1.29**	1.30**	1.30**	1.34**	1.36**	1.42**	1.43**
Race								
Black		0.67**	0.61**	0.62**	0.67**	0.72**	0.66**	0.63**
White		1.00	1.00	1.00	1.00	1.00	1.00	1.00
Grade								
Sophomore		1.62**	1.64**	1.66**	1.65**	1.59**	1.75**	1.76**
Senior		1.00	1.00	1.00	1.00	1.00	1.00	1.00
Parent Responding								
Mother		1.18**	1.07	1.09*	1.08	1.07	1.07	1.08
Father		1.00	1.00	1.00	1.00	1.00	1.00	1.00
Family Social Class								
Blue Collar			1.00	1.00	1.00	1.00	1.00	1.00
White Collar			0.83**	0.84**	0.90*	0.92*	0.97	0.98
Parent's Education								
High School or Less			1.00	1.00	1.00	1.00	1.00	1.00
Some Post-High School			0.78**	0.78**	0.94	0.94	0.93	0.96
College Degree			0.70**	0.71**	0.97	0.98	1.05	1.06
Female Roles								
Traditional				1.00	1.00	1.00	1.00	1.00
Liberated				0.90*	0.95	0.94	0.94	0.95
Educ. Aspirations of Parent								
Less Than College Degree					1.00	1.00	1.00	1.00
College Degree					0.59**	0.65**	0.87*	0.89*
Graduate or Prof. Degree					0.46**	0.56**	0.81*	0.85*

	1	2	3	4	5	6	7	8
Occup. Aspirations of Parent								
No Paid Occupation					0.87	0.85*	0.88	0.85*
Blue Collar					1.00	1.00	1.00	1.00
Skilled					0.90	0.89	0.94	0.89
Low Professional					0.74**	0.77**	0.84**	0.86**
High Professional					0.52**	0.60**	0.81**	0.86
Expect. Age of Trans.-Parent								
19 or Earlier						1.88**	1.73**	1.75**
20–22						1.26**	1.27**	1.30**
23–25						1.00	1.00	1.00
26 or Later						0.71**	0.69**	0.75*
No Opinion						1.04	0.96	0.96
Educ. Aspirations of Student								
Less Than College Degree							1.00	1.00
College Degree							0.51**	0.52**
Graduate or Prof. Degree							0.30**	0.34**
Occup. Aspiration of Student								
No Paid Occupation								1.14
Blue Collar								1.00
Skilled								1.16*
Low Professional								0.89
High Professional								0.74**
Intercept (× 10)	1.12**	0.79**	1.07**	1.10**	1.47**	1.06**	1.03**	0.95**
Improvement in Fit								
χ^2	843.6	208.2	103.4	7.5	384.8	102.5	442.5	48.4
Degrees of Freedom	1	3	3	1	6	4	2	4
Probability Level	.000	.000	.000	.006	.000	.000	.000	.000

*p < .05
**p < .001

Table 1b. Effects of Variables on the Expected Rate of School Completion: Males

Independent Variables	Model							
	1	2	3	4	5	6	7	8
Duration	1.23**	1.26**	1.28**	1.28**	1.32**	1.34**	1.38**	1.38**
Race								
Black		0.86*	0.78**	0.78**	0.79**	0.80**	0.79**	0.76**
White		1.00	1.00	1.00	1.00	1.00	1.00	1.00
Grade								
Sophomore		1.79**	1.80**	1.80**	1.78**	1.73**	1.76**	1.77**
Senior		1.00	1.00	1.00	1.00	1.00	1.00	1.00
Parent Responding								
Mother		1.16*	1.04	1.04	1.00	1.00	0.96	0.97
Father		1.00	1.00	1.00	1.00	1.00	1.00	1.00
Family Social Class								
Blue Collar			1.00	1.00	1.00	1.00	1.00	1.00
White Collar			0.70**	0.70**	0.80**	0.81**	0.82**	0.81**
Parent's Education								
High School or Less			1.00	1.00	1.00	1.00	1.00	1.00
Some Post-High School			0.84**	0.84**	0.94	0.94	0.96	0.95
College Degree			0.64**	0.64**	0.85*	0.84*	0.86*	0.87*
Female Roles								
Traditional				1.00	1.00	1.00	1.00	1.00
Liberated				1.00	1.10*	1.08	1.08	1.08
Educ. Aspirations of Parent								
Less Than College Degree					1.00	1.00	1.00	1.00
College Degree					0.61**	0.69**	0.88**	0.91
Graduate or Prof. Degree					0.50**	0.60**	0.90	0.93

Occup. Aspirations of Parent							
No Paid Occupation				0.80*	0.89	0.99	1.03
Blue Collar				1.00	1.00	1.00	1.00
Skilled				0.79**	0.86*	0.87*	0.90
Low Professional				0.74**	0.82**	0.92	0.93
High Professional				0.45**	0.53**	0.81*	0.93
Expect. Age of Trans.-Parent							
19 or Earlier					1.89**	1.71**	1.73**
20–22					1.24**	1.22**	1.22*
23–25					1.00	1.00	1.00
26 or Later					0.82	0.84	0.88
No Opinion					1.18	1.05	1.06
Educ. Aspirations of Student							
Less Than College Degree						1.00	1.00
College Degree						0.63**	0.64**
Graduate or Prof. Degree						0.32**	0.35**
Occup. Aspiration of Student							
No Paid Occupation							0.71**
Blue Collar							1.00
Skilled							0.88*
Low Professional							0.93
High Professional							0.60**
Intercept (× 10)	1.14**	0.75**	1.07**	1.07**	1.46**	1.02**	1.06**	1.09**
Improvement in Fit							
χ^2	603.2	214.6	190.2	0.0	412.7	76.5	264.8	42.1
Degrees of Freedom	1	3	3	1	6	4	2	4
Probability Level	.000	.000	.000	1.000	.000	.000	.000	.000

*p < .05
**p < .001

Table 2a. Effects of Variables on the Expected Rate of Entry into First Regular Job: Females

Independent Variables	Model 1	2	3	4	5	6	7	8
Duration	1.09**	1.09**	1.10**	1.10**	1.13**	1.13**	1.14**	1.14**
Race								
Black		0.96	0.90	0.90	1.01	1.03	1.01	1.00
White		1.00	1.00	1.00	1.00	1.00	1.00	1.00
Grade								
Sophomore		1.12*	1.11*	1.11*	1.08	1.06	1.06	1.07
Senior		1.00	1.00	1.00	1.00	1.00	1.00	1.00
Parent Responding								
Mother		1.11*	1.03	1.03	1.03	0.98	0.97	0.98
Father		1.00	1.00	1.00	1.00	1.00	1.00	1.00
Family Social Class								
Blue Collar			1.00	1.00	1.00	1.00	1.00	1.00
White Collar			0.87**	0.87**	0.94	0.95	0.96	0.95
Parent's Education								
High School or Less			1.00	1.00	1.00	1.00	1.00	1.00
Some Post-High School			0.92	0.92	1.09	1.11*	1.13*	1.13*
College Degree			0.68**	0.68**	0.88*	0.94	0.98	0.99
Female Roles								
Traditional				1.00	1.00	1.00	1.00	1.00
Liberated				1.01	1.05	1.05	1.05	1.05
Educ. Aspirations of Parent								
Less Than College Degree					1.00	1.00	1.00	1.00
College Degree					0.62**	0.70**	0.84**	0.84**
Graduate or Prof. Degree					0.54**	0.62**	0.74**	0.75**

Occup. Aspirations of Parent						
No Paid Occupation				0.86	0.89	0.90	0.90
Blue Collar				1.00	1.00	1.00	1.00
Skilled				1.05	1.12	1.12	1.09
Low Professional				0.97	1.05	1.09	1.12
High Professional				0.68**	0.74**	0.84	0.86
Expect. Age of Trans.-Parent							
19 or Earlier					1.60**	1.49**	1.48**
20–22					1.10	1.08	1.07
23–25					1.00	1.00	1.00
26 or Later					1.05	1.02	1.03
No Opinion					1.19	1.13	1.13
Educ. Aspirations of Student							
Less Than College Degree						1.00	1.00
College Degree						0.67**	0.68**
Graduate or Prof. Degree						0.63**	0.66**
Occup. Aspiration of Student							
No Paid Occupation							0.83*
Blue Collar							1.00
Skilled							1.02
Low Professional							0.88
High Professional							0.83*
Intercept (× 10)	2.13**	1.89**	2.33**	2.32**	2.65**	1.90**	2.05**	2.15**
Improvement in Fit							
χ^2	118.0	16.5	83.5	0.1	215.4	65.8	73.0	18.1
Degrees of Freedom	1	3	3	1	6	4	2	4
Probability Level	.000	.001	.000	.823	.000	.000	.000	.001

*p < .05
**p < .001

Table 2b. Effects of Variables on the Expected Rate of Entry into First Regular Job: Males

Independent Variables	Model							
	1	2	3	4	5	6	7	8
Duration	1.12**	1.12**	1.13**	1.13**	1.16**	1.17**	1.18**	1.19**
Race								
Black		0.88*	0.84*	0.84*	0.86*	0.88*	0.86*	0.82*
White		1.00	1.00	1.00	1.00	1.00	1.00	1.00
Grade								
Sophomore		1.25**	1.21**	1.21**	1.16*	1.14*	1.12*	1.12*
Senior		1.00	1.00	1.00	1.00	1.00	1.00	1.00
Parent Responding								
Mother		1.04	0.97	0.96	0.95	0.95	0.94	0.93
Father		1.00	1.00	1.00	1.00	1.00	1.00	1.00
Family Social Class								
Blue Collar			1.00	1.00	1.00	1.00	1.00	1.00
White Collar			0.85**	0.85**	1.00	1.01	1.06	1.05
Parent's Education								
High School or Less			1.00	1.00	1.00	1.00	1.00	1.00
Some Post-High School			0.92	0.92	1.04	1.07	1.07	1.06
College Degree			0.71**	0.71**	0.90	0.95	0.97	0.95
Female Roles								
Traditional				1.00	1.00	1.00	1.00	1.00
Liberated				1.01	1.07	1.04	1.05	1.06
Educ. Aspirations of Parent								
Less Than College Degree					1.00	1.00	1.00	1.00
College Degree					0.64**	0.71**	0.84**	0.84*
Graduate or Prof. Degree					0.56**	0.66**	0.87	0.89

Occup. Aspirations of Parent							
No Paid Occupation				1.22	1.27*	1.39*	1.44*
Blue Collar				1.00	1.00	1.00	1.00
Skilled				0.90	0.96	1.03	1.04
Low Professional				0.81**	0.87*	0.99	1.00
High Professional				0.51**	0.60**	0.79*	0.92
Expect. Age of Trans.-Parent							
19 or Earlier					1.64**	1.53**	1.49**
20–22					1.24*	1.20*	1.18*
23–25					1.00	1.00	1.00
26 or Later					0.71*	0.67**	0.67**
No Opinion					1.18	1.07	1.04
Educ. Aspirations of Student							
Less Than College Degree						1.00	1.00
College Degree						0.67**	0.68**
Graduate or Prof. Degree						0.48**	0.56**
Occup. Aspiration of Student							
No Paid Occupation							0.76**
Blue Collar							1.00
Skilled							0.95
Low Professional							0.94
High Professional							0.57**
Intercept ($\times 10$)	1.77**	1.55**	1.94**	1.94**	2.37**	1.61**	1.68**	1.79**
Improvement in Fit							
χ^2	176.5	33.1	74.9	0.0	291.7	66.7	100.3	48.0
Degrees of Freedom	1	3	3	1	6	4	2	4
Probability Level	.000	.000	.000	.862	.000	.000	.000	.000

*p < .05
**p < .001

Table 3a. Effects of Variables on the Expected Rate of Independent Residence: Females

Independent Variables	1	2	3	4	5	6	7	8
Duration	1.32**	1.33**	1.33**	1.33**	1.34**	1.36**	1.37**	1.37**
Race								
Black		0.63**	0.60**	0.60**	0.63**	0.71**	0.71**	0.71**
White		1.00	1.00	1.00	1.00	1.00	1.00	1.00
Grade								
Sophomore		1.17**	1.17**	1.16**	1.12*	1.08	1.07	1.07
Senior		1.00	1.00	1.00	1.00	1.00	1.00	1.00
Parent Responding								
Mother		1.10*	1.06	1.05	1.05	0.98	0.96	0.96
Father		1.00	1.00	1.00	1.00	1.00	1.00	1.00
Family Social Class								
Blue Collar			1.00	1.00	1.00	1.00	1.00	1.00
White Collar			0.89*	0.89*	0.94	0.95	0.98	0.99
Parent's Education								
High School or Less			1.00	1.00	1.00	1.00	1.00	1.00
Some Post-High School			0.99	0.98	1.06	1.03	1.03	1.03
College Degree			0.85*	0.85*	0.98	0.96	0.99	0.99
Female Roles								
Traditional				1.00	1.00	1.00	1.00	1.00
Liberated				1.06	1.09*	1.08	1.10*	1.10*
Educ. Aspirations of Parent								
Less Than College Degree					1.00	1.00	1.00	1.00
College Degree					0.79**	0.84**	0.99	1.00
Graduate or Prof. Degree					0.70**	0.77**	0.93	0.94

Occup. Aspirations of Parent						
No Paid Occupation				1.08	1.04	1.09	1.07
Blue Collar				1.00	1.00	1.00	1.00
Skilled				1.13	1.16	1.19*	1.17
Low Professional				1.02	1.05	1.13	1.12
High Professional				0.85	0.92	1.07	1.08
Expect. Age of Trans.-Parent						
19 or Earlier					2.20**	2.10**	2.09**
20–22					1.45**	1.42**	1.42**
23–25					1.00	1.00	1.00
26 or Later					0.77*	0.73*	0.73*
No Opinion					1.19*	1.16	1.16
Educ. Aspirations of Student						
Less Than College Degree						1.00	1.00
College Degree						0.69**	0.70**
Graduate or Prof. Degree						0.65**	0.66**
Occup. Aspiration of Student						
No Paid Occupation							0.99
Blue Collar							1.00
Skilled							1.05
Low Professional							1.01
High Professional							0.93
Intercept (× 100)	9.56**	8.59**	9.66**	9.50**	9.51**	6.51**	6.65**	6.56**
Improvement in Fit						
χ^2	1153.8	84.9	25.1	2.1	78.2	184.1	64.0	3.1
Degrees of Freedom	1	3	3	1	6	4	2	4
Probability Level	.000	.000	.000	.148	.000	.000	.000	.543

*p < .05
**p < .001

Table 3b. Effects of Variables on the Expected Rate of Independent Residence: Males

Independent Variables	Model 1	2	3	4	5	6	7	8
Duration	1.26**	1.26**	1.26**	1.26**	1.27**	1.28**	1.28**	1.28**
Race								
Black		0.78**	0.77**	0.77**	0.78**	0.80**	0.79**	0.78**
White		1.00	1.00	1.00	1.00	1.00	1.00	1.00
Grade								
Sophomore		1.23**	1.21**	1.21**	1.20**	1.17**	1.16*	1.15*
Senior		1.00	1.00	1.00	1.00	1.00	1.00	1.00
Parent Responding								
Mother		1.10*	1.07	1.06	1.06	1.05	1.06	1.05
Father		1.00	1.00	1.00	1.00	1.00	1.00	1.00
Family Social Class								
Blue Collar			1.00	1.00	1.00	1.00	1.00	1.00
White Collar			0.93	0.93	0.98	0.98	1.00	1.01
Parent's Education								
High School or Less			1.00	1.00	1.00	1.00	1.00	1.00
Some Post-High School			1.05	1.05	1.08	1.06	1.07	1.06
College Degree			0.90	0.90	1.00	1.02	1.05	1.04
Female Roles								
Traditional				1.00	1.00	1.00	1.00	1.00
Liberated				1.02	1.06	1.05	1.04	1.04
Educ. Aspirations of Parent								
Less Than College Degree					1.00	1.00	1.00	1.00
College Degree					0.92	0.92	1.03	1.03
Graduate or Prof. Degree					0.87*	0.91	1.06	1.06

Occup. Aspirations of Parent					
No Paid Occupation			0.97	1.01	1.01
Blue Collar			1.00	1.00	1.00
Skilled			0.97	1.01	1.00
Low Professional			0.85*	0.91	0.91
High Professional			0.66**	0.74**	0.77*
Expect. Age of Trans.-Parent					
19 or Earlier			1.64**	1.62**	1.64**
20–22			1.35**	1.33**	1.33**
23–25			1.00	1.00	1.00
26 or Later			0.96	0.95	0.95
No Opinion			1.05	1.03	1.03
Educ. Aspirations of Student					
Less Than College Degree				1.00	1.00
College Degree				0.78**	0.80**
Graduate or Prof. Degree				0.73**	0.78**
Occup. Aspiration of Student					
No Paid Occupation					1.17
Blue Collar					1.00
Skilled					1.04
Low Professional					0.96
High Professional					0.85
Intercept (× 100)	8.60**	7.47**	7.94**	7.91**	8.52**	6.93**	6.94**	6.86**
Improvement in Fit					
χ^2	811.9	42.1	12.6	0.2	54.1	71.2	24.6	8.9
Degrees of Freedom	1	3	3	1	6	4	2	4
Probability Level	.000	.000	.006	.888	.000	.000	.000	.064

*p < .05
**p < .001

Table 4a. Effects of Variables on the Expected Rate of First Marriage: Females

Independent Variables	Model 1	2	3	4	5	6	7	8
Duration	1.38**	1.39**	1.40**	1.40**	1.41**	1.44**	1.44**	1.45**
Race								
Black		0.60**	0.57**	0.58**	0.64**	0.71**	0.71**	0.69**
White		1.00	1.00	1.00	1.00	1.00	1.00	1.00
Grade								
Sophomore		0.90*	0.91*	0.93	0.91*	0.88**	0.88**	0.89**
Senior		1.00	1.00	1.00	1.00	1.00	1.00	1.00
Parent Responding								
Mother		1.08	0.99	1.02	1.04	1.01	1.00	1.01
Father		1.00	1.00	1.00	1.00	1.00	1.00	1.00
Family Social Class								
Blue Collar			1.00	1.00	1.00	1.00	1.00	1.00
White Collar			0.89*	0.90*	0.95	0.94	0.97	0.97
Parent's Education								
High School or Less			1.00	1.00	1.00	1.00	1.00	1.00
Some Post-High School			0.86**	0.87*	0.95	0.98	0.99	1.01
College Degree			0.70**	0.71**	0.84*	0.88*	0.91	0.91
Female Roles								
Traditional				1.00	1.00	1.00	1.00	1.00
Liberated				0.84**	0.87**	0.86**	0.86**	0.87**
Educ. Aspirations of Parent								
Less Than College Degree					1.00	1.00	1.00	1.00
College Degree					0.76**	0.89*	1.00	1.02
Graduate or Prof. Degree					0.61**	0.76**	0.86*	0.88

	1	2	3	4	5	6	7	8
Occup. Aspirations of Parent								
No Paid Occupation					1.31*	1.25*	1.28*	1.22*
Blue Collar					1.00	1.00	1.00	1.00
Skilled					1.19*	1.21*	1.22*	1.13
Low Professional					1.14	1.28*	1.34*	1.31*
High Professional					0.85	0.98	1.09	1.10
Expect. Age of Trans.-Parent								
19 or Earlier						3.45**	3.37**	3.30**
20–22						1.64**	1.64**	1.63**
23–25						1.00	1.00	1.00
26 or Later						0.64**	0.65**	0.64**
No Opinion						0.97	0.98	0.98
Educ. Aspirations of Student								
Less Than College Degree							1.00	1.00
College Degree							0.78**	0.78**
Graduate or Prof. Degree							0.70**	0.75**
Occup. Aspiration of Student								
No Paid Occupation								1.58**
Blue Collar								1.00
Skilled								1.42**
Low Professional								1.10
High Professional								1.07
Intercept (× 100)	2.72**	2.83**	3.51**	3.65**	3.31**	2.11**	2.14**	1.70**
Improvement in Fit								
χ^2	1725.9	73.0	60.1	16.2	117.6	310.0	36.43	55.27
Degrees of Freedom	1	3	3	1	6	4	2	4
Probability Level	.000	.000	.000	.000	.000	.000	.000	.000

*p < .05
**p < .001

Table 4b. Effects of Variables on the Expected Rate of First Marriage: Males

Independent Variables	1	2	3	4	5	6	7	8
Duration	1.43**	1.43**	1.44**	1.44**	1.44**	1.47**	1.47**	1.47**
Race								
Black		0.65**	0.62**	0.64**	0.64**	0.68**	0.67**	0.67**
White		1.00	1.00	1.00	1.00	1.00	1.00	1.00
Grade								
Sophomore		1.20**	1.19**	1.22**	1.22**	1.17*	1.17*	1.17*
Senior		1.00	1.00	1.00	1.00	1.00	1.00	1.00
Parent Responding								
Mother		0.96	0.90*	0.92	0.92	0.93	0.93	0.92
Father		1.00	1.00	1.00	1.00	1.00	1.00	1.00
Family Social Class								
Blue Collar			1.00	1.00	1.00	1.00	1.00	1.00
White Collar			0.89*	0.89*	0.93	0.95	0.96	0.96
Parent's Education								
High School or Less			1.00	1.00	1.00	1.00	1.00	1.00
Some Post-High School			0.94	0.94	0.96	0.98	0.99	0.99
College Degree			0.72**	0.73**	0.78**	0.83*	0.83*	0.83*
Female Roles								
Traditional				1.00	1.00	1.00	1.00	1.00
Liberated				0.85**	0.86**	0.89**	0.89*	0.89*
Educ. Aspirations of Parent								
Less Than College Degree					1.00	1.00	1.00	1.00
College Degree					0.80**	0.81**	0.84*	0.83*
Graduate or Prof. Degree					0.88	0.94	0.97	0.98

Occup. Aspirations of Parent							
No Paid Occupation					1.54*	1.56**	1.58**	1.62*
Blue Collar					1.00	1.00	1.00	1.00
Skilled					1.06	1.09	1.10	1.12
Low Professional					1.04	1.12	1.13	1.17
High Professional					0.80*	0.88	0.89	0.97
Expect. Age of Trans.-Parent								
19 or Earlier						2.70**	2.66**	2.71**
20–22						1.45**	1.45**	1.44**
23–25						1.00	1.00	1.00
26 or Later						0.57**	0.57**	0.57**
No Opinion						0.73**	0.73**	0.73**
Educ. Aspirations of Student								
Less Than College Degree							1.00	1.00
College Degree							0.93	0.96
Graduate or Prof. Degree							0.96	1.05
Occup. Aspiration of Student								
No Paid Occupation								1.02
Blue Collar								1.00
Skilled								0.96
Low Professional								0.88
High Professional								0.78*
Intercept (× 100)	1.51**	1.43**	1.71**	1.76**	1.80**	1.58**	1.58**	1.60**
Improvement in Fit								
χ^2	1588.9	49.7	42.7	12.0	39.5	194.5	1.31	7.17
Degrees of Freedom	1	3	3	1	6	4	2	4
Probability Level	.000	.000	.000	.000	.000	.000	.522	.126

*p < .05
**p < .001

Table 5a. Effects of Variables on the Expected Rate of Having a Child: Females

Independent Variables	Model 1	2	3	4	5	6	7	8
Duration	1.44**	1.44**	1.45**	1.45**	1.47**	1.49**	1.50**	1.50**
Race								
Black		1.14	1.05	1.07	1.29*	1.24*	1.27*	1.27*
White		1.00	1.00	1.00	1.00	1.00	1.00	1.00
Grade								
Sophomore		1.05	1.07	1.09	1.06	1.06	1.06	1.05
Senior		1.00	1.00	1.00	1.00	1.00	1.00	1.00
Parent Responding								
Mother		1.14*	1.02	1.05	1.06	1.06	1.05	1.05
Father		1.00	1.00	1.00	1.00	1.00	1.00	1.00
Family Social Class								
Blue Collar			1.00	1.00	1.00	1.00	1.00	1.00
White Collar			0.83**	0.83**	0.92	0.92	0.96	0.97
Parent's Education								
High School or Less			1.00	1.00	1.00	1.00	1.00	1.00
Some Post-High School			0.88*	0.89*	1.04	1.04	1.06	1.08
College Degree			0.60**	0.61**	0.81*	0.87	0.93	0.93
Female Roles								
Traditional				1.00	1.00	1.00	1.00	1.00
Liberated				0.85**	0.89*	0.90*	0.90*	0.92
Educ. Aspirations of Parent								
Less Than College Degree					1.00	1.00	1.00	1.00
College Degree					0.59**	0.67**	0.80**	0.81**
Graduate or Prof. Degree					0.44**	0.52**	0.64**	0.64**

40

Occup. Aspirations of Parent							
No Paid Occupation				1.52**	1.36*	1.39*	1.36*
Blue Collar				1.00	1.00	1.00	1.00
Skilled				1.22*	1.20	1.19	1.18
Low Professional				1.12	1.15	1.23	1.27*
High Professional				0.94	1.06	1.25	1.34
Expect. Age of Trans.-Parent							
19 or Earlier					2.97**	2.76**	2.64**
20–22					1.39**	1.32**	1.31**
23–25					1.00	1.00	1.00
26 or Later					0.60**	0.59**	0.60**
No Opinion					0.73**	0.72**	0.73**
Educ. Aspirations of Student							
Less Than College Degree						1.00	1.00
College Degree						0.65**	0.68**
Graduate or Prof. Degree						0.54**	0.60**
Occup. Aspiration of Student							
No Paid Occupation							1.45**
Blue Collar							1.00
Skilled							1.11
Low Professional							0.98
High Professional							0.86
Intercept (× 100)	0.97**	0.85**	1.10**	1.14**	1.02**	0.95**	0.99**	0.87**
Improvement in Fit							
χ^2	1500.3	13.3	83.1	10.0	197.7	226.9	70.0	29.6
Degrees of Freedom	1	3	3	1	6	4	2	4
Probability Level	.000	.004	.000	.002	.000	.000	.000	.000

*p < .05
**p < .001

Table 5b. Effects of Variables on the Expected Rate of Having a First Child: Males

Independent Variables	Model							
	1	2	3	4	5	6	7	8
Duration	1.42**	1.43**	1.43**	1.44**	1.44**	1.45**	1.45**	1.45**
Race								
Black		1.08	1.02	1.06	1.09	1.13	1.12	1.11
White		1.00	1.00	1.00	1.00	1.00	1.00	1.00
Grade								
Sophomore		1.38**	1.36**	1.42**	1.41**	1.34**	1.35**	1.34**
Senior		1.00	1.00	1.00	1.00	1.00	1.00	1.00
Parent Responding								
Mother		1.02	0.92	0.96	0.95	0.95	0.95	0.95
Father		1.00	1.00	1.00	1.00	1.00	1.00	1.00
Family Social Class								
Blue Collar			1.00	1.00	1.00	1.00	1.00	1.00
White Collar			0.78**	0.80**	0.86*	0.88*	0.88*	0.89
Parent's Education								
High School or Less			1.00	1.00	1.00	1.00	1.00	1.00
Some Post-High School			0.83*	0.83*	0.88*	0.87*	0.88*	0.87*
College Degree			0.63**	0.65**	0.73**	0.77*	0.79*	0.79*
Female Roles								
Traditional				1.00	1.00	1.00	1.00	1.00
Liberated				0.76**	0.78**	0.80**	0.79**	0.79**
Educ. Aspirations of Parent								
Less Than College Degree					1.00	1.00	1.00	1.00
College Degree					0.77**	0.82*	0.90	0.90
Graduate or Prof. Degree					0.80*	0.88	0.99	0.99

Occup. Aspirations of Parent							
No Paid Occupation				1.48*	1.51*	1.57*	1.60*
Blue Collar				1.00	1.00	1.00	1.00
Skilled				0.97	1.02	1.05	1.07
Low Professional				0.86	0.92	0.96	0.99
High Professional				0.73*	0.79*	0.80	0.86
Expect. Age of Trans.-Parent							
19 or Earlier					1.58	1.54	1.53
20–22					1.56**	1.55**	1.55**
23–25					1.00	1.00	1.00
26 or Later					0.65**	0.65**	0.66**
No Opinion					0.70**	0.70**	0.70**
Educ. Aspirations of Student							
Less Than College Degree						1.00	1.00
College Degree						0.75**	0.77**
Graduate or Prof. Degree						0.87	0.93
Occup. Aspiration of Student							
No Paid Occupation							0.99
Blue Collar							1.00
Skilled							0.95
Low Professional							0.92
High Professional							0.81
Intercept (× 100)	0.80**	0.64**	0.87**	0.91**	0.99**	1.06**	1.06**	1.08**
Improvement in Fit							
χ^2	1045.2	34.0	69.0	22.5	46.4	98.3	11.4	2.5
Degrees of Freedom	1	3	3	1	6	4	2	4
Probability Level	.000	.000	.000	.000	.000	.000	.003	.651

*p < .05
**p < .001

effects of career plans are partialed out suggests that these rational planning considerations act to suppress the strong connections between developmental age and demographic statuses.

B. Control Variables

1. Sex of Parent Respondent

The coefficients of the variable for sex of the parent responding to the survey provide reassurance that the characteristics of the survey design do not seriously bias the results. In general, adolescents whose mothers responded to the parent survey expect somewhat higher transition rates (earlier ages), but these differences are never large and they decline to nonsignificant magnitudes with the introduction of controls for family socioeconomic characteristics.

2. School Grade Cohort

There are major differences between sophomores and seniors in the anticipated ages of early life transitions. For both sexes, sophomores expect much higher rates of school completion than seniors (Tables 1a and 1b). Even controlling for the different educational aspirations of the two groups, sophomores have anticipated rates of school completion that are 75 percent higher than those of seniors. It may be that the earlier ages at which sophomores expect to complete school partly result from heterogeneity within each of the educational aspiration categories, but this seems unlikely because the addition of educational aspirations to this model has no effects among males and actually increases differences among the females. A more likely explanation is that sophomores anticipate they will be able to finish any level of schooling expeditiously, whereas seniors (who are actually facing the costs involved in school enrollment) anticipate delays in completing their higher educations due to postponed or interrupted college enrollments.

The grade level differences in expected ages at first job and independent residence again show sophomores with higher rates, but the magnitude of these differences are quite moderate. Indeed, the introduction of controls for the educational and occupational aspirations of the parent and for the parent's own anticipation of age at the transition greatly reduces the differences among males and reduces them to nonsignificance among females. It thus appears that young persons may postpone the expected ages at first job and independent residence as they age in response to the formation of more ambitious educational and occupational plans.

School grade differences in family formation plans vary substantially by sex. Among females, sophomores expect a slightly lower rate (later age) of first marriage but expect about the same rate of first birth. It may be that the emotional attachments developed by some students during their junior and senior years cause them to plan to marry at an earlier age than they initially anticipated. The combination of an earlier expected age at marriage among seniors and no grade difference in expected age at first childbirth implies that seniors expect to have a longer first birth interval (time between marriage and parenthood) than the sophomores. To the extent that it is parenthood rather than marriage than creates difficulties in career achievements among females, the family formation plans of the seniors permit them to hope for career achievements without abandoning plans to marry a high school sweetheart. Among males the patterns are more straightforward. Male sophomores have an expected rate of first marriage that is about 20 percent higher and rates of family formation that are 34 percent higher. These different expectations are in part a function of the earlier ages at family formation expected by the parents of the sophomores. As with the females, among the males seniors expect a longer first birth interval than sophomores.

C. Subcultural Affiliations

1. Race

The transition plans of American high school students differ substantially by race. Blacks expect to take longer to finish formal schooling than do whites even controlling for racial differentials in educational aspirations. The anticipated age-specific rate of school completion among black females is about one-third lower than among white females (Table 1a), whereas the differential is no more than one-quarter among males (Table 1b). Although there are no racial differentials in the expected timing of first job among females, the rates anticipated by black males are slightly lower than those of whites. These results imply that blacks more frequently expect to begin working at a regular job prior to completing their formal schooling, perhaps as one means of paying for advanced schooling in the absence of other economic assistance. Among both males and females, blacks expect lower age-specific rates of independent residence. Such extended residence with the family of origin may be one strategy a black adolescent planning a post–high school education can use to reduce costs. In essence, extended residence in the parental household is a source of nonmonetary financial assistance to the young black adult. These expectations resemble the resource-sharing strategies of black kin networks described by Stack (1975).

Both black females and males anticipate age-specific rates of marriage that are about one-third below those of whites (Tables 4a and 4b). Overall, there are no racial differentials in the expected rates of first childbirth (Tables 5a and 5b, panel 2). However, when controls are introduced for racial differences in the educational and occupational aspirations of parents for their children, black females anticipate a rate of first childbirth that is one-fourth higher than that of whites. Coupled with the racial differentials in marriage plans, these findings about expected rates of parenthood indicate that blacks are much more likely than whites to anticipate becoming a parent prior to marriage (tabulations not shown).

2. Social Class

Both males and females of blue-collar origins anticipate earlier ages at each of the youth-to-adult transitions. These normative differences in plans for adulthood come about largely as the result of the lower educational and occupational aspirations of blue-collar parents for their children. Parents in white-collar families expect their children to attain higher levels of education and to have higher occupational attainments. The children of white-collar parents plan to delay their ages at school completion, first job, independent residence, and family formation in order to facilitate their career achievements. The intergenerational transfer of social class position thus may partly be accomplished through parental influences on adolescent strategies for the youth-to-adult transitions.

3. Parental Education

Higher parental education is associated with a later expected age at school completion among both males and females. In large part, this influence is mediated by the parents' educational aspirations for their children. Children of parents with a college degree expect later ages at first job and independent household, but again most of this differential is due to the higher aspirations for the children of better educated parents. Children of better educated parents expect to delay marriage and initial childbirth. Among both sexes this tendency is most pronounced among the children of college-educated parents. The planned delays in family formation among females is due to the higher educational and occupational aspirations of better educated parents for their daughters, as well as to the parents' expectations regarding the ages at which their daughters will marry and have children. Among males the same pattern is observed, but sons of college-educated parents expect to delay marriage and childbirth even after taking into account the aspirations of parents for their children. The effects of higher parental education are greater in the case of parenthood than marriage, indicating that the sons and daughters of college-educated parents expect a longer first birth interval than children of less educated parents. Such a difference would facilitate the career achievements of young persons.

4. Parental Sex Role Attitudes

Parental attitudes about appropriate female roles have rather limited effects on the career plans of their children but somewhat larger impacts on their family formation behaviors. Daughters of parents with liberated sex role attitudes have lower rates of anticipated school completion because of the higher educational and career aspirations such liberated parents have for their daughters (Table 1a). Daughters of liberated parents expect to leave the parental household earlier than daughters of traditional parents (Table 3a). Coupled with the significantly lower rates of marriage and childbirth anticipated by daughters of liberated parents (Tables 4a and 5a), the daughters of liberated parents more often expect to leave the parental home prior to marriage. Daughters growing up in households where traditional female roles are preferred more often anticipate remaining at home until marriage. Because the delays in marriage and parenthood plans associated with liberated parental sex role views are about equal, it does not appear that daughters socialized with liberated views of female roles plan to delay childbearing substantially once they marry.

Not surprisingly, the attitudes of parents about appropriate female roles do not affect the plans of sons about the timing of school completion and first job. However, sons of parents with liberated female sex role views expect to delay marriage and childbearing (Tables 4b and 5b). Of particular interest, sons who have been socialized with liberated views of female roles anticipate that they will delay childbearing after marriage. Such a finding suggests that at least some men from these cohorts will be comfortable marrying a career-oriented woman who wishes to delay childbirth in order to further her career.

D. Parental Influences

1. Parental Educational Aspirations

The effects of parental aspirations for the educational and occupational attainments of their children on transition plans are strong and statistically significant for all transitions and both sexes. Among both sons and daughters, the expected age-specific rate of school completion is lowered by parental aspirations for a college or professional degree. A major part of this difference is accounted for by the higher educational aspirations of the children of better educated parents. Among daughters, however, higher parental educational aspirations are associated with expected delays in school completion, even controlling for the daughters' own educational plans, perhaps indicating a somewhat stronger direct effect of parental aspirations on the transition plans of daughters. Similar observations characterize the relationship between parental educational aspirations and the plans of their children for age at first job. Daughters whose parents expect them to get a college degree anticipate a lower rate of leaving the parental home due to extended school enrollment. Sons plan to leave the parental household at about the same rate regardless of the educational aspirations of their parents. Daughters of parents with high educational aspirations expect to delay marriage as a result of their own educational and career aspirations. Daughters of parents with high educational aspirations anticipate delays in childbearing. These differences remain substantial even controlling for the daughters' own career aspirations. The effects of parental educational aspirations on the marriage and childbearing plans of sons are much more limited and do not show a consistent pattern.

2. Parental Occupational Aspirations

Children raised by parents who instill aspirations for professional occupations expect a later age at school completion and first job, due principally to the extended school enrollment such professional careers require. Even controlling for educational plans, professional career objectives imply a somewhat later age at school completion and first job insofar as such careers cannot begin until after attaining the professional degree. Children of parents who do not report occupational aspirations for their children or who think their children will have no paid occupation have plans for much earlier marriage and parenthood transitions. These differences persist even with controls for the adolescents' own career plans. This finding suggests the active career socialization of children by their parents is important for the formation of plans about the transition to adulthood. It seems that the career socialization process may prompt young persons to think about the connections between career objectives and early life transitions. Regardless of the level of career aspirations parents attempt to instill, this process of connecting educational and occupational plans to thoughts about the timing of youth-to-adult transitions results in planned delays in those transitions. In this way, the socialization of children by their parents prolongs the period of adolescence and delays the achievement of adult statuses. This socialization process separates the social achievement of adulthood from the physical and cognitive criteria for adult status.

3. Parental Transition Expectations

This process of socialization depends on the parents' own views about the expected age at which their children will undergo each transition, net of the influence of the normative considerations implicit in subcultural identities. For every transition, there is a direct association between the views of parents and children about the anticipated timing of the transition. Children whose parents expect a relatively early transition (age 22 or younger) have much higher anticipated rates of transitions than adolescents whose parents expect a later transition. Conversely, sons and daughters of parents who expect their children will be 26 or older at the time of the transition (including those expecting the transition will never happen) anticipate much lower rates (later ages) at the transition. Although the magnitude of the coefficients are large for every transition, the impact of parental transition expectations on their childrens' transition anticipations are larger for the decisions about family formation and independent residence. In particular, the family formation plans of daughters depend quite heavily on the views of their parents. These results indicate that direct parental socialization about the appropriate ages for early life transitions are quite important factors in the transition plans of their children, and the influence of parents is greatest in regard to those transitions (residence, marriage, and parenthood) in which they have the greatest expertise. Those transitions traditionally have been more important for the overall life course of women than men, and the influence of parents, correspondingly, is greater for the plans of their daughters.

E. Rational Planning Considerations

1. Educational Aspirations

The direct connections between level of schooling completed and the age at school completion produce a very strong relationship between educational aspirations and the expected age at school completion (Tables 1a and 1b, panel 7). For both males and females, higher educational aspirations are associated with expectations of lower age-specific rates of school completion. Among both sexes, the higher educational aspirations also are associated with lower rates of first job entry. This connection is a result of the usual expectation that labor force entry will await school completion and is therefore unaffected by the particular occupational aspirations of the students. Adolescents expecting to complete a college degree program have rates of anticipated independent residence that are about one-quarter lower than adolescents with lower educational ambitions. However, adolescents expecting to earn graduate or professional degrees have the same rate of expected independent residence as students with bachelor's degree plans. This implies that some young persons expect to live at home while attending college during their later teens and early twenties but do not expect to remain at home indefinitely, even if they prolong their school enrollments into their middle and later twenties. Once again we find that social considerations embodied in educational and career decisions serve to delay the early life transitions, while it seems that developmental considerations dictate that these delays will not be indefinite.

As discussed in the introductory sections, advanced educational and career achievements are inconsistent with early marriage and parenthood, and the association is greatest among females for whom the role conflicts involved are severe. As hypothesized, females take these role conflicts into account in their plans about the timing of marriage and parenthood. Young women who have high educational aspirations (college degree or later) expect rates of first marriage that are about one-quarter lower than those with lower educational aspirations (Table 4a). Women with college degree plans expect rates of first childbirth about one-third lower than those expecting less than a college education, and the difference is even larger among those with aspirations for a graduate or professional degree (Table 5a). Interestingly, the educational plans of males have no impact on their marriage plans and a mixed pattern of effects on their plans for parenthood.

This lack of association between the educational and family formation plans of males is surprising given the observed connections between educational attainments and family formation behaviors. However, the lack of connections between educational aspirations and family formation plans among males may not reflect a failure to plan the transition to adulthood in a rational fashion. Rather, the marriage and parenthood transitions of this cohort of American males already are delayed sufficiently that they usually will not interfere with plans for school completion. For example, 44 percent of the male high school seniors expect to remain unmarried until their twenty-fifth birthday and 68 percent expect to be childless. Consequently, there is a fairly high probability that a male will delay forming a family of procreation until after his education is likely to be completed, in the usual course of making the educational, marriage, and childbirth transitions, without any conscious effort to delay family formation until after the completion of schooling.

Among female high school seniors, in contrast, only 26 percent expect to be unmarried on their twenty-fifth birthday and 55 percent expect to be childless. Thus, the earlier family formation transitions characteristic of the females, as well as the greater role conflicts between parenthood and school enrollment among females, produce a situation in which an aspiration for advanced education results in rational plans for a delay in family formation.

2. Occupational Aspirations

The occupational aspirations of students have smaller, less systematic impacts on transition plans than educational aspirations. Among females who do not expect a paid occupation at age 30 (principally those expecting to be homemakers), the beginning of the first regular job (paid occupation or homemaker) is expected to be somewhat later, although the anticipated timing of school completion and independent residence are about average. Women expecting to be homemakers at age 30 plan first marriage and parenthood at rates about 50 percent higher than other women. Among women aspiring to a paid occupation, a traditional skilled female occupation (e.g., secretarial or sales) is associated with plans for a slightly earlier age at school completion and a much higher rate of marriage. However, women planning to enter conventional skilled female occupations expect to have a rate of first childbirth like that of other career women. Women planning a high-level professional occupation are hypothesized to develop transition plans that will facilitate these career achievements. Since such professional careers require advanced schooling and cannot begin until after formal certification is obtained, these high-aspirations women expect to complete school and begin work at a somewhat late age (lower rates of these transitions). However, contrary to my hypothesis, once the higher educational ambitions of these women are taken into account, their expected rates of family formation do not differ significantly from those of women with unskilled or low-level professional aspirations.

In practice, success in high-level professional careers (doctor, lawyer, college professor) depends to a greater extent on continuity in employment than success in lower level professions (school teacher, nurse) which are more easily interrupted. In essence, the traditional female occupations probably are more compatible with the competing demands of childbearing and parenthood than are the high-status professions that formerly were the domain of males. Recent research showing the upturn in first birth rates of women (Kitagawa, 1981) as well as popular discussions of "super moms" suggest that professionally oriented women in previous cohorts will not forego marriage and parenthood to ease the route to career success. Similarly, among the female high school students of 1980 there is a willingness to postpone marriage and parenthood so that schooling may be completed, but there is no evidence that career goals will cause extensive delays in childbirth or childlessness.

Men with aspirations for a high-level profession expect to have somewhat lower age-specific rates of school completion and job entry compared with men with lesser occupational ambitions. This represents the longer period of education (within the graduate or professional degree category) that such occupations require as well as the difficulties in beginning professional occupations before certification is obtained. These young men do not expect to postpone marriage in order to complete advanced education, but there is a tendency among men with aspirations for high-level professional careers to postpone marriage slightly. Again it may be argued that the relatively late marriage ages expected by this cohort in general weaken the need to postpone family formation further to achieve career objectives.

V. CONCLUSIONS

In this analysis data from a national random sample of 6,564 high school students and their parents have been analyzed to determine the effects of normative subgroup affiliations, the proximate social influences of parents, and the educational and occupational aspirations of the students on the formation of adolescent expectations about the timing of early life transitions. This analysis was designed to take into account the role of these early life demographic transitions in defining adult status, and the relationships of physical maturity and cognitive development (as indexed by chronological age) to these transitions and the achievement of adult status. Because the issues addressed by this analysis are complex, the results cannot be summarized simply. However, several consistent findings have emerged from this analysis and these provide a basis for a number of general observations about the ways in which adolescents plan their youth-to-adult transitions.

The tendencies of adolescents to plan for early assumptions of adult demographic statuses are modified by normative considerations arising from subgroup affiliations, the proximate social influences of parents, and the educational and occupational aspirations of the adolescents. All three aspects of social control are structured by the American system of social stratification. As young persons mature they interact with their parents, peers, and school counselors in planning the timing of the youth-to-adult transitions. As educational and career aspirations develop, adolescents begin to anticipate later demographic transitions. Thus, seniors generally anticipate lower rates of early life transitions than sophomores.

Adolescents growing up in homes of lower social class standing and whose parents have lower educations expect earlier youth-to-adult transitions. The differences in transition plans arise from socioeconomic subcultures because of the influence of parents as socializing agents on their children's plans for adulthood. Parents of lower social class standing and with lesser educations have lower educational and career aspirations for their children. These parental aspirations influence the adolescents' own educational and career plans. The analysis showed that adolescents who have high educational and career ambitions expect to delay the timing of the youth-to-adult transitions. Adolescents who develop less ambitious plans for adult socioeconomic attainments, on the other hand, assume adult demographic statuses at the earlier ages, in accordance with physiological developmental processes. However, it is noteworthy that even students with the highest socioeconomic ambitions do not expect to delay the assumption of adult statuses forever; most adolescents expect to marry and bear children no later than their upper twenties or early thirties, regardless of the negative career consequences of such decisions.

Parents hold views about the ages at which they expect their children to accomplish the early life transitions and these views directly influence the adolescents' plans for assuming adult statuses. This process of intergenerational transmission of expectations about the timing of early life events presumably is an important source of observed intergenerational continuities in the actual timing of these events. These parental influences on plans about the timing of the early life transitions are strongest in the cases of the marriage and parenthood transitions. The parents have substantial expertise in these matters because they have experienced these transitions themselves and have observed the family formation behaviors of their own peers. In contrast, the knowledge of parents about college enrollment and careers different than their own is more circumscribed, so that the school completion and labor force entry transitions depend more directly on the rational planning considerations implicit in aspirations about socioeconomic attainments.

The process of planning the youth-to-adult transitions differs substantially between whites and blacks and between males and females. The differences appear to arise from racial and gender differences in rational planning considerations about becoming an adult as well as from subcultural differences in what is regarded as normatively appropriate behavior. Blacks anticipate greater difficulties than whites in finishing a given level of schooling, in entering the labor force with regular jobs, and in establishing their own residences. In all three instances, financial constraints appear to be an important consideration. Young blacks have more negative perceptions about the American opportunity structure (in terms of the difficulty of going to college, finding a job, and becoming financially independent), which produce the expectations that it will be more difficult to assume adult roles. This analysis suggests that blacks more than whites expect to rely on their families for material assistance (in particular, a "free" place to live) while assuming adult statuses. Blacks expect to become parents at about the same rates as whites but they anticipate a later age at marriage. Racial differences in marriage plans result in more blacks expecting to have a child while unmarried. These racial differences in reliance on kin networks and the greater acceptance of parenthood by unmarried men and women are consistent with anthropological work on urban blacks in the United States. It is as yet an unresolved issue whether these racial differences result from cultural traditions or are culturally based reactions to conditions in the social environment (see Hogan and Kitagawa, 1985).

Female roles in American society have been changing for the last two decades and remain in a state of flux. This research has shown that plans of adolescent women about the timing of early life events depend more heavily on parental influences than is the case for men. In particular, daughters whose parents hold nontraditional views of female roles and who encourage them to complete college degree programs in preparation for paid occupational careers plan to delay their marriage and childbearing in order to facilitate the achievement of career goals. More frequently than men, however, such daughters expect to rely on parental encouragement and assistance. Other women grow up in families where female roles are traditionally defined. To the extent that these women develop educational aspirations and expect to be homemakers at age 30, they plan to marry and become parents relatively early. It appears that the daughters of traditional families more often expect to remain residentially dependent on their parents until marriage.

Thus, the evolution of nontraditional roles for American females has permitted adolescent women to form both career and family goals. As has been widely noted, the career and family life courses are more closely linked among females than among males. This analysis indicates that this is recognized by adolescent women whose family formation plans depend significantly on their aspirations for educational and occupational attainments. Although these young women evince a willingness to delay marriage and childbearing in order to complete their college or graduate degree programs, they do not expect to forego marriage and parenthood indefinitely. There is some evidence that the adolescent males who grow up in sexually liberated homes expect to delay marriage and parenthood in ways that will enhance the career prospects of their wives.

However, as present cohorts of young adults are demonstrating, many men and women expect to be able to achieve career objectives while simultaneously raising families. The role conflicts resulting from these twin goals principally arise from the structure of family and labor institutions in the United States. Although these young people will modify their plans somewhat to attempt to cope with these institutional constraints, they are not prepared to abandon their twin goals of career and family achievements. Other research has noted that these role conflicts cannot explain the greater difficulties faced by females in translating educational attainment into career achievements (Miller and Garrison, 1982). Thus, individual strategies will be developed to cope with the difficulties imposed by institutional constraints but cannot be expected to resolve all problems encountered. The reduction of the problems inherent in these role conflicts ultimately will depend on institutional reforms in the workplace and at home.

This research has shown that the ways in which American adolescents plan to become adults depend on normative considerations embedded in memberships in cultural subgroups, on the proximate social influences of parents, and on the rational planning of early life transitions to facilitate the achievement of socioeconomic success. These three aspects of social control are structured by the American system of social stratification. Educational and career attainments depend on the actual timing of school completion, labor force entry, and family formation. The social control of adolescents' plans for the timing of youth-to-adult transitions thus is an important source of intergenerational continuities in socioeconomic attainments.

ACKNOWLEDGMENTS

This paper was written while the author was a Fellow at the Center for Advanced Study in the Behavioral Sciences. Support for this research was provided by a grant from the Spencer Foundation and by the John D. and Catherine T. MacArthur Foundation. I thank Gerald Suttles, Wendy Griswold, David Featherman, and Glen Elder for helpful discussions of the ideas developed in this paper.

REFERENCES

Bayer, A. E.
    1969 "Life plans and marriage age: an application of path analysis." Journal of Marriage and the Family 31:551–558.
Bengston, Vern L. and K. Dean Black
    1973 "Intergenerational relations and continuities in socialization." Pp. 208–234 in Paul B. Baltes and K. Warner Schaie (eds.), Life-Span Developmental Psychology: Personality and Socialization. New York: Academic Press.

Blau, Peter and O. D. Duncan
  1967 The American Occupational Structure. New York: John Wiley & Sons.
Card, Josephina J. and Lauress L. Wise
  1978 "Teenage mothers and teenage fathers: the impact of early childbearing on the parents' personal and professional lives." Family Planning Perspectives 10:199–205.
Cherlin, Andrew J.
  1981 Marriage, Divorce, Remarriage. Cambridge, MA: Harvard University Press.
Coleman, James S.
  1961 The Adolescent Society. New York: Free Press.
Coleman, John C.
  1980 "Friendship and peer group in adolescence." Pp. 408–431 in J. Adelson (ed.), Handbook of Adolescent Psychology. New York: John Wiley & Sons.
Davis, Nancy J. and Larry L. Bumpass
  1976 "The continuation of education after marriage among women in the United States: 1970." Demography 13:161–174.
Duncan, Beverly
  1965 "Dropouts and the unemployed." The Journal of Political Economy 53:121–134.
Duncan, O. D., David L. Featherman, and Beverly Duncan
  1972 Socioeconomic Background and Achievement. New York: Seminar Press.
Elder, Glen H., Jr.
  1975 "Age differentiation and the life course." Pp. 165–190 in A. Inkeles, J. Coleman, and N. Smelser (eds.), Annual Review of Sociology, 1975, Vol. 1. Palo Alto, CA: Annual Reviews.
  1978 "Approaches to social change and the family." American Journal of Sociology 84:S1–S38.
  1980 "Adolescence in historical perspective." Pp. 3–46 in J. Adelson (ed.), Handbook of Adolescent Psychology. New York: John Wiley & Sons.
Elder, Glen H., Jr. and Jeffrey K. Liker
  1982 "Economic change and health in women's lives: historical influences across forty years." American Journal of Sociology 88:241–269.
Elder, Glen H., Jr. and R. W. Rockwell
  1979 "Economic depression and postwar opportunity in men's lives: a study of life patterns and health." Pp. 249–303 in R. G. Simmons (ed.), Research in Community and Mental Health. Greenwich, CT: JAI Press.
Fallo-Mitchell, Linda and Carol D. Ryff
  1982 "Preferred timing of female life events: cohort differences." Research on Aging 4:249–267.
Feather, Norman T.
  1980 "Values in adolescence." Pp. 247–294 in J. Adelson (ed.), Handbook of Adolescent Psychology. New York: John Wiley & Sons.
Featherman, David L.
  1971 "The socioeconomic achievement of white religioethnic subgroups: social and psychological explanations." American Sociological Review 36:207–222.
  1980 "Schooling and occupational careers: constancy and change in worldly success." Pp. 675–738 in O. G. Brim, Jr. and J. Kagan (eds.), Constancy and Change in Human Development. Cambridge, MA: Harvard University Press.
  1982 "The life-span perspective in social science research." Five Year Outlook on Science and Technology. Washington, DC: National Science Foundation.
Featherman, David L. and T. Michael Carter
  1976 "Discontinuities in schooling and the socioeconomic life cycle." Pp. 133–160 in W. H.

Sewell, R. M. Hauser, and D. L. Featherman (eds.), Schooling and Achievement in American Society. New York: Academic Press.
Featherman, David L. and Robert M. Hauser
 1978 Opportunity and Change. New York: Academic Press.
Featherman, David L. and Dennis P. Hogan
 1984 "Entry into adulthood: profiles of young men in the 1950's. Pp. 159–202 in P. B. Baltes and O. G. Brim, Jr. (eds.), Life-Span Development and Behavior, Volume 6. New York: Academic.
Foner, Anne and David I. Kertzer
 1978 "Transitions over the life-course: lessons from age-set societies." American Journal of Sociology 83:1081–1104.
Friedenberg, E. F.
 1963 Coming of Age in America. New York: Vintage Books.
Garn, Stanley M.
 1980 "Continuities and change in maturational timing." Pp. 113–162 in O. G. Brim, Jr. and J. Kagan (eds.), Constancy and Change in Human Development. Cambridge, MA: Harvard University Press.
Glenn, N. D.
 1980 "Values, attitudes, and beliefs." Pp. 596–640 in O. G. Brim, Jr. and J. Kagan (eds.), Constancy and Change in Human Development. Cambridge, MA: Harvard University Press.
Gross, Alan J. and Virginia A. Clark
 1975 Survival Distributions: Reliability Applications in the Biomedical Sciences. New York: John Wiley & Sons.
Haggstrom, G. W., T. J. Blaschke, D. E. Kanouse, W. Lisowski, and P. A. Morrison
 1981 Teenage Parents: Their Ambitions and Attainments. Rand Publication R-2771-NICHD.
Hannan, Michael T., Nancy B. Tuma, and Lyle P. Groeneveld
 1977 "Income and marital events: evidence from an income-maintenance experiment." American Journal of Sociology 82:1186–1211.
Hofferth, Sandra L. and Kristin A. Moore
 1979 "Early childbearing and later economic well-being." American Sociological Review 44:784–815.
Hoffman, Martin L.
 1980 "Moral development in adolescence." Pp. 295–343 in J. Adelson (ed.), Handbook of Adolescent Psychology. New York: John Wiley & Sons.
Hogan, Dennis P.
 1978a "The effects of demographic factors, family background, and early job achievement on age at marriage." Demography 15:161–175.
 1978b "The variable order of events in the life course." American Sociological Review 43:573–586.
 1981 Transitions and Social Change: The Early Lives of American Men. New York: Academic Press.
Hogan, Dennis P. and Evelyn M. Kitagawa
 1985 "The impact of social status, family structure, and neighborhood on the fertility of black adolescents." American Journal of Sociology 90:825–855.
Hollingshead, A.
 1949 Elmtown's Youth. New York: John Wiley & Sons.
Horn, John L. and Gary Donaldson
 1980 "Cognitive development in adulthood." Pp. 445–529 in O. G. Brim, Jr. and J. Kagan (eds.), Constancy and Change in Human Development. Cambridge, MA: Harvard University Press.

Kaestle, Carl F. and Maris A. Vinovskis
  1978 "From fireside to factory: school entry and school leaving in nineteenth-century Massachusetts." Pp. 135–185 in T. K. Hareven (ed.), Transitions: The Family and the Life Course in Historical Perspective. New York: Academic Press.
Katz, M. B. and I. E. Davey
  1978 "Youth and early industrialization in a Canadian city." American Journal of Sociology 84(Supplement):S81–S119.
Kett, J. F.
  1977 Rites of Passage: Adolescence in America 1790 to Present. New York: Basic Books.
Kitagawa, Evelyn M.
  1981 "New life-styles: marriage patterns, living arrangements, and fertility outside of marriage." Annals, AAPSS 453:1–27.
Kobrin, Frances E. and Calvin Goldscheider
  1978 The Ethnic Factor in Family Structure and Mobility. Cambridge, MA: Ballinger Press.
Lewin-Epstein, Noah
  1980 Youth Employment During High School. Report to National Center for Education Statistics, University of Chicago, National Opinion Research Center.
McCarthy, James
  1978 "A comparison of the probabilities of the dissolution of first and second marriages." Demography 15:345–359.
Mare, Robert D.
  1979 "Social background composition and educational growth." Demography 16:55–71.
Marini, Margaret Mooney
  1978 "The transition to adulthood: sex differences in educational attainment and age at marriage." American Sociological Review 43:483–507.
  1982 "Determinants of the timing of adult role entry." Paper presented at the Workshop of the Population Research Center of the Economic Research Center, National Opinion Research Center.
Marini, Margaret Mooney and E. Greenberger
  1978a "Sex differences in educational aspirations and expectations." American Educational Research Journal 15:67–79.
  1978b "Sex differences in occupational aspirations and expectations." Sociology of Work and Occupations 5:47–78.
Menken, Jane, T. James Trussell, D. Stempol, and O. Babakol
  1981 "Proportional hazards life table models: an illustrative analysis of socio-demographic influences on marriage dissolution in the United States." Demography 18:181–200.
Miller, Joanne and Howard H. Garrison
  1982 "Sex roles: the division of labor at home and in the workplace." Pp. 237–262 in R. H. Turner and J. F. Short, Jr. (eds.), Annual Review of Sociology, Vol. 8. Palo Alto, CA: Annual Reviews.
Miller, Patricia Y. and William Simon
  1980 "The development of sexuality in adolescence." Pp. 383–407 in J. Adelson (ed.), Handbook of Adolescent Psychology. New York: John Wiley & Sons.
Modell, John
  1980 "Normative aspects of American marriage timing since World War II." Journal of Family History 5:210–234.
Modell, J., F. F. Furstenberg, Jr., and T. Hershberg
  1976 "Social change and transitions to adulthood in historical perspective." Journal of Family History 1:7–32.
Moen, Phyllis
  1982 "Continuities and discontinuities in women's labor force activity." Revised version of a

paper prepared for presentation at the Social Science Research Council sponsored workshop on Life-Course Research with Panel Data, November, 1981.

Moen, Phyllis, Edward L. Kain, and Glen H. Elder, Jr.
   1981 "Economic conditions and family life: contemporary and historical perspectives." Paper presented for the National Academy of Sciences, Assembly of Behavioral and Social Sciences, Committee on Child Development Research and Public Policy.

Moore, Kristin A., Linda J. Waite, Steven B. Caldwell, and Sandra L. Hofferth
   1978 "The consequences of age at first childbirth: educational attainment." Working Paper No. 1146-01, The Urban Institute, Washington, DC.

Neugarten, Bernice and Nancy Datan
   1973 "Sociological perspectives on the life cycle." Pp. 53–69 in P. B. Baltes and K. W. Schaie (eds.), Life-Span Developmental Psychology: Personality and Socialization. New York: Academic Press.

Neugarten, Bernice L., Joan W. Moore, and J. C. Lowe
   1965 "Age norms, age constraints, and adult socialization." American Journal of Sociology 70:710–717.

Otto, Luther B.
   1977 "Antecedents and consequences of marital timing." Pp. 101–126 in W. R. Burr et al. (eds.), Contemporary Theories About the Family, Vol. 1. New York: The Free Press.

Petersen, Anne C. and Brandon Taylor
   1980 "The biological approach to adolescence." Pp. 117–155 in J. Adelson (ed.), Handbook of Adolescent Psychology. New York: John Wiley & Sons.

Potter, Robert G.
   1977 "The multiple decrement life table as an approach to the measurement of use effectiveness and demographic effectiveness of contraception." Paper presented at the Sydney, Australia Conference of the International Union for the Scientific Study of Population.

Riley, Matilda White
   1976 "Age strata in social systems." Pp. 189–217 in R. H. Binstock and E. Shanas (eds.), Handbook of Aging and the Social Sciences. New York: Van Nostrand Reinhold.

Ryder, Norman B.
   1965 "The cohort as a concept in the study of social change." American Sociological Review 30:843–861.
   1969 "The emergence of a modern fertility pattern: United States, 1917–1966." Pp. 99–123 in S. J. Behrman, L. Corsa, and R. Freedman (eds.), Fertility and Family Planning: A World View. Ann Arbor, MI: University of Michigan Press.

Sandefur, Gary D. and Wilbur J. Scott
   1981 "A dynamic analysis of migration: an assessment of the effects of age, family, and career variables." Demography 18:355–368.

Sewell, William H.
   1971 "Inequality of opportunity for higher education." American Sociological Review 36:793–809.

Sewell, W. H., A. Haller, and A. Portes
   1969 "The educational and early occupational attainment process." American Sociological Review 34:82–92.

Sewell, W. H. and R. M. Hauser
   1975 Education, Occupation, and Earnings. New York: Academic Press.
   1980 "The Wisconsin longitudinal study of social and psychological factors in aspirations and achievements." Research in Sociology of Education and Socialization 1:59–99.

Sewell, W. H. and V. P. Shah
   1968 "Social class, parental encouragement, and educational aspirations." American Journal of Sociology 73:559–572.

Sørensen, Aage B.
  1980 "Analysis of change in discrete variables." Pp. 284–299 in J. Clubb and E. Schuech (eds.), Historical Social Research. Stuttgart: Klett-Cotta.
Spenner, Kenneth I. and David L. Featherman
  1978 "Achievement ambitions." Pp. 373–420 in R. H. Turner, J. Coleman, and R. C. Fox (eds.), Annual Review of Sociology, Vol. 4. Palo Alto, CA: Annual Reviews.
Stack, Carol
  1975 All Our Kin: Strategies for Survival in a Black Community. New York: Harper and Row.
Sweet, James A.
  1973 Women in the Labor Forces. New York: Seminar Press.
Tanner, Nancy
  1974 "Matrifocality in Indonesia and Africa and among Black Americans." Pp. 129–156 in M. Z. Rosaldo and L. Lamphere (eds.), Women, Culture, and Society. Stanford, CA: Stanford University Press.
Teachman, Jay D.
  1982 "Methodological issues in the analysis of family formation and dissolution." Journal of Marriage and the Family 44:1037–1053.
Tittle, Carol Kehr
  1981 Careers and Family: Sex Roles and Adolescent Life Plans. Beverly Hills, CA: Sage Publications.
Tuma, Nancy B.
  1979 Invoking RATE. Department of Sociology, Stanford University.
  1982 "Nonparametric and partially parametric approaches to event-history analysis." Pp. 1–60 in K. F. Schuessler (ed.), Sociological Methodology 1982. San Francisco, CA: Jossey-Bass.
Tuma, Nancy B. and Michael T. Hannan
  1979 "Approaches to the censoring problem in analysis of event histories." Pp. 209–240 in K. F. Schuessler (ed.), Sociological Methodology 1979. San Francisco, CA: Jossey-Bass.
Tuma, Nancy B., Michael T. Hannan, and Lyle P. Groeneveld
  1979 "Dynamic analysis of event histories." American Journal of Sociology 84:820–854.
Wohlwill, Joachim F.
  1980 "Cognitive development in childhood." Pp. 359–444 in O. G. Brim, Jr. and J. Kagan (eds.), Constancy and Change in Human Development. Cambridge, MA: Harvard University Press.
Zelnik, Melvin and John Kantner
  1978 "First pregnancies to women aged 15–19: 1976 and 1971." Family Planning Perspectives 10:11–20.
  1980 "Sexual activity, contraceptive use and pregnancy among metropolitan-area teenagers: 1971–1979." Family Planning Perspectives 12:230–237.
Zelnik, Melvin, John F. Kantner, and Kathleen Ford
  1981 Sex and Pregnancy in Adolescence. Beverly Hills, CA: Sage Publications.

PROCESSES OF ACHIEVEMENT IN THE TRANSITION TO ADULTHOOD

Geoffrey Maruyama, Michael D. Finch, and Jeylan T. Mortimer

ABSTRACT

This research examines the continuity of high school achievement and attainment in the early work career using four waves of data from the "Youth in Transition" panel of young men. The study is distinguished from prior work on socioeconomic attainment by its consideration of an early period of the life course, general rather than goal-specific influences from others, and a dimension of the self-image with special relevance for attainment. Maximum likelihood structural equation techniques were used to estimate a causal model with educational attainment, occupational status, and earnings as final outcome variables. The findings demonstrate the importance of ability and the academic self-concept for high school achievement. The academic self-concept and grade point average were found to be reciprocally related, with earlier achievement fostering a high academic self-image and the latter stimulating subsequent achievement. Both academic self-concept and grades heightened aspirations, which in turn had significant implications for attainments. Furthermore, achievement in high school had direct positive effects on both educational and occupational outcomes. Aspirations and educational attainment were found to have negative effects on earnings. Because the men in this study were only five years beyond high school when the income data were collected, those with higher aspirations and educational attainment had not yet had time to translate their credentials into high earnings. The findings provide another link in the study of life span occupational achievement, one that shows the effects of socioeconomic background, parental support, academic self-concept, and grades on aspirations; the importance of high school achievement and aspirations for early educational and occupational attainment, and the negative effects of deferring entry to the job market on early career earnings.

I. INTRODUCTION

The movement from school to work is a major component of the transition to adulthood. Experiences during the years immediately preceding and following high school graduation have important implications for the achievement of future educational and occupational goals. Because of the linkages of education, occupation, and earnings, this period can be viewed as comprising a critical initial phase of a lifelong process of socioeconomic achievement (Featherman, 1980). This chapter examines the processes of achievement during high school and the five-year period following graduation using data from four waves of the "Youth in Transition" study (see Bachman et al., 1978).

This period of the life span is earlier than that considered in some past research on attainment which has examined the achievements of representative samples of adults (Blau and Duncan, 1967; Hauser and Featherman, 1977; Duncan et al., 1972; Schooler, 1980). Data obtained during the years in high school and shortly after graduation, however, make possible a closer assessment of the process of transition to work. Five years after high school some young adults are still in school and many are just beginning to work at regular jobs. Focusing on this earlier period of the life course enhances understanding of the manner in which important early influences shape attainments in young adulthood. Thus we sacrifice a long-range perspective for one that focuses on the degree of continuity of high school achievement and status attainment processes.

At the beginning of the transition from school to work, adolescents are dependent on their families for economic as well as emotional support. Orientations toward education and work are also nurtured in the family setting (Mortimer, 1975; Gecas, 1979; Gordon, 1972). The school is a second major institutional arena for socialization and development in the preadult years. A social influence perspective (Maruyama, 1983) draws our attention to the importance of parents and teachers for early achievement and provides one theoretical basis for conceptualizing and understanding the process of attainment. Though peers are also important in the development of achievement orientations, in this paper we confine our attention to parents and teachers as major interpersonal sources of influence.[1]

Social influences are not, however, the only factors determining the process of attainment. Investigators are increasingly recognizing that the level of performance and achievement is also important for the development of positive self-concepts and assessments of competence (Rosenberg, 1981; Gecas and Schwalbe, 1983; Kifer, 1975; Wiley, 1979: Chap. 7), which in turn may serve to stimulate further achievement and attainment. One particular component of the self-image may be of special pertinence to the attainment process: the academic self-concept (Reitzes and Mutran, 1980; Looker and Pineo, 1983). Adolescents' assessments of their abilities to perform well in high school may influence their estimations of the likelihood that they will be successful in higher educational settings. Given the relevance of educational attainment as a credential for occupational entry, such self-perceptions and evaluations would likely also affect occupational aspirations and plans. Thus, an additional concern of the present study is to assess the determinants and consequences of the academic self-concept. Along with Rosenberg and Pearlin (1978), we hypothesize that achievement in school, as indicated by grade point average, is an important source of the adolescent self-image.

In this chapter, we view parental and teacher influences, school grades, and the academic self-concept as affecting aspirations and attainment outcomes. But it is necessary to include two other independent variables in our analysis of early attainment; namely, family socioeconomic status and individual ability, for there is considerable evidence (Duncan et al., 1972; Jencks et al., 1972) that these are major determinants of the attainment process. To summarize, we explore the interrelations of socioeconomic background and ability, family and teacher influences, academic achievement, academic self-concept, aspirations, and educational, occupational, and income attainments during the period from late adolescence to early adulthood. A major objective is to examine the continuity of achievement processes over time.

The general context for this investigation is provided in three ways. First we briefly review prior research on attainment. Drawing on the prominent Wisconsin study (Sewell and Hauser, 1976), whose findings have been the subject of considerable attention and replication (Jencks et al., 1983), we describe the bivariate relations of the independent variables and selected adult attainments, discussing initially those determinants that we believe have causal precedence, then the causally intermediate sources of influence, and finally those factors that are temporally closest to educational, occupational, and income outcomes. Second, we review research that has attempted to delineate an attainment process, considering the relations among these key variables in a multivariate context. Finally, we describe the model to be tested here.

II. THE DETERMINANTS OF ADULT ATTAINMENTS: BIVARIATE RELATIONS

A. Family Socioeconomic Status

Family background characteristics, such as social class and "home atmosphere," have been found to be consistently related to children's preparedness for school and to their level of achievement in school (White, 1982). Indeed, Coleman et al. (1966) have argued that schools contribute little to a child's achievement that is independent of family background. Of major interest with respect to attainment, however, is the extent to which the early advantages of children of higher status parents endure over time. In fact, it has been widely established that family socioeconomic background, as indicated by the father's occupation, parents' education, and family income, have continuing importance for adult educational, occupational, and income attainments (Sewell et al., 1977; Schooler, 1980; Duncan et al., 1972; Jencks, 1972). For example, Sewell and Hauser (1976) report correlations of socioeconomic background indicators and educational attainment that typically approach .3 for their male panel seven years following high school. The correlations of these background variables with occupational attainments are somewhat lower.

B. Ability

Insofar as ability tests are typically constructed to measure learning potential in school, we should expect to find that measured ability is strongly related to school grades and educational attainments and, as a result, to occupational outcomes. Further, because ability is commonly viewed as being highly stable across the school years (Bloom, 1964), its implications for aspirations and attainments ought to be nurtured and developed over a long period of time. That is, children who are seen by parents, teachers, and peers as "smart" and who have high achievement in school have a long time to think about those future occupational opportunities and rewards that may be linked to their abilities. One might well view a child's ability as a cornerstone among variables that influence attainments because it may contribute to parental and teacher perceptions of the child, the child's school achievement and academic self-concept, the child's aspirations, and, finally, the child's attainments. Many of these effects of ability may be indirect, i.e., transmitted by other variables. Sewell and Hauser (1976) report correlations of ability and educational and occupational attainments for their male sample that approximate .4.

C. Family Support

Support can be defined either as a general phenomenon involving approval, acceptance, and favorable evaluations, or more specifically with respect to particular skills, activities, or goals. The Sewell approach has commonly defined "influence of significant others" in terms of particular educational goals (e.g., Sewell and Hauser, 1976), for example, encouragement to attend college. Sewell and Hauser report a correlation of .47 between parental encouragement of post–high school education and educational attainment and a correlation of .36 between such encouragement and occupational attainment.

We have chosen, however, to focus on more general perceptions of social support consistent with our broad focus on the attainment process. That is, we are interested in the effects of support on the developing academic self-concept, school achievement, and aspirations as well as on the attainments. Parental support has been found to be related to a host of child attitudes that would facilitate socioeconomic attainment: the need for achievement (Rosen and D'Andrade, 1959; Kerckhoff, 1974; Gordon, 1972; Komarovsky, 1976), self-esteem (Rosenberg, 1965; Bachman, 1970; Coopersmith, 1967), internal control (Scheck et al., 1973); and the potency dimension of the self-concept (Gecas, 1971; Thomas et al., 1974: Chap. 2). Mortimer et al. (forthcoming), studying a panel of young professional and managerial men, also report that paternal support influences an array of psychological dimensions that foster achievement.

D. Teacher Influence

The literature on teacher expectations documents the impact of teachers on classroom processes and student outcomes (e.g., Brophy and Good, 1974). For example, Taylor (1979) found that the teacher's expectations about students' ethnic/racial background affected teacher–student interactions. Further, teacher effectiveness is an important determinant of student learning. Rosenshine (1978) describes how teacher style and orientation to teaching can affect learning and Johnson et al. (1981) demonstrate the effects of classroom goal structure on student achievement outcomes. As was true of parental support, teacher support can be thought of as having a general component, indicating overall acceptance and approval, as well as subcomponents focused on specific goals. Sewell and Hauser (1976) found the correlation of teacher encouragement to attend college with educational attainment and occupational status, respectively, to be .41 and .33. Again, we focus on a more general teacher support dimension.

E. Academic Self-Concept

While most social psychological research on the self-concept has focused on an overall evaluative dimension, or self-esteem, the academic self-concept, reflecting individuals' assessments of their own academic accomplishments and abilities, may be particularly relevant to attainment processes. If the academic self-concept is in fact an influential factor in educational and occupational decision making, it could mediate the effects of school achievement on aspirations.

Looker and Pineo (1983) report a correlation of .53 between a measure of the academic self-concept (at age 17–18) and educational attainment (at age 21–22).

F. School Achievement

There is little doubt that school achievement is one of the major correlates of educational and occupational attainment. Insofar as grades in school are an important basis for admittance to higher educational institutions and educational credentials are central criteria for occupational entry, these associations are to be expected. Looking again at the data reported by Sewell and Hauser (1976), high school grades were found to correlate .51 and .41, respectively, with educational and occupational attainment.

In this paper we examine three dimensions of early adult attainment: years of school completed, occupational status, and income. Of these three criterion variables, earnings have been all but neglected in the preceding discussion. Whereas earnings have been included in some studies of attainment (e.g., Featherman and Carter, 1976; Sewell and Hauser, 1976; Spaeth, 1976), the variables generally used in status attainment models are relatively poor predictors of income. Sewell and Hauser (1976) and Featherman and Carter (1976) were able to account for only about 7 and 10 percent, respectively, of the variance in earnings (see also Jencks et al., 1983).

Why is the prediction of earnings so much poorer than the prediction of educational and occupational attainments? Spaeth (1976:175) has argued that different kinds of variables determine income: "To the extent that income is a result of successful job performance, the relative failure of settings and qualifications as predictors may not be very surprising." Nevertheless, we include income in our study because it is one important dimension of attainment.

III. THE STATUS ATTAINMENT PROCESS

The preceding section has described the bivariate relations of a number of antecedent variables with educational and occupational attainments. In this section we examine some multivariate patterns of relations among these variables. The status attainment literature attempts to explain how these variables are interrelated with one another and with the attainments by specifying the nature of the causal relations among them.

Blau and Duncan and their colleagues initiated a series of path-breaking studies of attainments with their research on a large representative sample of American men (Blau and Duncan, 1967; Duncan, 1969; Duncan et al., 1972), demonstrating the importance of a multivariate approach to an understanding of this process. Sewell and his colleagues developed a second major program of research (Alexander et al., 1975; Sewell et al., 1969, 1970; Sewell and Hauser,

1976, 1977; Wilson and Portes, 1975) adding social psychological variables and social influences to the earlier attainment model. To obtain their data, these investigators generally followed panels of high school seniors, making their findings particularly pertinent for the present study.

In the Sewell and Hauser (1976) model, the exogenous variables, i.e., variables whose causes are not analyzed, are measures of social class: father's education, mother's education, father's occupational status, and family income. Causally intermediate variables within the model are mental ability; rank in high school class; significant others' influence, including parents' encouragement, teachers' encouragement, and peer plans (all as perceived by the individuals whose attainment is being studied); college plans; and occupational aspirations. The associations between social class background and attainments have been found to be largely mediated by ability, academic performance, social influences, and aspirations (see Hauser et al., 1983; Featherman, 1980). Ability and academic achievement, significant others' influences, plans and aspirations have been found to have direct effects on attainments (Sewell and Hauser, 1976; Sewell et al., 1969; Hauser et al., 1976).

Educational attainment has been found to be of crucial importance to the process of occupational and income achievement. Sewell and Hauser (1976:15) argue that "the model shows the fundamental role of educational attainment in determining occupational achievement; educational attainment has a large direct effect on occupational status, and it mediates most of the effects of variables preceding it (with the notable exception of level of occupational aspiration)."

In summary, Sewell and his colleagues have provided a model of status attainment processes which considers the effects of family background, ability, family, teacher and peer influences, educational achievement and aspirations on attainments. The variables included in their model were found to account for over half the variance in educational attainment and two-fifths of the variance in early occupational status (Sewell and Hauser, 1976). The Sewell model provides the present study with a point of departure because it includes structural, social, and psychological determinants of attainment and the respondent panels are of similar ages. Our study is different from theirs in its focus on a somewhat earlier period, including the high school years and five years beyond. Our model also includes general, rather than goal-specific, measures of social influence and a dimension of the self-concept that we believe has special relevance for attainment.

IV. DATA SOURCE

The respondents in the present study were 765 young white men from the Youth in Transition study (Bachman et al., 1978) for whom there were complete data available on all measures in the model to be tested.[2] The panel was followed from 1966 to 1974. We used data collected in the Fall of the sophomore year of high school (tenth grade), in the Spring of the junior year, in the Spring of the senior year, and, finally, during the Spring and Summer five years after high school graduation. The longitudinal nature of these data allowed us to use temporal sequencing to "causally" order the constructs.

Because data were collected over an eight-year period, it is not surprising that there was some sample attrition. Still, 73.5 percent of the participants in the initial study were included in the final wave (Bachman et al., 1978:5). Moreover, it appears that attrition did not appreciably alter the characteristics of the panel. Bachman and O'Malley (1977:368) noted that although there were differences between persons who were lost from the study and those who remained until the end, "the sample remains reasonably representative of the original population, particularly with regard to relationships among variables."

By the time of the last survey, most of the men were recent graduates of colleges or other higher educational institutions, and had recently entered the full-time labor force. Others had been in the work force for a longer period of time. Clearly, these men are at the beginning of the socioeconomic career.[3]

V. THE MEASURES

The measures are described under the conceptual or underlying variables that they were intended to represent. In many instances, these measures constitute a subset selected from a broader array of available indicators. Consistent with some of the work on status attainment, we aggregate measures of social class background (Hauser, 1973) but consider separately the different sources of social influence. We also aggregate our measures of aspirations. Departing from the research that has created weighted or unweighted linear composite variables used in regression analyses, however, we employ confirmatory factor analysis/structural equation techniques to extract the "underlying" constructs whose relations are examined (Long, 1976; Maruyama and McGarvey, 1980).

Socioeconomic Status of the Family:

- Father's educational attainment (eight categories ranging from less than high school to postgraduate degree)
- Mother's educational attainment (same as above)
- Father's occupational status (Duncan Socioeconomic Index)

Ability (for a description of measures, see Bachman, 1970:46–47):

- Ammons' Quick Text
- General Aptitude Test Battery (GATB), vocabulary (Part J)
- Matrices (constructed test, similar to Raven's Progressive Matrices)

Parent Support:

- These days my parents really help out; they don't let me down.
- How close do you feel to your father?
- How close do you feel to your mother?

Teacher Support

- How often are your teachers willing to listen to problems and help find solutions?
- Do many of your teachers seem to take a personal interest in you?
- How often are teachers at this school friendly and easy to approach?

Academic Self-Concept:

- How intelligent do you think you are compared with others (other boys) your age?
- How good a reader do you think you are compared with others (other boys) your age?
- How do you rate yourself in school ability compared with those in your grade in school?

School Achievement: Self-report of high school grade point average. In the Fall of the sophomore and Spring of the junior years, the question referred to grade point average over the preceding year. In the Spring of the senior year, the question referred to grade point average during that year.

Aspirations:

- Likelihood of attending college
- Likelihood of going to graduate school
- Aspired occupational status (Duncan SEI)

Attainments:

- Years of schooling completed (eight categories range from 10 to 17 or over)
- Occupational status (SEI)
- Before-tax earnings for last year

Because all of the relevant measures were not collected in the senior year, we include constructs representing family and teacher support and the academic self-concept for the tenth and eleventh grade only. The analyses reported in this chapter also utilize measures of socioeconomic status and ability obtained in the tenth grade, school achievement (grade point average) in all three years of high school, aspirations in the senior year, and the attainments five years after high school.

VI. MODEL SPECIFICATION AND METHODOLOGY

The predominant "causal" influences in the model (see Figure 1) flow from family socioeconomic status and ability, to the social influences, to the self-concept and school achievement constructs, to aspirations, to educational attainment, and, finally, to early occupational status and earnings. Maximum likelihood structural equation techniques were used to estimate this model using the computer program Linear Structural Relations—LISREL (Joreskog and Sorbom, 1978). These techniques produce simultaneous estimation of causal paths linking the constructs, of relations between the constructs and the measures used to define them, of residuals for both constructs and measures, and of any residual covariation. Also produced are confidence intervals for all parameter estimates and an overall goodness-of-fit statistic comparing the predicted and observed covariance structures.

Because the data are longitudinal, it is necessary to analyze a covariance matrix which allows for change in variability over time. However, to facilitate interpretation of the findings, a standardized solution is presented.

Although we have described general patterns of influence, we have thus far not provided information about specific measurement parameters and causal paths. The measurement model interrelating constructs and measures was quite straightforward (See Table 1). Except for school achievement and the three attainments, all constructs had three indicators (observed measures). With three indicators, it is possible to freely estimate the relations of the latent constructs with the indicators and the residuals of the measures (Maruyama and McGarvey, 1980). Further, when the same measures were collected at more than one point in time, residual covariation among them at contiguous intervals was estimated to capture any unique or indicator-specific variance.

Because there were only single measures of school achievement (self-reported grade point average), educational attainment, earnings, and occupational prestige, we assumed perfect measurement, fixing the factor loadings (λ coefficients) at 1. The implications of this procedure are not altogether clear. The assumption that school achievement is perfectly measured is doubtful because grades were collected via self-report (as opposed to school records, utilized by Sewell and Hauser, 1976; see Campbell, 1983). Our findings, however, are quite robust, even when this assumption of perfect measurement is relaxed.[4]

Initially, we attempted to aggregate the aspiration and attainment variables so that each would be represented by a single construct. This attempt was only partially successful. The aspiration measures defined a single construct as we had expected (see Table 1). The attainments, however, did not display the expected pattern. That is, even though educational attainment, occupational status, and

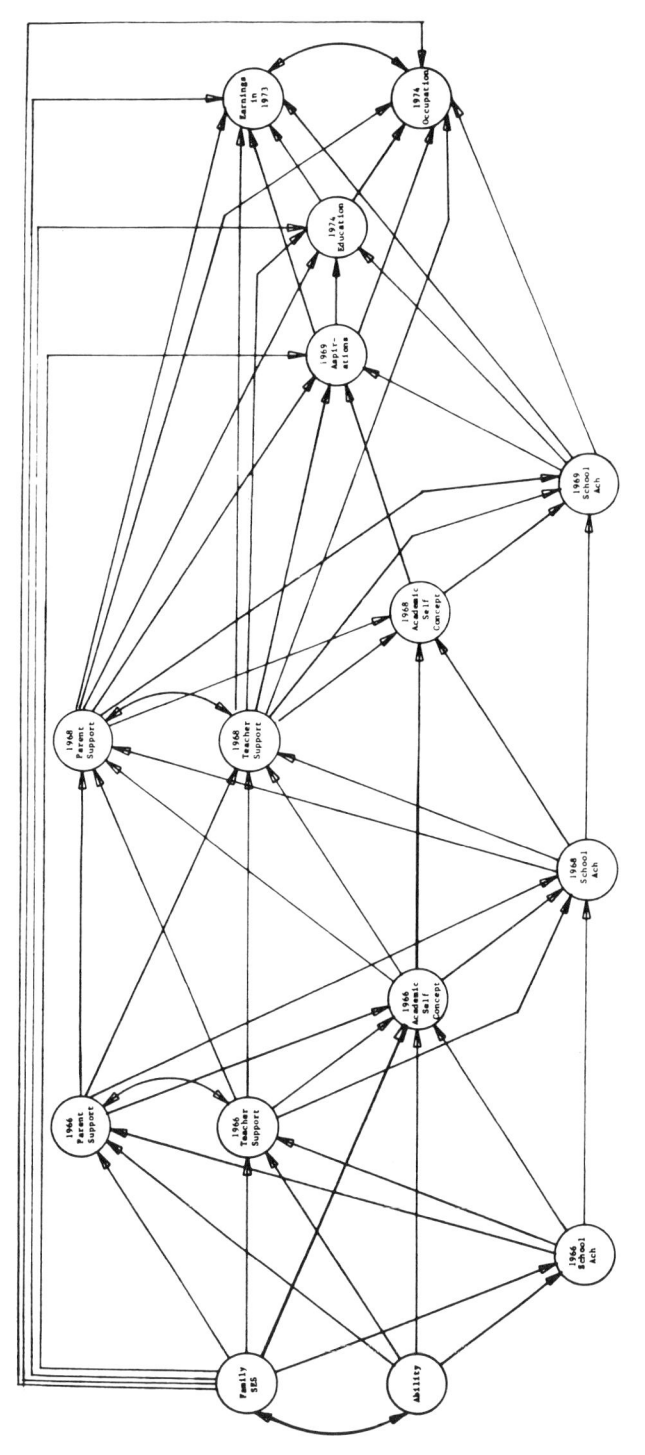

Figure 1. Causal Model of Attainment Including all Estimated Paths

Table 1. Scaled Factor Loadings
(LISREL Standardized Solution)

Latent Variable	Measures	1966	1968	1969	1974
Family SES	Father's Education	1.84			
	Mother's Education	.99			
	Father's Occupational Status	1.73			
Academic Ability	Ammon's Quick Test	.73			
	GATB J	5.09			
	Matrices	2.00			
School Achievement	GPA	.68	.69	.71	
Parent Support	Parents Help	.64	.65		
	Close to Father	.66	.70		
	Close to Mother	.58	.58		
Teacher Support	Teacher Help	.50	.64		
	Teacher Interest	.41	.41		
	Teacher Friend	.82	.58		
Academic Self-concept	School Ability	.55	.61		
	Intelligence	.68	.71		
	Reading Skill	.67	.70		
Aspirations	Go to College			.88	
	Go to Graduate School			.71	
	Aspired Occupation			1.75	
Education					1.86
Earnings in 1973					3.33
Occupational Status					2.45

Note: The scaled solution standardizes factors rather than measures. Since a covariance matrix was input, loadings (from standardized factors to unstandardized measures) do not fall between 0 and ±1.

earnings were defined conceptually in terms of a single construct, the loading of the earnings measure on this construct had a sign opposite to the others; earnings were negatively related to the latent construct, while education and occupational status had positive loadings.

On reflection, the negative relation of earnings with educational and occupational attainments should perhaps have been expected because the respondents were only five years beyond high school graduation at the time the attainment measures were obtained. Persons highest in income at that time were likely to be those with less education, who entered the work force shortly after high school and had already had several years of work experience and accumulated seniority, for example, in skilled blue-collar work or sales occupations. Persons attaining more education and higher occupational status were still deferring material gains until a later stage of their careers.

Given this pattern, we disaggregated the attainment construct into its three

Achievement in the Transition to Adulthood 73

components (see Figure 1). Thus, the analyses examine a model with one aspiration construct (containing both educational and occupational aspirations) and three attainment variables—educational attainment, occupational status, and earnings. Further, because the completion of formal education generally precedes full-time entry to the job market, we viewed educational attainment as causally prior to occupational status and earnings. Finally, because we had no basis for establishing a causal sequence for occupational status and earnings, we estimated their relation through residual covariation.

Several general considerations governed the causal model specification. First, even though family socioeconomic status and ability were measured during the tenth grade, at the same time as the initial social influence and individual outcome variables, they are depicted as exogenous. There is considerable discrepancy in the attainment literature as to whether ability is specified as an exogenous variable (Kerckhoff, 1974; Duncan et al., 1972:90; Hauser, 1971) or an endogenous one (Sewell and Hauser, 1975; Gordon, 1972). (For a discussion of the causal processes that may underly the association of social class background and measures of ability, see Jencks et al., 1972:77–81). Since our focus is not on this issue, we have chosen, for the purposes of this analysis, to consider socioeconomic background and ability as correlated exogenous variables.

Socioeconomic background and ability are predictors of the tenth grade achievement, social influence, and self-concept constructs. Because all constructs appearing more than once in the model were thought to be significantly stable, there are paths from the tenth to eleventh grade social influence and self-concept constructs and between the achievement constructs. It is assumed that the effects of the exogenous determinants on these dependent variables, measured after the tenth grade, flow through their stability paths. Moreover, the effects of ability on aspirations and attainments were expected to be mediated by prior social influence, self-concept, and school achievement. (It should be noted that while school grades indicate the level of performance in the school context, they may also suggest the potential for performance in many occupational contexts.) As a result, there are no direct paths from ability to the attainment variables.[5]

Socioeconomic status, in contrast, was expected to have both direct and indirect effects on aspirations and attainments. Social class background could affect the character of social influences, self-concept, and achievement, and it may also more directly influence attainment outcomes, for example, through the ability of parents to finance higher education. Therefore, we estimate direct paths from socioeconomic background to the aspirations and the attainments.

Social influences (parental and teacher support) are viewed as causally prior to the psychological and behavioral variables, i.e., the academic self-concept and school achievement. The specification of paths from social influences to individual attitudes and behavior is consistent with much earlier work that has examined significant others as sources of achievement (Maruyama, 1983) and psychological development (Mortimer and Finch, 1983; Mortimer and Lorence,

1981). Thus, paths were estimated from the social influence constructs to the academic self-concept within each time (tenth and eleventh grades). Parent and teacher support in the tenth grade predict achievement measured in the eleventh grade (including grades over the preceding year); these social influences in the eleventh grade predict achievement in grade twelve. There are also direct paths from eleventh grade social influences to the aspirations and attainments.

Reflecting a dynamic, reciprocal process of influence, paths were also estimated from prior achievement and self-concept to subsequent social influences. These lagged paths from the individual variables to the social influences reflect the assumption that individuals are not just passive recipients of environmental forces; they also affect the social environment that shapes their behavior (Mortimer et al., 1982; Rosenberg, 1981). (Note that tenth and eleventh grade achievements, respectively, are considered temporally prior to the tenth and eleventh grade self-concept and social influences because they represent grade point average over the previous year.)

Because we could not justify viewing one support variable as causally preceding another, their synchronous (within time) relations were depicted as residual covariation. Their cross-time relations were estimated by lagged causal paths.

Like the social influence and individual variables, self-concept and school achievements were also expected to be reciprocally related (Reitzes and Mutran, 1980). Consistent with much work in educational psychology, it was hypothesized that the academic self-concept influences later achievement (Wiley, 1979:405). In addition, following Rosenberg and Pearlin (1978) and Kifer (1975), earlier achievement was specified as "causing" the subsequent self-concept (Wiley, 1979:396–99).

The path from twelfth grade achievement to aspirations is based on the supposition that doing well in school heightens the expectation of success in higher educational settings and therefore strengthens aspirations (Spenner and Featherman, 1978). Grades in high school are important determinants of college admission and, as a result, influence occupational entry, and these processes are likely to be understood by the student. Further, we hypothesized that the academic self-concept, independent of achievement, would have a positive effect on aspirations (Reitzes and Mutran, 1980). Consistent with much prior work, aspiration level in turn was considered to have direct effects on all three attainments. Finally, we expected that educational attainment would influence both occupational status and earnings.

All estimated parameters are designated by arrows in Figure 1. In Figure 2, significant standardized paths ($p < .05$) are presented; nonsignificant paths are not shown.

VII. THE FINDINGS

Before describing the results of the analysis, there is one caution to the reader. Obviously, the findings are based on a matrix of covariances, which cannot be

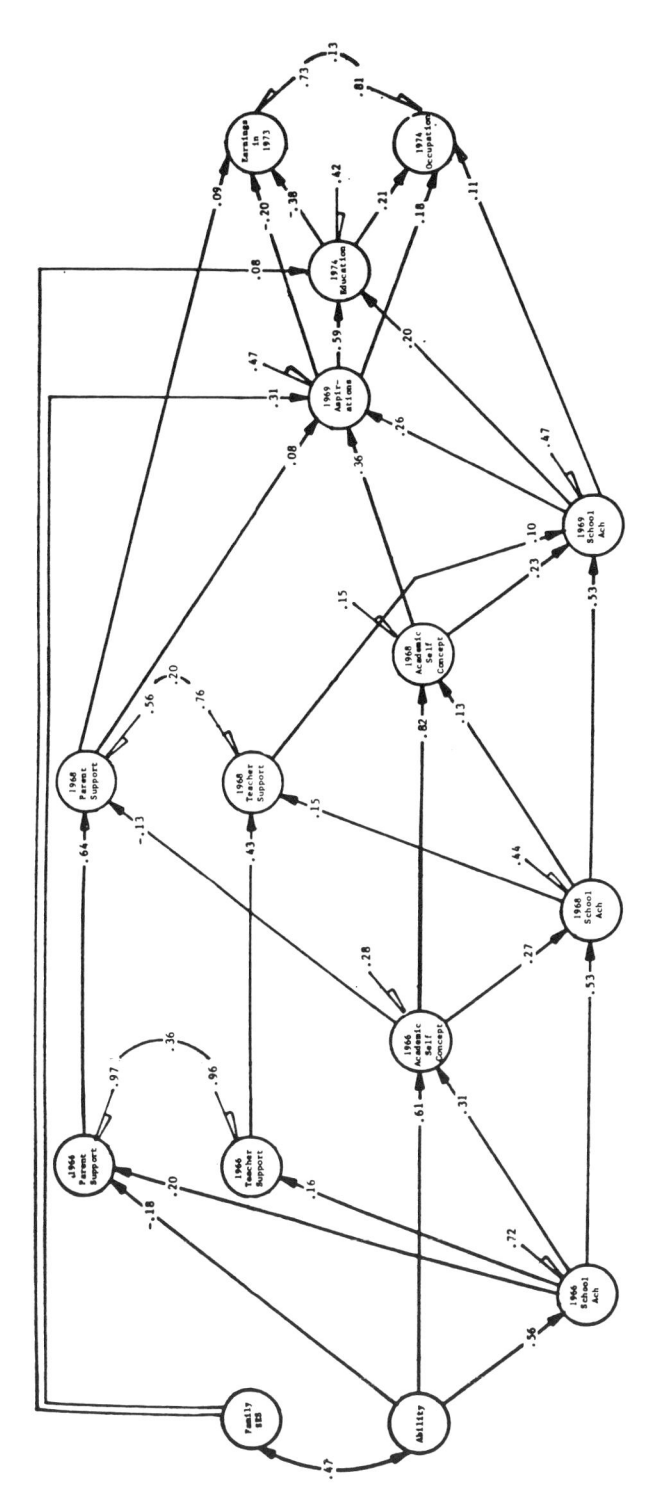

Figure 2. Standardized Estimates for Causal Model of Attainment (significant paths only): $\chi^2 = 960.52$; df = 434; n = 765

used to establish causality. There is causal influence only insofar as the model depicts true patterns of causal relations. Our use of the language of causality should not be construed as implying that our model is necessarily accurate or that true causality is depicted. Instead, one might view the findings as a "best guess" based on our conceptual framework, assumptions, and prior research. When we speak of causes or influences we are designating specified causal paths; this language clearly distinguishes those relations from noncausal correlations among measures or constructs.

Let us first examine the achievement process during the earlier high school period, assessing the determinants and consequences of grade point average and the academic self-concept (see Figure 2). The stability paths show that these outcome variables are quite stable over time. Standardized paths of .53 connect the achievement constructs during the first and second time intervals. The academic self-concept manifests a higher (.82) level of persistence. These stability estimates highlight the importance of longitudinal data in examining causal influences on individual achievement and self-image, because only when the stability of these constructs is controlled can such influence be demonstrated.

Consistent with much prior research, there is a significant correlation (.47) between socioeconomic status and ability. The effects of ability on school achievement (.56) and on academic self-concept (.61) are rather sizable. It thus appears that students of higher ability have higher grades and perceive themselves as more intelligent and capable academically, even when grades are controlled. It is somewhat surprising, however, to find that ability has no significant impact on teacher support and a negative effect on parental support (−.18). This negative coefficient probably is not attributable to the multicollinearity of the predictors (ability and achievement) since the zero-order correlation is also negative (−.06). It may be that students of higher ability gain greater independence from parents in adolescence; hence they may view them as less supportive. However, in a prior analysis (Mortimer and Finch, 1983) ability bore no relation to a measure of family autonomy.

It is noteworthy that net of ability socioeconomic background has no significant influence on the tenth grade social support, achievement, and self-concept variables. There is a moderately strong positive correlation between social background and self-concept (.40), but this diminishes to insignificance when ability is controlled. It is apparent that of the two exogenous variables, ability is a much more potent predictor of the initial elements in our achievement model.

The parent and teacher influence variables had relatively few significant effects. Eleventh grade support from teachers has a positive effect (.10) on twelfth grade achievement. But teacher support was found to have no significant impact on the academic self-concept in either period. Parent support had no significant effects on either of these outcomes. It must be concluded that these quite stable support variables have only negligible consequences for academic self-concept and achievement.

We argued earlier that the level of actual achievement in school, as well as social influence processes, are likely to affect the self-concept during the adolescent years. The positive effects of grades on the academic self-concept (.31 and .13 over the two intervals) is supportive of this view. Consistent with Rosenberg and Pearlin's (1978) hypothesis, it seems clear that students derive their estimation of their abilities at least partially from their demonstrated achievement, as indicated by grades in school. These is also substantial evidence that the academic self-concept fosters achievement in both the first (.27) and second (.23) intervals.

School achievement also strengthens the perception of teacher support in both periods (.16 and .15, respectively). Students may view their teachers as more supportive when they are rewarded by them with higher grades, and teachers may in fact be more encouraging of their "better" students. Academic achievement also appears to strengthen perceptions of parental support at the beginning of high school (.20). Parental support in the eleventh grade is likewise influenced by the academic self-concept in the tenth, but this effect is negative ($-.13$). Like the negative path from ability to tenth grade parental support, we find this coefficient rather perplexing.

These relations demonstrate the complex interweaving of ability, social influences, self-concept, and individual achievement processes during the period of adolescence. The findings highlight the importance of ability and the academic self-concept as early determinants of school achievement and the stability of the key interrelated individual outcome variables over time. Moreover, there is evidence for some dynamic, reciprocal processes of influence. Both tenth and eleventh grade school achievement strengthen the academic self-concept, which in turn fosters subsequent achievement. In the first two years of high school, grade point average increases the perception of teacher support, which in turn strengthens achievement in the last year.

Let us now turn to the aspirations and attainments. As in other analyses of the attainment process, aspirations were found to be dependent on family background (.31) and school achievement (.26). The strength of the effect of socioeconomic background on aspirations was somewhat unexpected given prior research (see Sewell and Hauser, 1976). The significant path from senior year grades to aspirations is consistent with our reasoning that school achievement is an important consideration in high school students' assessments of their potential for subsequent success. But we find that the academic sclf-concept has an even greater positive direct effect on aspirations (.36).

It is noteworthy that we also find a significant path from parental support in the twelfth grade to aspirations (.08). Even when social class background, academic self-concept, and grades are controlled, the supportiveness of parents exerts a significant positive effect on male adolescents' aspirations. It thus appears that parental influence on attainments is partially mediated by student aspirations. This finding, though weak in absolute magnitude, is consistent with the results of

Mortimer and her colleagues (forthcoming) obtained in a study of professional and managerial men.

There is also a direct path from parental support to earnings (.09). Adolescents who perceived their parents as supportive during the last year of high school are found to have higher earnings five years later. This direct effect, as well as the indirect linkages through aspirations, suggests that a more general dimension of parental support, in addition to the more specific encouragement to attend college, deserves attention in subsequent research on attainment.

Twelfth grade aspirations, not surprisingly, are a strong determinant of educational attainment (.59). School achievement likewise influences educational attainment both directly (.20) and indirectly, through its effect on aspirations. Educational attainment thus appears to be dependent on both the desire to achieve, i.e., the level of aspiration, and one's previous academic success. We find that socioeconomic background also has a positive effect on educational attainment (.08) but no significant impact on subsequent attainments. Thus, as depicted by the model, socioeconomic status is important for the attainment process because of its effects on aspirations and educational attainment.

Earlier, we described the unexpectedly negative relation of earnings with the other attainments. Yet once earnings are disaggregated from educational attainment and occupational prestige, the pattern of causal relationships seems to be fairly plausible for the age group under study. Lower earnings are the consequence of high aspirations ($-.20$) and high educational attainment ($-.38$). Because aspirations and educational attainment both reflect academic involvement, their negative relations with earnings should be expected. That is, persons who have high academic aspirations and educational attainment have deferred entry to the labor market to attain their educational goals and therefore sacrifice early economic rewards.

Occupational status five years after high school was found to be increased by high grades in school (.11), by high aspirations (.18), and by high educational attainment (.21). The finding that occupational attainment was not affected by our social influence variables is consistent with the Sewell and Hauser (1976) study. The fact that educational attainment does not completely mediate the effects of high school achievement and aspirations on occupational status is also compatible with their work (Sewell and Hauser, 1976:19).

Finally, the positive residual covariation (.13) between earnings and occupational status shows that once the negative effects of aspirations and educational attainment are removed, earnings and occupational attainment become positively related.

Having examined the model in some detail, we find that the results are quite plausible; they confirm past findings and extend them in very straightforward ways. Another way of assessing the model is by its goodness of fit to the data. By this criterion, the model appears to be very acceptable. The overall goodness-of-fit statistic is quite good; with a sample of 765, a χ^2 to degrees of freedom ratio of 2.2 is definitely acceptable (Wheaton et al., 1977).

A third way to evaluate the model is by examination of the percentage of variance in aspirations and attainments that is explained by the predictors. Fifty-three percent of the variance in aspirations, 58 percent of the variance in educational attainment, 27 percent of the variance in earnings, and 19 percent of the variance in occupational status are explained by the model. For educational attainment, this figure is comparable to those reported by others. Our model has more predictive power for earnings than previous work, but it is poorer for occupational attainment. It is difficult to determine why the prediction of earnings is so much better here than in other studies, such as those by Featherman and Carter (1976) or Sewell and Hauser (1976). It may well be, however, that the answer again lies in the life stage at which the men were observed. If we had collected earnings information five years later, we also might have found only weak prediction of earnings because the positive effects of educational and occupational status on earnings might have only then been starting to emerge. Moreover, at that time earnings may be substantially determined by work performance, organizational and industrial context, and other variables beyond the confines of our model. Later in the work career, the associations of earnings with educational and occupational status become clearly positive. For example, in this study a measure of earnings in the family of origin loaded positively on the family socioeconomic background construct. Our relatively poor prediction of occupational status, in comparison with past studies, may occur because the college and in particular the professional school populations have not yet settled into regular jobs.

VIII. SUMMARY AND CONCLUSION

To summarize a rather complex model we will highlight the influences of key variables through the attainment process. First, socioeconomic background was found to have no significant effects on the early social influences, academic self-concept, and achievement variables, net of ability. Because we have chosen to depict the substantial association of socioeconomic background with academic ability as noncausal (unlike Sewell and Hauser, 1976), any "indirect" relations with other variables that occur through the covariation of social class with ability cannot be interpreted causally. But insofar as socioeconomic background does influence ability, its effects on secondary school achievement would appear to be largely mediated by this variable. We do find, however, that social background has a considerable impact on aspirations, and it likewise affects the level of educational attainment five years beyond high school. The latter influence on education is particularly noteworthy given that the large effect of aspirations on educational attainment has been controlled.

Ability, the second exogenous variable, was found to exert a strong impact on both the academic self-concept and grades. Thus, at the early stage in their careers in which the men in this panel were studied, ability seems to shape attainments by determining the level of academic achievement and self-concept. These individual variables, in turn, were found to have great significance in the attainment process both because of their positive, reciprocal interrelations over time, and their direct effects on aspirations. Grades were also found to have direct impacts on educational and occupational attainments.

The analysis suggests that net of the other variables, parental support has little effect on the secondary school achievement process. Parental support was found to be related, however, to aspirations and earnings. These direct effects argue for the importance of family support as a source of influence on attainment (Mortimer et al., forthcoming, report a similar pattern of findings). Teacher support had only a modest impact on the achievement process, fostering higher school grades in the senior year. Although the findings for the influence variables are weaker than those sometimes reported (see Sewell et al., 1969), the differences may result from our tapping general rather than goal-specific influence from others. Our earlier work and our interest in exploring the consequences of social influence for a range of outcomes led us to examine a general dimension of influence.

Given its lack of attention in most prior research, the findings with regard to the academic self-concept are of particular interest. This dimension of the self-image had positive effects on school achievement at both times. Much theorizing in the social sciences has viewed the academic self-concept as critical in shaping educational success and, consequently, status attainment (Purkey, 1970; Scheirer and Kraut, 1979), and our findings are consistent with this view. Moreover, the academic self-concept measured in the eleventh grade had a rather substantial effect on twelfth grade aspirations. It is noteworthy that a previous analysis of the data (Mortimer and Finch, 1983) found much weaker relationships between self-esteem, an overall self-evaluative dimension, and school grades. The findings taken together support Rosenberg's (1979) contention that the self-concept is a multidimensional phenomenon whose components have distinct consequences for attitudes and behaviors.

School achievement exerted a wide range of influences throughout the model. Grades in school were found to have positive effects on parental support, teacher support, and the academic self-concept. Insofar as these variables foster subsequent achievement (as in the case of teacher support and the academic self-concept), a pattern of "dynamic stability" is observed (Mortimer and Lorence, 1981). That is, high achievement early in the high school years fosters a high academic self-concept and teacher support, which in turn serve to enhance school achievement in subsequent periods. Moreover, achievement in the senior year of high school exerted a substantial positive effect on aspirations and significant influences on educational and occupational attainment.

Finally, as has been shown in many previous studies, educational attainment contributed positively to occupational status. The negative effect of schooling on earnings, initially unexpected given the findings of past research, assumes considerable interest when viewed in the context of a lifespan process of attainment. The men in this study were only five years beyond high school when the income data were collected, in contrast to the Sewell and Hauser study (1976) which measured earnings 10 years after the senior year of high school. The persons earning the least in the Youth in Transition panel were those with the most education because they were likely to be recent entrants to the full-time labor force or still in school. Whereas later in the career the relations of earnings with education and occupational status become positive, at this early stage these relations are substantially negative. Those who entered the labor force shortly after high school have higher earnings, whereas those with greater educational attainment and, presumably, careers with higher income ceilings have not yet had enough time to translate their credentials into higher earnings.[6]

But if in fact earnings and occupational status have not yet stabilized, some might wonder whether it is worthwhile to examine status attainment processes in such a young population. Our view is that it is definitely worthwhile. The transition from school to work covers a period of years, involves changes occurring at different rates for different individuals, and cannot be dated with precision (see, for example, Duncan, 1967). Featherman (1980) has argued that the influence of high school achievement processes and college education on occupational achievement diminishes later in the career. Thus, it is important to capture the transition process at a number of points in time in order to examine how it progresses. By tapping early occupational achievement, the present study may provide a starting point for assessing the changing effects of educational achievements on later attainments.

In concluding, it is useful to place the present findings within a broader, life course perspective. Occupational status and earnings are obviously of major importance throughout the adult years. These attainments are shaped by numerous prior influences. The impacts of specific determinants seem likely to change over time, as their salience increases or diminishes, and their influence may sometimes change in direction. We have chosen to focus on what may be seen as a crucial stage of status attainment, during which period the transition from student to worker generally occurs. By focusing on early attainment we have maximized our chances of finding continuity from high school achievement processes to attainment outcomes. It appears that we have discovered considerable continuity; the academic self-concept fostered achievement as well as high aspirations, and high school grades were directly related to aspirations and to two of the attainments. The findings provide another link in the study of life span occupational experience, one that shows clearly the impacts of ability and the academic self-concept on the process of high school achievement; the effects of socioeconomic background, parental support, the academic self-concept, and grades on aspirations; the importance of high school grades in early educational and occupational attainment, and the negative effects of deferring entry to the job market on early career earnings.

ACKNOWLEDGMENTS

This research was supported by grants from the National Institute on Aging (AGO 03325) and the University of Minnesota Computer Center. The data were made available by the Inter-University Consortium for Political and Social Research. The data for the Youth in Transition Project were collected by Jerald G. Bachman. Neither the collector of the data nor the consortium bear any responsibility for the analyses or interpretations presented here.

NOTES

1. Whereas the teacher expectation literature suggests that teachers exert a positive influence on students' educational and occupational goals, the effects of peers have been the subject of some controversy (Lewis and St. John, 1974; Sewell and Hauser, 1976; Coleman, 1961; and Bronfenbrenner, 1979). Although zero-order correlations between peer influence and achievement are commonly positive, causal modelling of this relationship has not found that peers influence achievement (Maruyama, 1983; Maruyama and McGarvey, 1980). This, in conjunction with earlier analyses of the present data that found peer influence to be only trivially related to other variables (Maruyama and Finch, 1983), led us to exclude it from further analyses. We should note, however, that in the present study the measures available to operationalize peer influence (e.g., how would your friends feel if you dropped out of school?) were not ideal for our purposes. Responses to such items were highly skewed.

2. The original sample of 2,213 tenth grade boys was weighted to correct for school size (see Bachman, et al., 1978, for a description of the sampling procedures). All analyses reported in this paper are based on the weighted panel (N=2514 in grade 10). The exclusion of respondents with missing data yielded a weighted N of 765, or 45 per cent of the 1681 white respondents in the fifth wave. Given the extent of missing data (for example, approximately one-fourth of the white first-wave panel lacked information for father's occupational status), we decided to take the rather conservative approach of utilizing only those cases with complete information.

3. Since we are reporting the results of secondary analyses, one might well wonder whether prior analyses have examined these relationships. Bachman and O'Malley (1977) have reported an analysis of a path model focused on the determinants of self-esteem. That model, estimated using ordinary least squares regression, included social class, academic ability, ninth grade achievement, high school self-esteem, educational attainment, occupational status, and self-esteem five years after high school. These analyses are not directly comparable to ours for several reasons. First, they included the more general evaluative dimension of the self-concept, self-esteem, rather than the more specific variable of interest to us, the academic self-concept. Second, they included achievement (grades) obtained at the first data collection point, thereby having a longer causal lag from this independent variable to the dependent variables than we will report. Third, they omitted a number of determinants of attainments of interest to us, namely, the social support and aspiration variables. The omission of aspirations seems particularly critical, for aspirations are commonly seen as mediating the relation between academic achievement and attainments (Sewell and Hauser, 1976). Finally, their path analysis approach, which does not allow for measurement error, might well be expected to generate

coefficients differing from ours. Bachman, et al. (1978) have reported additional analyses that are also not directly comparable to ours.

4. We have attempted to extract measurement error in the achievement construct through a variety of procedures, and have explored the consequences of alternative achievement reliability estimates for the causal process (see Maruyama and Finch, 1983). However, estimating reliabilities from single indicator models gives rise to difficulties in interpretation (Wheaton, et al., 1977:100–105). Reducing the reliability of achievement raises the stability of this construct and tends to weaken the effects of the academic self-concept on achievement. The pattern of effects of grades on the aspirations and attainments, however, appear to be relatively unaffected by such change in the reliability estimate. Maruyama, et al. (1981), using a multiple indicator achievement construct, found the latter to be highly stable and unrelated to self-esteem. It should be noted, however, that their achievement construct was based on standardized achievement tests which might be expected to be more stable than grades (see Jencks, et al., 1972: 57, 60). Further, their self-concept construct was not the academic self-concept but overall self-esteem, which has been found to have a weaker relation to grades (Kifer, 1975; Mortimer and Finch, 1983; see also Wiley, 1979: 405–406).

5. In a prior analysis, we attempted to estimate the direct effects of ability on aspirations and the three attainments. Only the first path (to aspirations) was statistically significant. However, the high degree of association of some of the predictors led to problems of multicollinearity and findings that were difficult to interpret.

6. It is also pertinent to note that these respondents entered the labor market in the early seventies, a period in which the demand for college graudates was declining and the pool of college educated workers was large. As a result, the benefit of college education (in terms of occupational status and earnings) also declined (Freeman, 1976; Featherman, 1980: 712–13). Further research, on different cohorts, is necessary to ascertain whether the negative effect of education on earnings is specific to this historical period. Both career processes and labor market phenomena certainly contribute to the relationship between education and earnings.

REFERENCES

Alexander, Karl L., Bruce K. Eckland, and Larry J. Griffin
   1975 "The Wisconsin model of socioeconomic achievement: a replication." American Journal of Sociology 81:324–347.

Bachman, Jerald G.
   1970 Youth in Transition, Vol. II. The Impact of Family Background and Intelligence on Tenth-Grade Boys. Ann Arbor, MI: Survey Research Center, Institute for Social Research.

Bachman, Jerald G. and Patrick M. O'Malley
   1977 "Self-esteem in young men: a longitudinal analysis of the impact of educational and occupational attainment." Journal of Personality and Social Psychology 35:365–380.

Bachman, Jerald G., Patrick M. O'Malley, and Jerome Johnston
   1978 Adolescence to Adulthood—Change and Stability in the Lives of Young Men. Youth in Transition, Vol. 6. Ann Arbor, MI: Institute for Social Research.

Blau, Peter M. and Otis Dudley Duncan
   1967 The American Occupational Structure. New York: John Wiley and Sons.

Bloom, Benjamin S.
   1964 Stability and Change in Human Characteristics. New York: John Wiley and Sons.

Bronfenbrenner, Urie
   1979 The Ecology of Human Development. Cambridge, MA: Harvard University Press.

Brophy, Jere E. and Thomas L. Good
   1974 Teacher–Student Relationships: Causes and Consequences. New York: Holt, Rinehart, and Winston.

Campbell, Richard T.
  1983 "Status attainment research: end of the beginning or beginning of the end?" Sociology of Education 56:47–62.
Coleman, James S.
  1961 The Adolescent Society. Glencoe, IL: The Free Press.
Coleman, James S., Earnest Q. Campbell, C. J. Hobson, James McPartland, A. M. Mood, F. D. Weinfield, and Robert L. York.
  1966 Equality of Educational Opportunity. Washington, DC: Office of Education, H.E.W.
Coopersmith, Stanley
  1967 The Antecedents of Self-Esteem. San Francisco: W. H. Freeman & Co.
Duncan, Beverly
  1967 "Early work experience of graduates and dropouts." Demography 4:19–29.
Duncan, Otis Dudley
  1969 "Contingencies in constructing causal models." Pp. 74–112 in Edgar F. Borgatta (ed.), Sociological Methodology, 1969. San Francisco: Jossey-Bass.
Duncan, Otis Dudley, David L. Featherman, and Beverly Duncan
  1972 Socioeconomic Background and Achievement. New York: Seminar Press.
Featherman, David L.
  1980 "Schooling and occupational careers: constancy and change in worldly success." Pp. 675–738 in Orville G. Brim, Jr. and Jerome Kagan (eds.), Constancy and Change in Human Development. Cambridge, MA: Harvard University Press.
Featherman, David L. and T. Michael Carter
  1976 "Discontinuities in schooling and the socioeconomic life cycle." Pp. 133–160 in William H. Sewell, Robert M. Hauser, and David L. Featherman (eds.), Schooling and Achievement in American Society. New York: Academic Press.
Freeman, Richard B.
  1976 The Overeducated American. New York: Academic Press.
Gecas, Viktor
  1971 "Parental behavior and dimensions of adolescent self-evaluation." Sociometry 34:466–482.
  1979 "The influence of social class on socialization." Pp. 365–404 in Wesley R. Burr, Reuben Hill, F. Ivan Nye, and Ira L. Reiss (eds.), Contemporary Theories about the Family. New York: The Free Press.
Gecas, Viktor and Michael L. Schwalbe
  1983 "Beyond the looking glass self: social structure and efficacy-based self-esteem." Social Psychology Quarterly 46:77–88.
Gordon, Chad
  1972 Looking Ahead: Self-Conceptions, Race, and Family as Determinants of Adolescent Orientation to Achievement. Rose Monograph Series. Washington, DC: American Sociological Association.
Hauser, Robert M.
  1971 Socioeconomic Background and Educational Performance. Rose Monograph Series. Washington, DC: American Sociological Association.
Hauser, Robert M.
  1973 "Disaggregating a social psychological model of educational attainment." Pp. 255–284 in Arthur S. Goldberger and Otis Dudley Duncan (eds.), Structural Equation Models in the Social Sciences. New York: Seminar Press.
Hauser, Robert M. and David L. Featherman
  1977 The Process of Stratification: Trends and Analyses. New York: Academic Press.
Hauser, Robert M., William H. Sewell, and Duane F. Alwin
  1976 "High school effects on achievement." Pp. 309–341 in William H. Sewell, Robert M.

Hauser, and David L. Featherman (eds.), Schooling and Achievement in American Society. New York: Academic Press.

Hauser, Robert M., Shu-Ling Tsai, and William H. Sewell
 1983 "A model of stratification with response error in social and psychological data." Sociology of Education 56:20–46.

Jencks, Christopher, Marshall Smith, Henry Acland, Mary Jo Bane, David Cohen, Herbert Gintis, Barbara Heyns, and Stephen Michelson
 1972 Inequality: A Reassessment of the Effect of Family and Schooling in America. New York: Basic Books.

Jencks, Christopher, James Crouse, and Peter Mueser
 1983 "The Wisconsin model of status attainment: a national replication with improved measures of ability and aspiration." Sociology of Education 56:3–19.

Johnson, David W., Geoffrey Maruyama, Roger T. Johnson, Deborah Nelson, and Linda Skon
 1981 "Effects of cooperative, competitive, and individualistic goal structures on achievement: a meta-analysis." Psychological Bulletin 89:47–62.

Joreskog, Karl G. and Dag Sorbom
 1978 LISREL IV: Estimation of Linear Structural Equation Systems by Maximum Likelihood Methods. Chicago: National Educational Resources.

Kerckhoff, Alan C.
 1974 Ambition and Attainment: A Study of Four Samples of American Boys. Rose Monograph Series. Washington, DC: American Sociological Association.

Kifer, Edward
 1975 "Relationships between academic achievement and personality characteristics: a quasi-longitudinal study." American Educational Research Journal 12:191–210.

Komorovsky, Mirra
 1976 Dilemmas of Masculinity. New York: W. W. Norton & Co.

Lewis, Ralph and Nancy St. John
 1974 "Contribution of cross-racial friendship to minority group achievement in desegregated classrooms." Sociometry 37:79–91.

Looker, E. Dianne and Peter C. Pineo
 1983 "Social psychological variables and their relevance to the status attainment of teenagers." American Journal of Sociology 88:1195–1219.

Long, J. Scott
 1976 "Estimation and hypothesis testing in linear models containing measurement error." Sociological Methods and Research 5:157–206.

Maruyama, Geoffrey
 1983 "Understanding the process of educational achievement." Pp. 165–197 in L. Bichman (ed.), Applied Social Psychology Annual, Vol. IV.

Maruyama, Geoffrey and Michael D. Finch
 1983 "Social influence, academic self-concept, and school achievement." Paper presented at the American Psychological Association meeting.

Maruyama, Geoffrey and Bill McGarvey
 1980 "Evaluating causal models: an application of maximum-likelihood analysis of structural equations." Psychological Bulletin 87:502–512.

Maruyama, Geoffrey, Rozalyn A. Rubin, and Gage G. Kingsbury
 1981 "Self-esteem and educational achievement: independent constructs with a common cause?" Journal of Personality and Social Psychology 40:962–997.

Mortimer, Jeylan T.
 1975 "Occupational value socialization in business and professional families." Sociology of Work and Occupations 2:29–53.

Mortimer, Jeylan T. and Michael D. Finch
 1983 "Autonomy as a source of self-esteem in adolescence." Paper presented at the 1983 American Sociological Association meeting.
Mortimer, Jeylan T., Michael D. Finch and Donald Kumka
 1982 "Persistence and change in development: the multidimensional self-concept." Pp. 263–312 in Paul B. Baltes & Orville G. Brim, Jr. (eds.), Life-Span Development and Behavior, Vol. 4. New York: Academic Press.
Mortimer, Jeylan T. and Jon Lorence
 1981 "Self-concept stability and change from late adolescence to early adulthood." Pp. 5–42 in Roberta G. Simmons (ed.), Research in Community and Mental Health, Vol. 2. Greenwich, CT: JAI Press.
Mortimer, Jeylan T., Jon Lorence, and Donald Kumka
 Forth-coming Work, Family, and Personality: Transition to Adulthood. Norwood, NJ: Ablex Publishing Corporation.
Purkey, William Watson
 1970 Self-Concept and School Achievement. Englewood Cliffs, NJ: Prentice-Hall.
Reitzes, Donald C. and Elizabeth Mutran
 1980 "Significant others and self-conceptions: factors influencing educational expectations and academic performance." Sociology of Education 53:21–32.
Rosen, Bernard C. and Roy G. D'Andrade
 1959 "The psychosocial origin of achievement motivation." Sociometry 22:185–218.
Rosenberg, Morris
 1965 Society and the Adolescent Self-Image. Princeton, NJ: Princeton University Press.
Rosenberg, Morris
 1979 Conceiving the Self. New York: Basic Books.
Rosenberg, Morris
 1981 "The self-concept: social product and social force." Pp. 593–624 in Morris Rosenberg and Ralph H. Turner (eds.), Social Psychology: Sociological Perspectives. New York: Basic Books.
Rosenberg, Morris and Leonard I. Pearlin
 1978 "Social class and self-esteem among children and adults." American Journal of Sociology 84:53–77.
Rosenshine, Barak V.
 1978 "Academic engaged time, content covered and direct instruction." Journal of Education 160:38–66.
Scheck, Dennis C., Robert Emerick, and Mohamed M. El-Assal
 1973 "Adolescents' perceptions of parent–child relations and the development of internal–external control orientation." Journal of Marriage and the Family 35:643–654.
Scheirer, Mary Ann and Robert E. Kraut
 1979 "Increasing educational achievement via self-concept change." Review of Educational Research 49:131–150.
Schooler, Carmi
 1980 "Psychological and social perspectives on status attainment." Paper presented at the Social Science Research Council, Japan–U.S. Conference on Social Stratification and Mobility, January 3–7.
Sewell, William H., Archibald O. Haller, and George W. Ohlendorf
 1970 "The educational and early occupational status attainment process: replication and revision." American Sociological Review 35:1014–1027.
Sewell, William H., Archibald O. Haller, and Alejandro Portes
 1969 "The educational and early occupational attainment process." American Sociological Review 34:82–92.

Sewell, William H. and Robert M. Hauser
 1975 Education, Occupation, and Earnings: Achievement in the Early Career. New York: Academic Press.
 1976 "Causes and consequences of higher education: models of the status attainment process." Pp. 9–27 in William H. Sewell, Robert M. Hauser, and David L. Featherman (eds.), Schooling and Achievement in American Society. New York: Academic Press.
Sewell, William H., Robert M. Hauser, and Wendy C. Wolf.
 1977 Sex, Schooling, and Occupational Careers. Working Paper 77–31, University of Wisconsin, Madison: Center for Demography and Ecology.
Spaeth, Joe L.
 1976 "Characteristics of the work setting and the job as determinants of income." Pp. 161–176 in William H. Sewell, Robert M. Hauser, and David L. Featherman (eds.), Schooling and Achievement in American Society. New York: Academic Press.
Spenner, Kenneth I. and David L. Featherman
 1978 "Achievement ambitions." Annual Review of Sociology 4:373–420.
Taylor, Marylee C.
 1979 "Race, sex, and the expression of self-fulfilling prophecies in a laboratory teaching situation." Journal of Personality and Social Psychology 37:897–912.
Thomas, Darwin L., Viktor Gecas, Andrew Weigert, and Elizabeth Rooney
 1974 Family Socialization and the Adolescent. Lexington, MA: D.C. Heath.
Wheaton, Blair, Bengt Muthen, Duane F. Alwin, and Gene F. Summers
 1977 "Assessing reliability and stability in panel models." Pp. 84–136 in D. R. Heise (ed.), Sociological Methodology, 1977. San Francisco: Jossey-Bass.
White, Karl R.
 1982 "The relation between socioeconomic status and academic achievement." Psychological Bulletin 91:461–481.
Wiley, Ruth C.
 1979 The Self-Concept. Rev. ed. Vol. 2. Theory and Research on Selected Topics. Lincoln: University of Nebraska Press.
Wilson, Kenneth L. and Alejandro Portes
 1975 "The educational attainment process: results from a national sample." American Journal of Sociology 81:343–363.

AGE, COHORT, AND REPORTED JOB SATISFACTION IN THE UNITED STATES

Norval D. Glenn and Charles N. Weaver

ABSTRACT

Data from nine U.S. national surveys conducted from 1972 to 1982 are used to estimate the contribution of age- and cohort-related influences to the often observed positive relationship between age and reported job satisfaction. A combination of relatively informal and relatively rigorous techniques of analysis, applied separately to data for males and females, reveals very persuasive, although not absolutely conclusive, evidence for important cohort effects, whereby each birth cohort which has reached adulthood in recent decades has been less inclined to be satisfied with work than the one before it. There may also have been important positive age effects, but the evidence for them is less compelling than the evidence for cohort effects. Given the nature of the apparent cohort effects, demographic change during the next few decades is likely to be unfavorable to positive attitudes toward work and perhaps to high job performance as well.

I. INTRODUCTION

One of the most consistent findings of research on attitudes toward work in the United States has been a positive relationship between age and reported job satisfaction.[1] Recent research has revealed a similar moderately strong positive relationship between age and reported enjoyment of work for both 1955 and 1980 (Glenn and Weaver, 1982a).

Why older workers have tended to view their work and their jobs more favorably than have younger workers, according to their self-reports, is not clear. The most common interpretation of the data is that workers tend to become more satisfied with their work as they grow older and become more experienced, perhaps because they tend to change jobs, and sometimes occupations, until they find work they like. Wright and Hamilton (1978) report some evidence which supports this explanation, but there is no conclusive evidence that the variations by age in reported job satisfaction are not largely cohort effects. There may have been changes in preadult formative experiences in recent decades which have made each successive birth cohort which has reached adulthood somewhat less inclined to be satisfied with their work than the one before it. One change which may have had this effect is the successively smaller percentage of the members of each cohort who have grown up on farms, where involvement in the adult world of work typically begins at a young age.[2] Furthermore, the large size of the post-World War II "baby boom" cohort and the increased labor force participation of women have placed members of that cohort in a relatively unfavorable position with respect to opportunities to do highly rewarding work. And if, as some observers believe, the baby boomers have expected more from their work than have members of earlier cohorts (Jones, 1980), relatively low job satisfaction and enjoyment of work in that cohort would be expected.

Still another possibility is that the relationship between age and attitudes toward work reflects primarily compositional effects (see Glenn, 1977:12–13; 1980:600–601). Responses to questions about job satisfaction and enjoyment of work are meaningful only for persons who are currently working, and those at each age level who are currently working may be an unrepresentative sample of their birth cohorts. The potential for selectivity bias is great for women at all age levels and is great for men at both the younger and older adult ages. For instance, the men most likely to have favorable attitudes toward work may be those who do not enter the labor force until their midtwenties and later, and the men with the least favorable attitudes toward work may begin to leave the labor force in substantial numbers after about age 50. Dissatisfied workers may also be somewhat more prone than other workers to early death. If so, mortality and movement of live individuals into and out of the labor force might largely account for the positive relationship between age and favorable attitudes toward work.

The possibility which is perhaps most disturbing to researchers who deal with self-reports of emotions and feelings is that the age variation in reported work attitudes reflects little more than intercohort differences in stoicism. The ideal that one should "keep a stiff upper lip" and put up a cheerful front in the face of adversity and unsatisfactory conditions may well have weakened in recent decades, and thus may be stronger among older people, although we know of no direct evidence on the issue. At least one might suspect that younger people have often been influenced by the self-help literature of popular psychology, which has encouraged people to express their "true feelings" and thus would be less inclined than older people to give a perfunctory favorable response to a question about their feelings toward their work. This explanation cannot be dismissed out of hand, and evidence relating to it must be examined along with the evidence relating to other explanations.

If either the aging or the birth cohort explanations should be correct, that fact would have some very important implications for the future of American society. The mean age of employed workers is projected to rise for at least the next 20 years and is likely to remain high relative to the present mean age for an indefinite period. If older workers have more favorable attitudes toward work because they are older or more experienced, the increase in the proportion of employed workers in the older age ranges has positive implications for the quality of life and probably for productivity and proficiency of work performance as well. If, on the other hand, the younger cohorts are inherently less inclined to view their work favorably because of the nature of their formative experiences and other aspects of their "cohort situation," the demographic changes in the work force during the next few years will be influences toward a lower quality of life and probably toward lowered productivity and quality of job performance. For instance, if the baby boom cohort is fated to have low job satisfaction and enjoyment of work throughout its life span, the fact that it will constitute a very substantial proportion of the labor force for the next 30 years does not augur well for the near future.

In this paper, we report and interpret tabulations and analyses of job satisfaction data from U.S. national surveys conducted annually from 1972 through 1978 and in 1980 and 1982. From these data we estimate the extent to which the cross-sectional positive relationship between age and reported job satisfaction reflects age, cohort, and compositional effects, and we consider possible reasons for the effects we estimate. Finally, we consider the implications of the findings for the future of work and the quality of life in America.

II. A SEARCH FOR AGE, COHORT, AND COMPOSITIONAL EFFECTS

The data in Table 1, which are pooled from the nine U.S. General Social Surveys conducted from 1972 through 1982,[3] show the usual positive, monotonic relationship between age and reported job satisfaction. The indicated relationship is

Table 1. Responses (in Percent) to a Question on Global Job Satisaction,[a] by Sex and Age, Employed Workers, Pooled Data from U.S. National Surveys Conducted in 1972, 1973, 1974, 1975, 1976, 1977, 1978, 1980, and 1982

Age	Very Dissatisfied	A Little Dissatisfied	Moderately Satisfied	Very Satisfied	Total (N)	Index[b]
Males:						
18–19	6.8	27.3	39.8	26.1	100.0 (88)	1.61
20–29	5.2	13.0	40.8	41.1	100.0 (1,123)	2.18
30–39	4.5	9.9	38.7	46.9	100.0 (1,064)	2.28
40–49	3.0	8.4	36.9	51.7	100.0 (868)	2.37
50–59	2.8	6.0	34.7	56.4	100.0 (812)	2.45
60–69	0.6	4.5	24.8	70.0	100.0 (330)	2.64
70 and older	0.0	2.9	14.7	82.4	100.0 (68)	2.80
Total	3.7	9.5	36.7	50.0	100.0 (4,353)	2.33
Females:						
18–19	8.6	17.2	50.0	24.1	100.0 (58)	1.90
20–29	5.3	14.6	42.5	37.7	100.0 (911)	2.13
30–39	3.6	8.6	35.7	52.1	100.0 (756)	2.36
40–49	2.3	6.9	35.6	55.1	100.0 (606)	2.43
50–59	1.6	4.9	33.5	60.0	100.0 (553)	2.52
60–69	1.3	6.7	30.5	61.5	100.0 (239)	2.52
70 and older	2.4	0.0	12.2	85.4	100.0 (41)	2.81
Total	3.4	9.3	36.8	50.6	100.0 (3,164)	2.35

[a]The question is: "On the whole, how satisfied are you with the work you do—would you say you are very satisfied, moderately satisfied, a little dissatisfied, or very dissatisfied?"

[b]The index is constructed by scoring very satisfied 3, moderately satisfied 2, a little dissatisfied 1, very dissatisfied 0, and by taking the mean score for the respondents.

similar for males and females, being strong enough to be important for both sexes—even if one ignores the youngest and oldest age levels, for which the N values are rather small. For instance, the percentage of "very dissatisfied" workers was more than twice as great at the younger ages than at the older ones.

Some simple additional tabulations of these data allow us to rule out some plausible explanations for the positive relationship between age and reported job satisfaction. For instance, we mention above that one reason for a cohort effect on attitudes toward work might be that successively smaller percentages of the persons in the cohorts that have recently reached adulthood have grown up on farms, and a farm background may be conducive to positive attitudes toward work. Therefore, we divided the respondents into those who lived on farms at age 16 and those who did not (Table 2).

Reported job satisfaction *was* somewhat higher at the younger ages for the farm origin workers, the difference at ages 20-29 being statistically significant for both males and females.[4] Aside from the oldest and youngest age levels shown in the table, for which the number of cases is not sufficient for reliable estimates, reported job satisfaction differed little by age among the farm origin workers—an intriguing finding which may provide a lead worth pursuing in later research. However, the differences in reported job satisfaction between persons with farm and nonfarm origins can account for virtually none of the relationship between age and reported job satisfaction among workers of all origins; standardizing the data for all workers at each age level to the origins distribution of workers of all ages (see the data under the heading of "Standardized Total" in Table 2) resulted in data very similar to the unstandardized data. Similarly, standardizing the responses at each age level to the same educational distribution made little difference.

We must turn, then, to more complex tabulations and analyses to find clues as to the kinds of effects reflected in the cross-sectional relationship between age and reported job satisfaction. Since the pooled data conceal some apparently important changes during the 10-year period, we report the percentage of "very satisfied" responses by year and age in Table 3 and by year and birth cohort in Table 4. The data in these two tables are, however, too detailed to be digested through visual inspection alone. In order to tease from them the information they can yield about causal processes, we first turn to a simple technique for "smoothing" the trends shown by the data, and then we perform multiple regression analyses for a somewhat more rigorous approach.

The "smoothed" data in Tables 5 and 6 are simply three-year running averages of the percentages in Tables 3 and 4. This smoothing procedure lessens the fluctuation due to sampling variability and any short-term influences on the responses, and makes easier the detection of any systematic change through the 10-year period.

If the data reflected pure age and/or compositional effects, the pattern of variation by age would be approximately the same at the different dates and there

Table 2. Percentage of Employed Workers Who Said They Were Very Satisfied with Their Work, by Age, Sex, and Farm–Nonfarm Origins, Pooled Data from U.S. National Surveys Conducted in 1972, 1973, 1974, 1975, 1976, 1977, 1978, 1980, and 1982

	Males				Females			
Age	Nonfarm Origin (N)	Farm Origin (N)	Total (N)	Standardized Total[a]	Nonfarm Origin (N)	Farm Origin (N)	Total (N)	Standardized Total[a]
18–19	26.8 (82)	16.7 (6)	26.1 (88)	24.6	22.6 (53)	20.0 (5)	22.4 (58)	22.2
20–29	39.3 (971)	52.0 (150)	41.1 (1,121)	42.0	36.1 (828)	53.8 (80)	37.7 (908)	39.1
30–39	45.5 (877)	53.8 (186)	46.9 (1,063)	47.3	52.1 (658)	53.1 (96)	52.1 (754)	52.3
40–49	50.6 (656)	55.5 (211)	51.7 (867)	51.6	55.8 (495)	52.3 (111)	55.1 (606)	55.2
50–59	57.0 (574)	54.9 (237)	56.4 (811)	56.6	59.0 (398)	62.3 (154)	60.0 (552)	59.6
60–69	70.7 (215)	69.0 (113)	70.0 (328)	70.3	60.6 (165)	63.5 (74)	61.5 (239)	61.1
70 and up	84.0 (45)	75.0 (24)	82.4 (69)	82.1	85.2 (27)	85.7 (14)	85.4 (41)	85.3

[a] What the percentage for workers of all origins at each age level would be if the proportion with rural origins were the same at each age level as for workers of all ages.

94

Age, Cohort, and Reported Job Satisfaction

Table 3. Percentage of Employed Workers Who Said They Were Very Satisfied with Their Work, by Sex, Age, and Year, U.S. National Surveys

Age	1972 (N)	1973 (N)	1974 (N)	1975 (N)	1976 (N)	1977 (N)	1978 (N)	1980 (N)	1982 (N)
Males:									
20–29	34.7 (147)	39.8 (113)	44.6 (121)	46.5 (114)	40.8 (125)	42.6 (129)	41.0 (139)	36.8 (106)	43.4 (129)
30–39	51.3 (113)	53.6 (125)	44.3 (97)	54.4 (103)	56.0 (109)	40.7 (123)	45.5 (132)	40.1 (147)	39.1 (115)
40–49	48.2 (137)	45.5 (101)	54.0 (100)	57.8 (90)	54.4 (77)	58.1 (104)	55.7 (97)	47.0 (83)	58.2 (79)
50–59	51.9 (131)	59.1 (93)	53.5 (99)	61.4 (83)	58.3 (84)	53.3 (90)	62.5 (80)	53.4 (88)	57.8 (64)
60–69	72.7 (55)	60.0 (40)	73.7 (38)	69.7 (33)	77.1 (35)	75.0 (36)	87.5 (30)	80.0 (35)	85.7 (28)
Total[a]	48.6 (605)	49.6 (488)	51.1 (470)	55.7 (442)	53.5 (452)	47.6 (496)	50.5 (491)	46.2 (476)	48.3 (433)
Females:									
20–29	32.0 (75)	36.6 (82)	38.6 (83)	37.6 (93)	44.3 (97)	27.9 (104)	47.7 (128)	36.9 (122)	34.6 (127)
30–39	50.0 (56)	60.0 (55)	45.2 (73)	70.8 (72)	60.8 (74)	52.0 (102)	49.5 (105)	45.2 (93)	45.2 (126)
40–49	58.2 (67)	58.3 (72)	52.3 (65)	61.8 (68)	49.2 (59)	52.1 (73)	50.8 (61)	52.2 (67)	59.5 (74)
50–59	56.4 (55)	51.6 (64)	60.4 (53)	58.2 (55)	63.3 (49)	65.6 (90)	66.2 (65)	61.8 (55)	55.2 (67)
60–69	60.0 (25)	55.2 (29)	63.0 (27)	60.7 (28)	68.4 (19)	70.4 (27)	56.5 (23)	62.1 (29)	59.4 (32)
Total[a]	50.2 (285)	50.3 (312)	49.5 (309)	54.8 (330)	51.9 (314)	50.5 (404)	52.8 (396)	48.0 (377)	47.6 (437)

[a]Includes persons ages 18–19 and 70 and older.

would be no systematic change through time at each age level.[5] In fact, however, the pattern of variation shown by the data is not the same for the different periods and there were some systematic changes from the earlier to the later periods at some age levels. For males, for instance, the running averages at ages 30–39 distinctly decrease, and at ages 60–69 they distinctly increase. For females, there is also a decrease at ages 30–39 and a less definite one at ages 40–49. There is no

Table 4. Percentage of Employed Workers Who Said They Were Very Satisfied with Their Work, by Sex, Birth Cohort, and Year, U.S. National Surveys

Date of Birth	1972 (N)	1973 (N)	1974 (N)	1975 (N)	1976 (N)	1977 (N)	1978 (N)	1980 (N)	1982 (N)
Males:									
1943–1952	34.7 (147)	41.1 (124)	46.9 (128)	46.7 (120)	43.9 (139)	39.6 (134)	42.9 (161)	35.5 (157)	39.1 (115)
1933–1942	51.3 (113)	52.5 (120)	43.8 (89)	58.7 (104)	63.4 (93)	46.4 (110)	50.5 (107)	48.8 (80)	58.2 (79)
1923–1932	48.2 (137)	50.0 (94)	50.0 (112)	58.4 (89)	46.2 (78)	48.5 (101)	60.3 (78)	50.0 (80)	57.8 (64)
1913–1922	51.9 (131)	56.3 (96)	58.3 (84)	65.2 (66)	71.2 (73)	63.8 (69)	64.8 (54)	66.7 (54)	60.7 (28)
Females:									
1943–1952	32.0 (75)	38.8 (80)	41.7 (96)	48.4 (91)	50.0 (92)	39.8 (118)	48.3 (120)	45.4 (108)	45.2 (126)
1933–1942	50.0 (56)	59.3 (59)	43.8 (64)	66.7 (78)	60.6 (71)	51.9 (79)	47.3 (74)	47.1 (70)	59.5 (74)
1923–1932	58.2 (67)	56.9 (72)	59.3 (59)	54.1 (61)	47.3 (55)	65.0 (80)	61.7 (60)	62.7 (59)	55.2 (67)
1913–1922	56.4 (55)	53.4 (58)	62.5 (56)	62.7 (51)	66.7 (45)	67.7 (65)	65.9 (44)	57.1 (35)	59.4 (32)

systematic increase at ages 60–69, but there seems to be a slight increase at ages 50–59.

The running averages in Table 5 are useful for detecting apparent trends at each age level, but there are no statistical tests which can be applied to them to test the null hypothesis that there was no systematic change. In order to apply such tests, we used the cells in each row of Table 3 as the units of analysis for correlation-regression analyses in which year was the independent variable and percentage of workers who said they were very satisfied with their work was the dependent variable. Only three of the correlation coefficients computed in this way are statistically significant, the one for males for the 30–39 age level ($r = -.708$; $p < .05$), the one for males for the 60–69 age level ($r = .774$; $p < .02$), and the one for females for the 30 39 age level ($r = -.779$; $p < .01$).

More powerful tests might reveal other statistically significant trends, but the three trends revealed by this method are sufficient for us rather confidently to reject the notion that there are only age and/or compositional effects reflected in

Age, Cohort, and Reported Job Satisfaction 97

Table 5. Smoothed Trend Data Computed from the Data in Table 3 (Three-Year Running Means of the Percentage of Employed Persons Who Said They Were Very Satisfied with Their Work)

Age	1972, 1973, 1974	1973, 1974, 1975	1974, 1975, 1976	1975, 1976, 1977	1976, 1977, 1978	1977, 1978, 1980	1978, 1980, 1982
Males:							
20–29	39.7	43.6	44.0	43.3	41.5	40.1	40.4
30–39	49.7	50.8	51.6	50.4	47.4	42.1	41.6
40–49	49.2	52.4	55.4	56.8	56.1	53.6	53.6
50–59	54.8	58.0	57.7	57.7	58.0	56.4	57.9
60–69	<u>68.8</u>	<u>67.8</u>	<u>73.5</u>	<u>73.9</u>	<u>79.9</u>	<u>80.8</u>	<u>84.4</u>
Total	49.8	52.1	53.4	52.3	50.5	48.1	48.3
Females:							
20–29	35.7	37.6	40.2	36.6	39.9	37.5	39.7
30–39	51.7	58.7	58.9	61.2	54.1	48.9	46.6
40–49	56.3	57.5	54.4	54.4	50.7	51.7	54.2
50–59	56.1	56.7	60.6	62.4	65.0	64.5	61.1
60–69	<u>59.4</u>	<u>59.6</u>	<u>64.0</u>	<u>66.5</u>	<u>65.1</u>	<u>63.0</u>	<u>59.3</u>
Total	50.0	51.5	52.1	52.4	51.7	50.4	49.5

Table 6. Smoothed Trend Data Computed from the Data in Table 4 (Three-Year Running Means of the Percentage of Employed Persons Who Said They Were Very Satisfied with Their Work)

Date of Birth	1972, 1973, 1974	1973, 1974, 1975	1974, 1975, 1976	1975, 1976, 1977	1976, 1977, 1978	1977, 1978, 1980	1978, 1980, 1982
Males:							
1943–1952	40.9	44.9	45.8	43.4	42.1	40.7	40.5
1933–1942	49.2	51.7	55.3	56.2	53.4	48.6	52.5
1923–1932	49.4	52.8	51.5	51.0	51.7	52.9	56.0
1913–1922	55.5	59.9	64.9	66.7	66.6	65.1	64.1
Females:							
1943–1952	37.5	43.0	46.7	46.1	46.0	44.5	46.3
1933–1942	51.0	56.6	57.0	59.7	53.3	48.8	51.3
1923–1932	58.1	56.8	53.6	55.5	58.0	63.1	59.9
1913–1922	54.1	59.5	64.0	65.7	66.8	63.6	60.8

the data. We cannot, however, be equally confident about what effects *are* reflected. Since the two significant trends for males are in different directions, the most plausible explanation for the pattern of variation is that it reflects cohort effects. According to this explanation, as there was complete replacement of one 10-year birth cohort by another at each age level during the period covered by the data, reported job satisfaction went either up or down if there were any differences between the replaced and the replacing cohorts in their inclinations to be satisfied with their work. At ages 30–39, a cohort relatively inclined to be satisfied was replaced by one relatively disinclined to be satisfied, whereas at ages 60–69, the replacing cohort was more inclined to be satisfied with its work than was the replaced one. The only other explanation for the data would be a rather improbable (in our opinion) age–period interaction whereby period influences produced a decrease in job satisfaction at ages 30–39 but produced an increase at ages 60–69. We cannot be sure, of course, that such an age–period interaction did not occur, but the data by birth cohort in Tables 4 and 6, to which we now turn, also tend to support the cohort explanation.

The running averages in Table 6 reveal the smoothed trends within 10-year birth cohorts of the percentage of respondents who said they were very satisfied with their work. To the extent that there were positive age and/or compositional effects not offset by negative period effects, the running averages in each cohort should indicate an increase. For males, the data show an increase within each of the two older cohorts, but only a small one within the 1923–1932 cohort. For females, there is an indication of an increase within both the youngest and the oldest cohorts, but not a very pronounced one in either case.

Again, we must turn to correlation–regression analysis of the unsmoothed trends (shown in Table 4) in order to apply statistical tests. None of the within-cohort trends is statistically significant at even the .10 level, although the increase for women in the youngest cohort comes close. Of the remaining seven correlation coefficients, three are positive and more than negligible in magnitude, two are positive and negligible, and two are negative and negligible. Since all of the larger coefficients are in the predicted direction, it is quite likely that there are positive age and/or compositional effects reflected in the data, but unless there were offsetting negative period effects, those effects could hardly have been very strong.

The evidence examined so far suggests that the cross-sectional relationship between age and reported job satisfaction in this country in recent years reflects cohort effects to a large extent but probably age and/or compositional effects as well. But since the evidence is far from conclusive, we need to examine the data from a different perspective to gain additional clues.

If in successive sets of cross-sectional data from the same population there is a particular and persistent *nonlinear* pattern of variation of a dependent variable by age, the only plausible explanation for the pattern is that it reflects, largely or entirely, age effects and/or compositional effects (Glenn, 1981a). On the other

Age, Cohort, and Reported Job Satisfaction

hand, if successive samples are drawn at different times from the same set of adjacent birth cohorts (as in Table 4), and if there is a particular and persistent *nonlinear* pattern of variation by cohort, the only plausible explanation is that the pattern reflects, largely or entirely, cohort effects. Such simple patterns of variation with such unambiguous meanings are rarely found, unfortunately, but a search for them should always be an early step in the examination of cohort data.

In Table 7, we report the deviations from the linear regression line of the percentages in each column of Table 5, when percentage very satisfied is regressed on age and when the age levels (cells in each column) are the units of analysis. In Table 8, we report the deviations from the linear regression line of the percentages in each column of Table 6, when percentage very satisfied is regressed on year of birth and when the birth cohorts (cells in each column) are the units of analysis.

The data in Table 7 show that the variation by age was consistently nonlinear but generally not in a consistent fashion from the earlier to the later dates. For males, there is a tendency for the deviations from the regression line to vary systematically from the earlier to the later dates, except at ages 40–49, where the deviations go from negative to slightly positive and then back to negative. The deviations are consistently negative for ages 50–59 and consistently positive for ages 60–69, but the magnitude of the deviations tends to increase from the earlier to the later dates at both levels. The trend at both of the two youngest age levels is perfectly monotonic—precisely the pattern to be expected as a result of cohort

Table 7. Deviations from the Linear Regression Line,[a] Computed from the Smoothed Trend Data in Table 5

Age	1972, 1973, 1974	1973, 1974, 1975	1974, 1975, 1976	1975, 1976, 1977	1976, 1977, 1978	1977, 1978, 1980	1978, 1980, 1982
Males:							
20–29	−0.1	+0.2	+0.3	+0.6	+2.4	+4.7	+5.7
30–39	+3.6	+1.8	+1.5	+0.8	−0.4	−2.9	−3.5
40–49	−3.2	−2.1	−1.1	+0.4	−0.5	−1.0	−2.0
50–59	−4.0	−2.1	−5.3	−5.6	−7.3	−7.8	−8.1
60–69	+3.7	+2.2	+4.1	+3.8	+5.8	+4.4	+8.0
Females:							
20–29	−5.8	−8.0	−5.6	−7.4	−2.8	−2.3	−1.7
30–39	+5.0	+8.9	+8.2	+11.1	+5.3	+2.4	−0.2
40–49	+4.5	+3.5	−1.2	−1.8	−4.3	−1.4	+2.0
50–59	−0.9	−1.5	0.0	+0.1	+3.9	+4.7	+3.5
60–69	−2.8	−2.8	−1.5	−1.9	−2.1	−3.4	−3.6

[a]Regression of reported satisfaction with work (percentage "very satisfied") on age, computed with the cells in the columns as the units of analysis.

replacement if the replaced and replacing cohorts differed in their inclinations to be satisfied with their work. For females, the deviations are perfectly consistent in sign only at the oldest and youngest age levels, and there is a monotonic decline in the size of the negative deviations at ages 20–29. Furthermore, the rather consistent negative deviations at ages 60–69 do not strongly suggest age and/or compositional effects in the absence of consistent deviations at the next lower age level.

For males, the search for evidence for cohort effects in Table 8 is more fruitful than the search for evidence for age or compositional effects in Table 7. Of the 28 deviations shown, only two prevent the signs of the deviations from being perfectly consistent for each birth cohort, and both of those values are near zero. There is no monotonic trend for any of the cohorts, as there should be if there were any substantial nonlinear age effects. Thus the data suggest the presence of some fairly substantial nonlinear cohort effects. In contrast, the data for females in Table 8 hardly fall into a discernible pattern at all, partly, no doubt, because of smaller N values and greater sampling variability, but probably also because a steep increase in the labor force participation of women during the period covered brought about some complex compositional effects.

Thus, at this point, the evidence for cohort effects underlying the cross-sectional positive relationship between age and job satisfaction remains stronger than the evidence for age or compositional effects. However, our methods of examining the data have been rather informal,[6] and one might reasonably ask for evidence from the application of more rigorous methods. However, the confounding of age, period, and cohort effects (and sometimes compositional ef-

Table 8. Deviations from the Linear Regression Line,[a] Computed from the Smoothed Trend Data in Table 6

Date of Birth	1972, 1973, 1974	1973, 1974, 1975	1974, 1975, 1976	1975, 1976, 1977	1976, 1977, 1978	1977, 1978, 1980	1978, 1980, 1982
Males:							
1943–1952	−1.3	−0.5	−0.6	−1.2	−0.6	+0.5	−1.6
1933–1942	+2.6	+1.7	+3.6	+5.1	+3.5	+0.6	+2.9
1923–1932	−1.6	−1.8	−5.6	−6.6	−5.3	−2.8	−1.0
1913–1922	+0.1	+0.7	+2.5	+2.7	+2.4	+1.6	−0.3
Females:							
1943–1952	−4.1	−3.5	−1.4	−2.5	0.0	+0.2	−0.5
1933–1942	+3.7	+5.1	+4.1	+5.7	+0.6	−2.6	−0.7
1923–1932	+5.1	+0.3	−4.2	−4.0	−1.4	+4.5	+2.7
1913–1922	−4.6	−1.9	+1.4	+0.8	+0.7	−2.1	−1.6

[a]Regression of reported satisfaction with work (percentage "very satisfied") on date of birth, computed with the cells in the columns as the units of analysis.

fects) in cohort data means that rigorous methods cannot be routinely and mechanically applied to separate the effects (Glenn, 1976, 1977), and at least one authority on cohort analysis appears to argue, in effect, that the rigorous methods should not be used (Rodgers, 1982). We agree that extreme caution should be exercised in interpreting statistical tests of cohort models, but occasionally one can defend the assumption that either age, period, or cohort effects are absent, in which case the remaining two kinds of effects can be estimated through straightforward application of linear regression, log linear analysis, or some similar technique.

In this case, there is reason to believe that there were no monotonic period effects of any importance from 1972 through 1982. According to the data in Table 3, the overall level of reported job satisfaction was about the same in 1972 and in 1982 for males, and although it was somewhat lower in 1982 than in 1972 for females, cohort replacement alone could have accounted for the small decline. A rather general up–down pattern in the "very satisfied" percentages during the decade at specific age levels almost certainly reflects period effects, but nonlinear ones which apparently left little if any net change. Over a longer period of time, such changes as those in management styles and in specialization of work tasks may have brought about important period effects on job satisfaction, but there is little reason to believe that such changes from 1972 to 1982 were substantial enough to produce pronounced effects. Nevertheless, the estimates of age and cohort effects from the model which assumes no period effects must be viewed with caution.

For testing the regression model, we entered age and cohort as sets of dummy variables, with each dummy representing a 10-year age level or a 10-year birth cohort. The age categories begin at 18 and extend through 57—the older ages being excluded because of small N values and the probability of substantial compositional effects due to retirement. The included birth cohorts are those within that age range in 1972 and/or in 1982. We regressed reported job satisfaction, scored according to the values in footnote *a* of Table 9, on age and cohort simultaneously and computed from the regression results the adjusted mean job satisfaction scores reported in Table 9.

It is apparent from a cursory examination of the data that both age and cohort effects are indicated. It is difficult to compare the magnitude of these effects, however, because five birth cohorts but only four age levels are represented. In order to make a comparison, we computed the summary effect scores in Table 10, which are derived by expressing the standard deviation (among the age levels or cohorts) of the mean job satisfaction scores as a percentage of the standard deviation of the midpoints (in years) of the age levels or birth cohorts.

For the first time as we have examined the evidence, there is an indication that age and/or compositional effects were greater than cohort effects, the summary effect score for age being more than twice that for birth cohort in the case of females and moderately higher than that for birth cohort in the case of males.

Table 9. Regression of Reported Global Job Satisfaction on Age and Birth Cohort, by Sex, Employed Workers, Pooled Data from U.S. National Surveys Conducted in 1972, 1973, 1974, 1975, 1976, 1977, 1978, 1980, and 1982

	Adjusted Mean Job Satisfaction Scores[a]			
	Regression I[b]		Regression II[c]	
	Males	Females	Males	Females
Age:				
18–27	2.20	2.16	2.20	2.15
28–37	2.26	2.32	2.26	2.32
38–47	2.34	2.38	2.34	2.38
48–57	2.38	2.45	2.39	2.46
Date of Birth:				
1915–1924	2.42	2.39	2.43	2.41
1925–1934	2.32	2.36	2.33	2.36
1935–1944	2.32	2.36	2.32	2.37
1945–1954	2.23	2.26	2.22	2.25
1955–1964	2.20	2.23	2.22	2.23

[a] Very satisfied is scored 3, moderately satisfied 2, a little dissatisfied 1, and very dissatisfied 0. The adjustment is for the "effects" of other variables entered simultaneously in the regression.
[b] Age and cohort are the only variables entered simultaneously in the regression.
[c] Years of school completed is entered simultaneously with age and cohort.

According to the scores, cohort effects were stronger for males than for females in agreement with the other evidence we have examined), whereas age and/or compositional effects were stronger for females than for males. Since there has been much more movement of females than of males into and out of the employed labor force in the age range covered except at the very youngest adult ages, it seems likely that greater compositional effects largely account for the greater "age" effects indicated for females.

The estimated age effects for males in the first column of Table 9 are monoto-

Table 10. Summary Effect Scores Computed from the Data in Table 9

Independent Variable	Regression I		Regression II	
	Males	Females	Males	Females
Age	.62	.96	.65	1.02
Birth cohort	.55	.44	.56	.50

nic and very nearly linear, and the estimated age effects for females in the second column are monotonic but distinctly nonlinear, most of the variation being between ages 18–27 and 28–37. One might suspect that most of this latter difference is a compositional effect because many of the women who are not satisfied with their work as very young adults are able to leave the labor force by the time they reach their late twenties and early thirties. Some of the difference for males between ages 18–27 and 28–37 may also be a compositional effect since many of the men most likely to be very satisfied with their work—i.e., professionals—are out of the labor force much of the time until they reach their middle or late twenties. However, the difference between the two middle age levels should be an age effect because most men have almost continuous labor force participation from age 28 through age 47, and that difference is the greatest of the estimated differences between age levels. The data suggest, therefore, that something associated with growing older and accumulating work experience *is* conducive to enhanced job satisfaction among American men, as most interpreters of the cross-sectional relationship between age and job satisfaction have believed.

The estimated cohort effects on job satisfaction are nonlinear for both males and females. For both sexes, the adjusted mean job satisfaction scores are identical for the 1925–1934 and 1935–1944 cohorts, are lower and similar for the two baby boom cohorts, and are highest for the 1915–1924 cohort. It is hardly surprising that the reported job satisfaction of persons born from 1945 to 1964 is relatively low because the crude birth rate was 20 or higher throughout that period and the large number of cohort members has stiffened competition for the more rewarding kinds of work. It is also possible that the baby boomers generally had early formative experiences which caused them to approach work and other adult roles with unrealistic expectations (Jones, 1980).

We must now consider the implications if the assumption of no systematic period effects should not be correct. Positive additive period effects from 1972 to 1982 would appear in our estimates about equally as positive age effects and as positive (from earlier to later dates of birth) cohort effects. On the other hand, negative 1972–1982 period effects would appear about equally as negative age effects and as negative cohort effects. Thus, if there were positive period effects, the real positive age effects were smaller than those estimated (and could conceivably have been zero) and the real negative cohort effects were larger. And if there were negative period effects, the real positive age effects were larger than the ones estimated and the real negative cohort effects were smaller or nonexistent.

Any period effects would have to have been very strong, however, to have accounted completely for either the estimated positive age effects or the estimated negative cohort effects. The estimated effects are spread over several 10-year cohorts and age levels, whereas all of the period effects would have been concentrated in one 10-year period and only about half of the period effects would have appeared in the estimates of either the age or the cohort effects. If period effects of such a magnitude had occurred, the level of reported job satisfaction in the total work force could hardly have remained about constant, as it apparently did (Table 3). The level of reported job satisfaction in the total work force could have remained about constant in the face of substantial period effects only if cohort succession (cohort effects) had offset the period effects, and the extent to which cohort succession could have affected the total work force during the 10-year period is quite limited.

A limited empirical test of the accuracy of the allocation of age and cohort effects can be performed by adding to the regression a variable known to be largely cohort related rather than age related, or vice versa. For instance, adding a cohort-related variable to the regression equation should affect only the estimates of the cohort effects and not the estimates of the age effects if the allocation of age and cohort effects is accurate. Years of school completed is a cohort-related variable because at the individual level years of school cannot decrease with aging, and yet this variable relates negatively to age. To the extent that aging does affect level of education, the effect must be positive.

Formal education apparently has a positive (although modest) effect on job satisfaction (Glenn and Weaver, 1982b), and thus removing the indirect effect through education of age on job satisfaction should, if it makes any difference, weaken the estimated positive effect of age. In contrast, removing the indirect effect through education of cohort on job satisfaction should strengthen the estimated negative effect of cohort.

However, the data in Tables 9 and 10 show that adding years of school completed to the regression equation strengthens the estimated effects of both age and cohort—an indication of error in the allocation of the effects. It appears that some rather substantial negative cohort effects are misallocated by the regression model and appear as estimated positive age effects.[7] This evidence and the fact that an unknown but possibly substantial proportion of the estimated age effects reflect compositional effects leave us with no really strong and compelling evidence for positive age effects of an important magnitude.

We return, then, to essentially the same conclusion we tentatively made after our more informal examination of the data: There is convincing, although not conclusive, evidence that the birth cohorts now in adulthood vary in their tendency to be satisfied with work, the earliest (oldest) cohorts being most inclined to be satisfied and the youngest ones being least inclined to do so. There may well be important positive age effects on job satisfaction as well, but we cannot conclude with confidence that there are.

III. POSSIBLE SOURCES OF COHORT EFFECTS

We have already mentioned that a likely reason for relatively low satisfaction in the baby boom cohort is simply the greater competition for the more desirable jobs and lines of work, and we have noted that some observers of the cohort think that its members reached adulthood with unusually high expectations for work (as well as for marriage and other aspects of life) which would have been hard to fulfill even under more favorable circumstances.

Although some characterizations of the baby boom cohort seem to us to be overdrawn and exaggerated (e.g., Jones, 1980), there are some reasons to think that members of the post–World War II cohorts, including perhaps the persons born after the end of the so-called baby boom, have reached and are reaching adulthood with expectations which are, on the average, rather unrealistic. These are the first cohorts who have grown up with television and there is much speculation (but little direct evidence, so far as we are able to tell)[8] that viewing television during the formative years tends to whet the appetite for glamorous and adventurous living and affluent life-styles and to undermine the patience and persistence required to put in sustained effort to attain long-term goals. Whatever the consequences may be, television has tended to portray the world of work unrealistically. As their work is portrayed on television, doctors, lawyers, police officers, newspaper reporters, and even persons in such relatively mundane lines of work as teaching school have work lives full of challenge, excitement, and frequent overcoming of obstacles and the consequent gratification and feelings of fulfillment. The viewer rarely gets a sense of the persistent frustrations and of the many hours devoted to relatively uninteresting tasks even by persons in the more glamorous occupations. And unlike most children and adolescents of a century ago, persons who have reached adulthood in recent years have formed their early impressions of work to a large extent from the mass media because few of them have learned of the world of work firsthand by working with their parents, and observing their parents work, on farms or in family-owned businesses.

A difference between the baby boom cohort and the next earlier one is apparently not the only cohort difference in tendency to be satisfied with work, since, according to our estimates, the 1915–1924 cohort has been more inclined toward satisfaction than the 1925–1934 or the 1935–1944 cohort. There probably has been, therefore, a long-term intercohort trend rather than a sharp one-time change beginning with the baby boomers. Perhaps fluctuations in fertility have brought about fluctuations around the long-term trend line, with low-fertility cohorts (such as the Great Depression cohort) being above the trend line and high-fertility cohorts (such as the baby boomers) being below the line.

If so, what accounts for the long-term intercohort trend? The mass media may be partly responsible because the media which existed prior to television, such as radio and the movies, may have had effects similar to, but weaker than, those of television. One of the more plausible explanations for the trend traces it back to the separation of place of residence and place of work which began with industrialization. Offspring of farmers and of some small-business owners still grow up with ample opportunities to observe and participate in the world of work, but the lives of most children and adolescents today intersect with the adult world of work only in some of its very specialized corners (such as with school teachers) except in very superficial ways. Self-esteem and self-actualization come from play activities, school accomplishments, and the like, but usually not from work of the kind engaged in by adults. Thus when the person goes into the world of work—sometimes as late in the life span as the middle or late twenties—work is unlikely suddenly to become as central in the person's life as it would have been had he or she begun relying on it for self-actualization much earlier. The lack of a strong and consistent relationship between farm origins and reported job satisfaction (Table 2) casts some doubt on this explanation but does not by itself disprove it.

We cannot be absolutely sure, of course, that any intercohort difference in the tendency to report high job satisfaction is anything except just that—a tendency to say one is satisfied regardless of true feelings. A stoicism born of frontier conditions may have become somewhat less prevalent in each successive cohort as the cohort members became, on the average, further away generations-wise from the frontier. If so, the intercohort differences are still important, but their implications are of course different from those of authentic differences in the tendency to be satisfied with work.

IV. IMPLICATIONS FOR THE FUTURE

Statements about the implications of the findings reported here must be tentative, of course, because we cannot be absolutely certain that there have been any important cohort effects, and in turn we cannot be certain that any cohort effects have not been differences in stoicism and the feeling that one should be satisfied with work rather than in a genuine tendency to be satisfied. However, such a need for tentativeness is the rule rather than the exception when one is dealing with social scientific issues, and thus implications should be drawn on the basis of the best available evidence, even though that evidence is not conclusive. And we believe that the best available evidence indicates a long-term intercohort trend toward a lesser tendency to be satisfied with work, with a distinct difference between persons born in 1945–1964 and those born during the previous 20 years.

If this conclusion is correct, one should view with skepticism the often heard predictions that the American work force will become as a whole more satisfied and productive as the average age of workers in it increases during the next couple of decades. Even if these are some positive age effects on job satisfaction, the effects of changes in the age distribution of the work force are likely to be more than offset by the effects of cohort succession, whereby retiring older workers relatively inclined to be satisfied with work will be replaced by young workers relatively disinclined to be satisfied. Demographic changes alone are very unlikely, we believe, to produce a work force with more favorable attitudes toward work.

There is not a very strong relationship between job satisfaction, as it is measured here, and job performance, at least at the individual level (Berg et al., 1978), and thus we can make no strong conclusions about probable trends in job performance on the basis of probable trends in job satisfaction. However, we *can* say that there is little or no reason to believe that trends in job satisfaction during the next several years will contribute positively to job performance and productivity.

ACKNOWLEDGMENTS

The data reported here are from the 1972–1982 General Social Surveys conducted by the National Opinion Research Center (James A. Davis, principal investigator) with funds from the National Science Foundation. The authors are solely responsible for the analyses and interpretations reported here. The research was supported in part by National Science Foundation Grant SES-7907917. Computer time for portions of the project was provided by the Computation Center at the University of Texas at Austin.

NOTES

1. The many publications reporting this relationship include Vollmer and Kinney (1955), Hulin and Smith (1965), Sheppard and Herrick (1972), Quinn et al. (1974), Glenn et al. (1977), Wright and Hamilton (1978), Janson and Martin (1982), and Kalleberg and Loscocco (1983). An excellent summary of most of the literature relating to age and attitudes toward work is in Doering et al. (1983).

2. Elsewhere we speculate that a difference by age in reported enjoyment of work reflects to a large extent the smaller proportion of persons with farm origins at the younger ages (Glenn and Weaver, 1982a).

3. The General Social Surveys are surveys of the civilian, noninstitutionalized population of the 48 contiguous United States age 18 and older. The interviews were conducted face-to-face with about 1,500 respondents for each survey selected through standard multistage cluster sampling techniques. See Stephenson (1979) for a detailed description of the sample designs.

4. At the .05 level on a two-tailed test. We multiplied the standard errors by 1.3 as a correction for the effects of the complex design of the samples.

5. We assume that the reader is familiar with the concepts and the logic of cohort analysis. For a concise discussion of these topics, see Glenn (1981b).

6. And the last method we employed is, of course, adequate only for detecting *nonlinear* effects. It would never detect linear effects.

7. The reason for this misallocation is probably that there were systematic positive period effects from 1972 to 1982. Testing the cohort model with years of school completed in the regression equation would be complicated if there were a strong tendency for persons with little education to retire or drop out of the labor force at a younger age than persons with more education. However, we conducted a cohort analysis with years of school completed as the dependent variable and found no appreciable increase in the educational distributions of cohorts which aged beyond 50.

8. There is much controversey concerning the effects of television among persons who have done research on the topic. For a discussion of much of the relevant evidence, see Comstock et al. (1978) and Liebert and Schwartzberg (1977).

REFERENCES

Berg, Ivar, Marcia Freedman, and Michael Freeman
   1978   Managers and Work Reform: A Limited Engagement. New York: Free Press.

Comstock, George, Steven Chaffee, Nathan Katzman, Maxwell McCombs, and Donald Roberts
   1978   Television and Human Behavior. New York: Columbia University Press.

Davis, James A.
   1982   General Social Surveys, 1972–1982: Cumulative Codebook. Chicago: National Opinion Research Center.

Doering, Mildred, Susan R. Rhodes, and Michael Schuster
   1983   The Aging Worker: Research and Recommendations. Beverly Hills: Sage.

Glenn, Norval D.
   1976   "Cohort analysts' futile quest: statistical attempts to separate age, period, and cohort effects." American Sociological Review 41:900–904.
   1977   Cohort Analysis. Beverly Hills: Sage.
   1980   "Attitudes, beliefs, and values." Pp. 596–640 in Orville Brim and Jerome Kagan (eds.), Change and Continuity in Human Development. Cambridge, MA: Harvard University Press.
   1981a   "Age, birth cohorts, and drinking: an illustration of the hazards of inferring effects from cohort data." Journal of Gerontology 36:362–369.
   1981b   "The utility and logic of cohort analysis." Journal of Applied Behavioral Science 17:247–257.

Glenn, Norval D., Patricia A. Taylor, and Charles N. Weaver
   1977   "Age and job satisfaction among males and females: a multivariate, multisurvey study." Journal of Applied Psychology 62:189–93.

Glenn, Norval D. and Charles N. Weaver
   1982a   "Enjoyment of work by full-time workers in the U.S., 1955 and 1980." Public Opinion Quarterly 46:459–470.
   1982b   "Further evidence on education and job satisfaction." Social Forces 61:46–55.

Hulin, Charles L. and Patricia Smith
   1965   "A linear model of job satisfaction." Journal of Applied Psychology 49:209–216.

Janson, Philip and Jack K. Martin
   1982   "Job satisfaction and age: a test of two views." Social Forces 60:1089–1102.

Jones, Landon Y.
   1980   Great Expectations: America and the Baby Boom Generation. New York: Coward, McCann, and Geoghegan.

Kalleberg, Arne L. and Karyn A. Loscocco
   1983   "Aging, values, and rewards: explaining age differences in job satisfaction." American Sociological Review 48:78–90.

Liebert, R. M. and N. S. Schwartzberg
   1977   "The psychological effects of mass media exposure." Annual Review of Psychology, 1977. Palo Alto, CA: Annual Reviews.

Quinn, Robert P., Graham L. Staines, and Margaret R. McCullough
   1974   Job Satisfaction: Is There a Trend? Washington, DC: U.S. Department of Labor.

Rodgers, Willard L.
   1982   "Estimable functions of age, period, and cohort effects." American Sociological Review 47:774–787.

Sheppard, Harold L. and Neil Q. Herrick
   1972   Where Have All the Robots Gone: Worker Dissatisfaction in the 70s. New York: Free Press.

Stephenson, C. B.
 1979 "Probability sampling with quotas: an experiment." Public Opinion Quarterly 43 (Winter):477–496.

Vollmer, M. H. and J. A. Kinney
 1955 "Age, education, and job satisfaction." Personnel 32:38–43.

Wright, James D. and Richard F. Hamilton
 1978 "Work satisfaction and age: some evidence for the 'job change' hypothesis." Social Forces 56:1140–1158.

OCCUPATIONAL STRUCTURE AND RETIREMENT

Melissa A. Hardy

ABSTRACT

The research literature on retirement has generally identified OASI and pension benefits as the major "pull" factors and mandatory retirement and health limitations as the major "push" factors determining retirement behavior. Descriptive data analyses of older workers suggested occupational differences in retirement determinants, and retirement studies that incorporated some form of occupational distinction into the analysis indicated some variation in retirement behavior. The research reported in this chapter was undertaken with the aim of developing systematic evidence relevant to this issue.

Using data from the National Longitudinal Surveys of Older Men, I analyzed information from 1973, 1976, and 1978 in order to examine determinants of retirement with respect to the question of variations by occupational category. A retirement model that included health limitations, compulsory retirement, second pension coverage, Duncan's index of socioeconomic status, education, job tenure, wage, and age eligibility variables was estimated by means of a logistic regression procedure within occupational groups. Occupational differences in retirement patterns primarily involved the pension-related variables; however, the similarity in the patterns of effects suggested that, once retirement age differences were controlled, the variables that influenced retirement behavior were fairly consistent across occupational categories.

I. INTRODUCTION

Recent investigations of retirement among older males have cited a variety of factors that influence retirement behavior, including, most commonly, health limitations, second pension coverage, eligibility for Old Age and Survivors Insurance (OASI) benefits or second pension benefits, mandatory retirement policies, and age (either directly or indirectly, since age is the frequently used indicator of eligibility for benefits and for enactment of mandatory retirement rules). In early studies of retirement conducted by the Social Security Administration (SSA), retired persons were generally asked why they had retired; "retired" was often synonymous with filing for OASI benefits (Wentworth, 1945; Stecker, 1951, 1955; Epstein and Murray, 1967; Reno, 1971). These studies emphasized the "push" factors involved in retirement behavior, e.g., poor health and mandatory retirement. More recent studies tend to analyze information on cohorts of older workers, defining retirement relative to labor force participation and/or labor supply. These studies focus on differences in the characteristics of the retired vs. those still working rather than on the relative frequencies of factors cited as the reasons for retirement. Although some of these studies (e.g., Bowen and Finegan, 1969; Boskin, 1977) elevate the importance of "pull" factors, such as retirement income from OASI and other pension plans, while minimizing the impact of poor health, others (Quinn, 1975; 1977; Hardy, 1982a) emphasize the combined effects of both push and pull factors in increasing the likelihood of retirement. When retirement is defined directly in terms of work activity, the argument for the impact of retirement income variables is a straightforward application of microeconomic principles. OASI and private pension plans provide alternative income sources, and depending on the worker's earnings history and whether he or she qualifies for benefits other than OASI, the rate at which retirement income can replace earnings is more or less satisfactory. In general, the existence of plans and the amount of benefits provided by those plans increases with occupational status (Kolodrubetz, 1973). Given that living expenses generally drop after retirement,[1] persons with low earnings may actually improve their financial situation by retiring. To the extent that poor health makes continued employment more difficult, retirement becomes an increasingly attractive alternative.

With few exceptions these previous investigations have been based on samples of older workers without regard to the occupational categories in which the workers were employed. That is, the implicit working assumption has generally been that the influence of variables such as health and retirement policy should be more or less uniform across occupational groups. Such an assumption may, of course, be correct. However, it is also plausible that the pattern of retirement determinants may differ by occupational category. The research reported in this chapter was undertaken with the aim of developing systematic evidence relevant to the issue.

II. PREVIOUS STUDIES AND SPECULATIONS

There are various reasons that would lead one to expect that occupational differences should correlate with differences in retirement behavior. The most obvious reason is that occupations are not uniformly characterized by the key retirement factors cited above. To a large degree, opportunities for retirement income are accumulated throughout the work career. Pension coverage is more common in upper white-collar occupations, and in blue-collar occupations it is generally the more highly paid, highly skilled workers who have this provision (Kolodrubetz, 1970). Some occupations, e.g., professional and technical, have a higher incidence of mandatory retirement policies (Reno, 1976). Pension coverage and mandatory retirement are often dual policies of a particular work place (U.S. Department of Labor, 1965). Provisions of compulsory retirement and pension coverage are most common among professional/managerial and skilled blue-collar workers. Reno (1972) reported that retirees whose former jobs had compulsory retirement policies usually had higher preretirement earnings. Because OASI benefits are based on preretirement earnings, men in these same occupations are more likely to qualify for maximum OASI benefits, thereby providing these workers with generally superior retirement income (Kolodrubetz, 1976b).

To the extent that certain occupations are more physically demanding or more hazardous than others, these occupations may be associated with a higher incidence of health limitations among its workers. Many studies investigating the impact of health on retirement must rely on self-reported measures of health that are based on respondents' assessments of their health relative to the kind or amount of work they can do. It is natural to assume that the evaluative context in which this assessment is made will reflect respondents' current employment. Not only are health limitations more likely to occur in certain occupations, but particular limitations are more disruptive of work activity in certain occupations. For example, an inability to lift heavy objects may have no effect on the performance of a college professor, but a manual laborer would be severely curtailed. Schwab's (1974) analysis of the Retirement History Survey (RHS) showed that the incidence of reported work limitations was higher for manual workers than for nonmanual workers, a finding reproduced in the National Longitudinal Survey data (Parnes, 1974) and in the Social Security Survey of the Disabled (Haber, 1968). Reporting health limitations occured most frequently among laborers and service workers, and least often among professionals (Schwab, 1974).

The occurrence of health limitations has also been linked to other retirement factors. When levels of education and training are controlled, Parnes (1970) reported that men with health limitations have lower hourly and annual earnings (a factor that inhibits savings/investment behavior and results in lower retirement income) and higher unemployment than men without limitations. Other studies (Rubin, 1976; Hardy, 1982b) have also reported that men with health limitations are less likely than those reporting no limitations to be covered by second pensions and consequently must rely on OASI benefits for retirement income.

These reasons for anticipating occupational differences in patterns of retirement determinants are largely documented by descriptive data analyses provided by the SSA. However, there are other arguments that can be brought to bear on the matter. Studies of occupational mobility have produced findings that suggest differences among occupations in characteristics relevant to labor supply. Although retirement has often been defined simply as a nonwork role, it can also be thought of as a category of occupational structure that is conditioned by the previous positions the worker occupied. As noted above, retirement income derives directly from employment history—both the continuity and the kind of employment involved. Workers' health status in later years is, to some extent, a function of previous job activities, the environmental conditions of their employment, and the amount of physical strain required for satisfactory job performance. The kind of activities in which retired workers engage may also be related to the special context in which retirement was viewed by coworkers, the availability of retirement counseling programs, and the existence of social networks that retired workers move into once they exit the labor force. In these ways, retirement is an extension of one's earlier career in terms of relative income (Henretta and Campbell, 1976) and general activities. Given this view of retirement, it seems likely that some of the same characteristics that affect the movement of people in the labor force from one category to another will also influence retirement from the labor force. For example, in analyzing income after retirement, Henretta and Campbell (1976) reported that the factors which determine income in retirement are the same as those that determine income before retirement. Indeed, the "dollar value" of both occupational status and education appears to be even greater in old age.

The fact that the modern social process of allocating individuals throughout social space is predominantly one of education and occupational structure leads one to expect that the process of reallocating people to positions outside the mainstream of activities involved in producing essential goods and services should show residual features of the basic allocation process. One component of this reallocation process is likely to be experience. Studies of differences among working men, e.g., studies of wage differentials and occupational mobility, frequently include "experience" as a correlate of noted inequalities along dimensions of income and prestige. Experience, however, can be translated into different kinds of procedural knowledge, depending on the occupation to which it is applied. A commonly invoked occupational distinction is that of white-collar/blue-collar jobs. Traditionally, the former have been identified more with the use of social management skills and the latter with mechanical skills. The impact of technological advance on mechanical knowledge has generally been an elaboration of equipment such that an increasingly complex machine takes over more of the work task, leaving the worker with a task of smaller proportion, narrower dimension, and increasing specialization. In order to minimize the cost of labor, management's tendency has been to rely on less skilled workers as operators of the new equipment rather than the more highly skilled, more highly paid experienced workers, who thereby tend to be displaced. Under such circumstances, experience with any particular technology is quickly discounted once a new technology becomes available; one would therefore expect manual workers to experience some pressure from employers to vacate positions once they reach retirement age (Slavick and Wolfbein, 1960; Friedman and Orbach, 1974). This is not to say that older workers cannot be retrained, simply that their labor tends to be more expensive.[2]

The situation for white-collar workers may be somewhat different. In time, however, one would expect this historical process to continue in white-collar as it does in blue-collar positions. For example, the situation for clerical workers should be somewhat analogous to that of skilled manual workers or operatives: clerical workers seem to be increasingly under the same technological pressure as manual workers—most noticeably, in recent years, from the computer. More generally, the social management skills of white-collar workers are, in large part, knowledge of the bureaucratic process, and since bureaucratic operations generally involve rational calculation, much of this activity reduces to paperwork. Given the inertia of bureaucracies, skill in managing situations, largely gained through experience, may be less susceptible to the kind of changes that affect manual workers. However, to the extent that preferred styles of management mirror the same underlying structural process driving other kinds of technological changes in the marketplace, certain styles of doing business may be defined as outmoded and in need of "new vitality," a phrase generally synonomous with a preference for younger rather than older workers.

Research on older workers that attends to occupational differences has suggested that the occupational category, and more specifically the kind of job task and the skill level involved in performing that job, may significantly influence the retirement decision. At the most general level, Schwab's (1974) analysis of data for older men (age 58–63 in 1969) indicated that the percentage of older workers who continued to work differed by occupational category: labor force participation rates were highest for professions, managers, salespersons, and farmers, and lowest among laborers. From a 1969–1970 national survey of employed Americans, Sheppard (1976) reported that the desire to continue working even if one had enough money to live comfortably was stronger among white-collar than blue-collar workers; only half of the blue-collar workers but three-quarters of the white-collar workers replied that they would continue working under such conditions. Several studies have shown that once occupational differences are taken into account, education has little relationship to labor force participation (Sheppard, 1976).

There is some evidence that the impact of health on retirement is not uniform across occupational groups. Analysis of the RHS indicated not only that manual workers has a higher rate of work limitations, but also that manual workers with limitations were much more likely than nonmanual workers to be out of the labor force at an early age (Schwab, 1974). This suggested interaction between health limitation and occupation may be evidenced in a finding from Rubin's (1976) study of newly entitled workers, although a compositional explanation of the result cannot be ruled out: men with no limitations who worked beyond age 65 were more likely to be technical, professional, or managerial workers and unlikely to be laborers; however, men with health limitations retiring at age 62 were most likely to be semiskilled or unskilled workers and least likely to be upper white collar or crafts. Craftsmen and operatives experiencing limitations were presumed to be less likely to continue working because their occupations were less adaptable in terms of physical demands.

In analyzing white male blue-collar workers only, Sheppard (1972) included a measure of perceived autonomy/responsibility/variety of the job and found that the lower the quality of task level, the greater the percentage in each age group reporting that they would retire immediately if assured adequate income. Quinn (1975) also reported that low job autonomy increased the likelihood of retirement. In a study of male British factory workers age 55–64, Jacobson (1972) found that the more physically demanding the job the lower the "ideal" retirement age and the poorer the reported health status; he also reported that men in more rigidly defined work patterns, i.e., mechanized line operators, were more likely to be willing to retire at the company's retirement age than men whose work role was less mechanized and characterized by more automony.

Several other studies have concentrated on specific groups of workers. Barfield and Morgan (1970) analyzed the retirement plans of a sample of United Automobile Workers and reported that expected pension income was the principal factor in the retirement decision and that poor health correlated with plans for early retirement. Using 1970–1971 data from the UAW, Sheppard found that lower skilled auto workers retired prior to reaching age 65 at a rate much higher than that obtained from the highest skilled workers.

Finally, Rogers and Friedman's (1980) study of printers allows a more detailed look at how the older members of one particular group of workers responded to a major technological change in the workplace. These workers faced no mandatory retirement age and had been guaranteed job security; as an alternative to retraining workers, management offered those who would take immediate retirement a cash bonus of $2,500 plus six months "sabbatical" salary (to be taken at the same time), amounting to approximately an $11,000 total. Most who took the bonus were over age 65; they included among their reasons for retirement failing health, preference for leisure, and financial situation.

III. PURPOSE OF THE STUDY

The major purpose of this investigation is to examine determinants of retirement with respect to the question of variations by occupational category. Occupational differences can be studied either by using nominal occupational categories as an organizing framework or by including detailed characteristics that relate to the specific features of occupations that one suspects will produce differences in retirement behavior. The latter strategy requires a very detailed data base, but it allows one to specify the particular occupational characteristics that affect the retirement responses of older workers. The former strategy allows the occupational title to serve as a surrogate for a whole range of characteristics and provides an appropriate first step in the investigation of the role of occupational structure in molding retirement patterns. In modern industrial societies, occupational structure serves as an important foundation for the main dimensions of social stratification. Hierarchies of prestige strata as well as hierarchies of economic classes are based in the occupational structure. As sources of income, occupations are tied to class; as sources of prestige, occupations are tied to status; and as sources of authority, occupations are tied to power. The concept of occupational structure is generally used to represent an aggregation of jobs in which similar tasks are performed, but it also refers to an inequality of rewards and requirements. Occupations imply differences in technical requirements (i.e., differences in necessary training and, more generally, in the kinds of human resources that are related to job performance) and in the rewards gained by incumbents.

Alba Edwards's (1933) classification of occupations delineates six major categories: professionals; proprietors, managers, and officials (including farmers); clerks and kindred; skilled workers and foremen; semiskilled; and unskilled (including farm laborers, nonfarm laborers, and "servant" classes). This basic classification was meant to be representative of similar life-styles and similar social and economic characteristics. The Bureau of the Census classification modifies the Edwards scheme by treating farmers and salespersons as separate categories and by elaborating the blue-collar workers. The twelve categories are professional, technical, and kindred; managers, officials, and proprietors; clerical and kindred; sales workers; craftsmen, foremen, and kindred; operatives and kindred; private household; service workers, except private household; farmers and farm managers; farm laborers and foremen; laborers, except farm and mine; armed forces. Clearly, these categories represent real categories in the social world. People call themselves, are called by others, and are hired by employers according to an occupational category. For all these reasons it is sensible to undertake this initial investigation on the basis of the nominal occupational categories. Thus, in this study the strategy is to define the factors that discriminate retired from nonretired workers within any given occupational group and then to compare these patterns of effects across occupational groups.

IV. METHOD OF STUDY

A. Sample and Data

For purposes of this analysis I have restricted the population to white males who are or were employed in wage and salary positions. The decision to exclude self-employed workers seemed appropriate for several reasons. Because self-employed workers may not be subject to the same process of wage determination as wage and salary workers, one can argue that the income earned by the self-employed is not comparable to the earnings of wage and salary workers. Also, several studies (e.g., Quinn, 1980; Hardy, 1982a; Fuchs, 1982) have reported that self-employed workers tend to retire later than wage and salary workers, the most common explanation being that self-employed workers usually have more flexibility in setting work schedules and work tasks than do wage and salary workers. Self-employed workers generally do not qualify for second pensions and must rely instead on their own accumulated financial resources. Non-eligibility for private pensions represents a different kind of constraint for wage and salary workers than it does for self-employed workers. Retirement behavior as enacted by self-employed workers seems subject to a set of options and constraints structurally different from those that apply to wage and salary workers. Consequently, I opted for increasing the homogeneity of the analysis sample by focusing initially on wage and salary workers only. The decision to restrict the sample to whites resulted from similar reasoning, i.e., from a desire to limit the major dimension of structural variation to occupational categories and not to introduce race as a confounding influence.

Data are from the National Longitudinal Surveys of Older Men. These men were aged 45–59 at the time of the initial survey in 1966. I analyze information from 1973, 1976, and 1978. The 1973 wave is the first wave in which a sufficiently large number of men are retired, thereby making it possible to estimate retirement models within occupational categories.

In order to look at the structure of retirement influences as they operate within particular occupational categories, workers must be organized into subgroups that reflect the occupation of current or last employment; such occupational grouping provides a context in which retirement decisions are made. To this end, a slightly modified version of the census classification is used:[3] four white-collar categories (professional, technical, and kindred; managers and administrators;

clerical workers; salespersons) and four blue-collar categories (craftspersons; operatives; service workers[4]; laborers[5]).

B. Variables

1. Retirement

Defining "retirement" requires a framework that makes the interpretation of results as unambiguous as possible. In this paper, retirement is measured by means of a discrete state framework. In defining the retired category, information on labor force status at the time of the interview and on the amount of labor supply provided during the prior 12-month period is used. It is advisable to classify respondents in terms of current labor force status because information relating to current occupation, current health status, retirement policies, and the like refer to the respondent's situation at the time of the interview. If the respondent was retired at the time of the interview (in this data set, being coded as retired required that the respondent was not currently working or looking for work) or if he had worked zero hours during the previous year and was classified as being out of the labor force at the time of the interview, he was considered "retired." The remaining men were classified as "not retired." By defining the retirement category on the basis of labor force status at the time of the interview, we can eliminate the differences in past year's labor supply that result from labor force withdrawal at some point during the previous year. In other words, full-year part-time workers and workers who retired completely some time during the previous year will be in different categories; the latter will be "retired" whereas the former will be "part-time employed" and in the labor force at the time of the interview. Although there is still considerable variation in work schedules of men in the labor force, clarity has been added to the retired category.

2. Health

Respondents were asked to report whether the kind or amount of work they could do was limited by considerations of health. As has been indicated in other studies and in other data sets, the blue-collar members of this sample more often reported work-restricting conditions of health than did the white-collar members of the sample. There is also a tendency for upper white-collar workers to report fewer limitations than lower white-collar workers and for upper blue-collar workers to report fewer limitations than lower blue-collar workers. But in general, the incidence of work-limiting health conditions increases as one moves from upper white-collar to lower blue-collar jobs. Because health limitations are more of a problem for blue-collar workers, health may play a more important role in their retirement decisions. To the extent that certain categories of blue-collar workers are more likely to qualify for second pensions, the effect of health might be especially pronounced for men in occupations with higher levels of second pension coverage.

3. Retirement Policies

Compulsory retirement, coverage by a second pension (i.e., other than OASI) and eligibility for Social Security benefits are the policies included in this study. Since eligibility for Social Security has become nearly universal, its main relevance involves the worker's age relative to eligibility ages for benefit claims. This factor is handled by age variables that signify reduced-benefit eligibility (ages 62–64) and full-benefit eligibility (65 and older).

Since the beneift eligibility variables are defined by contiguous age categories, including these two categories leaves those younger than 62 as the reference groups. It should be noted that membership in either the oldest or the youngest group is only partly consistent from one wave to the next. That is respondents aged 45–49 in 1966 are always in the youngest group (i.e., in 1978 they are 57–61 years old) and respondents aged 58–59 in 1966 are always in the oldest age group (by 1973 they are already 65 or older). However, as we move from 1973 to 1976 to 1978, the composition of the youngest category changes: the age range becomes narrower, as younger workers age from 52 to 61 years old in 1973 to 57 to 61 years old in 1978. In contrast, the age range of the oldest age group becomes wider, expanding from those who are 65–66 in 1973 to those who are 65–71 in 1978. The actual composition of the middle-age group–those aged 62–64—is largely different from one wave to the next; the ages of respondents at the time of the initial wave (i.e., 1966) for this category as it is defined in the 1973, 1976, and 1978 waves are 55–57, 52–54, and 50–52, respectively. The actual comparison being made in the different waves therefore involves a reference group that is not constant across time. However, given that the lack of constancy is due to aging, one might anticipate that the differences between this age group and the 62–64 age group would be less pronounced in later waves because the younger ages are no longer included in the comparison. It is also important to realize that, although the main relevance of these age categories is assumed to be benefit eligibility, the older category in particular includes elements of mandatory retirement (since age 65 is the most common mandatory retirement age) and social definitions of "appropriate" retirement ages, although the latter may be considered largely derivative of the age structure set up for OASI benefits.

Retirement policies also serve as a basis for planning work behavior prior to the criterion age. Whether or not one argues that pensions influence labor supply decisions *throughout* one's career (Burkhauser, 1977), the anticipatory effects of retirement policies may depress labor supply prior to key criterion ages. Because pension policies and compulsory retirement policies are not independent policies from the standpoint of the firm, these variables are defined as cells in a two-by-two matrix, with compulsory retirement on one axis and pension coverage on the other. (The absence of pension coverage defines the reference category.[6])

This sample again yields information consistent with that supplied by the SSA. White-collar workers are more likely to face compulsory retirement and more likely to be covered by second pensions. Within the white-collar category, upper white-collar men are more often covered by these policies than are lower white-collar men. Among blue-collar workers, craftsmen and operatives are more likely to be covered by second pensions, but compulsory retirement appears to be equally likely across blue-collar occupations. Since these policy variables are included in estimations as policy combinations, we can also look at the distribution of the joint policies of compulsory retirement with pension coverage (CRAPE) and pension coverage without compulsory retirement (PENCR). White-collar workers are more likely to be subject to both mandatory retirement and pension policies, with professional, technical, and kindred workers having the largest proportion of workers in this joint category. Clerical workers and laborers have the lowest percentage of workers in this joint category. Craftspersons and operatives are more likely to be both eligible for second pensions and not subject to compulsory retirement.

4. Wage

Hourly wage rate is relevant to the cost of terminating employment and to financial resilience. Studies of labor supply among middle-aged males have shown that wage rate generally has a negative effect on labor supply. This may not hold for older workers, however, because older workers may make labor supply decisions with reference to a time frame that extends into their retirement years and that includes calculations of expected retirement income from OASI and private pensions. Other studies of retirement (e.g., Quinn, 1977) have reported that wage rate is not a key determinant of retirement behavior.

Since wage rates are not reported for workers who have withdrawn from the labor force, it is necessary to calculate for these individuals wage rates that are representative of the wages they could be earning had they remained in positions comparable to the ones they left. For these individuals, hourly wage rates will be imputed on the basis of multivariate estimations of log hourly wages for those respondents reporting wage information.[7]

5. Job and Worker Characteristics

Three variables tapping paricular characteristics of workers or their jobs are included in the analyses as controls for the different positions workers occupy in the occupational and labor market structures: (1) Duncan's socioeconomic index (SEI), which serves to control the effects of variable status within any given occupational category; (2) job tenure, which affects retirement options insofar as it is involved in eligibility requirements for private pension benefits, and it is also a measure of accumulated experience with a given employer; (3) years of education, which, though related to SEI, indexes the additional dimension of generalizable skills and knowledge that may increase the ability of workers who have retired from career jobs to relocate in other jobs.

C. Estimation Procedure

The main analysis involves estimating a series of binary choice models within occupational groups and then comparing estimations across occupational groups for each wave. Since the dependent variable is dichotomous, the chosen functional form for the model is the cumulative logistic probability function, defining P_i as the probability that a given individual is retired, and $(1 - P_i)$ as the probability that an individual is in the labor force; estimated values for the dependent variable will therefore represent conditional probabilities. This model can be written as

$$P_i = \frac{1}{1 + e^{-(\alpha + \beta X_i)}}. \tag{1}$$

However, actual estimation is based on

$$\log \frac{P_i}{1 - P_i} = \alpha + \beta X, \tag{2}$$

where the dependent variable is the log odds in favor of retirement (Pindyck and Rubinfeld, 1976; Hanushek and Jackson, 1977).[8] Since logistic coefficients are not interpretable in an intuitively appealing manner, coefficients of major interest have been transformed into proportional effects. In this case, proportional effects estimate the predicted change in the proportion of cases retired (as opposed to nonretired) for a unit change in an independent variable. For those variables of interest that are dummy-coded, this proportional effect estimates a category contrast.[9] Due to the nonlinearity of the estimation technique, the proportional effect will be a function of the probability itself; therefore, effects will be evaluated at the mean of the dependent variable, recognizing that the mean of this dichotomous variable relates the proportion of cases falling into the retired category. Allowing for the approximation that for any y, $\Delta \log y \approx \Delta y/y$, the proportional effect can be calculated as

$$\Delta P_i \approx B_k [P_i (1 - P_i)], \tag{3}$$

where B_k is the logistic coefficient, P_i is the proportion retired, and $1 - P_i$ its complement (Pindyck and Rubinfeld, 1976).

The logistic coefficients for the binary choice models are presented in appendix tables. The set of independent variables used in the estimations includes health limitations (coded "1" if the respondent reported that his health limited the kind or amount of work he could do); Duncan's index of socioeconomic status; job tenure (number of years with the same employer); years of education; compulsory retirement with second pension coverage (CRAPE), and second pension coverage without compulsory retirement (PENCR), the reference category for both CRAPE and PENCR consisting of those not covered by a second pension; ages 62–64, an index of eligibility for reduced Social Security benefits; ages 65 and older, indicating eligibility for full Social Security benefits; and log hourly wage.

Based on theoretical considerations as well as empirical results from other studies, the direction of the effect can be predicted for most of these variables. Health limitations, CRAPE, and the benefit eligibility variables are expected to have positive effects on the likelihood of retirement because they constitute the major push and pull factors that have been identified to date. Job tenure and wage are expected to have positive effects on retirement because they represent major considerations in the determination of pension benefits, i.e., the amount of retirement benefits for which workers qualify (assuming they are eligible for such plans) is a positive function of earnings and service. Duncan's SEI and years of education should have negative effects on retirement because more highly educated workers and workers in higher status jobs tend to retire later; and, although many face mandatory retirement, the specified age is not infrequently older than 65. The only variable effect for which an argument of direction is more ambiguous is PENCR: on the one hand, pensions are an inducement to retirement, therefore the effect should be positive; on the other hand, in the absence of compulsory retirement there may be some tendency toward delayed activation of pension, therefore the effect could be negative.

Because the hypotheses for all variables but PENCR specify direction, one-tailed tests of significance will be used in the following sections. It will be apparent from information supplied in the tables whether any given coefficient estimate also meets the criterion for a two-tailed test.

At this point, it may be useful to make some cautionary statements about comparisons across waves. There is considerable overlap in sample members from one wave to the next, and those workers who are retired in one wave are most likely retired in subsequent waves. One can imagine the retirement process as captured in this analysis as a flow of individuals from a state of wage and salary employment to a state of retirement (or into self-employment), with a slight countercurrent that moves individuals from retirement back into a state of some work activity in a wage and salary position. At each wave we take a snapshot of the distribution of workers between these two states. During the interim between waves, respondents are lost because of death, because of noninterviews for reasons other than death, and, to a much smaller degree, because of mobility into a self-employed position. When compared with an earlier wave, findings from any later wave may differ because of the characteristics of those workers who join the ranks of the retired, or because of the changes in the characteristics of those consistently retired, e.g., appearance of a health limitation, or because of some shift in the retirement process itself or some combination of the above. The appearance of a "difference" between or across waves is further complicated by an indeterminancy in the structure of errors and their correlation across waves. Given this design, it is not possible to discriminate unambiguously among alternative explanations for what may appear to be differences from one wave to another; therefore, the discussion of results will concentrate on how different occupational categories compare in their patterns of retirement determinants and, to a much smaller degree, on the consistency of this relative standing across waves.

V. RESULTS OF ANALYSIS

A. Baseline Estimations

In order to provide a baseline for comparison, a single retirement equation was estimated in each of the three waves without regard to occupational differences. Results of these estimations, shown in Table 1, are consistent with most of the empirical literature. Reporting health limitations, being subject to mandatory retirement in conjunction with a second pension, and being eligible for either reduced or full OASI benefits increased the likelihood of retirement. Although these four variables register the strongest, most consistent effects across all three waves, job tenure also had a consistently small positive effect; and in the later two waves (where the proportion of retired workers was higher) socioeconomic status significantly influenced the probability of being retired: the higher the SEI of one's job, the lower the probability of retirement; but the longer the tenure with a given employer, the higher the likelihood of retirement.

Of the remaining variables, coefficients for education were uniformly negative, but only the 1973 coefficient achieved significance; wage had a positive and significant effect in 1976; and PENCR achieved significance in none of the estimations, although its sign was uniformly positive. In general, then, these three variables appear to have little or no explanatory power.

Two summary statistics are presented in Table 1. As a goodness-of-fit measure the "likelihood ratio statistic" is defined as twice the difference between the log likelihood at convergence and the log likelihood at zero. It provides a test of the hypothesis that all parameters are zero. Under the null hypothesis, it is χ^2-distributed with degrees of freedom equal to the number of estimated parameters. The critical χ^2 value for the specified model is 29.6 at the .001 level of confidence. Clearly, for all waves we can reject the null that all parameters are zero.

Table 1. Logit Coefficient Estimates
for Wage and Salary Workers
(all occupational groups combined)[a]

	1973	1976	1978
LIMIT	1.244	.828	1.264
	(.179)	(.137)	(.141)
	6.940	6.025	8.978
DUNCAN	.002	−.009	−.010
	(.005)	(.003)	(.004)
	.416	−2.685	−2.597
ED	−.074	−.035	−.027
	(.032)	(.023)	(.025)
	−2.329	−1.482	−1.090
TENURE	.013	.010	.010
	(.007)	(.005)	(.006)
	1.713	1.820	1.869
CRAPE	1.560	.628	1.302
	(.238)	(.163)	(.182)
	6.560	3.843	7.135
PENCR	.396	.010	.090
	(.259)	(.175)	(.177)
	1.531	.057	.507
LNWAGE	−.245	.398	.128
	(.187)	(.115)	(.126)
	−1.313	3.469	1.016
62–64	2.295	1.728	1.676
	(.199)	(.154)	(.176)
	11.520	11.190	9.534
65+	3.853	2.743	2.731
	(.245)	(1.59)	(.172)
	15.760	17.270	15.870
CONSTANT	−3.415	−2.580	−2.501
	(.383)	(.273)	(.318)
	−8.917	−9.436	−7.872
Likelihood rato statistic	1378	676	563
Percent correctly predicted	88	78	75
Sample N's	1687	1631	1389

[a] The values shown are coefficient estimate, standard error, and t statistic.

The second auxiliary statistic is "percent correctly predicted." A case is defined as "correctly predicted" when the alternative that was chosen is forecast to have the highest probability of being chosen. Considering that in the absence of any information we could successfully predict whether the sample members were retired or not at a rate of 50 percent, the success achieved by this model is quite respectable. It reduces our errors of prediction by half or more.[10]

B. Blue-Collar vs. White-Collar Comparisons

The remaining analyses will include all variables used in the foregoing estimations, although several of these variables (education, wage, PENCR, and Duncan's SEI) will be treated primarily as controls. Because the major factors identified in the baseline model are health limitations, CRAPE, and the two age eligibility variables, presentation of findings in this and in the subsequent section will attend mainly to these four variables.

Before disaggregating workers according to the eightfold occupational scheme, an intermediate analysis was undertaken on the basis of a simple white-collar/blue-collar dichotomy. The effects of the retirement factors were estimated within each of the two categories. Table 2 reports the logit coefficient estimates for white- and blue-collar workers for the three waves.

Consistent with results from the baseline model, four variables—health limitations, CRAPE, and the age eligibility variables—registered the strongest and most consistent effects. Health limitations, reduced-benefit eligibility, and full-benefit eligibility had large, positive, uniformly significant effects among both white-collar and blue-collar workers. In two of the three waves, health limitations had a slightly larger effect for blue-collar than white-collar workers, although the differences are statistically significant at the .05 level in the 1973 wave only.[11] CRAPE had a large positive net effect in all estimations but one (blue-collar, 1976), but with that one exception the effect of CRAPE did not vary between occupational categories. The second pension policy variable, PENCR, was significant in none of the estimations, suggesting that second pension coverage in the absence of compulsory retirement neither increased nor decreased the likelihood of retirement. The general failure of PENCR to contribute to the prediction of retirement implies that it was not the pension alone but compulsory retirement, and the interaction of compulsory retirement and second pension coverage, that encouraged retirement. With respect to this question of interaction it should be noted that when compulsory retirement is present, second pension coverage is almost always also present; moreover, second pension benefits tend to be higher when the coverage is joined with a policy of compulsory retirement than when it is not.

In estimations of the baseline model, both Duncan's SEI and job tenure had significant and oppositely signed effects on the likelihood of being retired. In 1973 and again in 1978, job tenure registered a small positive net effect on

Table 2. Logit Coefficient Estimates for White- and Blue-Collar Wage and Salary Workers[a]

	1973 White	1973 Blue	1976 White	1976 Blue	1978 White	1978 Blue
LIMIT	.812 (.307) 2.642	1.450 (.230) 6.310	1.172 (.236) 4.971	.677 (.174) 3.904	1.009 (.237) 4.265	1.401 (.180) 7.796
DUNCAN	.002 (.010) .194	.008 (.009) .911	−.018 (.007) −2.468	.004 (.006) .613	−.017 (.008) −2.062	.001 (.007) .116
ED	−.087 (.049) −1.781	−.052 (.043) −1.191	−.087 (.039) −2.267	.005 (.031) .152	−.017 (.039) −.442	−.017 (.033) −.531
TENURE	.007 (.012) .612	.018 (.010) 1.786	.006 (.008) .731	.011 (.007) 1.571	−.002 (.010) −.237	.018 (.007) 2.431
CRAPE	1.852 (.409) 4.531	1.296 (.304) 4.265	1.035 (.279) 3.704	.345 (.209) 1.645	1.358 (.300) 4.522	1.253 (.236) 5.302
PENCR	.130 (.471) .277	.454 (.323) 1.404	−.153 (.314) −.486	.034 (.218) .115	−.507 (.307) −1.654	.368 (.225) 1.634
LNWAGE	−.364 (.273) −1.332	−.137 (.274) −.499	.661 (.183) 3.607	.245 (.154) 1.586	.280 (.188) 1.486	−.044 (.187) −.236
62–64	2.111 (.330) 6.393	2.409 (.255) 9.452	1.695 (.270) 6.284	1.805 (.192) 9.406	1.565 (.300) 5.210	1.798 (.223) 8.070
65+	3.630 (.399) 9.091	4.140 (.327) 12.650	2.669 (.274) 9.746	2.919 (.204) 14.310	2.909 (.290) 10.020	2.730 (.224) 12.190
CONSTANT	−2.894 (.763) −3.791	−4.014 (.528) −7.608	−2.148 (.575) −3.736	−2.887 (.363) −7.952	−2.130 (.622) −3.423	−2.814 (.446) −6.309
Likelihood ratio statistic	550	839	302	99	399	335
Percent correctly predicted	89	88	80	78	76	75
Sample N's	669	1018	633	998	547	842

[a] See note to Table 1.

retirement for blue-collar but never for white-collar workers; in 1976 and in 1978, Duncan's SEI had a weak negative net effect on retirement for white-collar but never for blue-collar workers. Although the metrics of these two variables are scaled in small units (by comparison to the dummy coding of health, for example), the effects are still quite small.

Years of education had a small negative effect in 1973 and 1976, and log hourly wage registered a positive effect only once, among white-collar workers in 1976. In general, then, these two variables, along with PENCR, offered virtually no net contribution to the explanation of retirement in these estimations.

For reasons previously noted, it is risky to make too much of cross-wave comparisons. However, it is apparent from Table 1 that the results reported for 1976 are somewhat peculiar: coefficients for CRAPE, education, and log hourly wage obtain in the white-collar estimation but not in the blue. In addition, for blue-collar workers the effects of health limitations and CRAPE are noticeably lower in 1976 than in either 1973 or 1978. Perhaps in these respects the 1976 results are partly mirroring consequences of the 1974–1975 recession, which may well have had different impacts on blue-collar and white-collar workers relative to the question of retirement. The analysis design of this study does not allow us to test this hypothesis, however, so our speculation must be left at that.

To summarize, although there were some slight variations in the effects of retirement determinants across white- and blue-collar categories, the overall pattern seems to have been one of little or no difference. As in Table 1, the variables of major importance were the two age eligibility variables, CRAPE, and health limitations, with the 65-and-older category registering the strongest effects for both white- and blue-collar workers. There is some indication, however, that the relative importance of health was higher for blue-collar workers; and job tenure had a weak positive effect on retirement among blue-collar workers but none among white-collar workers. These differences are nevertheless small in magnitude and do not substantially modify the overall conclusion.

C. Comparisons Among Eight Occupational Categories

The distinction between white- and blue-collar occupations is admittedly crude. It masks considerable variation among occupations in terms of the kinds of activities involved in job performance, the presence of retirement inducements, the significance of work-limiting health problems, and other factors that may be relevant to the retirement decision. It seems plausible to expect, for example, that retirement among unskilled workers should be especially sensitive to health limitations because the occupation of laborer generally requires more physical stamina than other manual occupations. Also, because of the lower rates of second pension coverage and the lower wage scale—two factors that predict relatively low levels of retirement income—eligibility for reduced OASI benefits and mandatory retirement/pension coverage policies should be less of an incentive for the unskilled. In contrast, skilled workers should be more susceptible to retirement benefit inducements because they are more likely to have second pension coverage and high primary insurance amounts under the Social Security program (Kolodrubetz, 1976a:159). Therefore, we would expect the effects of the eligibility variables and the retirement policy variables (especially CRAPE because it also indicates higher pension benefits) to be particularly important for craftspersons. In addition, within the crafts category the effect of the 62–64 age eligibility variable may also reflect the impact of special early-retirement features of those private pension plans (e.g., the UAW plan) that provide high benefits for workers who retire earlier than the minimum age for OASI eligibility (Barfield and Morgan, 1970).

Similar arguments would lead one to expect different patterns in retirement determinants across the several white-collar occupational categories. For example, professionals have the highest incidence of second pension coverage, and the benefit levels associated with these plans are much higher than those available to other occupational groups (Kolodrubetz, 1976b). Thus, we would expect CRAPE to be an especially significant factor in predicting retirement for this occupational group. Professionals are also more likely than other categories of workers to face a mandatory retirement age of 70, and research has indicated that professional workers tend to retire relatively late; therefore, the coefficients for the two eligibility variables should reflect this tendency toward delayed retirement. Given that coefficients for both the age eligibility variables are relative to the youngest age group, the difference between the two coefficients indicates whether being within the 62–64 age range increases the likelihood of retirement at a level comparable to the effect of being within the 65 or older age range, or, as would be relevant to the argument here, whether the impact of the 65-plus age range is significantly stronger.

With such considerations in mind, then, the basic equation was reestimated within each of the eight occupational categories previously described. Complete results of the logistic regressions are reported in the Appendix. The following discussion will refer primarily to the subset of results presented in Table 3. This table reports the logistic coefficients for four variables—health limitation, CRAPE, and the age eligibility variables—and, for each variable, its proportional effect as calculated at the category mean. The proportional effect metric provides a useful basis for comparison within occupational groups. However, because the size of the proportional effect is contingent on where it is evaluated (in this case, at the category mean), and because the proportion retired differs by category (and, therefore, so do category means), differences in proportional effects reflect both the size of the coefficient and the frequency of retirement for a particular category.[12]

Estimations are complete for all occupational groups in the 1976 and 1978

Table 3. Logit Coefficient Estimates and Proportional Effects of Key Variables, by Occupational Category[a]

	White	Prof	Man	Cler	Sales	Blue	Crafts	Op	Service	Labor
1973										
LIMIT	.812**	—	1.143**	.426	—	1.450**	1.401**	2.117**	1.814**	1.113
	.095		.137	NS		.201	.190	.250	.333	NS
CRAPE	1.852**	—	1.948**	.869	—	1.296**	1.755**	1.698**	1.022	.368
	.216		.234	NS		.179	.238	.201	NS	NS
62–64	2.111**	—	1.615**	2.041**	—	2.409**	2.270**	2.405**	2.344**	3.544**
	.246		.194	.298		.334	.308	.285	.430	.531
65+	3.630**	—	3.682**	3.394**	—	4.140**	4.157**	4.419**	5.971**	3.380**
	.423		.442	.495		.533	.563	.523	1.095	.506
1976										
LIMIT	1.172**	1.331**	.337	1.919**	2.366**	.677**	.900**	.376	.415	1.104**
	.239	.249	NS	.453	.434	.155	.208	NS	NS	.258
CRAPE	1.035**	3.797**	1.131**	−.119	.692	.345	.792**	.066	−.309	.218
	.211	.685	.233	NS	NS	NS	.183	NS	NS	NS

62–64	1.695**	1.605**	1.826**	1.288**	2.762**	1.805**	1.666**	2.467**	1.847**	1.208**
	.346	.289	.377	.304	.507	.418	.384	.540	.435	.282
65+	2.669**	3.385**	2.626**	2.502**	3.771**	2.919**	3.461**	2.900**	2.635**	2.379**
	.545	.610	.541	.591	.692	.668	.798	.635	.620	.556
1978										
LIMIT	1.009**	1.210**	1.259**	−.025	2.021*	1.401**	1.546**	1.173**	1.310**	2.059**
	.237	.287	.280	NS	.397	.349	.385	.293	.324	.514
CRAPE	1.358**	2.935**	1.302**	−.406	2.765**	1.253**	1.268**	.956*	2.097**	1.364**
	.319	.697	.289	NS	.543	.312	.316	.239	.518	.341
62–64	1.565**	1.439**	1.175**	2.702**	3.713**	1.798**	2.010**	1.701**	2.871**	1.086
	.367	.342	.261	.670	.730	.448	.501	.424	.710	NS
65+	2.909**	4.869**	2.425**	3.001**	2.078**	2.730**	2.942**	3.442**	2.745**	1.694**
	.683	1.156	.539	.744	.585	.680	.733	.859	.679	.423

[a]The logit coefficient estimates for the full equations are reported in the Appendix. Proportional effects are given below the logistic regression coefficients.
**Significant at the .05 level or better in a two-tailed test or a one-tailed test.
*Significant at the .05 level or better in a one-tailed test only.

waves; in 1973, however, it was not possible to estimate retirement models for two of the eight groups (professional, technical, and kindred; sales) because the frequency of retirement was too low. Also, the 1973 estimates for clerical workers and laborers are based on small ratios of retirees to nonretirees.

Given the results reported in Table 3 (as well as in the Appendix), we can make several observations. The effect of health limitations tended to be slightly higher among lower white-collar than upper white-collar workers, but the differences are not statistically significant. There is some indication of the same tendency among blue-collar workers, although in this case it is more a difference between laborers and other blue-collar categories.

Concerning the retirement policy variables, we find nothing in these more detailed results that disputes the earlier finding that mandatory retirement is an important determinant of retirement. Pension coverage by itself shows no consistent results. The effect of CRAPE was somewhat stronger for professionals (in 1976, in particular) than for other white-collar occupations, and it was consistently nonsignificant for clerical workers. Among the blue-collar occupations, the effect of CRAPE was most consistent for craftsmen. The effects of the combined policies of mandatory retirement and second pension coverage are therefore strongest and most consistent for the occupational categories in which pension benefits are typically most lucrative: managers and officials and the professional and technical workers enjoy much higher pension payments than other occupational groups (Kolodrubetz, 1976b).

As for the age eligibility variables, the effect of reduced-benefit eligibility tended to be somewhat greater for lower than for upper white-collar occupations; among the blue-collar categories, its effect was consistently significant for craftsmen, operatives, service, and in two of the three waves it was significant for laborers. Full-benefit eligibility had a consistently strong positive effect in all occupational categories. The one notable variation pertains to the professional category, for whom in 1978 the magnitude of effect of full-benefit eligibility was especially large. Also, the difference between the coefficients for reduced- and full-benefit eligibility was largest for professionals: in 1976 and 1978 coefficients for ages 65 and older were two to three times as large as the coefficients for reduced-benefit eligibility. Previously it was suggested that the data should reflect a tendency of professionals to retire later. Given the difference between the coefficients for the two age eligibility variables, a difference that is particularly large in 1978, it is apparently the case that the differential in the propensity to be retired relative to the benefit eligibility ages is larger for professionals than for other occupational categories.

In these estimations, unlike those reported in Tables 1 and 2, Duncan's SEI no longer discriminated between the retired and nonretired; so it seems that its previous success was largely due to differences in gross occupational categories.

However, the previously noted effect of job tenure does persist in one occupational category. Recall that in the baseline estimations job tenure had a small positive effect; and in the white-collar/blue-collar comparison, we noted that the influence of job tenure was confined to the blue-collar category. As an inspection of the Appendix shows, job tenure had a small positive effect for operatives in both 1976 and 1978 and for service workers in 1978. One explanation for the relevance of job tenure to retirement among semiskilled workers concerns pension benefits. The amount of benefits to which a worker is entitled is a function of earnings and length of employment in the pension job or with the same employer. Lower wage earners with long tenure can have a greater wage replacement ratio than high-wage earners (Kolodrubetz, 1976b:179); therefore, for workers in these occupations, job tenure may be a key indicator of expected pension benefits, whereas for other categories of workers earnings may be the better indicator; hence the absence of job tenure effects on retirement.

As before, results for log hourly wage and education are generally nonsignificant. However, in keeping with the preceding argument concerning the effect of job tenure, the reader may note that the wage coefficient was significant for salesmen in 1976 and 1978, for professionals in 1978 (though it approached significance in 1976), and for clerical workers in 1976.

The summary statistics reported at the bottom of each panel of the Appendix show only small variations by occupation in the overall power or fit of the retirement equation. In 1973 the percentage correctly predicted is quite high (ranging from 86 to 92 percent), with only marginal differences among the six categories for which the equation was estimated. The percentage values are somewhat more variable in the later waves—in both instances they range from 74 to 87 percent—but the only consistent patterns of occupational difference involve the professionals and salesmen, for whom the equation had slightly stronger "predictive power," and the laborers, for whom it had the lowest rate of correct predictions.

VI. DISCUSSION

This chapter began with a variety of arguments offered in support of the plausibility of occupational differences in retirement behavior. Having completed a detailed analysis of retirement within an eightfold scheme of occupational categories, we are struck by the consistency of findings. Although there were some occupational differences in the magnitude of effects of certain retirement determinants and some variation in the model's success in predicting retirement, these differences were overshadowed by the general consistency of effects registered by health limitations, CRAPE, and the age eligibility variables.

The largest occupational differences in retirement determinants were generally found in the age eligibility variables. Such differences can also be seen in the occupation-specific rates of retirement. Table 4 reports the proportion retired in 1976 and 1978 for each of the eight occupational categories, and for the white-collar/blue-collar aggregations, within three age categories—61 and younger, 62–64, and 65 and older. These figures indicate, first, that blue-collar workers were in general more likely than white-collar workers to be retired, and that this difference occurred primarily within the 62–64 and 65-and-older age groups. Second, although overall rates of retirement among the four blue-collar categories were similar, among the white-collar categories the clerical workers were distinguished by a relatively high rate of retirement. Indeed, the proportion retired among clerical workers was closer to the average for blue-collar than to the average for white-collar workers. Of course, comparisons of the overall rate of retirement may be confounded by age compositional variations among the occupational categories; but, in fact, the age compositions were highly uniform across all occupational categories (except the service workers, who were slightly older). And if we compare retirement rates within the age categories shown in Table 4, we continue to find evidence of a similarity in retirement behavior between clerical workers and blue-collar workers (although there is in general more variation among both the blue-collar and the white-collar categories when we control for age). Clerical workers had relatively high rates of retirement in all three age groups and actually resembled craftsmen more than any other group.

How are these occupational differences in age-specific retirement rates reflected in estimations of the retirement model? In order to answer this question, we must first recall that the age categories in which retirement rates were calculated in Table 4 are the same age categories used in the estimations to denote

Table 4. Proportion Retired, by Age and Occupation (1976 and 1978 Waves)

	1976 Wave				1978 Wave			
	−61	62–64	65+	All Ages	−61	62–64	65+	All Ages
All white-collar:	13	41	58	29	14	40	66	38
Professional	11	33	54	24	11	34	80	39
Managerial	13	45	58	29	15	33	55	33
Clerical	21	45	72	38	24	67	82	54
Sales	10	38	50	24	5	32	50	27
All blue-collar:	15	50	74	35	19	55	75	47
Crafts	16	48	84	36	20	61	79	47
Operatives	11	58	65	32	18	51	82	48
Service	13	46	68	38	11	56	63	45
Laborers	18	39	71	37	31	47	62	49

reduced and full-benefit eligibility: the youngest category serves as the reference group for the two older categories. Age-specific differences in retirement rates are thereby captured relationally by the coefficients for the age eligibility variables and the constant. Using the information reported in Table 4, we can return to Table 3 and add to the earlier discussion of the age eligibility coefficients. For example, among professionals the coefficients for reduced-benefit eligibility are roughly the same in both waves; so is the relationship between the age-specific retirement rates for men 61 and younger and men aged 62–64. The relatively large size of the coefficient for full-benefit eligibility in 1978 tells us that professionals aged 65 and older had a much higher rate of retirement than the younger age groups; and we see in Table 4 that the proportion of retired professionals in the oldest age group was quite high, higher than for any other white-collar group (except clerical workers) and higher also than the lower blue-collar groups.

Taking a closer look at the laborer category, we can see that the relatively small 1976 coefficient for reduced-benefit eligibility and the nonsignificant coefficient in 1978 do not mean that relatively few laborers retired early. These coefficients do tell us that the rate of retirement among 62–64 year olds was not that much different from the rate of retirement among laborers aged 61 and younger. However, the similarity derives from the fact that retirement before age 62 was not uncommon for laborers: in 1978, laborers were characterized by the highest proportion retired in the age category of 61 and younger.

The resemblance between clerical workers and craftsmen is suggested in these coefficients as well: for both categories the differences between the effect of reduced eligibility and the effect of full-benefit eligibility was smaller than it was for, say, professionals, because the proportions of clerks and craftsmen aged 62–64 who were retired were much higher than the proportion of professionals. Whether lower white-collar workers are more similar to upper white-collar or to blue-collar workers has been a frequently debated issue in the sociological literature. Because lower white-collar workers enjoy more prestige and a more pleasant work environment, they have often been set apart from the working class. But it can also be argued that other characteristics such as relations of authority make lower white-collar workers very similar to members of the working class. In a recent study of the relationship between occupational categories and social classes (Wright et al., 1982:721–22), e.g., the authors concluded that "clerical occupations have class profiles that are much closer to those of manual operatives and laborers than to higher status white-collar positions." Evidence from the current study suggests a similarity between clerical workers and blue-collar workers in their rates of retirement, although the similarity is with craftsmen rather than operatives; and in the estimations of the retirement models, clerical workers were distinguished from other white-collar categories by the absence of significant effects for the mandatory retirement/second pension variable.

Nevertheless, the age category variables were so overwhelmingly important in the retirement estimations for all occupational groups that we must start from that observation and raise some additional questions. Once we control for age differences in retirement rates, what else matters? First of all, health limitations was clearly an important correlate of retirement; and although there is some suggestion that it was relatively more important for certain categories of blue-collar workers, its effects can be noted in virtually all occupational categories (the one most likely exception being the clerical category). Second, among upper white-collar workers and craftsmen, in particular, being subject to mandatory retirement and covered by a second pension was an important determinant of retirement. For operatives, job tenure had a small positive effect, but the impact of tenure here as elsewhere was swamped by the variables already mentioned. In general, then, once differences in retirement age are controlled, the structure of retirement determinants operates rather uniformly across occupational categories, with some variation in the relative magnitude of effects.

In recent decades, normative patterns of behavior have established retirement as the expected culmination of the work career, and the age structures that govern sources of retirement income have specified a relatively narrow range of ages at which retirement "typically" occurs. It may be that OASI eligibility and health considerations (in conjunction with mandatory retirement and second pension eligibility) are so overwhelmingly important to older workers that the only major difference among workers *is* one of timing, i.e., whether they retire before age 62, at ages 62–64, or later. The present study was not designed to answer that question; rather the purpose of this study was to identify the factors that discriminate the retired from the nonretired and determine whether the pattern of retirement determinants differed by occupation. Although this study suggests some small though interesting differences, sample size within particular occupational groups is not sufficiently large for us to compare *age-specific* retirement patterns across occupational groups. Obviously, a major determinant of timing is OASI eligibility; however, to say that OASI eligibility influences the timing of retirement does not preclude the possibility that other retirement determinants may operate more or less strongly within particular age ranges. Previous research (Quinn, 1975; Hardy, 1982) has suggested that certain retirement determinants may be more strongly related to early retirement as opposed to later retirement. But there may be a variety of other occupationally related factors that are involved in the timing issue. In the present study, the occupational variable was simply a nominal measure, and these occupational categories were treated as surrogates for more detailed occupational differences; it may be that the differences of primary relevance to retirement were not sufficiently captured by that nominal variable. Therefore, it would certainly be advisable to take a closer look at a more detailed set of job characteristics, characteristics that might well distinguish retirement behavior among older workers on dimensions other than age.

APPENDIX:
LOGIT COEFFICIENT ESTIMATES WITHIN OCCUPATIONAL GROUPS

1973[a]

	Prof.	Manag.	Clerks	Sales	Crafts	Operatives	Service	Labor
LIMIT		1.143	.426		1.401	2.117	1.814	1.113
		.490	.651		.345	.464	.801	.760
		2.334	.654		4.065	4.560	2.264	1.464
DUNCAN		.019	−.017		.010	−.021	−.006	.036
		.023	.027		.014	.025	.037	.121
		.857	−.637		.663	−.831	−.159	.302
ED		−.078	−.097		−.069	−.114	.003	.099
		.092	.098		.069	.086	.138	.169
		−.840	−.992		−.999	−1.328	.025	.587
TENURE		−.010	.033		.013	.020	.034	.024
		.018	.029		.015	.021	.040	.033
		−.568	1.154		.879	.977	.862	.737
CRAPE		1.948	.869		1.755	1.698	1.022	.368
		.669	.929		.536	.618	.892	.979
		2.911	.935		3.273	2.749	1.146	.376
PENCR		.056	.091		1.099	.417	−1.027	1.119
		.771	.968		.533	.617	1.243	1.201
		.073	.094		2.061	.676	−.826	.932

(*continued*)

APPENDIX (Continued)

1973^a

	Prof.	Manag.	Clerks	Sales	Crafts	Operatives	Service	Labor
LNWAGE		.033	−.231		−.363	−.214	2.080	−.924
		.453	.653		.440	.637	.838	.777
		.072	−.353		−.826	−.336	2.482	−1.188
62–64		1.615	2.041		2.270	2.405	2.344	3.544
		.559	.691		.382	.501	.930	.882
		2.888	2.952		5.943	4.806	2.520	4.020
65+		3.682	3.394		4.157	4.419	5.971	3.380
		.677	.919		.518	.748	1.135	1.019
		5.436	3.693		8.029	5.908	5.260	3.317
CONSTANT		−4.463	−1.802		−3.793	−3.520	−7.487	−4.576
		1.721	1.839		.927	1.069	2.024	1.735
		−2.593	−.980		−4.092	−3.294	−3.699	−2.638
Likelihood ratio statistic		207	87		386	287	107	91
Percent correctly predicted		88	86		89	91	92	89
Sample N's		258	124		464	321	124	109

138

1976[a]

LIMIT	1.331 (.531) 2.507	.337 (.392) .859	1.919 (.546) 3.519	2.366 (.833) 2.842	.900 (.282) 3.190	.376 (.345) 1.090	.415 (.499) .832	1.104 (.474) 2.330
DUNCAN	−.017 (.019) −.880	−.013 (.015) −.890	−.017 (.025) −.684	.062 (.035) 1.750	.001 (.010) .134	−.022 (.020) −1.065	.018 (.027) .667	.021 (.079) .271
ED	−.117 (.084) −1.386	−.037 (.065) −.561	−.158 (.010) −1.601	−.105 (.129) −.815	−.005 (.050) −.107	−.021 (.062) −.341	.050 (.094) .536	.085 (.080) 1.069
TENURE	−.006 (.018) −.308	.010 (.014) .667	.025 (.021) 1.226	.021 (.027) .753	−.007 (.011) −.607	.029 (.015) 1.936	.028 (.028) 1.016	.019 (.020) .968
CRAPE	3.797 (1.248) 3.043	1.131 (.451) 2.509	−.119 (.640) −.186	.692 (.843) .822	.792 (.359) 2.208	.066 (.415) .158	−.309 (.546) −.567	.218 (.551) .395
PENCR	2.460 (1.256) 1.959	−.109 (.491) −.223	−.241 (.744) −.324	−1.883 (.916) −2.056	.145 (.360) .402	−.108 (.419) −.257	−.129 (.630) −.204	.315 (.612) .515

(*continued*)

APPENDIX (Continued)

	1976[a]							
	Prof.	Manag.	Clerks	Sales	Crafts	Operatives	Service	Labor
LNWAGE	.545	.202	1.441	1.029	.278	.783	-.166	-.046
	(.335)	(.306)	(.745)	(.516)	(.311)	(.357)	(.524)	(.314)
	1.625	.659	1.933	1.995	.893	2.195	-.317	-.145
62–64	1.605	1.826	1.288	2.762	1.666	2.467	1.847	1.208
	(.617)	(.432)	(.598)	(.961)	(.292)	(.388)	(.597)	(.560)
	2.602	4.225	2.154	2.873	5.712	6.364	3.095	2.158
65+	3.385	2.626	2.502	3.771	3.461	2.900	2.635	2.379
	(.619)	(.474)	(.654)	(.965)	(.358)	(.416)	(.562)	(.583)
	5.472	5.540	3.826	3.909	9.678	6.965	4.686	4.084
CONSTANT	-4.253	-1.899	-2.653	-7.823	-2.705	-3.535	-2.748	-3.060
	(1.936)	(1.077)	(1.977)	(2.577)	(.692)	(.818)	(1.061)	(1.021)
	-2.197	-1.763	-1.341	-3.036	-3.910	-4.322	-2.590	-2.997
Likelihood ratio statistic	116	98	57	68	201	141	44	47
Percent correctly predicted	87	79	80	85	80	80	74	76
Sample N's	178	228	128	99	446	290	124	132

1978[a]

LIMIT	1.210	1.259	-.025	2.021	1.546	1.173	1.310	2.059
	.555	.389	.628	1.064	.289	.356	.566	.511
	2.181	3.241	-.040	1.898	5.343	3.295	2.317	4.027
DUNCAN	-.028	-.004	-.090	.045	-.013	-.014	.031	-.036
	.023	.019	.037	.045	.011	.022	.033	.075
	-1.231	-.234	-2.452	1.010	-1.176	-.609	.923	-.479
ED	-.151	-.035	-.003	-.318	-.024	-.053	-.018	.032
	.093	.067	.115	.217	.055	.064	.099	.093
	-1.634	-.521	-.023	-1.467	-.425	-.817	-.180	.342
TENURE	-.031	-.012	.013	-.003	.014	.030	.075	-.003
	.021	.014	.031	.046	.011	.016	.037	.022
	-1.475	-.803	.414	-.058	1.274	1.860	2.033	-.119
CRAPE	2.935	1.302	-.406	2.765	1.268	.956	2.097	1.364
	1.004	.478	.856	1.328	.395	.490	.734	.642
	2.924	2.724	-.474	2.082	3.210	1.951	2.857	2.126
PENCR	1.247	-.280	-3.374	.223	.516	.605	-.532	-.631
	.953	.502	1.040	1.065	.366	.476	.651	.643
	1.308	-.558	-3.245	.209	1.409	1.272	-.818	-.980

(*continued*)

APPENDIX (Continued)

	1976[a]							
	Prof.	Manag.	Clerks	Sales	Crafts	Operatives	Service	Labor
LNWAGE	.952	.280	.486	.520	−.482	.258	−.743	.323
	.443	.311	.660	.212	.336	.394	.677	.407
	2.148	.901	.736	2.447	−1.433	.656	−1.097	.793
62–64	1.439	1.175	2.702	3.713	2.010	1.701	2.871	1.086
	.637	.520	.876	1.575	.335	.449	.863	.669
	2.257	2.261	3.085	2.357	6.004	3.788	3.328	1.623
65+	4.869	2.425	3.001	2.978	2.942	3.442	2.745	1.694
	.830	.464	.790	1.453	.352	.468	.846	.668
	5.868	5.226	3.797	2.050	8.368	7.349	3.242	2.534
CONSTANT	−2.306	−2.461	2.651	−5.332	−1.494	−2.963	−3.563	−2.822
	1.965	1.242	2.051	2.908	.848	.964	1.446	1.219
	−1.173	−1.981	1.293	−1.834	−1.761	−3.074	−2.464	−2.314
Likelihood ratio statistic	101	80	56	87	165	117	60	39
Percent correctly predicted	87	76	82	90	79	78	82	74
Sample N's	152	201	101	93	370	245	114	113

[a]See note to Table 1.

ACKNOWLEDGMENT

This research was supported by a grant from the National Institute on Aging (1-R01-AG-02974-01).

NOTES

1. Because of differences in transportation, clothing, and housing costs, some economists have estimated substantial reductions in living expenses after retirement. However, these estimations implicitly assume that no other comparable activities are substituted for work, i.e., that transportation costs decline because retired workers go out less frequently than employed workers.
2. Actually, some studies have reported the successful retraining of older workers (Belbin and Belbin, 1968; Mullan and Gorman, 1972) and have suggested that the quality of work performed by older workers may be superior to that of younger workers (Butler, 1975).
3. Farm owners and farm managers were effectively excluded as a category since they are almost uniformly self-employed.
4. Although service workers can be divided into "household" and "other than household service," they are treated together in this study. The number of household service workers was very small, less than one percent of the service category.
5. Farm and non-farm laborers were combined in the general laborer category. Approximately 30 percent of the laborers were farm laborers.
6. It is true that respondents who indicated coverage by a second pension are not a homogeneous group. Only one dimension of difference is incorporated into these policy variables, namely mandatory retirement policies—a difference that may also indicate a basis for variation in benefit levels. Other factors such as tenure, earnings, and work history will also affect pension levels; job tenure and wage are included directly in the equation, and work history is to some limited degree implied in job tenure. Combining those not covered by pensions, regardless of the mandatory retirement policy, was necessary since only 5 percent of the sample were subject to mandatory retirement but not covered by a pension.
7. One issue involved in these estimations is whether estimates should be based on the sample of men currently in the labor force, i.e., estimated on the subsample of men actually reporting wage and salary (income), or whether some correction for sample selection should be included. If one is interested in identifying the factors that produce differences in observed wage rates and assessing the relative impact of each factor on wage differentials, then to the extent that factors involved in the wage estimation are also the factors that influence membership in the subsample (i.e., variables that predict labor-force participation) estimated coefficients will be biased. However, in this study the object is simply to predict the wage rates that would most likely apply to men who are now retired if they had chosen instead to remain in the labor force. Still, in order for the imputed wages to serve as measures of wages forgone due to retirement, we must assume that an actual relocation of currently retired men back into the labor force, with employment in jobs similar to their last jobs, would not significantly alter the market wage structure. Equations for imputed wage measures included education, job tenure, Duncan's SEI, age, and wage in 1965 as predictor variables.
8. Equations were estimated by QUAIL, a program designed by Daniel McFadden and Hugh Wills.
9. For example, if 20 percent of the respondents are retired and the coefficient for health limitations is 2.0, then the expected difference in the proportion retired for those with limitations versus those without is .32, i.e., the proportion of men with limitations who are retired is expected to be 32 percent higher than the proportion of men without limitations who are retired.
10. The reader may note that the percent correctly predicted declines from one wave to the next (especially from the 1973 to the 1976 wave). This decline is largely a function of the changing

proportion of sample members who were retired at any given wave, a proportion that increased from 15 percent in 1973 to 33 percent in 1976 and to 43 percent in 1978 (i.e., the variance in the dependent variable almost doubled between 1973 and 1976). It should also be noted that, whereas the percent correctly predicted is sensitive to the variance in the dependent variable, the likelihood ratio statistic is sensitive to sample size. This latter statistical characteristic means that, in any given set of estimations, the likelihood ratio statistic will generally be higher for the category with the larger sample size (e.g., it will be larger for the blue-collar than for the white-collar category since the sample size for blue-collar is greater).

11. It is possible to treat the estimated coefficients for the various occupational groups as variables that are normally distributed around coefficient value. Given that assumption, differences between pairs of coefficients can be assessed within a t-test framework. This t-test is essentially equivalent to testing the significance of dummy-variable interaction terms in a regression (performed on the pooled categories) that contains all independent variables specified in the model, a dummy-variable indicating group membership, and interaction terms defined by the product of the dummy-variable with each independent variable. The t-test used to test for differences between groups in this dummy-variable regression framework is:

$$t = \frac{b_1 - b_2}{[2(V_1 se_{b_1}^2 + V_2 se_{b_2}^2)/(V_1 + V_2)]^{1/2}}, \qquad (3)$$

where se is the standard error, V_1 and V_2 are the degrees of freedom, and b_1 and b_2 the regression coefficients for groups 1 and 2, respectively.

12. For example, for a coefficient of 1.00, the proportional effect for a category with 20 percent retired would be .16, whereas the proportional effect for the same coefficient in a category with 40 percent retired would be .24.

REFERENCES

Barfield, R. E. and J. N. Morgan
    1970 Early Retirement: The Decision and the Experience and a Second Look. Ann Arbor, MI: Institute for Social Research, University of Michigan.

Belbin, E. and R. M. Belbin
    1968 "New careers in middle age." Pp. 341–346 in B. Neugarten (ed.), Middle Age and Aging. Chicago: University of Chicago Press.

Boskin, M. J.
    1977 "Social Security and retirement decisions." Economic Inquiry 15(January):1–25.

Bowen, W. G. and T. A. Finegan
    1969 The Economics of Labor Force Participation. Princeton, NJ: Princeton University Press.

Burkhauser, R. V.
    1977 "An asset maximization approach to early Social Security acceptance." Discussion Paper No. 463-77, Institute for Research on Poverty. University of Wisconsin, Madison.

Butler, N.
    1975 Why Survive? Being Old in America. New York: Harper and Row.

Edwards, A. M.
    1933 "A social-economic grouping of the gainful workers of the United States." American Statistical Association Journal 28:377–387.

Epstein, L. A. and J. H. Murray
    1967 The Aged Population of the United States: The 1963 Social Security Survey of the Aged. U.S. Department of Health, Education and Welfare, Social Security Administration. Of-

fice of Research and Statistics, Research Report No. 19. Washington, DC: U.S. Government Printing Office.

Friedmann, E. and H. L. Orbach
- 1974 "Adjustment to retirement." Pp. 609–645 in S. Arieti (ed.), American Handbook of Psychiatry, Vol. 1, 2nd ed. New York: Basic Books.

Fuchs, V.
- 1982 "Self-employment and labor force participation of older males." Journal of Human Resources 17(Summer):339–357.

Haber, L. D.
- 1968 "Disability, work, and income maintenance: prevalence of disability, 1966." Social Security Bulletin (May):14–23.

Hanushek, E. A. and J. E. Jackson
- 1977 Statistical Methods for Social Scientists. New York: Academic Press.

Hardy, M. A.
- 1982a "Social policy and determinants of retirement: a longitudinal analysis of older white males, 1969–75." Social Forces 60(June):1103–1122.
- 1982b "Job characteristics and health: the differential impact on benefit entitlement." Research on Aging 4(December):457–478.

Henretta, J. C. and R. T. Campbell
- 1976 "Status attainment and status maintenance: a study of stratification in old age." American Sociological Review 41(December):981–992.

Jacobson, D.
- 1972 "Willingness to retire in relation to job strain and type of work." Industrial Gerontology 13:65–74.

Kolodrubetz, W.
- 1970 "Employee benefit plans in 1968." Social Security Bulletin (April):35–47.
- 1973 "Private retirement benefits and relationship to earnings: survey of new beneficiaries." Social Security Bulletin 36(May):16–36.
- 1976a "Characteristics of workers with pension coverage on the longest job." Pp. 151–167 in Reaching Retirement Age. U.S. Department of Health, Education and Welfare, Research Report No. 47. Washington, DC: U.S. Government Printing Office.
- 1976b "Earnings replacement from private pensions." Pp. 169–186 in Reaching Retirement Age. U.S. Department of Health, Education and Welfare, Research Report No. 47. Washington, DC: U.S. Government Printing Office.

Mullan, C. and L. Gorman
- 1972 "Facilitating adaptation to change: a close study in retraining middle-aged and older workers at Aer Lingus." Industrial Gerontology 15:20–39.

Parnes, H. S., et al.
- 1970 The Pre-Retirement Years. Manpower Research Monograph No. 15. Columbus, OH: Center for Human Resource Research, Ohio State University.
- 1974 The Pre-Retirement Years: Five Years on the Work Lives of Middle-Aged Men, Vol. 4. Columbus, OH: Center for Human Resource Research, Ohio State University.

Pindyck, R. S. and D. L. Rubinfeld
- 1976 Econometric Models and Economic Forecasts. New York: McGraw-Hill.

Quinn, J. F.
- 1975 The Microeconomics of Early Retirement Behavior. Unpublished Ph.D. dissertation, Massachusetts Institute of Technology.
- 1977 "The micro-economic determinants of early retirement: a cross-sectional view of white married men." Journal of Human Resources 12(3):329–346.
- 1980 "Labor force participation patterns of older self-employed workers." Social Security Bulletin 43(April):17–28.

Reno, V.
 1971 "Why men stop working at or before age 65." Survey of New Beneficiaries. Social Security Administration, Office of Research and Statistics, Report No. 3. Washington, DC: U.S. Government Printing Office.
 1972 "Compulsory retirement among newly entitled workers." Social Security Bulletin (March):3–15.
 1976 "Retirement patterns of men." Pp. 31–40 in Reaching Retirement Age. U.S. Department of Health, Education and Welfare, Research Report No. 47. Washington, DC: U.S. Government Printing Office.
Rogers, T. F. and N. S. Friedman
 1980 Printers Face Automation: The Impact of Technology on Work and Retirement Among Skilled Craftsmen. Lexington, MA: D. C. Heath.
Rubin, L.
 1976 "Disabling health conditions among men." Pp. 65–74 in Reaching Retirement Age. U.S. Department of Health, Education and Welfare, Research Report No. 47. Washington, DC: U.S. Government Printing Office.
Schwab, K.
 1974 "Early labor force withdrawal of men: participants and nonparticipants aged 58–63." Social Security Bulletin (August):24–38.
Sheppard, H. L.
 1972 Where Have All the Robots Gone? Worker Dissatisfaction in the 1970s. New York: The Free Press.
 1976 "Work and retirement." Pp. 286–309 in R. H. Binstock and E. Shanas (eds.), Handbook of Aging and the Social Sciences. New York: Van Nostrand Reinhold.
Slavick, F. and S. L. Wolfbein
 1960 "The evolving work-life pattern." Pp. 298–329 in C. Tibbetts (ed.), Handbook of Social Gerontology. Chicago: University of Chicago Press.
Stecker, M.
 1951 "Beneficiaries prefer to work." Social Security Bulletin 14(January):15.
 1955 "Why do beneficiaries retire? Who among them return to work?" Social Security Bulletin 18(May):3.
U.S. Department of Labor
 1965 The Older American Worker: Age Discrimination in Employment. Washington, DC: U.S. Government Printing Office.
Wentworth, E.
 1945 "Why beneficiaries retire." Social Security Bulletin 8(January):15–20.
Wright, E. O., C. Costello, D. Hachen, and J. Sprague
 1982 "The American class structure." American Sociological Review 47(December):709–726.

PLANNED AND ACTUAL RETIREMENT:
AN EMPIRICAL ANALYSIS

Richard V. Burkhauser and Joseph F. Quinn

ABSTRACT

Research on retirement has concentrated either on retirement plans or on actual retirement behavior. Here we link these two aspects of the retirement decision by analyzing those factors which determine the accuracy of retirement plans. Using 10 years of data from the Retirement History Study we find that workers on the verge of retirement (age 58–63) in 1969 were reasonably accurate in predicting their actual age of retirement over the next decade.

Those who planned to retire at a specified age were far more accurate than those who said they would never retire, as were those on their jobs since at least middle age and those with pension or mandatory retirement rules on their job. Even for workers in our sample who were

Current Perspectives on Aging and the Life Cycle
Volume 1, pages 147-168
Copyright © 1985 by JAI Press Inc.
All rights of reproduction in any form reserved.
ISBN: 0-89232-296-9

on long-term jobs, their plans were not etched in stone. These plans often changed over time, and in predictable ways in response to health and financial circumstances.

I. INTRODUCTION

No change in work patterns over the last three decades is more dramatic than the fall in labor force participation rates of older men. In the first four decades of this century few workers had the financial independence to leave their jobs in old age and the great majority stayed in the work force as long as physically possible. Over the last several decades major changes have occurred in the institutional arrangements found in the workplace. The Social Security system was created in the late 1930s. Though it was still a small program well into the third decade of its existence (only $11 billion in expenditures in 1960), by 1984 it was the single largest social welfare program in the country with a budget of $218 billion. Private pensions, once a rare phenomenon, are now much more widespread. While estimates vary, private beneficiaries have increased from fewer than 2 million in 1960 to as many as 9 million in 1980. Nearly two out of three full-time male workers in the private sector with more than one year of service are currently covered by private pensions.[1] These two sources of retirement income have allowed workers to withdraw from the workplace at earlier and earlier ages.[2]

Institutionalized savings and retirement programs, such as employer pensions, civil service retirement plans, and Social Security, serve a number of purposes. One is to reduce the amount of financial uncertainty concerning the future. Social Security and defined benefit pensions make promises concerning benefit levels upon retirement. Defined contribution plans make no such promises and are more subject to the vagaries of investment markets. In all of these, the eventual benefit amount is subject to change because Congress and firms can always alter the benefit calculation rules. But as employees approach retirement, they should have a better and better idea of what they can expect.

We suspect that the introduction of these pension plans has had a number of labor market effects. First, they change the planned retirement age of those covered. Those with the financial means to retire will plan to do so earlier than those without. Second, these plans may tighten the linkage between planned and actual behavior. If these arrangements do reduce uncertainty about the future, then those who are covered will be more able to follow through on plans made prior to retirement age. The net result of these impacts—on initial plans and on the ability to follow them—is the observed change in actual retirement behavior.

Both retirement plans and retirement behavior have been studied in the literature, though the latter much more so than the former. This paper analyzes the middle link—the relationship between planned and actual behavior. We are interested in whether people retire earlier than they had planned, later, or on time, and what other characteristics correlate with these outcomes.

II. RETIREMENT DETERMINANTS

Although the recent trend of male workers toward earlier retirement is unmistakable, the factors which influence these decisions are still the subject of heated debate. Many of the early discussions of retirement emphasized the impact of poor health and implied that people generally continued to work until health deterioration dictated retirement. They then turned to whatever retirement income sources were available, such as savings, Social Security, or employer pensions. These income sources were not thought to induce retirement but rather to soften the financial blow when it occurred. These conclusions were drawn largely from a series of Social Security Administration surveys (USDHEW 1976a,b) in which retired respondents were asked why they retired. The overwhelming response was always health.

More recent analyses of retirement, mostly by economists, have concentrated not on why people say they retire, but on their objective circumstances at the time of the decision. In these econometric studies, retirement income sources always play a major role. Eligibility for Social Security and other pensions, the size of the benefits for which one is eligible, and the rules and regulations concerning changes in benefits if their acceptance is postponed all appear to be important determinants. Three excellent recent reviews of this literature (Clark et al., 1978; Danziger et al., 1981; and Mitchell and Fields, 1982) show that economic variables do affect the timing of retirement. In addition, health remains important, despite problems in defining objective measures.

Another aspect of the debate concerns the relevance of retirement expectations. Barfield and Morgan (1969) and Hall and Johnson (1980) have used a worker's planned retirement age as the dependent variable in their analyses of the retirement process. Barfield and Morgan used a dichotomous variable i.e., whether the worker planned to retire prior to age 65 or not. They found that a primary determinant was the amount of retirement income expected. For many workers, that is largely Social Security and employer pension benefits. Poor health also seemed to encourage early retirement.

Hall and Johnson (1980) expanded the analysis of retirement plans in a number of ways. They divided the expected age of retirement into four categories: before 62, 62–64, 65 or after, and never. They had four categories of explanatory variables: expected income sources (Social Security, private pensions, government pensions), current economic variables (wage rate, assets and nonwage income, and dichotomous variables for a working spouse and home ownership), health (subjectively defined relative to peers), and other individual characteristics (education, self-employed status, compulsory retirement age, and suburban or rural residence). Variables in all four categories were significant determinants of planned retirement ages for men and women aged 58–63 in 1969. Social Security eligibility had the largest positive increase on the probability of retiring in the 62–64 age range. (The authors were unable to estimate the size of expected Social Security benefits.) The amount of private or government civil service pensions expected was also important and had monotonically increasing impacts on earlier and earlier planned retirement ages. Those with poor health, those with a compulsory retirement constraint, and male homeowners were more likely to plan an early retirement; the self-employed were more likely to have no planned retirement age at all.

As Hall and Johnson (1980) point out, plans can change for at least two reasons. There may be systematic changes over time, even if objective circumstances remain the same. Retirement may become more or less attractive as one approaches it. Or, the circumstances determining the original plans may change. Assets or retirement income may turn out to be unexpectedly high or low, health may deteriorate, or a spouse may die. These linkages between plans and final outcomes have received very little attention.

Some preliminary work on this has been done by Goudy (1982) using the Social Security Administration's Longitudinal Retirement History Study—the same data source employed by Hall and Johnson and by us (see below). Goudy asks whether workers in 1971 expected to stop working in the future or not. By 1975, they had either stopped working, expected to stop, or did not expect to stop. The 2 × 3 matrix creates six categories of workers. Goudy asks what antecedent factors correlate with each of these six types. Some reasonable findings emerge. Those who initially (in 1971) expect to stop working and then (by 1975) either do stop or still expect to stop are the most likely to have pension coverage, mandatory retirement, and high current income. The self-employed are more likely to plan to continue working and then to do so. The most surprising finding was the relative unimportance of health in differentiating among the groups. One plausible explanation for this is that the sample chosen (those still working in 1971, at ages 60–65) eliminates most of those with health problems, and the health distinctions remaining are too small to be important.

In our work below, the time frame of the analysis is expanded in both directions—back to 1969 and forward through 1977 and 1979. In addition, we concentrate not only on whether people plan to retire, but on when. This enables us to differentiate among those who retired before, after, or when they planned.

A final and related aspect of the retirement debate concerns the relevant time period over which retirement decisions are made. Many empirical models of retirement assume workers are myopic in choosing a retirement age. For instance, they analyze a worker at age 65 and argue that his choice is either to leave the job and take retirement benefits or to continue working and postpone these benefits for another year. These models usually ignore whether the worker's prior behavior may have anticipated this choice. Many of the variables treated as exogenous at age 65 may in fact by endogenous, i.e., simultaneously determined along with the earlier decision to retire at 65. In addition, many models ignore how economic and health variables may change in the future depending on the worker's retirement decision. For example, many studies of retirement use a replacement rate concept (the ratio of potential retirement benefits to potential earnings) as a predictor of retirement. Others use dichotomous dummy variables for Social Security or pension eligibility (see Barfield and Morgan, 1969; Quinn, 1977). These single-year measures of income or eligibility take no account of how benefits change if postponed. With Social Security and most pension plans, future annual benefits increase if one works an additional year. In some cases, the future increases are more than sufficient to compensate for the year's benefits foregone. In other cases they are not. These institutional details embody strong financial incentives to work or to retire, and are important in explaining and predicting behavior. Yet they are totally ignored in much of the earlier retirement literature.

The single-period framework has since been modified by those who argue that workers are concerned with their well-being over all future years. In deciding whether to retire at a given age, a worker considers the wealth value (the present discounted value) of all future pension and Social Security benefits and how this value would change depending on the decision made. In Burkhauser and Quinn (1983b) we suggest that total compensation paid to a worker in any period includes not only wage and salary income received but also the change in retirement wealth that occurs during that year of work. For most workers, pension wealth builds at younger ages. During these years, wage and salary data alone underestimate total compensation. But eventually, Social Security and pension wealth peak and begin to fall. When this occurs, wage and salary data overestimate actual net compensation. In other research (Burkhauser and Quinn, 1983a) we show that workers respond to these changes in retirement income wealth and that firms may use this institutional mechanism to induce workers to leave the job.

Recent economic theory has stressed broadening the time frame in which labor market decisions are modeled. This life cycle view argues that work and retirement plans are made far in advance of the actual age of eligibility for retirement benefits and that workers consider pension and Social Security benefits in their work decisions at all ages. Burkhauser and Turner (1978), for example, argue that the work disincentives of the Social Security earnings test not only discourage work at older ages, but encourage it in earlier years. Workers who anticipate the wage penalty ahead will concentrate their work effort in the years before the penalty goes into effect. Such rational behavior on the part of workers is no more surprising than the fact that anyone offered a higher hourly wage before lunch than after would spend more time working in the mornings.

Lazear (1979) takes a similar life cycle view in arguing that mandatory retirement rules may be necessary to enforce implicit long-term labor contracts between employers and employees. According to their "contracts," at younger ages workers are paid less than their true value to the firm. This is then made up by payment in excess of productivity at older ages. Both workers and employers can benefit from this arrangement if it reduces turnover (and its attendant costs) or increases the work effort of employees. But the agreement requires an explicit cutoff year at the point where lifetime compensation to the worker equals lifetime productivity to the firm. A mutually agreed upon mandatory retirement year enforces this termination. We (Burkhauser and Quinn, 1983b) have argued that even if such implicit life cycle contracts exist, mandatory retirement rules are not necessary to enforce them. Pension plans which fall in value if postponed past some age could also ensure that lifetime compensation to the worker equaled lifetime productivity. Life cycle models stress the point that worker and employer behavior must be viewed in a multiperiod framework and that expectations about the future are an important aspect of work choices.

A major problem with multiperiod models is that few data sets provide detailed information on behavior over time. A notable exception is the Retirement History Study (RHS), a 10-year longitudinal survey of men and nonmarried women aged 58–63 in 1969. [See Irelan (1976) for details on this extraordinary data set.] In this paper, we utilize the RHS:

- To analyze the relationship between retirement plans and actual retirement age over a 10-year period
- To compare the accuracy of various types of individuals in predicting their retirement age, especially those who could be considered long-term workers
- To show the effect of subsequent health on the plans of long-term workers

We do this first through a series of tables which show the relationship between various characteristics of a worker and the outcome of his or her retirement plans, and second through the use of multinominal logit estimations which test the significance of these characteristics in the accuracy of retirement plans.

III. ACCURACY OF THE RETIREMENT PLANS OF LONG-TERM WORKERS

Table 1 describes a sample of over 3,000 male non-self-employed workers, aged 58–63 and in the labor force in 1969.[3] In 1969 these workers reported a planned retirement age. Using data from subsequent RHS surveys every two years through 1979, we traced the workers to ages 68–73 and separated them into four groups: those who left the labor force before they planned to (early); those who

Table 1. Accuracy of Retirement Plans of Long-Term Career and Short-Term Career Non-Self-Employed Male Workers (percentages)[a]

	Started Current Job Before Age 50		Started Current Job After Age 50		
Retirement Outcome	Reported a Definite Retirement Age	Will Never Retire	Reported a Definite Retirement Age	Will Never Retire	Total Sample
Early	24%	80%	24%	78%	42%
On Time	60	NA	48	NA[b]	38
Late	16	NA	27	NA	13
On Schedule	0	20	1	22	7
Total	100	100	100	100	100
Number	1,499	490	558	482	3,029
(%)	(75)	(25)	(54)	(46)	(100)

Data: Retirement History Study (1969–1979).
[a] See Appendix for full definition of all terms. Sample consists of males aged 58 through 63 who were not self-employed and in the labor force in 1969. Actual retirement decisions are known through 1979.
[b] NA = not applicable.

retired within a year of their stated retirement age (on time); those who retired later (late); and those who have not reached their stated retirement age (including "never") and are still working (on schedule).

The last column in Table 1 shows that workers' predictions in 1969 were wrong (early or late) 55 percent of the time. They were three times more likely to retire before they said they would (42 percent) than after (13 percent). This crude comparison shows that retirement plans are a reliable predictor of actual behavior for less than one-half of the sample. A further look at Table 1, however, provides a useful insight into variations in the accuracy of plans across respondents and shows that for some workers such plans are quite accurate.

A. Length of Tenure

We disaggregate workers into two categories. The first includes workers who in 1969 were still on the same job they held at age 50. The second group consists of workers on jobs first started after age 50. Although 50 is an arbitrary cutoff age we felt it provided one description of Lazear's long-term contract worker. The majority of workers in this first group have been on the same job 20 years or more. We further subdivide workers based on their initial planned retirement age response. Those who gave a specific age of retirement are separated from those who said they would never retire. This disaggregation is continued in all subsequent tables. Notice that those who claimed they would never retire cannot logically end up on time or late.

The results are interesting. Long-term career workers appear to be more accurate than short-term workers because 60 percent of the former and only 48 percent of the latter retired on time. Both groups of workers are equally likely to be early but long-term workers are much less likely to be late. The vast majority of workers who planned to retire at a specific age chose an age no older than 65. Since by 1979 all the workers in our sample were age 68 or older, the on-schedule category is therefore quite small. In addition, those who give a specific retirement age are much more likely to be accurate than those who say they will never retire. Only about 20 percent of workers who planned never to retire in 1969 were still working 10 years later in 1979. Such plans, it appears, are not to be believed.

Long-term workers are not only more likely to be accurate than short-term workers but are also more likely to give a planned retirement age. Three out of four have a specific age planned in comparison with only about half of short-term workers. Workers whose current job tenure began during prime age appear to be more aware and able to predict their retirement than those whose jobs began later.

We believe that the distinction between long-term workers and those who must find new employment past age 50 may be an important one in the analysis of the subsequent labor market decisions of older workers. Life cycle modeling of retirement behavior that assumes long planning horizons appears to be more applicable to employees with long tenure with a single firm. Such workers are more likely to follow through on their original plans. We suspect that this is less likely for those who changed jobs late in life. The fact that long-term workers are more accurate in their retirement plans provides some evidence for this view.

B. Planning Horizon

A planned retirement age can be viewed as a target. When workers were questioned in 1969 they were different numbers of years away from their targeted retirement age. We expected that the shorter the time span between 1969 and the expected retirement year, the more accurate would be the retirement prediction. In Table 2 we look at the subsample of long-term workers and compare the accuracy of retirement predictions. As expected, those with more distant targets were less likely to hit them. Nearly three workers out of four whose retirement age was less than four years away were on time. The level of accuracy fell to 59 percent for targets which were four or five years away and to 45 percent for those six or seven years away. For those with targets eight or more years away, over three-quarters were early. Note, however, that all workers in this last (8+) group must have aimed at an age past 65. This small group (only 4 percent of those giving a specific age) looks very similar to those who claim they will never retire.[4]

Table 2. Accuracy of Retirement Plans Reaching Various Years into the Future for Male Long-Term Career Workers (percentages)[a]

Years Before Planned Retirement	Retirement Outcome					Row Population	
	Early	On Time	Late	On Schedule	Total	Number	Vertical %
0–1	0	68	32	0	100	135	9
2–3	10	74	16	0	100	494	33
4–5	26	59	16	0	100	465	31
6–7	43	45	12	0	100	345	23
8 or more	77	10	3	10	100	60	4
Planned to retire	24	60	16	0	100	1,499	75
Never planned to retire	80	NA	NA	20	100	490	25
Total	38	45	12	5	100	1,989	100

Data: Retirement History Study (1969–1979).
[a]See Appendix for full definition of all terms. Sample consists of workers age 58–63 in 1969 who had been on this job since age 50.

IV. CORRELATES OF ACCURACY

A. Pensions and Mandatory Retirement

As we have discussed, Lazear (1979) argues that mandatory retirement is an integral part of a long-term contract that increases worker productivity. We have suggested that pension plans can achieve the same goal by reducing net compensation for work past some agreed upon age. In the following tables we look at the accuracy in planning of those who have a mandatory retirement age or pension plans on their current job.

Over 72 percent of the long-term career workers in our sample were eligible for a pension on their current jobs (Table 3). When we segment the sample into those not eligible for a pension, those eligible on this job, and those eligible on a previous job, we find that those with pension coverage are much more likely to predict their retirement age accurately (62 percent on time) than others (44 percent on time). Of those in error, those with pensions are twice as likely to be early than late. Those without pensions are more likely to err on the late side.

Because we have argued that pension plans discourage older workers from extending their job tenure past a set age, we find it noteworthy that only 13 percent of those workers who are eligible for a pension on their current job retire late. In contrast, 34 percent of those with no pension are late. Additional evidence is provided by those who claim they will never retire. Those without a pension are nearly twice as likely to be in the work force 10 years later as those with a pension. Thus, for long-term career workers, pension plans are associated

Table 3. Pension Eligibility and Accuracy of Retirement Plans for Long-Term Career Workers (percentages)

	A Definite Retirement Age			Will Never Retire	
Retirement Outcome	Not Eligible for a Pension	Eligible for a Pension on Current Job	Eligible for a Pension from Some Other Job	Not Eligible for a Pension	Eligible for a Pension on Current Job	Eligible for a Pension from Some Other Job
Early	22	25	24	71	83	100
On Time	44	62	62	NA	NA	NA
Late	34	13	13	NA	NA	NA
On Schedule	0	0	1	29	17	0
Total	100	100	100	100	100	100
Number	195	1,156	148	172	286	32

Data: Retirement History Study (1969–1979). Total Sample Size 1,989.

both with more accurate planning of retirement and with a tendency to undershoot rather than overshoot planned retirement age.

Table 4 disaggregates this sample by mandatory retirement status. Lazear has stressed that mandatory retirement provides a mutually agreed upon end point for long-term contracts. Over half of those who have a mandatory retirement age on their current job retired on time compared with about a third of those with no mandatory retirement age. The next three columns disaggregate those with mandatory retirement age into workers whose planned retirement comes before their mandatory retirement age, workers who plan to retire at their mandatory retirement age, and workers who plan to retire after their mandatory retirement age.

Only 16 percent of those with a mandatory retirement age plan to work beyond that age. A few of these pick a specific later age; the vast majority claim they will never retire. Interestingly, nearly 90 percent of this group end up retiring early. Workers who plan to retire before mandatory retirement are on time in over two out of three cases whereas those who plan to retire at mandatory retirement are on time 57 percent of the time. Contrast these workers with those with retirement plans but without a mandatory retirement age. Each group has about the same likelihood of being on time, but those with a mandatory retirement age are much less likely to be late. Note also that only 15 percent of workers with a mandatory retirement age on their current job plan never to retire compared with over 36 percent of workers without this constraint.

A mandatory retirement age appears to be a clearly understandable signpost which guides long-term workers in planning retirement. As was the case with pension plans, those workers who had a mandatory retirement age were more likely to be accurate in their plans. Also, like pension plans, a mandatory retirement age appears to prevent workers from delaying retirement. It was much more likely for such workers who did change plans to retire early than late.

B. Health

The importance of health in the retirement decision has been the subject of much debate. In Table 5 we analyze whether poor health is related to the accuracy of retirement plans. We divide our long-term workers into two health-related groups. The first group reported continuous good health prior to their planned or actual retirement age, whichever came first.[5] The second group reported bad health in at least one interview year prior to this time. Our findings suggest that bad health does indeed affect planned retirement age.

Those reporting continuous good health were more likely to be on time, both because the healthy group of those reporting a specific retirement age was slightly more on time than those in poor health and because a greater share of those with poor health had planned never to retire. A more important finding is that those in bad health who report a definite retirement age are 50 percent more likely to retire early than those in good health. By the same token, those in good

Table 4. Mandatory Retirement Age and the Accuracy of Retirement Plans for Long-Term Career Workers (percentages)

	\multicolumn{5}{c	}{Retirement Plans}			
	\multicolumn{5}{c	}{With a Mandatory Retirement Age}	\multicolumn{3}{c	}{Without a Mandatory Retirement Age}
Retirement Outcome	Total	PRA before MR[a]	PRA at MR[b]	PRA after MR[c]	Will Never Retire (No PRA)[d]	Total	With a Planned Retirement Age	Will Never Retire (No PRA)
Early	36	15	36	70	89	41	21	76
On Time	53	68	57	20	NA	35	56	NA
Late	9	17	6	10	NA	15	23	NA
On Schedule	2	0	1	0	11	9	0	24
Total	100	100	100	100	100	100	100	100
Number	1,076	410	498	10	158	912	581	331

Data: Retirement History Study (1969–1979). Total Sample 1,988.
[a]Planned retirement age is before mandatory retirement age.
[b]Planned retirement age is the same as mandatory retirement age.
[c]Planned retirement age is after mandatory retirement age.
[d]No planned retirement age, will never retire.

Table 5. Health and the Accuracy of Retirement Plans for Long-Term Career Workers (percentages)

Retirement Outcome	Continuous Good Health			Bad Health		
	Total	Reported a Definite Retirement Age	Will Never Retire	Total	Reported a Definite Retirement Age	Will Never Retire
Early	34	20	80	44	30	80
On Time	47	61	NA	42	58	NA
Late	14	18	NA	9	13	NA
On Schedule	5	1	20	5	0	20
Total	100	100	100	100	100	100
Number	1,117	866	251	872	633	239
%		(78)	(22)		(73)	(27)

Data: Retirement History Study (1969–1979). Total Sample 1,989.

health are much more likely to retire late. Thus, health appears to be an important ingredient in explaining differences in planned and actual retirement behavior. Not only may bad health lead to earlier than expected retirement, but good health may lead to later than expected retirement.

C. Other Characteristics

Other economic characteristics found to be important in explaining retirement behavior include current earnings, Social Security wealth, and pension wealth.[6] We have found that current earnings are negatively correlated with job exit while Social Security and pension wealth are positively correlated (Burkhauser and Quinn, 1983a). Hall and Johnson (1980) find that earnings and the age of eligibility for Social Security or pension benefits affect planned retirement age.

The expected relationship between these three economic variables and *accuracy* of retirement plans is not obvious. If workers underestimate the value of Social Security or pension wealth in formulating their original retirement plans, then we would expect a tendency toward earlier retirement as the more favorable situation is realized. If the absolute size of the windfall is important, we would further expect this tendency to rise with the absolute amount of the wealth source which was underestimated.

It is very likely that eventual Social Security wealth was substantially underestimated by those making retirement plans in 1969. Table 6 shows the annual Social Security benefits for the median worker turning 65 (with a 65-year-old wife) between 1969 and 1981.

Benefits increased over the period for two reasons. First, nominal wages increased, and this increased the average monthly earnings of those who con-

Table 6. Yearly Social Security Benefits for a Worker with Median Earnings Aged 65 with a 65-Year-Old Dependent Spouse

Year[a]	Yearly Benefit (current dollars)	Yearly Benefit (1967 dollars)	Change in Real Terms from Previous Year (%)
1959	1,886	2,160	—
1960	1,903	2,145	−0.7
1961	1,920	2,143	−0.1
1962	1,933	2,134	−0.4
1963	1,951	2,128	−0.3
1964	1,970	2,121	−0.3
1965	2,132	2,256	6.4
1966	2,157	2,219	−1.6
1967	2,186	2,186	−1.5
1968	2,218	2,129	−2.6
1969	2,546	2,319	8.9
1970	2,985	2,567	10.7
1971	3,342	2,755	7.3
1972	3,401	2,714	−1.4
1973	4,157	3,123	15.1
1974	4,238	2,869	−8.1
1975	4,799	2,977	3.8
1976	5,343	3,134	5.3
1977	5,878	3,239	3.4
1978	6,448	3,300	1.9
1979	7,009	3,224	−2.3
1980	7,851	3,179	−1.4
1981	9,136	3,366[a]	5.9
1959–1968			−1.4%
1968–1981			+58.1%

[a]Assumes worker and wife are aged 65 on January 1. Benefits are based on Social Security rules as of January 1 of each year.

tinued to work. Second, and much more important, Congress dramatically changed the formula relating average monthly earnings to the size of the benefit. In 1969, workers basing their expected benefits on the level of benefits provided by the system over the previous decade had good reason to expect little change. In fact, between 1959 and 1968, real Social Security benefits remained virtually constant, falling 1.4 percent in real terms over the period.

Such expectations for subsequent years would have substantially underestimated what was to come. Between 1968 and 1973 real Social Security benefits rose by 47 percent, and by another 8 percent by 1981. Unless workers anticipated this unprecedented increase in Social Security wealth, we would expect this windfall to be correlated with earlier than planned retirement.

Planned and Actual Retirement

Table 7. Accuracy of Retirement Plans of Long-Term Career Workers with Various Levels of Social Security Wealth (percentages)

Social Security Wealth in 1969	Reported a Definite Retirement Age				Vertical Percentage
	Early	On Time	Late	On Schedule	
0	27	61	11	1	12
1–10,000	29	50	21	0	2
10,001–20,000	26	52	22	0	14
20,001–22,500	27	52	20	2	8
22,501–25,000	28	54	17	1	18
25,001–27,500	28	58	14	0	19
27,501–30,000	19	67	14	0	11
30,001–35,000	15	72	13	0	14
35,001–40,000	10	81	10	0	2
Total	364	893	236	6	100

Data: Retirement History Study (1969–1979). Total Sample 1,499.

Table 7 documents the accuracy of retirement plans for our sample of long-term workers who report a definite planned retirement age in 1969. It does appear that those with higher Social Security wealth are less likely to overshoot their planned retirement age. Between 10 and 14 percent of those with Social Security wealth of $25,000 or more retired later than planned compared with 20–22 percent of those with positive wealth below $22,500. Those with higher

Table 8. Accuracy of Retirement Plans of Long-Term Career Workers with Various Levels of Pension Wealth (percentage)

Pension Wealth in 1969	Reported a Definite Retirement Age				Vertical Percentage
	Early	On Time	Late	On Schedule	
0	22	44	34	0	14
1–5,000	22	56	21	1	6
5,001–10,000	28	64	8	0	10
10,001–15,000	23	66	10	1	12
15,001–20,000	27	65	8	0	10
20,001–25,000	20	69	11	0	10
25,001–30,000	26	57	16	1	7
30,001–40,000	30	63	7	0	12
40,001–50,000	17	69	14	0	6
50,000 or more	23	59	18	1	13
Total	331	831	208	5	100

Data: Retirement History Study (1969–1979). Total sample 1,375.

Table 9. Accuracy of Long-Term Workers
Across Various Earning Levels (percentages)

Earnings in 1969	Reported a Definite Retirement Age				Vertical Percentage
	Early	On Time	Late	On Schedule	
0– 4,000	19	54	27	0	8
4,001– 6,000	25	59	15	1	17
6,001– 7,000	23	62	14	1	14
7,001– 8,000	32	59	9	0	15
8,001– 9,000	25	63	12	0	11
9,001–10,000	24	59	17	0	11
10,001–12,000	21	65	14	0	11
12,001–15,000	13	67	19	1	6
15,001–20,000	32	45	22	1	5
20,001 or over	20	47	33	0	2
Total	364	893	236	6	100

Data: Retirement History Study (1969–1979). Total sample 1,499.

Social Security wealth, however, were more likely to be on time and less likely to be early than those with lower Social Security wealth. This last finding is unexpected.

During the 1970s, the opposite phenomenon may have occurred with respect to private pensions. Most private sector pension benefits are not automatically or fully adjusted for inflation after retirement. [Federal government pensions are fully indexed, and most state pensions are partially so (see Quinn, 1982).] The unexpected inflation of the 1970s reduced pension wealth and may have caused workers to reconsider their pension plans. If the size of the windfall loss is the determining factor, we would expect those with larger pensions to be more likely to retire later than planned and less likely to retire early.

Table 8 displays the relationship between retirement plan accuracy and level of pension wealth. The hypothesis mentioned above receives little support in this bivariate analysis. It is difficult to discern any pattern at all as pension wealth increases.

Table 9 shows the accuracy of retirement plans of long-term workers at different earnings levels. No obvious pattern appears. However, as we will see below, this is not the case when we are able to hold other variables constant.

V. AN EMPIRICAL ANALYSIS OF PLANNED AND ACTUAL RETIREMENT

We have shown that the accuracy of retirement plans varies systematically across individuals. Whereas only 45 percent of all workers in our sample were on time or on schedule, the proportion was much higher for certain groups. In this section we use multinominal logit estimation to determine which characteristics of workers affect the accuracy of retirement plans.[7] This multivariate analysis is important because many of the variables we have discussed are correlated. The tables above, though enlightening, do not hold other factors constant.

The data for this analysis is a sample of 1,841 male non-self-employed workers, aged 58–63, who were in the labor force in 1969 and who reported a specific planned retirement age in 1969. In Table 1 we had 2,057 workers with specific retirement plans. The other 216 observations were lost due to bad data responses to other variables used in our logit estimates. The definitions of all variables used and their mean values for this sample are contained in the Appendix.

Table 10 presents the results of our logit estimates. Because there are three possible outcomes we need two estimating equations. (The third could be derived from these two.) In the first equation (equation A) the coefficients of the inde-

Table 10. Logit Equations

	Late vs. On Time			
A.	B	t-stat	B	t-stat
Constant	−.267	1.08	−.166	0.67
Years Away	−.203	8.81	−.210	9.22
Bad Health (0,1)	−.306	3.49	−.311	3.60
Tenure (years)	−.016	4.50	−.023	6.38
Earnings ($1,000) per year	.023	3.41	.024	3.14
Social Security Wealth ($10,000)	−.092	1.99	−.152	3.15
Pension Wealth ($10,000)	—	—	−.048	2.29
Pension on Current Job (0,1)	−.373	3.71	—	—
Mandatory Retirement on Job (0,1)	−.451	4.61	—	—

	Early vs. On Time			
B.	B	t-stat	B	t-stat
Constant	−4.104	11.43	−4.002	11.14
Years Away	.389	16.09	.395	16.31
Bad Health (0,1)	.277	3.13	.278	3.15
Tenure (years)	.009	2.57	.012	3.42
Earnings ($1,000) per year	−.014	1.79	−.019	2.09
Social Security Wealth ($10,000)	.052	1.05	.090	1.76
Pension Wealth ($10,000)	—	—	.043	2.03
Pension on Current Job (0,1)	.111	1.03	—	—
Mandatory Retirement on Job (0,1)	.364	3.64	—	—
Likelihood Ratio Index	.236		.222	
Percent Correctly Predicted	61.5		60.7	

pendent variables represent the importance of the variable in differentiating between an actual retirement age that is late and one that is on time. In the second equation (equation B) the coefficients represent the importance of that variable in differentiating between early and on time. We use two specifications, one which includes dichotomous variables mandatory retirement and pension eligibility, and another which substitutes pension wealth for these two dummy variables.

Many of the variables which appeared to be important in the cross-tabulations remain so in the multivariate equations. The most significant factor is years away—the number of years between 1969 and the planned retirement year. Those with a distant target are more likely to be early and less likely to be late. Bad health and long tenure on the job also encourage earlier than planned retirement and discourage a late exit. Despite the absence of any discernible pattern in Table 9, high potential earnings appears to increase the probability of a delay in retirement. As expected, high Social Security wealth decreases the likelihood of late retirement and increases the probability of withdrawal earlier than planned. One interpretation of these results is that those with higher Social Security wealth enjoyed the largest windfall gains in the early 1970s and responded to this unexpected change in circumstances by moving their retirement date forward.

In the first specification (column 1), pension eligibility and mandatory retirement are entered as dummy variables. Both significantly reduce the likelihood of late retirement, and mandatory retirement also increases the probability that a worker will retire early. In the second column, pension wealth is included, and behaves much like Social Security wealth—encouraging earlier and discouraging later retirement. This contradicts the inflation hypothesis, which would have predicted just the opposite, i.e., those with the most pension wealth lost the most because of the unexpected levels of inflation in the 1970s and therefore decided to delay their plans. An alternative explanation is that as the retirement date approached, people investigated the details of pension plans and discovered that even earlier treatment was to their financial advantage.[8]

VI. CONCLUSIONS

Previous work on retirement concentrated either on those factors affecting retirement plans or on actual retirement behavior. In this paper we have attempted to link these two aspects of the retirement decision by analyzing those factors which determine the accuracy of retirement plans. In our initial sample of workers, 55 percent retired either more than a year before or more than a year after their planned age. Yet the accuracy of plans within subgroups of our population was much more accurate. Those who planned to retire at a specific age were far more likely to hit that target than those who said they would never retire. The great majority of the latter retired during the 10 years following that statement. This may mean that the "work forever" response was often made without a great deal of thought.

Within the subgroup of workers who had a specific planned retirement age, we found that those who had been on the job since middle age and those with a mandatory retirement or pension on their job were more likely to be on time than to overshoot their target. Such findings are consistent with the argument that institutional aspects of the job facilitate a long-term contract between employees and employers with regard to work life. In addition, we found that subsequent health affects the accuracy of job plans. Those who suffered poor health at the time of their statement or later were more likely to retire earlier than anticipated. Those in consistently good health were more likely than others to delay their retirement beyond the anticipated date.

Using multinominal logit estimations we were able to show that the presence of a mandatory retirement age or pension plan on a job decreases the likelihood of overshooting a specific retirement age. In addition, it is likely that workers underestimated Social Security wealth in 1969 and that this may have induced earlier retirement.

Such results suggest that multiperiod models of retirement are necessary to capture the effect of institutional variables on the retirement decision. For many workers, especially those with long seniority on the job, the actual retirement decision is dependent on plans made years before. Nonetheless, it must be recognized that about one-third of the employed workers in our study (aged 58–63 in 1969) were not on the same job they held at age 50. Although some of these workers voluntarily left the job they had in their prime working years, others were bumped from their life cycle planning path by unexpected forces (such as plant closings, health changes, and so on). Such workers are much less accurate in their retirement plans. They could be a large subgroup for whom life cycle models, and their assumptions of perfect foresight, may be of little use in analyzing behavior.

Furthermore, even for workers in our sample who were on long-term jobs, their plans are not etched in stone. These plans often change over time, and in predictable ways in response to changes in health and financial circumstances. The latter are affected by public policy initiatives regarding Social Security and pension rules, and these labor market impacts should be included in the evaluation of legislative proposals.

APPENDIX: DEFINITION OF VARIABLES, AND MEAN VALUES FOR THE LOGIT EQUATIONS

Early (.24)	Early equals 1 if respondent's actual retirement age is less than one year prior to his stated retirement age in 1969; otherwise 0.
On time (.56)	On time equals 1 if respondent's actual retirement age is within one year of his stated retirement age in 1969; otherwise 0.
Late (.20)	Late equals 1 if respondent's actual retirement age is more than one year after his stated retirement age in 1969; otherwise 0.
On schedule (NA)	On schedule equals 1 if respondent's stated retirement age in 1969 has not been reached by 1979 and the person is still working; otherwise 0.
Bad health (.44)	Bad health equals 1 if respondent answers yes to the question, "Do you have a health condition that limits the kind or amount of work that you do?" in 1969 or in any other year prior to the earlier of either the year of expected retirement or the year of actual retirement; otherwise 0.
Mandatory retirement (.54)	Mandatory retirement equals 1 if respondent has a mandatory retirement age on his current job; otherwise 0.
Pension plan (.65)	Pension plan equals 1 if the respondent is eligible to receive a pension on his current job; otherwise 0.
Tenure (20.4)	Tenure is the number of years worked on respondent's current job.
Earnings ($8428)	Earnings are wage and salaries earnings on current job in 1968.
Social Security wealth ($21,450)	The present discounted value of all future Social Security benefits based on respondent's earning history through 1968. For a full discussion of the derivation of this variable, see Burkhauser and Quinn (1983b).
Private pension wealth ($21,337)	The present discount value of all future private pension benefits. For a full discussion of this variable, see Burkhauser and Quinn (1983b).

NOTES

1. See Burkhauser and Turner (1982) for an overview of this change in institutional arrangements in the workplace and Hatch (1981) or Kotlikoff and Smith (1983) for a detailed look at the current private pension structure in the United States.

2. By 1980, nearly 80 percent of men aged 70 were out of the labor force, along with 76 percent of those 68, 65 percent of 65, nearly half of men aged 63, and over a quarter of those aged 60. Retirement prior to age 65, a rare phenomenon only 30 years ago, is now the norm for American men. For a more detailed time series on labor force participation rates, see Quinn and Burkhauser (1983).

3. Individuals in the 1969 RHS but excluded here are females, self-employed workers, those not responding to questions concerning retirement plans, and those who died between 1969 and 1979.

4. The patterns for the short-term workers are similar. For those two or three years away, 54 percent were on time. This drops to only 9 percent in the 8+ category.

5. In explaining behavior, it is important to consider only circumstances which occurred prior to the behavior being explained. For example, a worker who planned to retire at 65 retires at 60. At 62, a health problem arises. Although he suffered bad health prior to the planned retirement age, this person should (and would) be in the "good health" column of Table 5. By looking at health status only up to the earlier of planned or actual retirement, we avoid the effects of retirement on health or of coincidental changes in health after the decision.

6. Social Security (or pension) wealth is the present discount value of the future stream of benefits a worker is eligible to receive evaluated at his current age.

7. Regression analysis is inappropriate when the dependent variable is dichotomous. The primary reason is that predicted values of the dependent variable (best interpreted as probabilities) are logically bounded by 0 and 1 whereas the predictions from a regression are not. In logit estimation, the impact of explanatory variables tapers off as the predicted probabilities near 0 or 1, and the predictions are thereby kept in the unit interval. Unfortunately, the estimated coefficients cannot be interpreted as first derivatives, as can regression coefficients. For more detail, see Kmenta (1971).

8. In separate logit equations not shown, we added pension wealth to our first logit equation and our pension dummy to our second logit equation. In both equations the pension dummy was highly significant but pension wealth was insignificant at the 5 percent level. Mandatory retirement continued to be significant at the 1 percent level.

REFERENCES

Barfield, Richard E. and James N. Morgan
    1969 Early Retirement: The Decision and the Experience. Ann Arbor, MI: University of Michigan, Institute for Social Research.

Burkhauser, Richard V. and Joseph F. Quinn
    1983a "Is mandatory retirement overrated? Evidence from the 1970s." Journal of Human Resources 18(3):337–358.
    1983b "The effect of pension plans on the pattern of life-cycle compensation." Pp. 395–415 in Jack E. Triplett (ed.), The Measure of Labor Cost: Conference on Research in Income and Wealth, Studies in Income and Wealth, Vol. 48. Chicago: University of Chicago Press, National Bureau of Economic Research.

Burkhauser, Richard V. and John Turner
    1978 "A time series analysis on Social Security and its effects on the market work of men at younger ages." Journal of Political Economy 18(4):701–716.
    1982 "Labor market experience of the almost old and the implications for income support." American Economic Review 72(2):304–308.

Clark, Robert, Juanita Kreps, and Joseph Spengler
    1978 "Economics of aging: a survey." Journal of Economic Literature 16(3):919–962.

Danziger, Sheldon, Robert Haveman, and Robert Plotnick
    1981 "How income transfers affect work, savings, and income distribution." Journal of Economic Literature 19(3):975–1028.

Goudy, Willis J.
    1982 "Antecedent factors related to changing work expectations." Research on Aging 4(2):139–157.

Hall, Arden and Terry Johnson
    1980 "The determinants of planned retirement age." Industrial and Labor Relations Review 33(2):241–254.

Hatch, Sara
- 1981 "Financial retirement incentives in private pension plans." Urban Institute Report to the Department of Labor, No. J-9-P-0-0163, September.

Irelan, Lola M.
- 1976 "Retirement history study: introduction." In Almost 65: Baseline Data from the Retirement History Study. Social Security Administration, Office of Research and Statistics, Research Report No. 49. Washington, DC: U.S. Government Printing Office.

Kmenta, Jan
- 1971 Elements of Econometrics. New York: MacMillan.

Kotlikoff, Laurence J. and Daniel E. Smith
- 1983 Pensions in the American Economy, Chicago: University of Chicago Press, National Bureau of Economic Research.

Lazear, Edward P.
- 1979 "Why is there mandatory retirement?" Journal of Political Economy 87(6):1261–1284.

Mitchell, Olivia and Gary Fields
- 1982 "The effects of pensions on retirement: a review essay." Pp. 115–155 in Ronald Ehrenberg (ed.), Research in Labor Economics, Vol. 5. Greenwich, CT: JAI Press.

Quinn, Joseph F.
- 1977 "Microeconomic determinants of early retirement: a cross-sectional view of white married men." Journal of Human Resources 12(3):329–346.
- 1982 "Pension wealth of government and private sector workers." American Economic Review 72(2):283–287.

Quinn, Joseph F. and Richard V. Burkhauser
- 1983 "Influencing retirement behavior: a key issue for social security." Journal of Policy Analysis and Management 3(1):1–13.

U.S. Department of Health, Education and Welfare, Social Security Administration
- 1976a "Reaching retirement age: findings from the Survey of Newly Entitled Beneficiaries 1968–1970." Washington, DC: U.S. Government Printing Office.
- 1976b Almost 65: Baseline Data from the Retirement History Survey. Office of Research and Statistics, Research Report No. 49. Washington, DC: U.S. Government Printing Office.

NONMARRIED WOMEN APPROACHING RETIREMENT:
WHO ARE THEY AND WHEN DO THEY RETIRE?

Gayle Thompson Rogers

ABSTRACT

The labor force participation and work lives of American women have increased substantially over the last few decades. Consequently, retirement from work has or will become a central life cycle event in many of their lives. This article examines women's retirement behavior and the personal and economic resources which they bring to that life period by studying the cohort of women entering retirement in the 1970s. Using data from the Retirement History Study, it compares men and nonmarried (formerly and never married) women with respect to their preretirement characteristics and when and why they retire. It thus provides a baseline with which to compare the behavior of future cohorts of retiring women.

As they approached retirement, the nonmarried women studied generally had less favorable preretirement labor market characteristics than men and, as a result, they had accumulated fewer financial resources to support them in retirement. Specifically, their shorter work lives, different occupational structures, and lower earnings were reflected in lower potential Social Security benefits and lower probability of second pension eligibility. Despite some expected improvements in women's occupations, earnings, and work lives, future cohorts of retiring women are likely to remain financially less well off in retirement than their male counterparts.

The nonmarried women studied were a little more likely than the men to retire at the earliest possible age. The factors related to retirement age, defined as the age at which Social Security benefits were first received, were about the same for nonmarried women as for men.

I. INTRODUCTION

Over the last few decades, American women have been entering the labor force in increasing numbers and staying for longer periods of time than ever before (Fullerton and Byrne, 1976; Bednarzik and Klein, 1977; Maymi, 1982; Smith, 1982). As a result, retirement from work is becoming a central life cycle event in the lives of many American women. More and more women approach late middle age with the need to make decisions about their own retirement from the world of work: decisions about their finances and living arrangements, decisions about when to retire and whether to retire completely or partially, and decisions about how to spend their leisure time.

One indication of the growing importance of retirement to women is the increasing proportion of them who are eligible for retired worker benefits under the Social Security program (Lingg, 1975). Persons are eligible for retired worker benefits if they have worked long enough in employment covered under the program. The specific amount of covered employment required depends on the year of birth. Aged women who are not eligible for their own worker benefits may qualify for benefits, either as wives or widows, on the basis of their husbands' work records. Between 1960 and 1978, the proportion of women beneficiaries who were receiving retired worker benefits rose from 43 to 54 percent. During the same period, the proportion receiving benefits only on the basis of their husbands' work records declined from 56 to 44 percent.

Women's retirement behavior and the personal and economic resources which they bring to that period of their lives have not been widely studied. This article contributes to knowledge in these areas by examining the cohort of women workers entering retirement in the 1970s and the ways in which they differ from men entering retirement at the same time. Specifically, it compares women and men with respect to (1) their preretirement labor force, financial, and health characteristics; (2) the age at which they retire; and (3) some of the economic factors related to their retirement timing decisions. It thus provides baseline data with which to compare data on future cohorts of retiring women. It also provides useful information to policymakers currently considering proposals to alter the nation's retirement income policy in general and the Social Security system in particular.

The analysis focuses on women who were not married at the time they retired, i.e., widowed, divorced, separated, and never married women. In 1970, 34 percent of the women aged 62-64 and 46 percent of those aged 65-72 were not married. In other words, many women enter their retirement years without the financial, social, and psychological support of husbands. Therefore, their economic resources and retirement decisions are important subjects for study.

Retirement can be defined in many ways. For this analysis, retirement is defined as the receipt of retired worker benefits under the Social Security program and therefore the analysis is restricted to data on persons eligible for such benefits. Persons are defined as retired if they have begun to collect these benefits even if they continue to work or return to work at a later time. Retirement age is defined as the age at which persons first begin to collect benefits and preretirement characteristics as those possessed at age 60-61. Under the Social Security program, retired worker benefits may be collected as early as age 62. If benefits are collected before age 65, however, they are actuarially reduced for each month collected. The maximum reduction is 20 percent. Benefits received after attainment of age 65 are increased for each month they are deferred up to age 72.

II. DATA AND SAMPLE

The data for this analysis are drawn from the Social Security Administration's Retirement History Study (RHS), a 10-year panel study of the retirement process. The sample consists of a national sample of men of all marital statuses and nonmarried women (widowed, never married, divorced, and separated) born in the years 1905-1911.[1]

The first interview was conducted in 1969 and reinterviews were held every other year through 1979.[2] In 1969, the sample was aged 58-63. By 1979, the survivors were aged 68-73.

This article focuses on the 4,751 persons who were under age 62 at the time of the first interview and who were eligible for retired worker benefits.[3] Eighty-two percent of these persons were men and 18 percent were women.

In order to obtain information on retired workers' characteristics at age 60-61, data were selected from the 1969 or 1971 interviews depending on the initial age of the sample person. Retired workers aged 62-63 in 1969 are excluded because baseline data concerning their preretirement characteristics are not available.

Although the RHS provides valuable information about retirement behavior, the sample does not include married women and represents a specific birth cohort entering retirement at a particular point in time, the 1970s. The characteristics of future cohorts of retiring women undoubtedly will differ to some extent because of such things as anticipated increases in the length of their work lifes and in the number eligible for retirement benefits from private pension plans.

III. PRERETIREMENT CHARACTERISTICS

The preretirement characteristics of the men and nonmarried women retiring in the 1970s differed substantially. This section examines these differences and discusses whether or not some of them may persist into the future. The characteristics examined are family characteristics (marital status, living arrangements, and support patterns); employment characteristics (employment status, extent of weekly employment, length of the work life, and work-limiting health conditions); job characteristics (occupation and earnings); pension characteristics (size of the Social Security benefit and eligibility for second pension benefits); and financial characteristics (assets and total money income).

A. Family Characteristics

The vast majority (88 percent) of the men were married. The remaining 12 percent were equally divided among the widowed, divorced or separated, and never married. Widows constituted the largest group of nonmarried women. Forty-five percent of the women were widows, 29 percent were divorced and separated, and 26 percent were never married.

Many of the formerly married women had been without a spouse for a substantial period of time. The median years without a spouse were 13 years for widows and 17 years for divorced and separated women (Table 1).

Although most of the men shared a household only with their wives and most of the nonmarried women lived alone, a substantial minority of both sexes (38 percent) shared living arrangements with others. Never-married women were the most likely and widows were the least likely to have lived with others.

Nonmarried women were much less likely than men to have been providing either partial or total financial support to children or parents. The proportions providing such support were 12 and 33 percent, respectively (a 21 percentage point difference). Few of either group were receiving financial support from children although nonmarried women, particularly the divorced and separated, were more likely to do so than men.

B. Employment and Pension Characteristics

As they neared retirement, the vast majority of men and nonmarried women were employed (Table 2). Nonmarried women, however, were somewhat less likely than men to have had jobs. Moreover, if employed, women were more

Table 1. Preretirement Family Characteristics by Sex and Marital Status of Nonmarried Women: Percentage Distributions

	Men	\multicolumn{4}{c}{Sex and Marital Status}
		\multicolumn{4}{c}{Nonmarried Women}
		All	Widowed	Divorced or Separated	Never Married
Length of marital status (in years)— ever married women:					
Number	—	—	316	181	—
Total percent	—	—	100	100	—
1–3	—	—	7	7	—
4–5	—	—	13	5	—
6–10	—	—	24	16	—
11–15	—	—	18	16	—
16–20	—	—	15	18	—
21 or more	—	—	22	37	—
Median	—	—	13	17	—
Living arrangements:					
Number	3,920	830	378	239	213
Total percent	100	100	100	100	100
Alone or with spouse only	61	61	65	60	54
1 additional person	22	24	22	24	29
2 additional persons	9	6	5	7	8
3 or more additional persons	7	8	8	9	9
Support given to children or parents:					
Number	3,866	827	376	237	214
Total percent	100	100	100	100	100
Neither	67	88	90	85	91
Parents only	6	6	4	5	9
Children only	25	5	5	9	0
Both	2	1	1	1	0
Support received from children:					
Number	3,890	827	376	237	214
Total percent	100	100	100	100	100
Yes	1	5	5	9	1
No	99	95	95	91	99

inclined to work on a part-time basis. Divorced and separated women were the most likely and never married women were the least likely of the women to work part time.

Although the RHS does not contain detailed questions about functional disability, its measure of work limitations provides some estimate of the effect of health on work and retirement behavior. It measures whether or not persons consider themselves limited in the amount or kind of work they can perform. Widows and never-married women, but not the divorced and separated, were

Table 2. Preretirement Employment Status, Extent of Weekly Employment, Length of Worklife, and Work Limitations by Sex and Marital Status of Nonmarried Women: Percentage Distribution

	Sex and Marital Status				
		Nonmarried Women			
	Men	All	Widowed	Divorced or Separated	Never Married
Employment status:					
Number	3,920	831	378	239	214
Total percent	100	100	100	100	100
Employed	90	85	87	84	85
Not employed	10	15	13	16	15
Extent of weekly employment— employed persons:[a]					
Number	3,350	683	318	192	173
Total percent	100	100	100	100	100
Full-time	94	85	86	79	91
Part-time	6	15	14	21	9
Years elapsed since last regular job— nonemployed persons:[b]					
Number	200	66	—	—	—
Total percent	100	100	—	—	—
Less than 1	22	18	—	—	—
1–2	36	33	—	—	—
3–5	24	15	—	—	—
6 or more	17	33	—	—	—
Years without work since age 21:[c]					
Number	3,220	646	301	180	165
Total percent	100	100	100	100	100
10 or less	97	61	49	57	86
11–20	2	19	22	22	11
21–30	0	15	22	16	2
31 or more	1	5	7	5	1
Work limitations:					
Number	3,920	831	378	239	214
Total percent	100	100	100	100	100
Not limited	75	80	83	72	84
Limited	25	20	17	28	16

[a] Full-time workers are those who worked 35 or more hours per week.
[b] Tabulated only for those aged 60–61 in 1969. Not shown by marital status of women due to small sample size.
[c] Measured as of 1975.

less likely than men to consider themselves work-limited. However, work limitations, when they existed, appeared to have had a greater impact on women's preretirement employment status than it did on men's (Table 3). Among work-

Table 3. Preretirement Employment Status by Work Limitations and Sex: Percentage Distributions

| | \multicolumn{4}{c}{Work Limitations and Sex} |
Employment Status	Men Not Limited	Men Limited	Nonmarried Women Not Limited	Nonmarried Women Limited
Number	2,955	965	686	173
Total percent	100	100	100	100
Not employed	6	21	11	32
Employed	94	79	89	68

limited persons, 32 percent of the nonmarried women compared with 21 percent of the men were not employed.

For some without jobs, the nonwork status was temporary but for others it was of long duration (Rogers, 1983). The time elapsed since nonworkers had last held a regular job was longer for nonmarried women than for men. To illustrate, 33 percent of the women compared with 17 percent of the men without jobs at age 60–61 had not had a regular job for six or more years. The longer nonwork period of women may be partly due to the fact that some of them had only recently lost their husbands' earning power.

Regardless of employment status, nonmarried women had substantially shorter work lives than men. Few of the men (3 percent) had been without work for more than 10 of the years since they were aged 21 whereas a substantial proportion (39 percent) of the women had been without work for that long. Twenty percent of the women had been without work for 21 or more years. Never-married women had longer work lives than other nonmarried women. The length of their work life more closely resembled that of men than that of other nonmarried women. Widows had the shortest work lives.

Substantial occupational differences existed between the men and nonmarried women entering retirement in the 1970s (Table 4). A majority of the men working just prior to retirement age (57 percent) were employed in three occupational categories: managerial, craft, and operative occuptions. Nonmarried women, on the other hand, were concentrated in two traditionally female categories: the clerical and service occupations. Fifty-four percent of the women were employed in these two occupations, 28 percent as clerical workers and 26 percent as service workers. Never-married women, on the other hand, were more likely than any of the other groups, including the men, to have been professional workers.

Occupational differences between men and women are reflected in earnings differences. Nonmarried women, regardless of marital status, earned much less than men. Seventy-eight percent of the working women compared with 44 percent of the working men, a 34 percentage point difference, had earnings below

Table 4. Preretirement Occupation and Annual Earnings
Among Employed Persons by Sex and Marital Status of Nonmarried Women:
Percentage Distributions

		\multicolumn{4}{c}{Sex and Marital Status}
		\multicolumn{4}{c}{Nonmarried Women}
Occupation and Earnings	Men	All	Widowed	Divorced or Separated	Never Married
Occupation:					
Number	3,513	705	323	200	182
Total percent	100	100	100	100	100
White-collar workers:					
Professional and technical	9	15	12	12	23
Managerial and administrative	18	7	7	5	8
Clerical	5	28	32	18	33
Sales	4	7	5	6	9
Blue-collar workers:					
Craftsman	22	1	2	2	0
Operative	17	14	18	13	11
Nonfarm laborers	6	1	1	2	3/
Service workers	9	26	23	41	15
Farmworkers	10	1	3/	3/	1
Annual earnings:[a]					
Number	3,342	683	313	195	175
Total percent	100	100	100	100	100
1st quartile	20	48	44	59	40
2nd quartile	24	30	35	25	30
3rd quartile	28	15	16	13	17
4th quartile	28	7	5	3	13
Median[b]	$7,060	$4,450	$4,560	$3,940	$4,920

[a]Quartiles were determined from the earnings distribution of all retired workers studied. The quartile limits (in 1968 dollars) are: $4,320, $6,500, and $9,050.
[b]In 1968 dollars.
[c]Less than one percent.

the median for all retired workers studied. A great many of the women had earnings in the lowest quartile. Among women, the divorced and separated were the most likely and the never married were the least likely to have had earnings that low.

In the population as a whole, some women are moving into traditionally male-dominated fields. Nevertheless, the majority of women workers remain employed in traditionally female occupations. The proportion employed as clerical or service workers has not changed over the last few decades. In 1960, the proportion of women employed in these two occupations was 54 percent. In 1979, it was 55 percent (Maymi, 1982:198). Moreover, today's young women workers are about as likely as older women to be employed in these two occupations. In 1979, 50 percent of working women aged 30–39 compared with 53 percent aged 40–49 and 54 percent aged 50–59 were clerical or service workers.

Even when women are employed in the same broad occupation group as men (e.g., in professional jobs), they tend to hold lower status and lower earning positions. Among professional workers, for example, women predominate in elementary and secondary school teaching, registered nursing, social work, libraries, dietetics, physical therapy, and dental hygiene. Men, on the other hand, predominate among university educators, doctors, lawyers, engineers, and in many other prestigious, better paying occupations. There was little change in this situation over the 30-year period from 1940 to 1970 (Waldman and McEaddy, 1974). Given the relatively stable character of women's occupational structure, the occupational distribution of future cohorts of retiring women are not likely to change for some time.

Among year-round, full-time workers, women's earnings have remained at about 60 percent those of men for at least the last 25 years (Maymi, 1982:201). Given the fact that today's young women are about as likely as older women to work in female-dominated occupations, where earnings levels are generally lower than in traditionally male or heterogeneous occupations (Maymi, 1982:202), the male–female earnings differential will persist for some time. Thus, future cohorts of retiring women will continue to be less well off than their male counterparts with respect to earnings and aspects of retirement income which are a function of earnings.

Among persons retiring in the 1970s, sex and marital status differences in length of the work-life, earnings and occupation are reflected in differences in the size of Social Security benefits and eligibility for benefits from second pensions (Table 5).[4] The Social Security primary insurance amount (PIA) is the monthly amount payable to retired workers taking benefits at age 65. It is reduced for early retirement and increased for retirement after age 65. The size of the PIA is dependent on two factors: (1) length of time worked in employment covered by Social Security and (2) size of earnings. Because women have both shorter work lives and lower earnings than men, they have lower PIAs. In the sample studied, divorced and separated women had the lowest PIAs. As expected, given their comparatively longer work lives and higher earnings, never married women had higher PIAs than other nonmarried women. Nevertheless, like other women, their PIAs were below those of men.

Retired persons who receive benefits from second pension plans as well as from Social Security have substantially higher retirement income, a much lower probability of poverty, and a higher replacement of their preretirement earnings than those who receive Social Security benefits only (Fox, 1982). To be eligible for second pension benefits, workers must first be employed on jobs where pension plans are available. Once covered under plans, they must work long enough under them to qualify for benefits at retirement age.

Table 5. Social Security Primary Insurance Amount (PIA) and Eligibility for Second Pension Benefits by Sex and Marital Status of Nonmarried Women: Percent Distributions

		Sex and Marital Status			
			Nonmarried Women		
PIA and Second Pension Eligibility	Men	All	Widowed	Divorced or Separated	Never Married
Primary insurance amount (PIA):[a]					
Number	3,900	807	370	237	200
Total percent	100	100	100	100	100
1st quartile	22	41	36	55	31
2nd quartile	24	30	34	24	29
3rd quartile	27	16	16	14	18
4th quartile	27	13	14	7	22
Eligibility for second pension benefits:					
Number	3,920	831	378	239	214
Total percent	100	100	100	100	100
Not eligible	47	59	59	70	47
Eligible	53	41	41	30	53
At age 62 or earlier	41	30	27	21	46
After age 62	12	11	14	9	7

[a]The PIA is measured as of December 1978. The quartiles are determined from the distribution of all retired workers. The quartile limits are $246, $338, and $380.

Prior to passage of the Employee Retirement Income Security Act (ERISA) of 1974, there were no federally mandated vesting requirements[5] for private pension plans, and therefore persons with long service under plans could become ineligible for benefits if they left their jobs and plans prior to retirement age. In 1969, for example, 30 percent of the active participants in plans with 26 or more participants were in plans requiring 11–15 years of service for vesting and 11 percent were in plans requiring 16 or more years (Davis and Strasser, 1970:49). Since the birth cohort studied in this article attained requirement age before 1974, their work lives occurred prior to the imposition of federal vesting standards for private pensions by ERISA.

Women are more likely than men to be employed on jobs where pension plans are uncommon (Beller, 1981; Rogers, 1980). Moreover, once covered, women have shorter service under their plans and, therefore, are less likely than men to attain vested status and be eligible for benefits when they retire (Rogers, 1981b:25).

In the birth cohort studied, 41 percent of the nonmarried women compared with 53 percent of the men were eligible for a second pension in addition to Social Security benefits. The longer work life of never-married women is reflected in the fact that they were much more likely to be eligible for second pension benefits than widows or divorced and separated women. In fact, the proportion of never married women eligible for such benefits was identical to that of men.

Because of the continuing lengthening of the work life among women and the lowering of vesting requirements in private pension plans following the passage of ERISA, the male–female gap in the size of Social Security benefits and in second pension eligibility may close somewhat for future cohorts of retirees. Differences probably will continue to exist for some time, however, because women still work fewer years and because the majority, despite some advances, remain employed in traditionally female industries and occupations where earnings and the probability of second pension coverage are comparatively low.

C. Financial Characteristics

Social Security benefits are intended to provide a "floor" of income protection in retirement. Therefore, these benefits are likely to need supplementation from second pension benefits and income from personal savings if persons wish to maintain or approximate their preretirement standards of living. Among persons reaching retirement age in the early 1970s, women, as noted earlier, were less likely than men to have been eligible for second pension benefits. They also had accumulated fewer assets.

With respect to home ownership, women were less likely than men to have owned their own homes (Table 6). Only 47 percent of the women compared with 78 percent of the men, a 31 percentage point difference, had acquired equity in their homes.

Although women were about as likely as men to have received income from their asset holdings, they had accumulated fewer financial assets[6] and, therefore, they received less income from those assets (Table 7). Regardless of marital status, substantially more of them had assets falling in the first quartile.

The asset position of divorced and separated women was particularly poor.

Table 6. Percent Owning Home and Percent Receiving Income from Assets by Sex and Marital Status of Nonmarried Women

		Sex and Marital Status			
			Nonmarried Women		
Assets	*Men*	*All*	*Widowed*	*Divorced or Separated*	*Never Married*
Percent owning home	78	47	54	40	42
Percent receiving income from assets	58	54	55	46	65

Table 7. Size of Preretirement Assets and Total Money Income by Sex and Marital Status of Women: Percentage Distributions

		Sex and Marital Status			
			Nonmarried Women		
Assets and Total Income[a]	Men	All	Widowed	Divorced or Separated	Never Married
Financial assets:					
Number	2,951	646	290	199	157
Total percent	100	100	100	100	100
1st quartile	21	43	39	54	35
2nd quartile	24	29	33	27	26
3rd quartile	26	18	16	14	24
4th quartile	28	10	12	5	15
Income from assets (recipients only):[b]	1,914	365	166	93	106
Number	1,914	365	166	93	106
Total percent	100	100	100	100	100
1st quartile	27	30	30	40	22
2nd quartile	22	25	27	17	27
3rd quartile	24	25	22	28	28
4th quartile	26	20	21	15	23
Total money income[b]					
Number	3,182	671	308	193	170
Total percent	100	100	100	100	100
1st quartile	21	46	42	53	39
2nd quartile	23	32	37	29	29
3rd quartile	27	14	15	14	16
4th quartile	29	8	6	4	16

[a] The quartiles were determined from the distribution of all retired workers. The quartile limits, in 1968 dollars, are as follows: financial assets—$2,350, $8,600, and $21,620; income from assets—$100, $300, and $900; total money income—$3,800, $6,280, and $9,120.
[b] Income of individuals, not families.

They were less likely to have owned their own homes than either men or widows. In addition, they had accumulated fewer financial assets than any of the other groups studied and they received less income from those assets.

Nonmarried women have been shown to be worse off in labor market terms than men and to approach retirement with fewer assets. It thus is no surprise to find that their overall preretirement financial status, as measured by total money income, was substantially below that of men. Forty-eight percent of the women had total incomes in the lowest quartile of the distribution of the retired workers studied and an additional 32 percent had incomes in the next to lowest quartile. The comparable proportions for men were 21 and 23 percent, respectively. As with most of the other characteristics examined, the divorced and separated were the most disadvantage and the never married the least disadvantaged of the women.

IV. WHEN AND WHY WOMEN AND MEN RETIRE

A. Retirement Age

Retirement age is defined as the age at which persons first begin to collect Social Security retired worker benefits. In other words, it is defined in terms of benefit receipt, not work stoppage. Some persons stop work permanently when they begin to receive benefits whereas others may stop temporarily and then return at a later time. Some continue to work. Still others may not be working just before they collect benefits. Benefit receipt at ages 62–64 is referred to as early retirement and receipt at age 65 as normal retirement.

Nonmarried women retired at about the same age as men although they were a little more likely to retire at the earliest possible age, age 62 (Table 8). The majority of both groups, 61 percent of the nonmarried women[7] and 58 percent of the men, retired early. About one-fourth of each group retired at age 65. Few of either group deferred retirement until age 68 or later.

The retirement age distribution of nonmarried women varied by marital status. Although a majority of all nonmarried women retired early, regardless of marital status, widows were less likely to have retired at that time than never-married or divorced and separated women. Fifty-four percent of the widows as compared with 65 and 70 percent of the other two groups of women elected benefits at age 62–64.

Table 8. Age at Retirement by Sex and Marital Status of Nonmarried Women: Percentage Distributions

		\multicolumn{4}{c}{*Sex and Marital Status*}
		\multicolumn{4}{c}{*Nonmarried Women*}
Age at Retirement	Men	All	Widowed	Divorced or Separated	Never Married
Number	3,920	831	378	239	214
Total percent	100	100	100	100	100
62	31	37	29	48	36
63–64	27	24	25	22	29
65	26	25	29	20	25
66–67	9	10	14	6	7
68 or older	6	3	3	4	3

The remainder of this section examines some of the factors related to why men and nonmarried women reaching retirement in the 1970s retired when they did, with special emphasis on early retirement.[8] Attention is also given to the question of whether nonmarried women retired in response to the same influences as men and, if so, if those influences carry the same weight. The predictor variables examined are employment status just prior to age eligibility for retired worker benefits and, among the employed, size of the PIA[9] and preretirement earnings, work limitations, size of financial assets, and eligibility for second pension benefits.

B. Reasons for Retirement

Given the fact that many nonworkers had been without work for some time, it is not surprising that they were much more likely to elect benefits before age 65 than those who had jobs (Table 9). The effect of employment status on retirement age is about the same for nonmarried women as for men. Among nonemployed persons, 76 percent of the men and 77 percent of the nonmarried women took benefits at the earliest possible age and an additional 14 percent of both sexes took them at ages 63–64.

An earlier analysis of these data (Rogers, 1983) showed that about one-fifth to one-fourth of the nonemployed women and men were receiving second pension benefits. The availability of these benefits may have enabled them to retire before Social Security benefits become available. The vast majority of nonemployed men and women, however, were not receiving these benefits. Many of

Table 9. Age at Retirement
by Preretirement Employment Status and Sex:
Percentage Distributions

Age at Retirement	Men Not Employed	Men Employed	Nonmarried Women Not Employed	Nonmarried Women Employed
Number	392	3,528	133	726
Total percent	100	100	100	100
62	76	26	77	30
63–64	14	29	14	26
65	5	29	4	29
66–67	3	9	3	11
68 or older	2	7	2	4
	tau c = .191 $p < .001$		tau c = .262 $p < .001$	

these nonrecipients had health problems which, in their view, interfered with their ability to work. The financial status of the nonrecipients, particularly the work-limited, was substantially below that of pension recipients and employed persons. In short, many of these men and women without jobs were either physically or financially disadvantaged.

Among those who had jobs just prior to their age eligibility for retired worker benefits, earnings, financial assets, and PIA were all positively related to retirement age (Tables 10–12). The nature and magnitude of these relationships were the same for nonmarried women as for men. The multiple R^2 indicates that these three financial characteristics, all of which are interrelated, together account for 22 percent of the variance in retirement age among nonmarried women and 17 percent of the variance among men.

Persons at the upper ends of the earnings, PIA, and asset distributions were less likely to retire early than those at the lower ends. The major retirement age differences occurred between those falling in the lowest quartile of each of the three financial variables and those falling above that point. In other words, the most financially disadvantaged workers—those with the lowest earnings, the fewest assets, and the lowest potential Social Security benefits—retired the earliest.

The relationship between earnings and retirement age among men illustrates this point. Forty-five percent of the men whose earnings fell in the lowest quartile compared with 19–23 percent of those with earnings in the other three

Table 10. Age at Retirement Among Employed Persons by Preretirement Earnings[a] and Sex: Percentage Distributions

	\multicolumn{8}{c}{Earnings and Sex}
	\multicolumn{4}{c}{Men}	\multicolumn{4}{c}{Nonmarried Women}
Age at Retirement	1st quartile	2nd quartile	3rd quartile	4th quartile	1st quartile	2nd quartile	3rd quartile	4th quartile
Number	676	813	921	932	336	212	105	47
Total percent	100	100	100	100	100	100	100	100
62	45	22	23	19	42	21	23	—[b]
63–64	29	34	27	25	29	24	22	—[b]
65	18	31	33	30	21	35	36	—[b]
66–67	4	9	11	12	6	16	11	—[b]
68 or older	3	4	5	14	1	4	8	—[b]
	\multicolumn{4}{c}{tau c = .200}	\multicolumn{4}{c}{tau c = .219}
	\multicolumn{4}{c}{p < .001}	\multicolumn{4}{c}{p < .001}

[a]The quartiles were determined from the distribution of all retired workers. The quartile limits, in 1968 dollars, are $4,320, $6,500, and $9,050.
[b]Not shown: base fewer than 50 persons.

Table 11. Age at Retirement Among Employed Persons by PIA[a] and Sex: Percentage Distributions

	\multicolumn{8}{c}{PIA and Sex}
	\multicolumn{4}{c}{Men}	\multicolumn{4}{c}{Nonmarried Women}
Age at Retirement	1st quartile	2nd quartile	3rd quartile	4th quartile	1st quartile	2nd quartile	3rd quartile	4th quartile
Number	676	796	990	1,050	246	224	124	113
Total percent	100	100	100	100	100	100	100	100
62	45	33	34	2	52	25	19	3
63–64	28	37	36	16	28	34	23	14
65	16	24	23	45	15	32	38	42
66–67	7	4	5	19	3	8	18	25
68 or older	4	2	2	18	2	1	2	16
	\multicolumn{4}{c}{tau c = .380}	\multicolumn{4}{c}{tau c = .399}
	\multicolumn{4}{c}{p < .001}	\multicolumn{4}{c}{p < .001}

[a]The PIA is measured as of December 1978. The quartiles were determined from the distribution of all retired workers. The quartile limits, are $246, $338, and $380.

Table 12. Age at Retirement Among Employed Persons by Financial Assets[a] and Sex: Percentage Distributions

	\multicolumn{8}{c}{Financial Assets and Sex}
	\multicolumn{4}{c}{Men}	\multicolumn{4}{c}{Nonmarried Women}
Age at Retirement	1st quartile	2nd quartile	3rd quartile	4th quartile	1st quartile	2nd quartile	3rd quartile	4th quartile
Number	519	657	713	761	227	169	103	52
Total percent	100	100	100	100	100	100	100	100
62	37	28	24	24	42	30	26	21
63–64	31	29	28	25	26	30	21	27
65	22	31	30	29	21	30	34	38
66–67	6	8	13	10	7	8	14	8
68 or older	4	4	5	12	3	2	5	6
	\multicolumn{4}{c}{tau c = .121}	\multicolumn{4}{c}{tau c = .146}
	\multicolumn{4}{c}{p < .001}	\multicolumn{4}{c}{p < .001}

[a]The quartiles were determined from the distribution of all retired workers, including those with zero amounts. The quartile limits, in 1968 dollars, are $2,350, $8,600, and $21,620.

Women Approaching Retirement

quartiles retired as soon as they became eligible for benefits. Stated differently, the lowest earners were twice as likely as higher earners to retire at age 62.

Two factors probably contribute to the positive relationship between earnings and retirement age. The first is the progressive nature of the Social Security benefit computation formula, which, together with other features of the program, results in a much higher replacement of preretirement earnings for low than for high earners. Therefore, all other things being equal, high earners experience a much more drastic drop in their standard of living when they retire and have a greater incentive to remain at work longer.

The second potential contributing factor is the Social Security earnings test. The earnings test specifies the amount of earnings that can be received by persons under age 70 (under age 72 from 1954 through 1982) before benefits are withheld. The earnings test limit in effect at the time most of the cohort under study reached retirement age was $1,680. Persons earning that amount or less received their full Social Security benefit. Those earning over $1,680, however, had $1 of benefits withheld for each $2 of earnings between $1,680 and $2,880 and $2 of benefits withheld for each $2 of earnings over $2,880. Since persons earning under the earnings test limits can continue to earn the same amount at retirement and still receive their full Social Security benefit, they have an obvious incentive to take benefits at the earliest possible age. Persons earning substantially above the earnings test limit, however, cannot continue to earn at that level and receive benefits. Therefore, their retirement age decision is influenced by other factors such as the earnings replacement rate, the availability of other types of retirement income, health, and social-psychological factors such as pleasant work environment, control over the work flow, and attachment to work.

Before retirement, men were less likely than nonmarried women to have earned below or just above the earnings test limit. Four percent of the men compared with 11 percent of the women had preretirement earnings lower than $1,681. The proportions with earnings of $1,681–2,880 were 5 and 9 percent, respectively.

The effect of the earnings test on retirement age is partially illustrated by the data in Table 13. Among women, 64 and 54 percent of those with preretirement earnings under $1,681 and $1,681–$2,880, respectively, compared with 29 percent earning between $2,880 and the upper limit of the lowest earnings quartile retired as soon as possible. Stated differently, women earning under or near the earnings test limit were two to three times more likely to take benefits at age 62 than all other women.

Work limitations and second pension eligibility also had a bearing on the retirement age of men and women who were working just before attaining age 62. As expected, persons who in their opinion had health problems which interfered with their ability to work retired earlier than those who did not have these problems (Table 14). Although the nature and magnitude of the relationship

Table 13. Age at Retirement Among Employed Persons
with Preretirement Earnings in the Lowest Quartile by Earnings (in 1968 dollars)
and Sex: Percentage Distributions

| | Earnings and Sex ||||||
| Age at Retirement | Men ||| Nonmarried Women |||
	Under $1,681	$1,681– $2,880	$2,880– $4,320	Under $1,681	$1,681– $2,880	$2,880– $4,320
Number	130	169	377	76	65	195
Total percent	100	100	100	100	100	100
62	58	55	36	64	54	29
63–64	23	27	33	21	22	34
65	14	11	23	11	18	27
66–67	4	5	4	3	3	9
68 or older	1	2	4	1	3	1

between work limitations and retirement age was about the same for nonmarried women as for men, work-limited women were more likely to retire early than their male counterparts. Fifty-one percent of the work limited women compared with 38 percent of the work limited men retired at age 62.

Regardless of sex, the retirement age structure of persons not eligible for second pension benefits is somewhat similar to that of persons eligible for those benefits at age 62 or earlier although the ineligibles, particularly among women, tended to retire earlier (Table 15). Both of these groups retired much earlier than

Table 14. Age at Retirement Among Employed Persons
by Work Limitations and Sex: Percentage Distributions

| | Work Limitations and Sex ||||
| Age at Retirement | Men || Nonmarried Women ||
	Not Limited	Limited	Not Limited	Limited
Number	2,770	758	608	118
Total percent	100	100	100	100
62	23	38	26	51
63–64	29	29	27	22
65	29	25	30	19
66–67	10	6	12	6
68 or older	8	2	4	2
	tau c = −.144		tau c = −.154	
	p < .001		p < .001	

Table 15. Age at Retirement Among Employed Persons by Second Pension Eligibility and Sex: Percentage Distribution

		Second Pension Eligibility and Sex						
			Eligible				Eligible	
Age at Retirement	Not Eligible	All	After 62	At 62 or Earlier	Not Eligible	All	After 62	At 62 or Earlier
Number	1,639	1,889	445	1,444	409	317	89	228
Total percent	100	100	100	100	100	100	100	100
62	30	23	10	27	35	23	13	27
63–64	29	29	30	28	25	29	18	33
65	23	33	36	32	25	33	36	32
66–67	10	9	12	8	11	11	22	7
68	8	6	11	5	4	4	10	1
		$x^2 = 118.08$ $p < .001$				$x^2 = 50.3$ $p < .001$		

those who were eligible for benefits but not until after age 62. Among women, for example, 35 percent of those ineligible for benefits and 27 percent of those eligible at age 62 or earlier compared with 13 percent eligible after age 62 retired at the earliest possible age.

The relationship between second pension eligibility and retirement age becomes clearer when one considers the relationship between eligibility and earnings. Those ineligible for second pension benefits cluster in the lowest two earnings quartiles, particularly in the lowest, whereas those eligible for second pension benefits cluster in the highest two quartiles (Table 16). The retirement age of those ineligible for benefits may be affected by the fact that many in this

Table 16. Preretirement Earnings by Second Pension Benefits: Percentage Distribution Among Employed Persons

	Second Pension Eligibility		
Earnings	Not Eligible	Eligible After Age 62	Eligible at Age 62 or Earlier
Number	1,907	521	1,614
Total percent	100	100	100
1st quartile	42	15	8
2nd quartile	26	33	22
3rd quartile	16	27	36
4th quartile	16	24	34

group have very low earnings, some under the earnings test limit, and that low earners receive a moderate replacement of their preretirement earnings from Social Security.[10] Because many of those who are eligible for second pension benefits are high earners and thus receive a comparatively low replacement of their earnings from Social Security, they may not feel financially able to retire until those benefits are available to supplement their Social Security.

V. SUMMARY AND CONCLUSIONS

Work has become an integral part of many American women's lives over the last few decades. As more and more women enter the labor force and remain there for substantial portions of their lives, retirement from work and planning for the social-psychological and financial effects of that event will become increasingly important to them. Therefore, it is necessary that we understand the personal and economic resources which today's older women bring to retirement and how these may change over the next few decades as today's women enter that period of their lives. This is particularly important in view of changes in the retirement age under Social Security.

In order to provide baseline data against which to compare future cohorts of retiring women and estimate the effects of the various proposals to alter retirement behavior, this article has examined the characteristics of women retiring in the 1970s. Its specific objective was to compare men and nonmarried women with respect to (1) their preretirement family, health, labor force, and financial characteristics; (2) their retirement age; and (3) factors related to their retirement timing decision. Retirement age was defined as the age at which persons eligible for retired worker benefits under the Social Security program first began to collect those benefits.

As they approached retirement, nonmarried women were less likely to have been employed than men and, if employed, they were less likely to have worked full time. Among the employed, nonmarried women had shorter work lives than men and, because they were concentrated in traditionally female occupations, they had lower earnings. Their shorter work lives, occupational structure, and lower earnings were reflected in the fact that they had lower Society Security benefits than men and were less likely to have been eligible for second pension benefits. The same characteristics may also have resulted in their having accumulated fewer assets than men. In short, the more unfavorable labor market characteristics of women resulted in their having fewer financial resources to support them in retirement.

Whether tomorrow's cohorts of nonmarried women will fare any better in retirement depends in part on their labor market behavior. If they move into industries and occupations where earnings and the probability of second pension coverage are high and if they remain in the labor market for most of their adult lives, then the financial resources which they bring to retirement probably will be comparable to those of men. Women have increased their work lives considerably over the last few decades and some have moved into traditionally male occupations. Moreover, because of ERISA their chances of acquiring vested rights to their pension benefits have increased. Despite these improvements, however, women still have shorter work lives than men and remain primarily employed in female-dominated occupations and industries. As a result, their earnings and their chances of participating in second pension plans remain substantially below those of men. Therefore, when retired, they are likely to be in an improved but still less advantageous financial position than men.

Nonmarried women retired at about the same age as men although they were a little more likely to have retired at age 62. The majority of both sexes retired before age 65 and few waited until age 68 or later.

Retirement timing was related to employment status, earnings, financial assets, Social Security benefits, work limitations, and second pension eligibility. The nature and magnitude of these relationships were about the same for nonmarried women as for men.

As expected, the nonemployed, the vast majority of whom were work-limited or financially disadvantaged, were much more likely to retire early than the employed. Among persons with jobs just prior to their eligibility for retired worker benefits, the most disadvantaged—those with the lowest earnings, the lowest Social Security benefits, and the fewest assets and those ineligible for second pension benefits or work-limited—retired the earliest. The exception to this general rule is found among those who were eligible for second pension benefits at age 62 or earlier.

ACKNOWLEDGMENT

This article was written by the author in her private capacity. No official support or endorsement by the Social Security Administration is intended or should be inferred.

NOTES

1. For more details on the RHS and for preliminary analyses, See Irelan (1976).

2. Initial interviews were obtained from 11,153 persons and final interviews from 6,243 persons. Of those not completing a 1979 interview, 2,854 had died during the survey and 2,056 had dropped out for other reasons. According to Goudy (1982:i), the RHS "is relatively free of bias caused by respondent attrition."

3. Excluded are (1) retired workers for whom retirement age could not be calculated because of a missing or incorrect date of birth; (2) those who converted to retired worker status from another beneficiary type, e.g., from disabled worker; and (3) women who married between sample selection and ages 60–61.

4. Second pensions are defined as private and government employee pensions and military retirement pensions.

5. The term "vesting" refers to the nonforfeitable rights of employees to receive benefits based

on employer contributions, i.e., rights to benefits even if the employees should cease active participation in their plans prior to retirement age.

6. Financial assets include U.S. savings bonds, checking and savings accounts, stocks, bonds, mutual funds, and money owed by others. For a detailed discussion of the asset holdings of men and women RHS sample members, see Sherman (1976).

7. Mallan's Study (1974) of women in approximately the same birth cohort showed a higher proportion of women (70 percent) retiring early. Her results undoubtedly reflect the inclusion of married women in the sample.

8. For a discussion of the literature on the retirement decision, see Clark and Barker (1981:20–51).

9. The PIA was measured as of December 1978 and was obtained for all persons eligible for retired worker benefits, including those who had not claimed benefits by that date.

10. Fox (1982) estimated that Social Security alone replaces 49 percent of the preretirement earnings of men in the lowest earnings quintile and 21 percent of those in the highest quintile. The replacement rate for the highest earning men is estimated at 47 percent for those receiving both Social Security and second pension benefits, however.

REFERENCES

Bednarzik, Robert W. and Deborah P. Klein
  1977 "Labor force trends: a synthesis and analysis." Monthly Labor Review 100(10:3–12.
Beller, Daniel J.
  1981 "Coverage patterns of full-time employees under private retirement plans." Social Security Bulletin 44(7):3–12.
Clark, Robert L. and David T. Barker
  1981 Reversing the Trend toward Early Retirement. Washington, D.C.: American Enterprise Institute for Public Policy Research.
Davis, Harry E. and Arnold Strasser
  1970 "Private pension plans, 1960 to 1969—an overview." Monthly Labor Review 93(7):45–56.
Fox, Alan
  1982 "Earnings replacement rates and total income: findings from the Retirement History Study." Social Security Bulletin 45(10):3–23.
Fullerton, Howard N., Jr. and James J. Byrne
  1976 "Length of working life for men and women, 1970." Monthly Labor Review 99(2):31–35.
Goudy, Willis J.
  1982 The Retirement History Study: Two Methodological Examinations of the Data. Ames, Iowa: Sociological Studies in Aging, Department of Sociology and Anthropology, Iowa State University, Sociology Report 151.
Irelan, Lola M.
  1976 "Retirement history study: an introduction." Pp. 1–6 in Irelan, et al., Almost 65: Baseline Data from the Retirement History Study. Washington, D.C.: U.S. Department of Health, Education, and Welfare, Social Security Administration, Office of Research and Statistics, Research Report No. 49.
Lingg, Barbara A.
  1975 "Women Social Security beneficiaries aged 62 and older, 1960–74." Research and Statistics Note. Washington, D.C.: U.S. Department of Health, Education, and Welfare, Social Security Administration, Office of Research and Statistics, DHEW Pub. No. (SSA) 75-11701.

Mallan, Lucy B.
   1974   "Women born in the early 1900's: employment, earnings, and benefit levels." Social Security Bulletin 37(3):3–25.

Maymi, Carmen R.
   1982   "Women in the labor force." Pp. 181–205 in Phyllis W. Berman and Estelle R. Ramey (eds.), Women: A Developmental Perspective. Bethesda, Md.: U.S. Department of Health and Human Services, Public Health Service, National Institute of Health, NIH Publication No. 82-2298.

Rogers, Gayle Thompson
   1980   Pension Coverage and Vesting Among Private Wage and Salary Workers, 1979: Preliminary Estimates From the 1979 Survey of Pension Plan Coverage. Washington, D.C.: Social Security Administration, Office of Policy, Office of Research and Statistics, Working Paper No. 16.
   1981a   "Aged widows and OASDI: age at and economic status before and after receipt of benefits." Social Security Bulletin 44(3):3–19.
   1981b   "Vesting of private pension benefits in 1979 and change from 1972." Social Security Bulletin 44(7):13–30.
   1983   "Characteristics of retired workers: a comparison of early, normal, and late retirees under Social Security." Unpublished.

Sherman, Sally R.
   1976   "Assets on the threshold of retirement." Pp. 69–81 in Lola M. Irelan, et al., Almost 65: Baseline Data from the Retirement History Study. Washington, D.C.: U.S. Department of Health, Education, and Welfare, Social Security Administration, Office of Research and Statistics, Research Report No. 49.

Smith, Shirley J.
   1982   "New worklife estimates reflect changing profile of labor force." Monthly Labor Review 105(3):15–20.

Waldman, Elizabeth and Beverly J. McEaddy
   1974   "Where women work—an analysis by industry and occupation." Monthly Labor Review 97(5):124–134.

WORK AND RETIREMENT AMONG THE BLACK ELDERLY

James S. Jackson and Rose C. Gibson

ABSTRACT

This chapter explores the premise that the lifetime labor force experiences of black Americans may have both negative and positive effects on the retirement process. Retirement status for many blacks, while characterized by relatively low socioeconomic conditions, provides a stability of income and relief from the exigencies of life in an unfavorable labor market. The economic, labor force, and retirement literatures related to blacks are reviewed.

An analysis of the first full national probability sample of the black elderly reveals that many blacks must work well into older age because of poor early work experiences and inadequate resources for retirement. These data suggest that past and present work conditions may even affect the manner in which retirement is subjectively defined and experienced. Older black workers, although better off financially, are less well off psychologically than black retirees. Blacks who were retired reported greater feelings of global well-being, personal control, and sense of life accomplishment. The implication of the findings for research and policy are discussed.

I. INTRODUCTION

Black Americans' disadvantaged labor force positions over the life course may have profound and lasting effects on their physical, economic, social, and psychological well-being as they age. Thus, the retirement process in this group must be studied within the context of their life course experiences. This chapter explores the premise that continuity exists between the work and retirement experiences of blacks based on data from a new national probability sample of the black elderly. Moreover, their lifetime work experiences may have simultaneously negative and positive effects on various aspects of the retirement process.

The study of the minority experience of retirement is important for several reasons. First, minorities (including blacks of retirement age) constitute increasing proportions of their own populations and of the general older population as well. Increases in the numbers of these individuals living beyond traditional retirement ages demand that we learn something about the minority experience of aging and the impact of changes such as retirement. Second, if there is an important element of continuity in the work, retirement, and leisure experiences of black Americans, as we argue in this chapter, then their unfavorable labor force positions in today's economic situation portend bleak work and retirement futures for many of them.

The third reason is that knowledge gained by studying work and retirement among blacks, regardless of similarities to or differences from the majority population, will increase our understanding of these processes in the general population (Jackson, Tucker, and Bowman, 1982). Finally, understanding the dynamics of labor force participation and retirement experiences among a disadvantaged minority will have important implications for policy development and implementation.

In spite of the need, virtually no research has focused exclusively on the work and retirement of older blacks. A few work and retirement studies include some black/white comparisons (e.g., Parnes and Nestel, 1981; Abbott, 1977), but little research or writing has been devoted to an investigation of factors related specifically to work and retirement experiences *within* the black population (Gibson, 1982b). An assumption implicit in this omission is that the antecedents and process of retirement are invariant across the cultural and life course experiences of minority and nonminority members of this society. No other reason would appear to account for the paucity of research and absence of attention to this topic.

In some ways this lack of attention to the retirement of blacks is paralleled in the lack of research on women's retirement (Szinovacz, 1980, 1982). Szinovacz argues that it was the presumed unimportance of female labor force participation that resulted in the historical void of research on the retirement experiences of women. The increased numbers of women retirees over the last decade and their steadily increasing labor force participation are given as reasons for the rise of research on women's retirement.

Gibson (1982b) suggests that black women have been historically an important segment of the work force. Although the lack of research on this group leaves a serious gap in our knowledge, it is somewhat understandable that they were not included in the major retirement studies simply because they were women. The reasons for the lack of research on the antecedents, nature, and processes of retirement among black men, however, is more difficult to fathom. In fact, comparative data on blacks and whites in many of the longitudinal studies of males are not given. It is not clear whether this omission indicates a lack of blacks within the samples, a lack of differences between black and white data, or a general lack of interest in the black retirement experience.

The major purpose of the present chapter is to provide preliminary data on the work and retirement experiences among the black elderly from a recently conducted national sample survey of the black American population. Literature related to labor force participation and retirement among black Americans is reviewed and the importance of culturally determined life course experiences on the work and retirement process in the black elderly is highlighted. The chapter closes with implications for research, planning, and policy related to the black elderly.

II. WORK AND ECONOMIC EXPERIENCES OF BLACKS

There is little disagreement that blacks (as well as other racial and ethnic minorities) have been disadvantaged with regard to work and economic well-being in comparison to whites (Current Population Reports, 1980; Munnell, 1978; Abbott, 1980; Corcoran and Duncan, 1978; Gordon et al., 1982). There is also ample documentation that the poor economic situation of blacks will continue. A variety of explanations for this dire prognosis have been offered (Anderson and Cottingham, 1981; Hill, 1981; Kronus, 1978; Green et al., 1979; Hill, 1982). Census data (Current Population Reports, 1980) and other economic reviews (Abbott, 1980; Munnell 1978; Gordon et al., 1982) provide evidence of both longstanding and current trends in inequalities of economic conditions between blacks and whites. A recent report by the U.S. Commission on Civil Rights (Gordon et al., 1982) demonstrates that between 1970 and 1980, blacks were disadvantaged relative to whites in both unemployment and *under*employment. Gordon et al. (1982) argue further that current and projected trends do not bode well for improvement in employment and economic conditions among blacks. Abbott (1980) in an analysis on the National Longitudinal Survey of the labor market experiences of men aged 45–49 (for the period 1966–1971) also found little to support positive projections for black workers, particularly for *older* black workers.

Several authors note a modest improvement (over the last few decades) in the economic condition of the black population (Abbott, 1980; Munnell, 1978; Current Population Reports, 1980). Abbott (1977), however, points out that the improvement was mainly in younger age groups. Others assert that not only was there a lack of progress by blacks relative to whites over the past few years, but there was actually a loss of gains made during the 1960s (Gordon et al., 1982; Anderson and Cottingham, 1981). While some positive gains may be evident in the economic conditions of black Americans, these changes have not had a great impact on the vast majority of the black population (Current Population Reports, 1980; Corcoran and Duncan, 1978; Gordon et al., 1982).

The impoverishment of large numbers of black Americans and their handicapping work histories are inextricably bound. Research and theory suggest that even when blacks are able to find work it is part time, intermittent, irregular, and probably within the secondary segment of the labor market (Anderson and Cottingham, 1981; Hill, 1981; Montagna, 1977; Cain, 1976; Gordon et al., 1982). An analysis of unemployment and underemployment in the 1970 decade (Gordon et al., 1982), in fact, found that minorities were disadvantaged in every index of labor market activity. High unemployment, intermittent work, low pay, and overeducation for job levels formed consistent patterns of minority work experience over the decade, regardless of peaks in economic conditions. Disaggregating the minority data, Gordon et al. (1982) reported that blacks had the highest unemployment rates, particularly among the better educated, and the highest rates of intermittent employment.

Theorists have attempted to account for the objectively poor conditions of blacks in the labor market and their consequent deprived economic status. Explanations are of two types (Corcoran and Duncan, 1978). The first perspective suggests that blacks (and other minorities and women as well) earn less and hold less prestigious positions because they lack qualifications and job skills. The second explanation holds that blacks, independent of existing skills, are disadvantaged in work and economic conditions because of differential treatment compared with whites.

Differential treatment, according to some theorists, has resulted in early tracking of blacks into dead-end, secondary labor market jobs. Moreover, this tracking process has not undergone any significant changes over the years. In comparison with the primary sector the secondary market is relatively small, consisting of small, unprofitable, and unstable economic institutions. The secondary sector of the economy would have fewer opportunities for promotions and training than the primary sector (Cain, 1976; Montagna, 1978; Corcoran and Duncan, 1978). Because jobs in the secondary sector lack the opportunities for advancement and stability, placement in this sector at an early age would have negative consequences for job trajectory and improvement over the life course. The lack of on-the-job training opportunities and limited access to work situations with higher wage, salary, and benefit structures have ramifications for the present economic status of blacks and for the future availability of adequate retirement benefits and pensions (Abbott, 1980).

Particularly troubling in the findings on the relative deprivation of blacks compared with whites in the labor force and in economic conditions is that occupational and educational status do not fully explain these differentials. For example, Abbott (1980) reported that when occupation and education were held constant, blacks were still less likely to hold full-time, full-year jobs than whites; and, even when they did hold full-time, full-year jobs, their earnings were significantly lower than those of whites. Similar findings were reported in an analysis of the *Panel Study of Income Dynamics* (PSID) data (Corcoran and Duncan, 1978). Some of the recent data (Gordon et al., 1982), in fact, suggest a *negative* impact of increased education on the probability of black males finding employment. The prospect that the increasing educational levels of blacks may not decrease unemployment among them coupled with the fact of a current high unemployment rate (nearly 50 percent in some segments of the black population) do not bode well for future work and economic gains in this population.

Given blocked opportunities to engage in regular market activities within the economy, several writers suggest that some blacks participate in nontraditional subsistence and economic activities to supplement work that is available in the regular market (Jackson and Chatters, 1982; Lowenthal, 1975; Ferman et al., 1978). Blacks, finding themselves in poor economic straits, become enmeshed in networks of friends, neighbors, and acquaintances and participate in a variety of paid exchange (irregular economy) or social exchange (no monetary transfers) activities. Jackson and Chatters (1982) postulate that participation in these two supplementary networks begins in the preadult years and strengthens over the life course as a function of experience and economic necessity. Just as the secondary sector of the labor market provides lower wages, less change for advancement, and lower pension and retirement benefits, if any (Abbott, 1980), involvement in the irregular and social economies (Lowenthal, 1975) also provides little security or benefits to the aging worker. Two nonmonetary benefits of these alternative economic networks, however, might be social support and no mandatory retirement age.

Some researchers warn that the continued poor labor market conditions of blacks might have irreversible negative impact on the black family (Gibson, 1982b; Datcher, 1980; Corcoran and Duncan, 1978). The present labor market experiences of blacks will also affect their future work and ultimately their retirement experiences. Abbott (1980:17) admonishes:

> In the long run, however, any trend toward or the eventual achievement of black–white economic parity after retirement will depend on economic gains for blacks of all ages relative to whites during the pre-retirement years. Otherwise, the extent to which older black workers benefit less than young blacks in any current gains will be reflected for many years in lower aggregate benefits levels for blacks than whites when they retire or become disabled.

In short, blacks are less well off economically than whites; their economic deprivation is due, in the main, to their disadvantaged labor force positions over time; and there is no evidence that these positions are changing for the better. The constancy of handicapping work experiences over a lifetime will ultimately impact the retirement experiences of black Americans.

In the next section we review the retirement literature that is directly pertinent to our topic. This research is of three types: (1) major national studies that apparently do not include blacks but examine constructs that are central to the study of retirement in blacks; (2) studies that include a comparison of blacks and whites; and (3) one study that focuses exclusively on blacks. The studies, as a whole, examine issues of retirement definitions; major predictors of retirement, retirement age, and adjustment to retirement; and objective conditions after retirement.

III. RETIREMENT EXPERIENCES OF BLACKS

As research on retirement has progressed over the years and data have accumulated (Morgan, 1969; Atchley, 1976a, 1979, 1982b; Parnes and Nestel, 1981), the conceptualization of what constitutes retirement has become more complex (Atchley, 1979). The very nature of ways in which retirement should be defined has been debated extensively. Atchley (1976a) concludes that retirement can be conceived of as an event, a process, a social role, a phase of life, or some combination of these descriptions. Some argue that the most effective definition of retirement is still open to question (Parnes and Nestel, 1981). An overall conclusion is that retirement can be objectively or subjectively defined, or both.

The theoretical and empirical disadvantages of using subjective definitions of retirement alone have been pointed out (Murray, 1979; Depner and Ingersoll, 1982). Although Parnes and Nestel (1981) argue that subjective definitions are useful, many researchers use a more sophisticated version based on Atchley's (1976) three-part subjective–objective conceptualization: the receipt of retirement benefits, a decrease in time spent in paid work, and a view of oneself as retired.

There is controversy in the literature as to whether these subjective and objective indicators of retirement are correlated. In some of the longitudinal studies, for example, large discrepancies in the retrospective accounts of the time of retirement and more objective indicators of cessation of work were found (Parnes and Nestel, 1981). Murray (1979), in contrast, found in an analysis of the Retirement History Survey data, self-evaluations of two groups of individuals—the completely retired and the nonretired—to be closely related to the number of hours they were working (or not working). The reports of the partly retired, however, were not as clearly predictive of hours worked. More recently, research attention has turned to ways in which the predictors of retirement vary as a function of definition. Palmore et al. (1982), analyzing data from seven longitudinal data sets on retirement, found that the strongest predictors of retirement status were structural factors such as socioeconomic status and job characteristics. These structural predictors were also found to be important in predicting early retirement and age at retirement. On the other hand, the more subjective indicators, health and attitude measures, were found to be important only in predicting early retirement and age at retirement.

Another body of research has focused on the antecedents and consequences of retirement (Atchley, 1982b). Much of this research has shown that the retirement decision is shaped by the attitudes and behaviors of individuals prior to the event of retirement (Atchley, 1982b; Kimmel et al., 1978).

As early retirement benefits became available to workers, the investigation of factors that might predict retirement age rose to prominence in the research literature. In the Palmore et al. study discussed earlier (1982), age at retirement was predicted best by a balance of socioeconomic status, health, job, and attitudinal variables. The role of health as a predictor of retirement, however, has been under continuing debate (Minkler, 1981). Palmore et al. (1982) found health to be almost useless in predicting retirement among men over 65. Morgan (1980b) reported a similar finding; and Palmore et al. (1982), in support of Morgan's (1980b) analysis, found that health operated in conjunction with the availability of a pension and other financial resources in predicting retirement before age 62. According to Morgan (1980b), the best predictors of retirement before age 62 are illness, wives with pensions, home ownership with no mortgage payment, government employment, unenjoyable jobs, at least a high school education, and employment in high-paying union jobs. Retirement between the ages of 62 and 65 was predicted best by wages that just kept up with inflation and retirement at age 65 or later by the amount of income and whether the person was employed. In general, as Morgan indicated both in 1969 (Barfield and Morgan) and in 1981, the process of retirement, however defined, begins when poor health demands a cessation of work or when there is an expectation of financial readiness. Palmore et al.'s findings, then, also corroborate Morgan's in that structural factors appear to be important in predicting on-time retirement while a combination of structural and subjective factors are important in predicting early retirement.

A plethora of studies has examined subjective well-being after retirement. In the main, researchers have attempted to identify factors associated with happiness, life satisfaction, morale, and other indicators of "the good life." The majority of studies find that poor adjustment to retirement is linked to poor health, low income, earlier-than-expected retirement, lack of meaningful activities, and low marital satisfaction (Atchley, 1982b; Beck, 1982). Barfield and Morgan's finding nearly 15 years ago (1969) still stands: the major determinants of retirement satisfaction are adequate income and good health.

Kimmel et al. (1978) found that individuals who held positive attitudes about the retirement decision and retirement itself were more likely than others to be satisfied with retirement; these attitudes were, in fact, as important as good health in predicting postretirement satisfaction. A consistent finding in the retirement satisfaction literature is that the event of retirement influences activity level which in turn affects morale (Atchley, 1982b; Mutran and Reitzes, 1981).

While the research on retirement has shown a large increase over the last several years, work directly related to the retirement experiences of blacks and other racial minorities is sparse (Atchley, 1976a). There are some analyses of the major longitudinal data sets, however, that compare blacks and whites on these experiences (Bould, 1980; Morgan, 1980a, 1981; Parnes and Nestel, 1981; Abbott, 1977; Gibson, 1982a,b,c).

With respect to predicting age at retirement, most research shows that poor health is an important contributor to early retirement (see Minkler, 1981 for a rejoinder). Blacks, suffering disproportionately from physical disabilities, are found more likely than others to leave the labor force as early retirees and to report poor health as the main reason for retirement (Gibson, 1982b; Atchley, 1982a,b; Parnes and Nestel, 1981). The clearest race difference reported in the literature is, in fact, that blacks are more likely than whites to retire early for reasons of poor health (Atchley, 1982b).

With respect to reasons for retiring at any age, Parnes and Nestel (1981) in an analysis of the 10-year National Longitudinal Studies found few racial differences but reported some notable race effects. Black males were more likely than white males to report (1) retiring for health reasons; (2) mandatory retirement (primarily in manufacturing); (3) unemployment in the 12-month period prior to retirement; and (4) job search discouragement. Blacks were less likely to report voluntary retirement and to express satisfaction with their preretirement and postretirement (if working) jobs than whites. In contrast, Morgan (1980a) found no independent contributions due to race in the regression of the retirement decisions of heads of household from the Panel Study of Income Dynamics. In a similar analysis on the consequences and antecedents of retirement in the same data set, Morgan (1980b) made no particlar mention of race effects.

There has been slightly more research comparing blacks and whites on retirement satisfaction than on reasons for retirement. Parnes and Nestel (1981), examining the subjective experience of retirement, found that nearly one-third of black male retirees reported being dissatisfied with their retirement experiences compared with one-fifth of white retirees. The researchers expressed surprise at the small margin of difference between blacks and whites in reported levels of global satisfaction. Given the large disparities between black and white elderly in income and retirement benefits, it might be expected that reports of subjective well-being would be commensurate with these gaps. But despite limited resources, the black elderly, in the main, give positive subjective appraisals of the retirement experience (Parnes and Nestel, 1981; Beck, 1982). Beck (1982) in analyzing 30 years of data from the Retirement History Survey also found no significant differences in global satisfaction between black and white elderly; nor did he find interactions among race and other major variables in the study. His conclusion was that the same factors—health, income, and expected retirement—are positively associated with life satisfaction and happiness in retirement for both blacks and whites. As is the case with most comparative research in this area, the conclusion that the predictors of global satisfaction operate the same in whites and blacks was not evaluated by conducting separate analyses by race. The lack of a significant overall race effect in Beck's (1982) analyses indicates that mean levels of happiness and satisfaction are similar in blacks and whites. What is most interesting about this set of findings, and the findings of others in this area (Campbell, 1981; Jackson, Chatters, and Neighbors, 1982), is that blacks, despite their more limited resources compared with whites, do not show lower levels of global satisfaction than whites. There are at least three explanations of this phenomenon. First, as we have speculated elsewhere, this may be a cohort effect, limited to older blacks (Jackson, Herzog, and Chatters, 1977). Second, these higher levels of adjustment, as assessed in global measures (Beck, 1982), may mean that retired blacks, being relatively better off after retirement than before, are actually fairly satisfied with their current situations. Or it may mean, as Gibson (1982c) argues, that blacks, being more socialized to adapt to uncertainty and change within their lives, arrive at old age more fortified, more rehearsed, and better able to adapt to its exigencies, despite fewer economic and social resources (Jackson et al., 1977/78).

In regard to postretirement objective conditions among black and white male retirees, Parnes and Nestel (1981) reported that the absolute percentage reduction in black income was smaller than that of whites but at the same time, black retirement income was only 64 percent of white postretirement income. In an earlier analysis of black and white family units from the Retirement History Survey, Abbott (1977) had also pointed out the disadvantaged economic status of black elderly compared with their white counterparts. In the same study, blacks were found to also be both educationally and occupationally disadvantaged; and regardless of similarities in occupation or income, were less well off economically than whites. Parnes and Nestel (1981) explored further the issue of economic disparity and found that nearly half of white retirees received some form of pension compared with less than one-third of black retirees. Generally, OASHI and disability benefits were more important sources of support for blacks whereas pensions were more often available to whites. Abbott (1977) reported similar findings, i.e., regardless of income level, proportionately more retired blacks than whites received public assistance payments, while whites were more likely to rely on income from assets. Both the Parnes and Nestel and the Abbott studies found that black elderly were more likely to be working and relying on earned income for subsistence than whites; but even with these supplements the income of blacks was still substantially below that of whites.

The single widely cited and available research study focused specifically on the retirement experiences of blacks was conducted, unfortunately, on a small select sample of 101 black men and women (Lambing, 1972a,b). As indicated in Gibson's (1982b) review, a few dissertations have been conducted on the retirement experiences of blacks, but little published literature in major sources is available.

Caution must be exercised in summarizing the research on the retirement of blacks because the probability of error may be increased by the small numbers of blacks in the analysis groups, the lack of multivariate controls, and possible construct invalidity. In spite of these methodological inadequacies, a picture of blacks in retirement begins to emerge. Blacks are more disadvantaged than whites in all phases of the retirement process except perhaps in overall feelings of well-being. They are more likely to face mandatory retirement, to retire early because of poor health, to have been recently unemployed prior to retirement, to receive less in retirement income, to be dissatisfied with that income, and to be dependent on OASHI and public assistance.

Despite these findings, there are still large gaps in our knowledge of the retirement process among blacks. Research to date has not examined issues of retirement *within* the group of black elderly. Little is known, for example, of factors that are related to their subjective definitions of retirement. Based on the knowledge at hand, we might speculate that discontinuous work experiences earlier in life and the necessity to work in old age would make it difficult for some black individuals to draw a clear line between work and nonwork. If work and retirement cannot be clearly demarcated, could there be consequences for adjustment in later life? Is pension income, as Atchley (1979) and others suggest, a valid indicator of objective retirement in blacks, when few blacks receive pensions? And do individuals label themselves "retired" when, in old age, income from their own labor (albeit small) exceeds that from traditional retirement sources? How do blacks engage themselves during retirement? Is there a heterogeneity among the black elderly with respect to subjective appraisals of the retirement experience? The analysis of the National Survey of Black Americans (NSBA) data presented later in the chapter provides some insight into these issues.

IV. THE CONTINUITY OF WORK AND RETIREMENT EXPERIENCES AMONG BLACKS

A synthesis of the economic, work, and retirement literature reviewed earlier suggests strongly that a correlation exists between the experiences of blacks in the labor market and their experiences in old age—they are disadvantaged economically at all points along the life cycle. Abbott (1980:38) puts it succinctly: "In reality, inadequate income among many of the elderly (more likely for the black than for the white elderly) is not a new experience in old age. It is, instead, a lifelong condition."

Based on our review of the economic, work, and retirement literature, then, we propose that there exists a continuity between the lifelong work and economic conditions of blacks and their retirement experiences. Specifically, the poor work and economic conditions of youth remain over the life course and continue on into old age to maintain poverty and make it necessary for many older blacks to remain in the work force, and negatively affect objective socioeconomic conditions among the retired black elderly. The review of the retirement research suggested, however, that the economic deprivation of blacks does not result necessarily in their psychological maladjustment to retirement. Thus, we expanded our theoretical framework to include the proposition that the same poor work and economic conditions earlier in life that negatively impact objective conditions may positively affect subjective conditions among the retired black elderly.

As discussed earlier, inadequate income, lack of benefits, underemployment, unemployment, and tracking into secondary sectors of the economy characterize the life experiences of blacks from youth to old age. While many researchers and public policy analysts had speculated that these would be temporary phenomena, characterizing only the present cohorts of the young and the old (Abbott, 1977), current poor economic conditions that maintain high unemployment rates among blacks and the continuing tracking of blacks into secondary sector jobs upon initial entry into the labor market ensure that future cohorts of blacks as they enter the labor force and reach retirement age will be similarly disadvantaged (Gordon et al., 1982). Succinctly, the lack of private pensions and benefits and greater dependence on public assistance in comparison to whites may characterize the experience of the black elderly for many decades to come.

While income levels do not show significant upward shifts for retired blacks, retirement may be an advantage for them nevertheless, i.e., retirement income from governmental sources may be more realiable and regular than income earned by participation in the labor force (Gordon et al., 1982). Whether the retirement income is OASHI, SSI, or, for those fortunate enough, a private pension, there may be a greater sense of income security and peace of mind in retirement than in the work years spent in a capricious, unstable, and psychologically punishing labor market. Additionally, early and continuous participation in irregular and social economic activities, as pointed out earlier, may continue to provide sources of income and other forms of subsistence during retirement. For these reasons, we might expect higher levels of adjustment among retired blacks than would be expected given their objectively poor financial circumstances. In support of this argument Barfield and Morgan (1978) found high levels of postretirement satisfaction in the lowest income workers.

In sum, while handicapping labor force and economic positions over a lifetime negatively affect economic well-being in old age, the same handicapping positions may also influence retired blacks to positively appraise their current situations. Simply put, retirement pay from governmental sources is more reliable than pay from intermittent work, leaving the labor force eliminates certain strains and stresses, and thus older blacks may be better off psychologically *out* of than *in* the labor force.

V. ANALYSIS OF THE DATA FROM THE NATIONAL SURVEY OF BLACK AMERICANS

As discussed in the previous section, our major premise is that continuity exists between the lifetime work and economic experiences of blacks and their retirement experiences. Handicapping labor force and economic positions over the life course negatively affect economic well-being but positively affect psychological well-being in retirement. Since the National Survey of Black Americans (NSBA) data are cross-sectional and were not collected to test this hypothesis (we are aware of the shortcomings of testing a dynamic model without longitudinal data), the goal of the present analysis is not to directly test our theoretical notions but to provide a descriptive account of the nature and meaning of the retirement experience among blacks as this experience relates to certain elements of our proposed framework. The NSBA represents the first attempt to collect information on a national probability sample of the black elderly. The survey, therefore, provides good-quality, culturally sensitive data that allow the exploration of work and retirement issues, for the first time, *within* the black elderly.

Our present analysis is in three parts. First, definitional issues are examined. Given the same objective criterion of working less than half-time, who among the black elderly label themselves as retired? Are these definitions associated with the ability to draw a sharp line between lifetime and present work patterns? What are the income packages of older blacks and are these combinations of income sources related to self-definitions of retirement status? Next, differences between working and nonworking black elderly with respect to subjective appraisals of well-being are explored. Is there evidence suggesting that older blacks *in* the labor force are less well off psychologically than those who are *not* in the labor force? Finally, a profile of the black retired—behaviors, attitudes, and feelings—is presented.

A. The National Survey of Black Americans

The 544 black Americans, 55 years of age and older, used in the present analysis represent a subset of the NSBA. The NSBA sample is a multistage probability sample of the black population consisting of 2,107 respondents. The sampling design was based on the 1970 census and each black American residing in an individual household within the continental United States had an equal chance of being selected. The sample design is similar to that of most national surveys but has unique features of primary area selection and stratification to make it responsive to the distribution of the black population. Eligibility for selection into this household sample was based on citizenship and noninstitutionalized living quarters within the continental United States. Reflecting the nature of the distribution of the black population, more than half (44) of the 76 primary areas used for final selection of households were located in the southern United States. Two methods of screening were developed to guarantee inclusion of blacks (meeting our selection criteria) in both high- and low-density areas (Jackson and Hatchett, 1985). The sample had a 67 percent response rate and all face-to-face interviewing was conducted in 1979-1980 by black interviewers trained through the Survey Research Center of the University of Michigan's Institute for Social Research.

The questionnaire used in the NSBA was developed especially for use in the black population. Two years of pretesting and refinement preceded actual use in the field. The instrument contained both open- and closed-ended items and took approximately 2 hours and 20 minutes to administer. Although our present concern is restricted to the retirement, work, and demographic sections, the questionnaire also includes the broad areas of neighborhood life, health, mental health, family, social support, racial and self-identity, religious experiences, and political participation. Thus, the data available for analysis in the present chapter represent a rich, culturally relevant, and carefully collected source of information on the work and retirement experiences of the black elderly.

B. The "Retired" and "Nonretired" Black Elderly

1. Defining Retirement

Atchley (1976a) proposed a three-part definition of retirement that incorporates receiving retirement benefits, decreasing time in paid work, and labeling oneself as retired. This model of defining retirement, we argue, might not be entirely appropriate for blacks for two reasons. The first reason is that a sizable group of them may not be receiving retirement benefits. The second reason is that in view of their discontinuous lifetime work patterns and their need to work in old age, decreases in time spent in work may not be that clear to them. Additionally, lifetime involvement in "paid work" in the irregular economy and involvement in the social economy (Jackson and Chatters, 1982), which may not have ceased in old age, may also complicate self-categorizations of retirement.

Findings in the present NSBA analyses indicate that black elderly who were still working part time and who also had histories characterized by part-time work were less likely than others to label themselves retired. This lends credence to the idea that without dramatic changes in work patterns from youth through old age, self-definitions of retirement are difficult to make.

Three groups of the black elderly were formed for this analysis of retirement definitions. Group 1 (N = 142), the "working," were those 55 and over who were working 20 or more hours per week. Group 2 (N = 252), the "retired," were those not working at all or working less than 20 hours per week and when asked the reason not working or not working more, replied "retired." Group 3 (N = 150), the "nonretired," were also not working or working less than 20 hours per week, but when asked the reason for not working or not working more gave reasons other than retirement. The only difference, then, between the retired and the nonretired were their subjective labels of retirement. This operationalization of the retirement definition construct is consistent with previous definitions which attempt to include both subjective and objective aspects of the retirement experience.

2. Sources of Income of Retired and Nonretired Elderly

As shown in Table 1, black elderly who did not label themselves retired were more likely than the subjectively retired to derive income from their own or spouse's work in addition to another source (14.7 percent vs. 2.3 percent). The retired, in contrast, were more likely to have that combination made up of two types of retirement income (18.7 and 2.7 percent respectively). Table 1 shows these single and dual sources of financial support and brief summaries of the work histories of the retired compared with the nonretired. Regardless of self-definitions of retirement status, more black elderly reported income from single than from dual sources (239 and 163, respectively). The nonretired are more likely than the retired to receive support from single sources (64.0 vs. 56.7 percent). The major single source of income for both the retired and nonretired groups is either Social Security or SSI payments. The most important combination of income sources for the nonretired is work of self or spouse combined with some other form of payment; almost half of the nonretired elderly who receive income from two sources are in this category. In contrast, the most common income package of the retired black elderly is retirement benefits of some type combined with Social Security payments or a second type of retirement payments. Almost half of the retirees who receive income from dual sources are in this category. An important point to be made here is that individuals still contributing to their income through their own work may be less likely than individuals exclusively receiving retirement benefits to label themselves retired. The balance between income from work and from retirement payments, as we suggested earlier, may be an important consideration in developing definitions of retirement in blacks.

Contrary to popular opinion, and regardless of subjective retirement status, black elderly receive little financial support from relatives, friends, or children; they are predominantly self-supporting, with spouses providing, in a few cases, some significant portions of family income. It is clear that OASHI payments are the sole source of support of nearly one-third of the black elderly in this sample, and if their incomes are supplemented at all it is through their own work. As we will show later, a large proportion of black elderly who report one or more work-

Table 1. Sources of Income and Work Histories of 55-Year-Old and Older Retired and Nonretired Blacks

Category	Retired (N = 252)	Nonretired (N = 150)
Panel A: Sources of Income		
Single sources of 1978 income		
Welfare, ADC, AFDC, or food stamps	1.2[a]	7.3
Social Security or SSI	30.2	23.3
Work of self or spouse (for pay or goods)	2.3	14.7
Retirement pay, pensions, or annuities	11.9	7.3
Savings, investments, or rental properties	0.8	0.0
Children, parents, other relatives, friends	1.6	2.7
Other governmental (Workmen's Compensation, disability pay, unemployment pay, or other governmental pay)	0.8	2.7
Not ascertained	6.0	7.9
Total respondents	143	96
Dual sources of 1978 income[b]		
Work of self or spouse combined with another source, welfare, SSI, Social Security, retirement pay, family, or other government sources	10.7	17.3
Welfare combined with another source (SSI, Social Security, or retirement pay)	4.8	2.7
Retirement pay, pensions, annuities, combined with another source (SSI, Social Security, or a second type of retirement pay)	18.7	2.7
Savings, investments, or rental property combined with another source (retirement pay, SSI, Social Security or other governmental pay)	2.8	2.0
Other governmental pay combined with another source	2.3	7.3
Family or friends combined with another source	3.6	4.0
Social Security combined with SSI	0.4	0.0
Total respondents	109	54
Panel B: Work History		
Number of hours per week presently working		
0 hours	94.0	86.0
1–10 hours	3.6	4.7
11–19 hours	2.4	6.7
Total respondents	252	150
Previous work experience		
Never worked for pay	0.8	11.7
Worked for pay	99.1	88.2
Total respondents	237	128
Full-time work experience		
Never had full-time work	5.1	15.5
Had full-time job sometime in life	94.9	84.5
Total respondents	234	116

(*continued*)

Table 1. (*Continued*)

Category	Retired (N = 252)	Nonretired (N = 150)
Job permanency		
Never had regular, permanent job	3.1	0.0
Had regular, permanent job sometime in life	96.9	100.0
Total respondents	192	82
Type of job in life		
Worked mainly in different jobs in life	39.1	41.2
Worked mainly in same job/occupation	60.9	58.8
Total respondents	220	97
Part-time work		
Worked part-time some years since age 18	54.8	72.2
Worked full-time all years since age 18	45.2	27.8
Total respondents	221	97

[a] Percentages
[b] Within dual sources of income, the work category could include any of the other sources as a source second to work. All other categories exclude work as a second source.

limiting health problems are still working (see Table 2). As Gibson (1982b) suggested, many black elderly in poor health may have to continue to work out of economic necessity.

Quite expectedly, then, and in line with previous reports (Abbott, 1977, 1980), our analysis indicates that the black elderly are highly dependent on public funds as a single source of support and are likely to be working (despite infirmities) to supplement incomes. Surprisingly, however, they are not likely to receive financial assistance from relatives, friends, and children.

3. Work Histories of the Retired and Nonretired

Several findings indicate that black elderly who do not call themselves retired when compared with those who do call themselves retired tend to be currently working more than 10 hours a week, to never have worked for pay, to never have had a full-time job in life, and to have been part-time workers for some years since age 18. Job permanency and type of job in life do not seem to distinguish between the two groups (see Table 1). It may be that these current and past discontinuous types of work experiences made it difficult to draw a line between work and nonwork, as our framework suggests.

Future attempts to develop a model of ways in which blacks define retirement should certainly consider the possibility that two circumstances might complicate self-definitions of retirement: (1) an indistinct line between work patterns earlier in life and work patterns in old age, and (2) the tendency for their own work to contribute significantly to retirement income.

Table 2. Selected Characteristics of 55-Year-Old and Older Working, Retired, and Nonretired Blacks[a]

Category	Working (N = 142) (26.1%)	Retired (N = 252) (46.3%)	Nonretired (N = 150) (27.6%)
Total family income, 1978			
Less than $6000 a year	25.2[b]	65.4	72.9
$6,000–19,999	52.8	29.9	23.0
$20,000 or more	22.0	4.8	4.1
Total respondents	123	208	122
Number of grades of school completed			
0–8 years	33.3	61.7	69.1
9–11 years	27.7	14.5	18.1
12 years	26.2	12.9	9.4
Some college, college graduate	12.8	10.9	3.4
Total respondents	141	248	149
Occupation			
Professional, managerial	11.9	6.8	0.7
Clerical, sales, craftspersons	11.2	12.8	7.5
Operatives	18.2	17.6	10.2
Laborers, private household	26.0	34.3	35.6
Service	31.5	21.6	22.6
Not ascertained	0.7	1.2	2.0
Never worked	0.0	6.3	22.0
Total respondents	142	252	150
Marital status			
Married	42.3	37.3	37.3
Divorced, separated	24.7	12.7	16.0
Widowed	31.0	46.0	42.7
Never married	2.1	4.0	4.0
Total respondents	142	252	150
Age in years			
55–61	59.9	3.6	48.0
62–64	15.5	6.3	12.7
65–66	9.2	11.1	6.0
67 or older	15.5	79.0	33.3
Total respondents	142	252	150
Sex			
Male	48.6	42.5	18.0
Female	51.4	57.5	82.0
Total respondents	142	252	150
Urban/Rural			
Large Urban	47.9	46.0	34.7
Small Urban	28.2	29.0	25.3
Rural	23.9	25.0	40.0
Total respondents	142	252	150

(*continued*)

Table 2. (*Continued*)

Category	Working (N = 142) (26.1%)	Retired (N = 252) (46.3%)	Nonretired (N = 150) (27.6%)
Region			
Northeast	21.8	15.5	14.0
North Central	21.8	18.7	15.3
South	47.9	62.7	66.0
West	8.5	3.2	4.7
Total respondents	142	252	150
Number of health problems			
None	16.9	12.7	2.7
1 or more	83.1	87.3	97.3
Total respondents	142	252	150
Extent to which health problems limit work or daily activities			
No limiting health problems or have health problems that do not limit	57.0	31.0	18.0
Only a little	33.1	36.5	22.7
A great deal	9.9	32.5	59.3
Total respondents	142	252	150
Satisfaction with health status			
Satisfied (very or somewhat)	85.2	87.7	70.7
Dissatisfied (very or somewhat)	14.8	12.4	29.3
Total respondents	141	252	150
Better off financially now than 3 years ago			
Better	56.2	38.0	37.6
Same	32.8	47.6	39.6
Worse	10.9	14.4	22.8
Total respondents	137	250	149
Worry about bills			
Great deal	16.9	14.5	28.6
Little	25.7	23.8	25.9
None	57.4	61.7	45.6
Total respondents	136	248	147
Life satisfaction			
Very satisfied	44.7	54.4	46.0
Somewhat satisfied	43.3	33.6	36.0
Somewhat dissatisfied/very dissatisfied	12.1	12.0	18.0
Total respondents	141	250	150
Happiness			
Very happy	36.6	59.8	42.7
Pretty happy	54.2	32.9	46.7
Not too happy	9.2	7.2	10.7
Total respondents	142	249	150

(*continued*)

Table 2. (Continued)

Category	Working (N = 142) (26.1%)	Retired (N = 252) (46.3%)	Nonretired (N = 150) (27.6%)
Personal efficacy			
Low efficacy	39.6	33.3	43.2
Medium efficacy	19.4	22.0	27.7
High efficacy	41.0	44.7	29.1
Total respondents	139	246	148
Got what you hoped for out of life			
Mostly	69.5	79.4	68.7
Less	30.5	20.6	31.3
Total respondents	141	247	147

[a] Working means working 20 or more hours per week for pay. Retired means working less than 20 hours per week and giving the reason for not working as retired. Not retired means although working less than 20 hours per week, the reason for not working or not working more was given as something other than retired.
[b] Percentages

C. Comparing the Working, Retired, and Nonretired Elderly

About 26 percent of the 544 black elderly were working, 46 percent were retired, and 28 percent were nonretired (see Table 2). As might be expected, working black elderly were the most likely of the three groups to report family incomes in the higher brackets (see Table 2). Most of the nonretired black elderly were in the lowest income and education categories. Although all three groups of black elderly were or had been mainly laborers, private household and service workers, the working and retired were more likely than the nonretired to be or to have been professional, clerical, or skilled workers. Although the working elderly were slightly more likely than the retired and nonretired to be separated or divorced and less likely to be widowed (due more to the differing age structures in the three groups than to anything else), there were no notable differences among the three groups in the proportions that were married. The working elderly were younger than the retired elderly—79 percent of the retired were 67 years old or over. What is interesting, however, is that a fairly sizable proportion (33.3 percent) of the nonretired elderly were also 67 years of age or older. This suggests that blacks do not base the decision to call themselves retired largely on chronological age. There was a higher proportion of females in the nonretired than in the other two groups.

The two remaining demographic characteristics examined were degree of urbanicity and region of residence. The nonretired elderly were more likely than the other groups to live in rural locations and less likely to live in large urban locations. One might speculate that workers in rural areas might see the line between work and cessation of work even less clearly than urban workers and thus may be less likely than urban workers to call themselves retired. Related to the location finding, perhaps, is that the nonretired are more likely than individuals in the other two groups to live in the South (66.0 percent, in contrast to 47.9 percent of the workers and 62.7 percent of the retirees).

The nonretired were the most likely to have one or more health problems (97.3 percent) and the most likely to have health problems that limited their work or daily activities a great deal (59.3 percent). Over twice as many of the nonretired reported being dissatisfied with their health in comparison with the working and retired (29.3, 14.8, and 12.4 percent, respectively).

In examining the subjective appraisal of their financial situation, the working elderly were the likeliest of the groups to report being better off than three years ago (56.2 percent), whereas the nonretired elderly were the likeliest to report being worse off financially than three years before the interview (22.8 percent). In a related item, when asked how much they worried about bills, the nonretired were more likely to worry a great deal (28.6 percent) than the working (16.9 percent) or retired (14.5 percent). The retired on the other hand, were the most likely of the three groups to report having no worries about meeting their bills (61.7 percent).

Table 2 also shows the differences between the working, retired, and nonretired groups on a number of indices of adjustment and satisfaction. Those who were retired were found to be better off than either the nonretired or the working on several measures. These findings lend some support to the notion that life in retirement, by providing a regularity of income and relief from the vagaries associated with a disadvantaged labor force position, is happier than life in the work force when one is black and old. For example, on measures of global satisfaction (life satisfaction and happiness) the retired group was more likely than either the working or the nonretired group to say they were very satisfied or very happy with their lives. In contrast, the nonretired group was slightly more likely to report being dissatisfied with their lives. Examining perceived personal efficacy in the groups, the nonretired were more likely to report a lower sense of personal control whereas the retired were more likely to report higher levels of personal efficacy. Greater feelings of personal control among the retired than among the working is consistent with Gibson's (1982a) finding that feelings of control increased as black female heads of household retired from the labor force. Related perhaps to the personal efficacy finding is that the retired group, compared with the nonretired and working elderly, was also more likely to report that they had gotten what they had hoped for out of life (79.4, 68.7, and 69.5 percent, respectively).

What is clear from this brief description of the differences and similarities among our major groups is that the black elderly are heterogeneous with respect to their labor force attachment. There are the full-time workers, the part-time workers, and the nonworkers. Our findings in this analysis are in line with our major hypothesis, i.e., leaving the labor force when elderly promotes psychological well-being. Based on our findings, we might even speculate that morale varies in the present cohort of black elderly inversely with the number of hours spent in the labor force. The retired in our sample were the most likely not to be working and exhibited the best psychological adjustment whereas the full-time workers showed the least adjustment. As expected, the nonretired, part-time, and sporadic workers lay somewhere in between on this continuum of subjective well-being.

D. Profile of the Black Retired Elderly

We focus now on the group of retired black elderly whom we considered to be both objectively and subjectively retired. As indicated earlier, these are individuals who were working less than 20 hours per week and stated that they were retired. In general, our findings fit what is already known or suspected about retired blacks. They retire relatively early for reasons of poor health, find it necessary to supplement postretirement incomes with work, and rely heavily on governmental sources for income. Despite economic adversity, they were found to maintain moderately high levels of subjective well-being. About half of the retired sample had planned to retire and half had not. Most of those who retired unexpectedly did so because of poor health. While recent findings (Parnes and Nestel, 1981; Palmore et al., 1982) have called retrospective reports of reasons for retirement into question, analyses on longitudinal data sets (Gibson, 1982b) suggest that the proportion we found is not an unreasonable estimate of the number who actually do retire for health reasons.

In examining the activity patterns of the retired group, working in the house or garden was the predominant response. Only a small number indicated "doing nothing" in retirement. Given the purported centrality of religion in the lives of the black elderly, it was surprising that church and church-related activities were engaged in by only a small minority of our sample (10 percent). This finding is consistent, however, with Gibson's (1982c) finding that the use of prayer as a coping strategy is decreasing among elderly blacks. Forty percent of the women belonged to clubs and organizations, while only 20 percent of the men did. The men were slightly more likely than the women, however, to be involved in volunteer work (29 percent vs. 22 percent).

Although most retirees did not report returning to work once they retired, males were twice as likely as women to report returning to work at some point after reaching retirement status (38 vs. 19 percent). About half of black elderly retirees said that they were living about the same financially now as before their retirement whereas approximately 30 percent said that they were living worse. When asked what they liked best about retirement, a sizable proportion (30 percent) said "freedom"; females were more likely to give this response than males (32 and 16 percent, respectively). Males also named freedom from work, enjoying sports, hobbies, and reading as positive aspects of retirement. Men were more likely to see boredom as a major problem of retirement whereas women saw having no money as a problem. Only a small percentage (12 percent) of both sexes reported missing anything about their previous jobs. A considerable proportion of the sample indicated liking retirement (approximately 46 percent) providing another indication that life is better out of than in the labor force. Sixty percent of the men and 46 percent of the women, however, stated that they missed *people* at work. Overall, 23 percent of the men and 35 percent of the women reported that they had absolutely no problems with retirement. Among those who said they had problems with retirement, about half said that the problem was not being ready to retire. The vast majority, however, stated that finding things to do and financial arrangements (Social Security payments, etc.) were not problems for them.

Generally, this profile of the black retired elderly is in keeping with previous descriptions (Parnes and Nestel, 1981) of black male retirees, i.e., black retirees in our sample indicated fairly high satisfaction overall with retirement (particularly if planned and unrelated to health reasons), were fairly active, and missed only the social aspects of their previous jobs. Most saw their financial situations as fairly stable over the three-year period preceding our interview and indicated few problems with their retirement income. Although some gender differences appeared in activities, returning to work, and views on the best aspects of the retirement experience, these differences were generally small.

V. CONCLUSIONS AND IMPLICATIONS FOR RESEARCH, PLANNING, AND POLICY

In the present chapter we attempted to provide a preliminary model of the work and retirement experiences of the black elderly. We have conceptualized their retirement experiences not as a disjunctive change from previous work and life experiences, but as having important continuities and roots in their earlier experiences. Thus, the early tracking into dead-end, secondary sector jobs in the work histories of black youth (Corcoran and Duncan, 1978) are viewed as important beginnings of poor work histories, unemployment and underemployment in later adulthood, and economic difficulties in late life. This pattern of poor jobs with few benefits and little stability has implications for the types of resources and benefits available to blacks in retirement (Abbott, 1977, 1980). The lack of benefits and available resources may force some of the black elderly to work long past the average ages of other demographic groups in this society. A great deal of literature was cited to support this premise.

We also found the existing literature on work and retirement among the black elderly extremely limited, focusing most often on males and then only to compare them with whites. Although we do not argue that the retirement experience of blacks is definitely different from that of whites in this society, we do contend that before this possibility is rejected further empirical examination is needed.

The data reported in the present chapter provide a preliminary step in analyzing issues of work and retirement among the black elderly. Clearly further analyses of this data set as well as analyses of panel data sets (Gibson, 1982b, for example) are needed in order to understand the work and retirement process among blacks. While our data provide only a cross-sectional "snapshot" of the current black elderly, these data are unique and provide a beginning in studying the issues.

Although the black elderly suffer social and economic deprivations in comparison to their white counterparts in this society, our findings also clearly show that they are a heterogeneous group, with various subgroups such as the working, retired, and nonretired having significantly different characteristics with respect to financial conditions, health status, background, social status, and attitudes. The nonretired black elderly who work less than 20 hours per week but do not view themselves as retired are an important disadvantaged group in need of further research. They are financially less secure, less educated, less healthy, and worry more about bills and financial security than other groups of the black elderly.

In support of our major hypothesis, blacks who appeared to be objectively and subjectively retired reported the highest global well-being, feelings of personal efficacy, and sense of life accomplishment. We have argued that feelings of well-being in the black elderly are inconsistent with a resource-based notion of subjective well-being, but may well be consistent with the life experiences of a disadvantaged and oppressed minority. That is, retirement status, though often judged inferior to working status by others, may provide for blacks a stability of income and financial security not known during their years spent in a capricious and unsupportive labor market. Thus, a rise in subjective well-being with the onset of retirement status might be expected. While we were not able to examine directly this dynamic hypothesis in our cross-sectional data, we found clear differences in various black elderly groups at different points along the work/retirement continuum. In short, the greater the attachment to the labor force, the lower the morale. We expect that subsequent multivariate analyses and new data collections will both refine this hypothesis and provide further tests of the general thesis.

While we suggest that future analyses of this and other data sets are needed to clarify some of our initial hypotheses and findings, we feel that some policy implications stem directly from our literature review and from our analysis of the NSBA data.

VI. RECOMMENDATIONS FOR RESEARCH AND POLICY

Abbott (1977) argued that the plight of the black elderly—inadequate retirement benefits and the greater necessity to work in old age—would improve as more advantaged cohorts of blacks arrived at retirement age. We have suggested in the present chapter that advances made by younger black workers in the 1960s are now dissipating (Anderson and Cottingham, 1981; Gordon et al., 1982) and that continuing poor economic circumstances are creating cohorts of disadvantaged workers who will also have limited benefits and disadvantaged status when they reach retirement age. In other words, today's disadvantaged black worker is tomorrow's disadvantaged black retiree. Policies must be advanced that address the fundamental issues of early funneling of blacks into dead-end jobs and the concomitants of that funneling. The failure to attend to these issues will result in cohort upon cohort of black workers who will be destined for poor economic straits in retirement.

Our data as well as the findings of others (e.g., Abbott, 1977, 1980) indicate that black elderly are highly dependent on Social Security and public funds because they are often the sole sources of support in retirement. Thus, blacks will be more affected by decisions that influence the basic payment structures of Social Security and Supplemental Security Income. Currently proposed changes in these payments do not suggest that there will be greater liberalization of means tests, significant increases in the amount of benefits paid, or increases in the minimum levels—changes that would benefit blacks.

While some have argued that the raise in the age of eligibility under Social Security would be of benefit in several ways (Sheppard and Rix, 1977), our data suggest that many blacks are working in spite of significant health problems. An increase in the minimum age for Social Security benefits would impact significantly, differentially, and negatively on black Americans. Our data also suggest strongly that retirement may be a time of more financial stability in the lives of blacks who have experienced an unstable labor market. Any policy which increases the time that must be spent in this labor market without first addressing the fundamental problems of black employment and unemployment will have a negative impact on the black worker and eventually the black retiree.

Although we have not emphasized the issue in the current chapter, greater attention must be paid to various subgroups within the black population. As Gibson (1982b) pointed out in her analysis of the PSID data, the black female head of household is in particularly poor economic straits. Our data indicate that black females, a sizable proportion of the nonretired group, are particularly disadvantaged in the receipt of adequate retirement income. While recent census data (Current Population Reports, 1980) indicate movement of black women out of traditionally low-paying and service occupations to which benefits were not attached, it is not clear that the job levels within these occupations that are opening to them will provide adequate benefits and preparation for retirement. The possibility that exclusion from the higher levels within given occupations might also limit retirement benefits for black women in the future needs attention.

In general, the data suggest that more research needs to be devoted to the links between the lifetime work and retirement experiences of blacks with emphasis on their special life circumstances and cultural diversity. These cultural differences may cause divergences in the retirement processes of blacks and whites. Consequently, labor force and retirement policies in behalf of the two groups may in some ways need to be different. We cannot stress enough the importance of studying the retirement process within the context of the life histories and experiences of black Americans. Poor health care early in life combined with poor education, lack of job training, and tracking into dead-end secondary sector jobs are all factors which impinge on retirement decisions, resources, and experiences. While measures have been taken to ameliorate poverty in old age, such as indexed Social Security and SSI payments, unless the root causes of inadequate retirement income are addressed the disadvantaged position of blacks in future cohorts of elderly will persist and public support will be necessary.

ACKNOWLEDGMENTS

We would like to acknowledge with appreciation the assistance of Elizabeth Keough, Jackie Pearlman, Beverly Williams, and Sara Freeland in the analyses and preparation of this chapter. We also thank Toni Antonucci for reading an earlier draft. Support from the National Institute on Aging under grants AG-01294 and AG-03553 is also gratefully acknowledged.

REFERENCES

Abbott, J.
    1977 "Socioeconomic characteristics of the elderly: some black–white differences." Social Security Bulletin 40:16–42.
    1980 "Work experience and earnings of middle-aged black and white men, 1965–1971." Social Security Bulletin 43(12):16–34.
Anderson, B. E. and D. H. Cottingham
    1981 "The elusive quest for economic equality." Daedalus 110(2):257–274.
Atchley, R. C.
    1976a The Sociology of Retirement. New York: Schenkman Publishing Co.
    1976b "Selected social and psychological differences between men and women in later life." Journal of Gerontology 31(2):204–211.
    1979 "Issues in retirement research." The Gerontologist 19(1):44–54.
    1981 "Orientation toward the job and retirement adjustment among women." Pp. 153–168 in J. F. Gabrium (ed.), Time, Roles, and Self in Old Age. New York: Human Sciences Press.
    1982a "The process of retirement: comparing women and men." Pp. 199–219 in M. Szinovacz (ed.), Women's Retirement. Beverly Hills, Ca: Sage Publications.
    1982b "Retirement: leaving the world of work." The Annals of the American Academy 464:120–131.
Atchley, R. C. and J. L. Robinson
    1982 "Attitudes toward retirement and distance from the event." Research on Aging 4(3):299–313.
Barfield, R. E. and J. N. Morgan
    1969 Early Retirement: The Decision and the Experience and a Second Look. Ann Arbor, MI: University of Michigan Press.
    1978 "Trends in satisfaction with retirement." The Gerontologist 18(1):19–23

Beck, S. H.
  1982 "Adjustment to and satisfaction with retirement." Journal of Gerontology 37(5):616–624.
Blau, Z. S.
  1978 "Aging, social class, and ethnicity." Paper presented at the University of Michigan.
Bosse, R. and D. J. Ekerdt
  1981 "Change in self-perception of leisure activities with retirement." The Gerontologist 27(6):650–654.
Bould, S.
  1980 "Unemployment as a factor in early retirement decisions." American Journal of Economics and Sociology 39(2):123–136.
Bowman, P. J., J. S. Jackson, S. Hatchett, and G. Gurin
  1982 "Joblessness and discouragement among black Americans." Economic Outlook USA 9(4):85–88.
Burkhauser, R. V.
  1979 "Are women treated fairly in today's Social Security system?" The Gerontologist 19(3):242–250.
Burkhauser, R. V. and G. S. Tolley
  1978 "Older Americans and market work." The Gerontologist 18(5):449–453.
Cain, G. G.
  1976 "The challenge of segmented labor market theories to orthodox theory: a survey." Journal of Economic Literature 14:1215–1257.
Campbell, A.
  1981 The Sense of Well-Being in America. New York: McGraw-Hill
Chatfield, W. F.
  1977 "Economic and sociological factors influencing life satisfaction of the aged." Journal of Gerontology 32(5):593–599.
Clark, R. L.
  1982 "A symposium on pension policy. Introduction: Issues in the regulation of employer pensions." The Gerontologist 22(6):473.
Clark, R. L. and J. A. Menefee
  1981 "Federal expenditures for the elderly: past and future." The Gerontologist 21(2):132–137.
Cohn, R. M.
  1979 "Age and the satisfactions from work." Journal of Gerontology 34(2):264–272.
Corcoran, M. and G. J. Duncan
  1978 "A summary of Part I findings." Pp. 3–46 in G. J. Duncan and J. N. Morgan (eds.), Five Thousand American Families, Vol. 6. Ann Arbor, MI: Institute for Social Research, The University of Michigan.
Cottrell, W. F. and R. C. Atchley
  1969 "Women in retirement: a preliminary report." Paper presented to the Administration on Aging (January).
Current Population Reports
  1980 "The social and economic status of the black population." Special Studies P-23, No. 80.
Datcher, L.
  1980 "The effects of community and family background on the education and earnings of black and white men." Pp. 147–181 in M. S. Hill, D. H. Hill, and J. N. Morgan (eds.), Five Thousand American Families, Vol. 8. Ann Arbor, MI: Institute for Social Research, The University of Michigan.
  1981 "Race/sex differences in the effects of background on achievement." Pp. 359–390 in G. J. Duncan and J. N. Morgan (eds.), Five Thousand American Families, Vol. 9. Ann Arbor, MI: Institute for Social Research, The University of Michigan.
Depner, C. and B. Ingersoll
  1982 "Employment status and social support: the experience of the mature women." Pp. 1–24

in M. Szinovacz (ed.), Women's Retirement: Policy Implications of Recent Research. Beverly Hills, CA: Sage Publications.

Ferman, L. A., L. Berndt, and E. Selo
   1978 "Analysis of the irregular economy: cash flow in the informal sector." Report to the Bureau of Employment and Training, Michigan Department of Labor. Institute of Labor and Industrial Relations, The University of Michigan—Wayne State University (March).

Fischer, J. S., S. L. Carlton-Ford, and B. J. Briles
   1978 "Life-cycle career patterns: a typological approach to female status attainment." Paper presented at the 31st Annual Scientific Meeting of the Gerontological Society (November).

Fox, J. H.
   1977 "Effects of retirement and former work life on women's adaptation in old age." Journal of Gerontology 32(2):196–202.

George, L. K. and G. L. Maddox
   1977 "Subjective adaptation to loss of the work role: a longitudinal study." Journal of Gerontology 32(4):456–462.

Gibson, R. C.
   1982a "Race and sex differences in the work and retirement patterns of older heads of households." Paper presented at the Scripps Foundation Minority Research Associates Conference (February 8–11).
   1982b "Work and retirement: aging black women—a race and sex comparison." Final report to the Administration on Aging.
   1982c "Blacks at middle and late life: resources and coping." The Annals of the American Academy of Political and Social Science (November).
   1985 "Blacks in an aging society." Daedalvus 118. In press.

Gordon, H. A., C. A. Hamilton, and H. C. Tipps
   1982 Unemployment and Underemployment Among Blacks, Hispanics, and Women. Washington, DC: Clearinghouse Publication No. 74.

Goudy, W. J.
   1981 "Changing work expectations: findings from the Retirement History Study." The Gerontologist 21(6):644–649.

Graney, M. J. and D. M. Cottam
   1981 "Labor force nonparticipation of older people: United States, 1890–1970." The Gerontologist 21(2):138–141.

Green, R. L., J. T. Darden, J. Hirt, C. Simmons, T. Tenbrunsel, F. S. Thomas, J. M. Thomas, and R. W. Thomas
   1979 "Discrimination and the welfare of urban minorities." Background paper prepared for the Urban Policy Task Force of the Department of Housing and Urban Development, Michigan State University (December).

Havighurst, R. J., W. J. McDonald, L. Maeulen, and J. Mazel
   1979 "Male social scientists: lives after sixty." The Gerontologist 19(1):55–60.

Haynes, S. G., A. J. McMichael, and H. A. Tyroler
   1978 "Survival after early and normal retirement." Journal of Gerontology 33(2):269–278.

Hill, M. S.
   1982 "Trends in the economic situation of U.S. families and children: 1970–1980." Paper presented at the Conference of Families and the Economy (January).

Hill, R. B.
   1981 Economic Policies and Black Progress: Myth and Realities. New York: National Urban League.

Holzberg, C. S.
   1982 "Ethnicity and aging: rejoinder to a comment by Kyriakos S. Markides." The Gerontologist 22(6):471–472.

Ingersoll, B.
　1982　"Differences in the social supports of retired men and women." Paper presented at the Annual Meeting of the American Psychological Association, Washington, DC.
Jackson, J. S., J. D. Bacon, and J. Peterson
　1977/　"Life satisfaction among black urban elderly." Aging and Human Development 8:169–
　78　179.
Jackson, J. S. and L. M. Chatters
　1982　"The productive behavior of older black Americans." Unpublished manuscript, The University of Michigan.
Jackson, J. S., L. M. Chatters, and H. W. Neighbors
　1982　"The mental health status of older black Americans: a national survey." Black Scholar 13(1):21–35.
Jackson, J. S., R. Herzog, and L. M. Chatters
　1977　"The meaning and correlates of life-satisfaction in older (and middle-aged) blacks: a secondary analysis." Final report to the Division of Research and Analysis of the Administration on Aging of the Office of Human Development Series, Department of Health, Education and Welfare. Grant No. 90-A-1025: 10-1-76/12-31-77 project period.
Jackson, J. S., B. Tucker, and P. J. Bowman
　1982　"Conceptual and methodological problems in survey research on black Americans." Pp. 11–38 in W. T. Liu (ed.), Issues in Minority Research. Chicago, IL: Asian-American Mental Health Center; Psychological Association, Washington, DC.
Jackson, J. S. and Hatchett, S. J.
　1985　"Intergenerational research: Methodological considerations." In N. Datan, A. L. Green and H. W. Reese (eds), Intergenerational networks: Families in context. Hillsdale, N.J.: Erlbaum Associates, Inc.
Jaslow, P.
　1976　"Employment, retirement, and morale among older women." Journal of Gerontology 31(2):212–218.
Kahn, R. L.
　1982　"Work and leisure in the year 2000." Unpublished manuscript presented at the Conference on Mankind in 2000, University of Haifa, Israel.
Keating, N. C. and P. Cole
　1980　"What do I do with him 24 hours a day? Changes in the housewife role after retirement." The Gerontologist 20(1):84–89.
Kimmel, D. C., K. F. Price, and J. W. Walker
　1978　"Retirement choice and retirement satisfaction." Journal of Gerontology 33(4):575–585.
King, F. P.
　1982　"Indexing retirement benefits." The Gerontologist 22(6):488–492.
Kronus, S.
　1978　"Race, ethnicity, and community." Pp. 202–232 in D. Street and Associates (eds.), Handbook of Contemporary Urban Life. San Francisco, CA: Jossey-Bass.
Lambing, M. L. B.
　1972a　"Leisure-time pursuits among retired blacks by social status." The Gerontologist 12:363–364.
　1972b　"Social class living patterns of retired negros." The Gerontologist 12:285–288.
Lopata, H. Z. and K. F. Norr
　1980　"Changing commitments of American women to work and family roles." Social Security Bulletin 43(6):3–14.
Lowenthal, M. D.
　1975　"The social economy in urban-working class communities." Pp. 447–469 in G. Gappert and H. M. Rose (eds.), The Social Economy of Cities. Beverly Hills, CA: Sage Publications.

Markides, K. S.
　1982　"Ethnicity and aging: a comment." The Gerontologist 22(6):467–469.
McCluskey, N. G. and E. F. Borgatta
　1981　Aging and Retirement. Beverly Hills, CA: Sage Publications.
Minkler, M.
　1981　"Research on the health effects of retirement: an uncertain legacy." Journal of Health and Social Behavior 22:117–130.
Montagna, P. D.
　1977　Occupations and Society: Toward a Sociology of the Labor Market. New York: John Wiley & Sons.
Morgan, J. N.
　1980a　"Retirement in prospect and retrospect." Pp. 73–105 in G. J. Duncan and J. N. Morgan (eds.), Five Thousand American Families, Vol. 8. Ann Arbor, MI: Institute for Social Research, The University of Michigan.
　1980b　"Occupational disability and its economic correlates." Pp. 277–313 in G. J. Duncan and J. N. Morgan (eds.), Five Thousand American Families, Vol. 8. Ann Arbor, MI: Institute for Social Research, The University of Michigan.
　1981　"Antecedents and consequences of retirement." Pp. 207–244 in M. S. Hill, D. H. Hill, and J. N. Morgan (eds.), Five Thousand American Families, Vol. 9. Ann Arbor, MI: Institute for Social Research, The University of Michigan.
Munnell, A. H.
　1978　"The economic experience of blacks: 1964–1974." New England Economic Review (January/February):5–18.
Murray, J.
　1979　"Subjective retirement." Social Security Bulletin 42(11):20–25,43.
Mutran, E. and D. C. Reitzes
　1981　"Retirement, identity and well-being: realignment of role relationships." Journal of Gerontology 36(6):733–740.
Palmore, E. B., L. K. George, and G. G. Fillenbaum
　1982　"Predictors of retirement." Journal of Gerontology 37(6):733–742.
Parnes, H. S. and G. Nestel
　1981　"The retirement experience." Pp. 155–197 in H. S. Parnes (ed.), Work and Retirement. Cambridge, MA: MIT Press.
Patrick, C. H. and E. F. Borgatta
　1981　"Available data bases for aging research." Research on Aging 3(4):371–501.
Pollman, A. W.
　1971　"Early retirement: a comparison of poor health to other retirement factors." Journal of Gerontology 26(1):41–45.
Prentis, R. A.
　1980　"White-collar working women's perception of retirement." The Gerontologist 20(1):90–95.
Quinn, J. F.
　1979　"Wage determination and discrimination among older workers." Journal of Gerontology 34(5):728–735.
　1981　"The extent and correlates of partial retirement." The Gerontologist 21(6):634–643.
Roadburg, A.
　1981　"Perceptions of work and leisure among the elderly." The Gerontologist 21(2):142–145.
Schieber, S. J.
　1982　"Trends in pension coverage and benefit receipt." The Gerontologist 22(6):474–481.
Schiller, B. R. and D. C. Synder
　1982　"Restrictive pension provisions and the older worker." The Gerontologist 22(6):482–487.

Schulz, J. H.
   1976   The Economics of Aging. Belmont, CA: Wadsworth Publishing Co.
Sheppard, H. L. and S. E. Rix
   1977   The Graying of Working America. New York: The Free Press.
Strauss, H., B. W. Aldrich, and A. Lipman
   1981   "Retirement and perceived status loss: an inquiry into some objective and subjective problems produced by aging." Pp. 220–235 in J. F. Gabrium (ed.), Time, Roles and Self in Old Age. New York: Human Sciences Press.
Streib, G. F. and C. J. Schneider
   1971   Retirement in American Society. Ithaca, NY: Cornell University Press.
Stryker, S.
   1968   "Identity salience and role performance: the relevance of symbolic interaction theory for family research." Journal of Marriage and the Family 30:558–562.
Szinovacz, M. E.
   1980   "Female retirement: effects on spousal roles and marital adjustments." Journal of Family Issues 1(3):423–440.
   1982   "Women's retirement." Beverly Hills, CA: Sage Publications.

VARIATION IN SELECTED FORMS OF LEISURE ACTIVITY AMONG ELDERLY MALES

Herbert S. Parnes and Lawrence Less

ABSTRACT

Based on 1978 data collected from a representative national sample of men 57–71 years of age (National Longitudinal Surveys of Labor Market Experience), this study uses both tabular and multivariate analysis to explore factors associated with variations in patterns of leisure time activity of retired and nonretired members of the sample. Six forms of leisure activity are covered: exercise, reading, hobbies, home maintenance, visiting, and volunteer work.

Systematic relationships are found between the extent of leisure time activity and other characteristics of the men. As would be expected, retired men devote more time than nonretired men to the specified activites. Health, occupational level, and family income all bear positive relationships to the pursuit of leisure time activity. The fact that occupational level and family income have independent effects suggests that the type of work men do is related to leisure pursuits not only through income but through the character of interests associated with different occupational levels.

Current Perspectives on Aging and the Life Cycle
Volume 1, pages 223-242
Copyright © 1985 by JAI Press Inc.
All rights of reproduction in any form reserved.
ISBN: 0-89232-296-9

Among retired and nonretired men alike, participation in leisure activities is strongly associated with life satisfaction, controlling for a variety of other factors including health and income. The fact that the relationship is strong for men still at work as well as for retirees argues against the simplistic interpretation that leisure activities contribute to life satisfaction of retirees merely by substituting for their previous work activity.

I. INTRODUCTION

Gerontological literature contains numerous studies of the leisure activities of the elderly (Bossé and Ekerdt, 1981; Harris, 1981; Longino and Kart, 1982; Roadburg, 1981; Weiner and Hunt, 1981) and some have focused on the impact of retirement (Bell, 1975; Bossé and Ekerdt, 1981; Foner and Schwab, 1981; Palmore et al., 1979; Peppers, 1976; Simpson et al., 1966). Many of the studies have aimed at testing competing theories of aging. Disengagement theory (Cumming and Henry, 1961) views aging as an inevitable period of withdrawal desired by both the individual and society. In contrast, activity theory (Havighurst and Albrecht, 1953) holds that high activity levels maintained into old age increase life satisfaction and that if withdrawal from society occurs, the aging individual is the passive victim rather than the initiator of such disinvolvement. Kleemeier (1964) has pointed out that leisure activities may substitute for work "in creating good morale and high life satisfaction in the later years" (p. 183). Atchley (1971) in support of "continuity theory" suggests that leisure can have a great deal of positive value as a "bridge between pre- and post-retirement life" (p. 17). A comprehensive review of the literature on adjustment to retirement (Friedman and Orbach, 1974) concludes that "there is no basis for the assumption that retirement causes or necessarily results in a constriction of life space and activity."

Despite the considerable work that has been done, it is not easy to be satisfied with what is known about the patterns of leisure activity among the elderly and, in particular, about the differences in this regard between retired individuals and those who have remained at work. Except for the single tabulation provided by Foner and Schwab (1981), the limited number of studies of the latter issue have been based on very small samples that do not purport to be representative; moreover, none has raised the question of whether the factors related to variation in leisure activity are the same for retired and nonretired men.

In this paper we attempt to meet these shortcomings of previous research by utilizing a rich data bank representative of the total U.S. population of elderly males. Our purpose is to join two interrelated subjects of inquiry: (1) the pattern of leisure activity among retired and nonretired men and (2) the effect of the extent of leisure activity on life satisfaction. More specifically, we first describe the patterns of leisure activity among representative national samples of retired and nonretired men and identify the characteristics associated with variation in those patterns. Second, controlling for other differences between retired and nonretired men, we measure the nature and extent of the difference in leisure activity between the two groups, interpreting differences as reflecting the effect of retirement.[1] Third, the extent of leisure activity is used as an explanatory variable in exploring life satisfaction among both retired and nonretired men. Although our findings have some relevance to the disengagement theory/activity theory controversy and the identity crisis/identity continuity debate (Atchley, 1971), we do not explicitly deal with those issues.

A. The Data Set and Principal Variables

A representative sample of the United States civilian population of males between the ages of 45 and 59 was drawn by the U.S. Bureau of the Census in 1966. Blacks were overrepresented in a ratio of 3 or 4 to 1 in order to permit reliable interracial comparisons. The total sample numbered 5,020—3,518 whites and 1,420 blacks.[2] Interviews were conducted first in 1966 and periodically thereafter (every one or two years) through 1983, although as of this writing data are available only through 1980.[3] As of that year, 2,931 white and black men were interviewed.

Because attrition from the sample for reasons other than death appears to be substantially random and because sampling weights of those interviewed have been adjusted each year to compensate for differences in attrition by race, education, and geographic mobility, the respondents interviewed in 1980 may be regarded as representative of the noninstitutionalized civilian population of white and black men 59–73 years of age in that year.[4] Data relating to retirement should therefore reflect rather faithfully both the incidence of retirement and the character of the retirement experience of the cohort of men within that age range as of 1980. It must be kept in mind, however, that our sample of retirees cannot be construed to be representative of *all* retirees as of 1980. The fact that the oldest member of the sample is 73 means that individuals who had been retired for long periods of time are not represented.[5]

1. Retirement Status

Respondents were asked in each survey at what age they expected to stop working at a regular job. One of the precoded responses to this question was "already stopped," and persons who responded in this way have been classified as retired.[6] On the basis of the entire longitudinal record for each individual prior to retirement we have classified retirees into three categories: men who were involuntarily retired under a mandatory retirement plan (mandatory retirement); those whose retirement appears from the total record to have been dictated by poor health (health retirement); and the remainder, i.e., men who appear to have freely chosen retirement (voluntary retirement). The latter group is subdivided into those who retired prior to age 65 (early retirement) and those who retired at that age or later (normal retirement).[7]

2. Leisure Activities

No definition of leisure is universally accepted, although it generally connotes time spent in activities other than work for pay or personal maintenance (Kaplan, 1961; Kleemeier, 1964; Robinson, Chap. 4, 1977). This uncertainty gives rise to the question of whether the meaning of leisure changes once an individual loses or abandons his or her primary labor market role (Hendricks and Hendricks, 1977; Roadburg, 1981). In any case, most investigations of leisure time pursuits have attempted to obtain some measure of the amount of time—in either relative or absolute terms—that the individual has spent in a variety of specified activities (Harris, 1981; Bossé and Ekerdt, 1981). In the present case, the 1978 interview schedule asked respondents whether they had engaged in each of six different types of activity during the preceding 12 months: (1) sports or exercise, e.g., golf, tennis, swimming; (2) reading books, magazines, or newspapers; (3) hobbies, e.g., collections, woodworking, playing a musical instrument, or gardening; (4) visiting with friends or relatives; (5) working on home maintenance or home repairs around the house; (6) doing volunteer work. For each affirmative response, individuals were asked during how many weeks they engaged in the activity and, on average, about how many hours per week they were thus involved.

On the basis of the resulting data, we have constructed two variables for each type of activity: (1) a dichotomous variable indicating whether the respondent engaged in the activity and (2) the total number of hours (weeks × weekly hours) that he spent on the activity. The latter has also been summed across the six activities to provide an aggregate annual figure.

The limitations of these data are self-evident. To begin with, this method of obtaining information on the amount of time devoted to various activities is not as reliable as the use of time diaries (Robinson, 1977). Second, we clearly cannot claim that all forms of leisure activity are included in the data. On the basis of a recent national survey that included a larger number of activities (Harris, 1981), the most important omission from the NLS data is watching television. Because this is an activity that occurs predominantly in the home, it seems likely that its omission results in an understatement of the amount of leisure activity of retired as compared with nonretired men.

3. Life Satisfaction

To measure the degree of satisfaction with their life situations in 1980, respondents were asked whether they were very happy, somewhat happy, somewhat unhappy, or very unhappy with five aspects of life:[8] their housing, the local area in which they resided, their health condition, their standard of living, and their leisure time activities. In addition, they were asked to indicate by means of the same four response categories how they felt "taking things all together." By assigning values from 1 (very unhappy) to 4 (very happy) to the responses to each component and then summing them, these six questions have been combined into a single "satisfaction-with-life" index ranging from 6 to 24.[9]

II. VARIATIONS IN LEISURE ACTIVITIES

One of the presumed attractions of retirement is the opportunity it provides for greater leisure. However, the limited evidence thus far available suggests that retirees engage in substantially the same general types of leisure activities they pursued while working (Peppers, 1976), and at least one study (Bossé and Ekerdt, 1981) found no increase in perceived involvement in leisure activities as the result of retirement. As has been noted above, however, the issue has not yet been examined on the basis of a representative national sample.

A. Gross Relationships: Retirement Status and Race

Table 1 stratifies the total National Longitudinal Surveys (NLS) sample by retirement status and race, and shows for each group the degree of participation in the six types of leisure activity specified in the 1978 interview schedule. It must be borne in mind that the table displays *gross* differences among the several categories of men, i.e., unadjusted for differences in other characteristics that may be related to retirement status or race.

For the total sample, reading and visiting are by far the most popular leisure activities, engaged in by over 85 percent of the respondents. At the other extreme is volunteer work, which occupies only one in five of the men. Between these, in descending order of frequency, are home maintenance work (67 percent), hobbies (53 percent), and exercise (40 percent). Among those who engage in the activities there is less variation in average number of hours devoted to them, ranging from about 485 hours in the case of reading to about 150 each for home maintenance and volunteer work. Relatively little variation appears among the participants in the amount of time they devote to each activity, except for reading. In that case, the large majority of men who report spending some time reading are fairly equally divided between those who spend under 250 hours per year, those who spend between 251 and 500 hours, and those who read for more than 500 hours. In the case of each of the other activities, between two-thirds and four-fifths of the participants spend no more than 250 hours per year—or about five hours per week on the average. Black men are much less likely than whites to engage in each of the activities, the difference being about 20 percentage points or more in the case of reading, exercise, and hobbies.

Table 1. Number of Hours per Year Devoted to Specified Leisure Activities, by Retirement Status and Race, 1978 (percentage distributions)

Activity	Total (n = 2899)						Whites (n = 2087)						Blacks (n = 812)					
	Total	None	1–250 Hours	251–500 Hours	Over 500 Hours	Mean[a]	Total	None	1–250 Hours	251–500 Hours	Over 500 Hours	Mean[a]	Total	None	1–250 Hours	251–500 Hours	Over 500 Hours	Mean[a]
									Total									
Exercise	100	60	28	7	5	247	100	59	29	7	5	247	100	78	16	3	2	235
Reading	100	12	26	29	33	484	100	10	25	29	35	492	100	33	31	22	14	346
Hobbies	100	47	35	10	8	251	100	46	36	10	8	255	100	63	30	4	3	179
Visiting	100	14	61	13	12	257	100	13	62	13	12	258	100	22	55	11	12	240
Home maintenance	100	33	55	7	6	158	100	31	56	7	6	160	100	51	41	4	4	133
Volunteer work	100	80	16	2	2	144	100	80	16	2	2	145	100	86	12	2	1	127
						Retired men[b] (n: whites = 1254; blacks = 504)												
Exercise	100	62	25	6	7	273	100	60	26	7	7	273	100	80	14	3	3	261
Reading	100	14	24	27	35	490	100	12	23	28	37	497	100	36	30	20	13	355
Hobbies	100	46	35	11	9	273	100	44	35	11	10	279	100	65	29	3	3	159
Visiting	100	15	58	14	14	274	100	14	58	14	14	275	100	25	51	11	13	252
Home maintenance	100	37	50	7	6	170	100	35	52	7	7	173	100	59	34	4	3	134
Volunteer work	100	81	14	3	2	174	100	81	14	3	2	175	100	85	12	2	1	144
						Never retired men (n: whites = 833; blacks = 308)												
Exercise	100	58	32	7	3	176	100	57	33	7	3	176	100	75	20	4	1	189
Reading	100	10	29	31	31	431	100	8	29	32	32	437	100	28	32	25	15	342
Hobbies	100	50	37	8	5	202	100	50	37	8	5	202	100	60	30	6	4	204
Visiting	100	13	67	12	9	212	100	13	67	12	8	212	100	18	61	12	9	216
Home maintenance	100	27	63	7	4	129	100	26	64	7	4	129	100	40	52	4	5	132
Volunteer work	100	79	19	2	1	105	100	78	19	2	1	106	100	86	13	1	—[c]	97

Source: National Longitudinal Surveys.
[a] Excluding those who do not engage in the activity.
[b] Men who had retired between 1965 and 1978. For definition of retirement, see text, Section I.A.1.
[c] Less than 0.5%.

228

Leisure Activity Among Elderly Males 229

The relative popularity of the several types of activity is identical for retired and nonretired men and, indeed, there is little difference between the two groups in the incidence of each activity, except for the lesser participation of the retired men in home maintenance (63 percent vs. 73 percent). As would be expected, however, retired men spend more time at each activity than the nonretired, although this relationship does not hold for the black men.

Taking all of the activities together, the typical respondent estimated spending about 1,000 hours per year—in the neighborhood of 20 hours per week (Table 2). For black men, however, the amount of time was only two-thirds as great as for whites. As would be expected, the dispersion around this average is considerably greater than in the case of individual activities; one in seven of the men spent fewer than five hours per week on all activities combined, but one in five devoted as many as 29 hours a week to them. For both races combined, retired men spent more time on the specified activities than men who had never retired, but the difference was attributable solely to the whites. The very small difference among blacks was actually in favor of the never-retired men.

B. Multivariate Analysis

1. Total Sample

What characteristics of older men are associated with the variation in the amount of time devoted to the specified leisure time activities? This question is addressed for the entire sample of men as well as for the retirees and nonretirees separately by the data shown in Table 3. The table presents the results of three

Table 2. Total Number of Hours per Year
Devoted to Specified Leisure Activities, by Retirement Status and Race, 1978
(percentage distributions)

Number of Hours	Total			Retired Men			Never Retired Men		
	Total	Whites	Blacks	Total	Whites	Blacks	Total	Whites	Blacks
Total n	2703	1941	762	1638	1162	476	1065	779	286
Total percent	100	100	100	100	100	100	100	100	100
None	1	5	2	2	7	1	1	3	2
1–250	12	10	30	11	10	33	12	11	24
251–500	15	15	21	14	14	19	17	16	24
501–1000	32	33	23	28	28	18	39	39	30
1001–1500	20	20	12	20	21	13	19	19	11
1501–2000	10	10	4	11	12	5	7	8	3
Over 2000	10	10	6	13	14	6	5	5	5
Mean[a]	1001	1031	647	1100	1140	637	851	867	663

Source: National Longitudinal Surveys.
[a]Includes men who spent no time on any of the activities.

Table 3. Total Number of Hours per Year
Devoted to Specified Leisure Activities, by Selected Characteristics, 1978
(MCA results)

	\multicolumn{2}{c}{Total Sample}	\multicolumn{2}{c}{Retired Men}	\multicolumn{2}{c}{Never Retired Men}
Characteristic	n	Adjusted[a] No. of Hours (F-ratio)	n	Adjusted[a] No. of Hours (F-ratio)	n	Adjusted[a] No. of Hours (F-ratio)
Total sample	2703	1001	1638	1100	1065	851
Retirement status		(153.090)**				
Never retired	1065	778**	—[d]		—[d]	
Retired	1638	1147**				
Race		(10.195)**		(10.358)**		(0.576)
Whites	1941	1014**	1162	1119**	779	855
Blacks	762	841**	476	874**	286	804
Age		(1.230)		(0.209)		(3.001)*
57–61	1019	985	333	1110	686	848
62–66	941	990	639	1078	302	818
67–71	743	1038	666	1112	77	1000*
Marital status		(0.437)		(0.018)		(0.076)
Married	2226	1004	1312	1100	914	849
Nonmarried	477	977	326	1093	151	864
Physical or mental impairment, 1976[b]		(16.271)**		(5.468)**		(0.182)
None	1050	1068**	473	1150	577	856
Minor-moderate	1081	1023	672	1136	409	847
Substantial-severe	553	798**	483	975**	70	814
Total family income, 1977		(10.744)**		(6.220)**		(3.107)**
Less than $5,000	336	808**	293	946*	43	762
$5,000–9,999	520	945†	412	1072	108	728†
$10,000–14,999	382	1100**	241	1235**	141	801
$15,000–19,999	284	1153**	119	1283*	165	948*
$20,000 or more	498	1078*	179	1208	319	901†
Occupation		(16.858)**		(8.645)**		(9.347)**
Professional	229	1200**	126	1254*	103	1076**
Managerial	360	1182**	198	1327**	162	930*
Other white collar	265	1137**	152	1272**	113	934
Craft	759	837**	506	938**	253	718**
Other blue collar	479	847**	308	992*	171	668**
Other	603	990	344	1068	259	852
Region		(11.178)**		(4.724)*		(5.741)*
South	1038	928**	673	1037*	365	782*
Nonsouth	1665	1033**	965	1132*	700	877*
Size of community		(2.918)†		(4.442)*		(0.363)
Small	960	1008	597	1134	363	837
Medium	1111	1028†	689	1127	422	868
Large	632	937*	352	976**	280	839
Work activity, 1978				(3.344)†		
None	—[d]		1157	1135*	—[d]	
Some			477	1021*		
Hours worked, 1978						(0.194)
Less than 2000	—[d]		—[d]		233	844
2000 or more					817	854

(*continued*)

230

Table 3 (Continued)

Characteristic	Total Sample n	Adjusted[a] No. of Hours (F-ratio)	Retired Men n	Adjusted[a] No. of Hours (F-ratio)	Never Retired Men n	Adjusted[a] No. of Hours (F-ratio)
Attitude toward retirement, 1978[c]		—[d]		(8.524)**		—[d]
Favorable			495	1242**		
Ambivalent			630	1068		
Unfavorable			400	1011*		
Route into retirement		—[d]		(8.313)**		—[d]
Forced			60	1232		
Health			683	951**		
Voluntary early			678	1204**		
Voluntary normal			216	1151		
Adjusted R^2		0.12		0.14		0.07

Source: National Longitudinal Surveys.
[a] For nature of adjustment, see text note 10.
[b] For construction of impairment index, see Chirikos and Nestel (1981).
[c] See text note 11.
[d] Not included in regression.
**Significant at the .01 level.
*Significant at the .05 level.
†Significant at the .10 level.

separate multiple classification analyses (MCAs):[10] one for the total sample, in which retirement status is introduced as one of the explanatory variables; a second for retired men; and the third for nonretirees. In each of the latter two a work activity variable is included which, for the retirees, differentiates those who worked at all from those who did not and, for the nonretired men, distinguishes between men who worked at least 2,000 hours per year and those who worked less than that.

With other characteristics of the men controlled, retirement status makes a more substantial difference than is indicated by the bivariate relationship shown in Table 2. Retired men devote 47 percent more time than their nonretired counterparts to the types of leisure time activity we have inquired about—a differential of about seven hours a week in contrast to the less than 4.8-hour difference shown by the bivariate data.

The gross racial difference that has been observed for the total sample in the bivariate relationships shown in Table 2 is maintained even with other characteristics controlled. Other things being equal, black men in the age-group under consideration devote about three fewer hours per week than whites to the specified activities. This finding suggests that the standard questions on leisure time activities probably have a cultural bias and that a serious effort to explore racial differences in leisure activities would require a different approach. Consistent with this interpretation is Neulinger's (1981) observation that there are good theoretical reasons for expecting major differences in leisure behavior between whites and blacks. "Leisure behavior is part of one's cultural heritage, and the American black certainly had a cultural background different from the average white American . . . their job was to make leisure possible for everyone except themselves" (p. 126). Additional evidence of this phenomenon emerges from our own work; in an earlier version of the MCAs we stratified by race and found that few of the relationships for the whites prevailed for the blacks. The results that are presented here should therefore be interpreted as applying basically to white men.

Both family income and occupational level (of current job for the nonretirees and of preretirement job for those who have retired) bear pronounced positive relationships with the amount of time spent in leisure time activity, at least among white men. The difference between the professional and managerial categories at one extreme and blue-collar workers at the other amounts to more than 300 hours per year, or over six hours per week. With regard to income, a difference of about the same magnitude separates those with incomes under $5,000 per year and those earning over $10,000, although the highest income group ($20,000 or more) devotes slightly fewer hours to leisure time activity than the next lower category.

The fact that occupational level and income exercise independent effects on what might be described as the purposeful use of leisure time has important implications. It suggests that the kind of work that men do influences leisure activities not only through the income that it generates, but also by conditioning (or reflecting) their interests. If participation in leisure activities contributes to satisfaction, one might therefore expect men who have retired from high-level jobs to manifest above-average satisfaction with retirement even when such factors as income and health are held constant.

Neither age nor marital status shows a significant relationship to the measure of leisure time activity, but health condition manifests a strong effect. Men with substantial or severe impairments devote significantly less time to the specified activities than men with less serious (or no) handicaps. Certain aspects of residence also bear a relationship to the extent of leisure time activity. Men residing in the south spend less time than those residing elsewhere; similarly, residents of very large communities devote less time to the specified activities than those in areas with smaller populations.

2. Stratification by Retirement Status

An interaction between retirement status and some of the other variables is evident in Table 3. To begin with, the racial difference that prevails in the total sample is pronounced among retirees but does not exist among men who have not retired—another finding that supports the cultural difference hypothesis mentioned above. The health variable is also nonsignificant among the men who are not retired, presumably because even the relatively few who are classified as having substantial impairments are not handicapped to the same degree as men in that category who have stopped working. Size of community doesn't make the same difference among working men as it does for the retired group. There is also a curious interaction between retirement status and age. Whereas no significant age differences appear among the retired men, the oldest five-year age category of nonretirees devotes a significantly larger number of hours to the specified activities than the two younger groups. Finally, although the variable is defined differently for the retired and nonretired groups, the extent of work activity bears a significant negative relationship to leisure time activity among retired men but not among their nonretired counterparts.

Two additional variables have been used in the MCA for retirees to ascertain whether the circumstances under which retirement occurred and the respondent's general attitude toward retirement are related to the extent of their leisure activities. The reason for retirement turns out to be highly significant; men who retired for health reasons devote considerably less time to the specified pursuits than voluntary retirees—especially the subset of the latter who retired prior to age 65. Since this difference is net of the differences in the extent of impairments in 1976, it suggests either that the impairment index does not reflect the full extent of health differences among the several groups of retirees or that, irrespective of current state of health, men who were forced by bad health to retire were psychologically less disposed than other men to develop interests in the types of leisure activities covered by the survey.

The strong positive relationship between attitude toward retirement and extent of leisure time activity is difficult to interpret confidently because the two variables were measured at the same time, making the direction of causation ambiguous. However, because the attitudinal variable purports to measure a *generalized* reaction to the idea of retirement rather than the degree of satisfaction with the retired status,[11] it seems to us reasonable to conclude that men who hold favorable views of retirement are more likely to develop purposeful uses of leisure during their own retirements.

3. *Variation in Pursuit of Specific Activities*

We turn now to a disaggregation of the results just described. Separate MCAs, comparable to those displayed in Table 3, have been run for each of the six leisure activities. In each case the dependent variable has been specified in two forms: (1) a dichotomous variable indicating whether the respondent engaged in the specified activity and (2) a continuous variable showing, for those who had participated, the number of hours per year. Moreover, there are two versions of each MCA—one for retired and one for nonretired men. In each case the explanatory variables are identical to those shown in Table 3. We have also run a series of MCAs for the total sample using the retirement status variable. From these we have extracted the adjusted values for the retirement status variable, and these are presented in Table 4.

Retirement significantly increases the likelihood of engaging in physical exercise, hobbies, and volunteer work, but makes no significant difference in regard to reading, visiting, and home maintenance. When attention is confined to those who participate in each activity, retired men spend significantly more time than their nonretired counterparts on every activity. The difference is greatest in the case of exercise—137 hours per year, or a little over 2.5 hours per week. For each of the other five activities in which the difference is significant it is less than 100 hours per year.

The complete results of all 24 MCAs (six activities × two dependent variables × two samples) are too voluminous to present here. Table 5 contains summaries of these results, showing the relationships between all the explanatory variables and each dependent variable for every activity. To use the upper portion of the table as an illustration, we see that the retired married men (in row three) are significantly more likely than nonmarried men, other things being equal, to devote some time to hobbies, home maintenance activities, and exercise, but that otherwise there are no differences by marital status. Attitude toward retirement (in the last row) bears a significant positive relationship to the likelihood of participation in all forms of leisure time activity except volunteer work and reading.

The most important generalizations yielded by Table 5 may be summarized briefly:

1. By and large the relationships for retired men are fairly similar to those for the never retired sample, although the relationship of marital status to the incidence of the activities is a perplexing exception. Married retirees are more likely to engage in all activities except reading, visiting, and volunteer work, whereas nonretired married men are more likely to spend time visiting and on hobbies and home maintenance.

2. The explanatory variables are more strongly and consistently related to the likelihood of participation in the several forms of leisure time activity than to the amount of time that participants devote to them. This is consistent with our finding greater variation in the incidence of participation than in the number of hours devoted by the participants.

3. Within the 15-year age range represented by the NLS sample, age rarely manifests an independent relationship to participation in any of the leisure activities, but the negative relation with the likelihood of engaging in exercise is a prominent exception. On the other hand, older retirees devote more time to reading than their younger counterparts.

4. Inexplicably, degree of physical or mental impairment of retirees bears a strong negative relationship only with the likelihood of engaging in reading and home maintenance activities. However, such impairment does display a strong

Table 4. Adjusted[a] Incidence and Number of Hours of Participation in Specified Leisure Activities, by Retirement Status, 1978 (MCA results)

Activity	Adjusted[a] Percent Participating Retired	Never Retired	Adjusted[a] Hours of Participants Retired	Never Retired
Exercise	44**	35**	304**	167**
Reading	89	87	518**	437**
Hobbies	57**	46**	285**	193**
Visiting	87	85	283**	218**
Home maintenance	67	68	191**	115**
Volunteer work	21*	18*	178**	97**

Source: National Longitudinal Surveys.
[a]Adjusted for the effects of all of the variables used in the MCA for the total sample shown in Table 3. For nature of the adjustment, see text note 10.
**Significant at the .01 level.
*Significant at the .05 level.

negative effect on number of hours of exercise for both retired and never-retired men.

5. Occupational level and family income display the same independent effects on the likelihood of participating in many forms of leisure pursuits as have been noted in the case of total hours of leisure activity. Moreover, occupational level bears a strong positive relationship to number of hours devoted to reading. With this exception, the income and occupation variables display no regular relationship to the number of hours that participants devote to the activities in which they engage.

6. Among retirees black men are significantly less likely than their white counterparts to devote time to all activities except volunteer work and home maintenance. The racial difference is less pronounced among nonretired men and is strongly significant only for reading. Among the participants in each activity there is no racial difference in number of hours, except that black retirees devote fewer hours to reading than their white counterparts.

7. Retirees living in the south are less likely to engage in all activities except volunteer work (no relationship) and exercise (more likely to participate). Retirees living in larger communities are less likely to participate in most activities.

8. Among retirees, those who retired for health reasons are less likely than voluntary retirees to engage in all the activities except hobbies. Those with favorable general attitudes toward retirement are significantly more likely to engage in every type of activity except volunteer work.

Table 5. Relation Between Specified Leisure Activities and Selected Characteristics of Men 57–71 Years of Age, 1978 (summary of MCA results)[a]

Characteristic	Retired						Never retired					
	Exercise	Reading	Hobbies	Visiting	Home Maintenance	Volunteer Work	Exercise	Reading	Hobbies	Visiting	Home Maintenance	Volunteer Work
	Incidence of participation											
Race (being black)	−	−	0	−	0	0	0	−	0	0	0	0
Age	−	0	0	0	0	1	−	0	0	0	0	−
Being married	+	0	+	0	+	0	0	0	+	+	+	0
Owning home	b	b	b	b	+	b	b	b	b	b	+	b
Physical or mental impairment[c]	1	−	0	0	−	0	0	0	0	0	1	0
Family income	+	1	+	0	+	+	+	+	+	0	0	1
Occupational level	+	1	+	1	0	1	+	+	1	0	0	1
Living in south	+	−	−	−	−	0	0	−	+	−	−	0
Size of community	0	0	−	−	−	−	0	0	0	0	−	−
Work activity	0	0	0	0	0	0	0	0	+	0	0	0
Retired for health	−	−	0	−	−	−	b	b	b	b	b	b
Favorable retirement attitude	+	0	+	+	+	0	b	b	b	b	b	b

Number of hours

Variable												
Race (being black)	0	–	0	0	0	0	0	0	0	0	0	0
Age[a]	0	+	0	0	I	0	0	0	0	0	0	0
Being married	0	0	0	0	0	0	0	0	0	0	0	0
Owning home	b	b	b	b	+	b	b	b	b	b	b	b
Physical or mental impairment[c]	–	0	0	0	0	–	0	0	0	0	0	0
Family income	I	0	I	0	0	I	0	0	0	0	0	0
Occupational level	0	+	I	0	0	0	+	0	0	0	0	0
Living in south	0	0	0	0	0	0	0	0	0	0	–	0
Size of community	0	0	–	0	+	0	0	0	0	0	0	0
Work activity	–	0	0	0	0	0	–	0	0	0	0	–
Retired for health	0	0	0	0	0	0	b	b	b	b	b	b
Favorable retirement attitude	0	I	0	+	0	0	b	b	b	b	b	b

Source: National Longitudinal Surveys.

Note: Each symbol describes the relationship that has been found between the explanatory variable shown in the stub and the dependent variable in a multiple classification analysis that has been performed for each specified type of leisure activity (see text for further detail). A "+" signifies a positive relationship significant at the .05 level; a "–" signifies a negative relationship significant at the .05 level; a "0" signifies no significant relationship; an "I" signifies a significant irregular relationship.

[a] For description of MCA, see text note 10.
[b] Variable not included.
[c] For construction of impairment index, see Chirikos and Nestel (1981).

III. LEISURE ACTIVITIES AND LIFE SATISFACTION

We now inquire whether the forms of leisure time activity that we have measured make a net contribution to the degree of life satisfaction expressed by our sample of males. For this purpose we have run three MCAs: one for the total sample, one for the retirees, and one for the men who had not yet retired by 1980. The dependent variable in each of these is the index of life satisfaction as of 1980, which has been described earlier. Among the explanatory variables is the total number of hours of leisure activity reported in the 1978 survey. Control variables in all three versions of the MCA include race, age, and marital status; occupation and type of worker (government, private, self-employed); region and size of community of residence; and measures of health, assets, and family income. In the MCA for the total sample retirement status is introduced as an additional control variable. In the retirees' MCA, additional control variables are work status in 1980, reason for retirement, general attitude toward retirement (measured in 1978), and retrospective evaluation in 1980 of the respondent's retirement decision.

Table 6 presents the adjusted life satisfaction index according to extent of leisure time activity and thus shows the net relationship between number of hours of leisure time activity and degree of life satisfaction, controlling for all of the factors listed above. For retirees and nonretirees alike there is a strong and regular relationship, significant at the 1 percent confidence level, between the amount of time a man spends on the specified forms of leisure activity and degree

Table 6. Net Relation[a] Between Extent of Leisure Time Activity in 1978 and Degree of Life Satisfaction Expressed in 1980, by Retirement Status (MCA results)

Extent of Leisure Activity, 1978	Adjusted[a] Life Satisfaction Index		
	Total	Retirees	Nonretired Men
Total n	2810	1959	851
Mean life satisfaction index	20.4	20.1	20.9
300 hours or less	19.5**	19.3**	20.1**
301–600 hours	20.1*	19.9	20.7
601–900 hours	20.3	20.0	21.1
901–1200 hours	20.7**	20.5*	21.1
Over 1200 hours	20.8**	20.5**	21.2[†]
F-ratio	13.784**	8.429**	3.765**

Source: National Longitudinal Surveys.
[a]For the list of variables entering the MCA, see text. For description of MCA, see text note 10.
**Significant at the .01 level.
*Significant at the .05 level.
[†]Significant at the .10 level.

of life satisfaction. It is interesting that the relationship is strong for the men who are still at work as well as for the retirees. This suggests that it is perhaps an oversimplification to regard the leisure activities of retired men as contributing to life satisfaction merely by substituting for their previous work activity. Retirement, to be sure, tends to increase the amount of time devoted to the forms of leisure activity that we have investigated, but by less than one-fifth of the hours that had previously been spent at work. Moreover, retirement appears to make little difference in regard to either the pattern of leisure activity or the factors associated with variation therein.

IV. SUMMARY AND CONCLUSIONS

A representative national sample of men aged 57–71 spent an average of about 20 hours a week in 1978 on six forms of leisure time activities: exercise, reading, hobbies, home maintenance, visiting, and volunteer work. Participation rates range from 88 percent in the case of reading to 20 percent in the case of volunteer work. Among those participating in the several activities, the variation in average amount of time per year devoted to each is less extreme—from about 500 hours (reading) to 150 hours (volunteer work).

A multivariate analysis reveals systematic relationships between the extent of leisure time activity and other characteristics of men in this age group. As would be expected, retirees as a group devote more time than nonretired men to the specified leisure activities in the aggregate: they have significantly higher participation rates in exercise, hobbies, and volunteer work. Controlling for other characteristics increases the gross difference between the two groups; if one is willing to accept this kind of cross-sectional evidence,[12] it can be said that retirement adds an average of seven hours a week to the time that men spend on the specified activities.

Even with other characteristics controlled, black men are significantly less likely than whites to engage in each of the activities (except volunteer work), which suggests a cultural bias in the specific types of activity about which respondents were asked. Health, occupational level, and family income all bear positive relationships to the pursuit of purposeful leisure time activity. The fact that occupational level and family income have independent effects suggests that the type of work men do is related to leisure pursuits not only through income but through the character of interests associated with different occupational levels.

The characteristics that are associated with variation in total time devoted to the leisure activities also tend to be related to variation in the likelihood of participation in each. Moreover, these patterns are fairly similar for both retired and nonretired men. Additional characteristics of retired men relate to their participation in the leisure activities—the reason for retirement and their generalized attitude toward retirement. Men who had retired because of poor health were significantly less involved in leisure pursuits than those who had retired voluntarily even controlling for current state of health. Men with favorable views about the desirability of retirement were more heavily involved than those with unfavorable views.

Among retired and nonretired men alike, participation in leisure activities is strongly associated with life satisfaction, controlling for a variety of other factors including health and income. The fact that the relationship is strong for men still at work as well as for retirees argues against the simplistic interpretation that leisure activities contribute to life satisfaction of retirees merely by substituting for their previous work activity.

ACKNOWLEDGMENTS

This report was prepared under a contract with the Employment and Training Administration, U.S. Department of Labor, under the authority of the Comprehensive Employment and Training Act. Researchers undertaking such projects under government sponsorship are encouraged to express their own judgments. Interpretations or viewpoints contained in this document do not necessarily represent the official position or policy of the Department of Labor. The authors profited considerably from the comments of their colleagues at the Center for Human Resource Research on an earlier draft, and especially from the helpful advice of Joan Crowley, although none of these individuals bears responsibility for whatever shortcomings remain.

NOTES

1. The usual objections to interpreting cross-sectional data in this way carry much less weight when the research design permits statistical controls for other differences between retired and nonretired men, especially age and health (cf. Palmore, 1968:261).

2. The remaining 82 members of the sample represented other races and are excluded from our analysis.

3. As of 1985, data are available for a more complete description of the NLS, see Center for Human Resource Research (1982).

4. See Parnes et al. (1981:4).

5. For most of the analysis we use only those men who were retired as of the time of the 1978 survey because it was in that survey that information on leisure time activities was collected.

6. We have elsewhere used alternative criteria of retirement and have analyzed variation in both number and characteristics of retirees according to the retirement criterion used. See Parnes and Less (1985).

7. It is important to understand that we have included in the mandatory group only a subset of men who were covered by mandatory plans: viz., those who retired at the mandatory age *and* had reported in the survey preceding retirement that they would have preferred to work longer. In the absence of evidence that retirement was induced by poor health, we regard as voluntary retirees men under a mandatory plan who retire before they have to, or at the mandatory age if they have reported no desire to work longer. Retirees who did not qualify for inclusion in the mandatory retirement group are classified as having retired for health reasons if evidence of work-limiting health problems is found in the year preceding retirement. All others are regarded as voluntary retirees.

8. Campbell et al. (1976) note a difference between "satisfaction with life" and "happiness with life" measures, but conclude that the two items tap "somewhat the same state of mind" (p. 35) and behave in the same way where demographic correlates are concerned, except that older persons show more satisfaction than young persons, whereas measures of happiness vary inversely with age.

9. For a justification of this approach, see Campbell et al. (1976:79). We experimented with two other measures: (1) a weighted sum in which health and standard of living had a weight of 2 and the overall question had a weight of 3; and (2) a simple dichotomous variable based on the overall question: very happy = 1; all other = 0. We chose the unweighted version because neither a factor analysis nor a multiple regression analysis provided evidence that justified weighting the separate responses. We preferred this to the simple dichotomous measure because of its explicit reference to several important "domains of life experience" (cf. Campbell et al. 1976:63). Actually, the major findings are substantially the same irrespective of the form of the dependent variable.

10. Multiple classification analysis, like multiple regression analysis with all of the explanatory variables expressed in categorical form, avoids the assumption of linearity. The constant term in the multiple classification equation represents the grand mean of the dependent variable over all of the observations. The coefficient of each category of every explanatory variable represents a deviation from the grand mean. Use of these coefficients allows us to calculate "adjusted" values of the dependent variable for every category of each explanatory variable, e.g., the number of hours that retired men and nonretired men would have devoted to leisure activity had each group been average in terms of all the other variables entering into the analysis. The F-ratio tests the overall significance of the explanatory variable while the t statistic tests the significance of a particular code category against the grand mean of the explanatory variable (see Andrews et al., 1967.)

11. The index is based on respondents' reactions to the following statements: (1) work is the most meaningful part of life, (2) most people think more of someone who works than they do of someone who doesn't, (3) retirement is a pleasant time of life, (4) older workers should retire when they can, so as to give younger people more of a chance on the job, and (5) people who don't retire when they can afford to are foolish.

12. See note 1, above. A subsequent *longitudinal* estimate of the effect of retirement on hours of leisure has yielded an almost identical figure. See Parnes et al. (1985). p. 129.

REFERENCES

Andrews, Frank, James Morgan, and John Sonquist
    1967   Multiple Classification Analysis. Ann Arbor, MI: Institute of Social Research.
Atchley, Robert C.
    1971   "Retirement and leisure participation: continuity or crisis." The Gerontologist 11:13–17.
Bell, B. D.
    1975   "The limitations of crisis theory as an explanatory mechanism in social gerontology." International Journal of Aging and Human Development 6:153–168.
Bossé, R. and D. J. Ekerdt
    1981   "Change in self-perception of leisure activities with retirement." The Gerontologist 21:650–654.
Campbell, Angus, Philip E. Converse, and Willard L. Rodgers
    1976   The Quality of American Life. New York: Russell Sage Foundation.
Center for Human Resource Research
    1982   The National Longitudinal Surveys Handbook. Columbus, OH: Ohio State University.
Chirikos, Thomas N. and Gilbert Nestel
    1981   "Impairment and labor market outcomes: a cross-sectional and longitudinal analysis." Pp. 93–131 in Herbert S. Parnes (ed.), Work and Retirement: A Longitudinal Study of Men. Cambridge, MA: MIT Press.

Cumming, E. and W. E. Henry
   1961   Growing Old: The Process of Disengagement. New York: Basic Books.
Foner, Anne and Karen Schwab
   1981   Aging and Retirement. Monterey, CA: Brooks/Cole Publishing.
Friedman, Eugene A. and Harold L. Orbach
   1974   "Adjustment to retirement." Chapter 30 in Silvano Arieti (ed.), American Handbook of Psychiatry, Vol. 1. 2nd ed. New York: Basic Books.
Harris, Louis and Associates
   1981   Aging in the Eighties: America in Transition. Washington, DC: The National Council on the Aging.
Havighurst, R. J. and R. Albrecht
   1953   Older People. New York: Longmans, Green, and Co.
Hendricks, J. and D. Hendricks
   1977   Aging in Mass Society: Myths and Realities. Cambridge, MA: Winthrop Publishers.
Kaplan, Max
   1961   "Toward a theory of leisure for social gerontology." Chapter 13 in Robert W. Kleemeier (ed.), Aging and Leisure. New York: Oxford University Press.
Kleemeier, Robert W.
   1964   "Leisure and disengagement in retirement." The Gerontologist 4:180–184.
Longino, Charles F., Jr. and Cary S. Kart
   1982   "Explicating activity theory: a formal replication." Journal of Gerontology 6:713–722.
Neulinger, John
   1981   The Psychology of Leisure. 2nd ed. Springfield, IL: Charles C. Thomas.
Palmore, E. B.
   1968   "The effects of aging on activities and attitudes." The Gerontologist 8:259–263.
Palmore, E., et al.
   1979   "Stress and adaptation in later life." Journal of Gerontology 34:841–851.
Parnes, Herbert S., et al.
   1981   Work and Retirement: A Longitudinal Study of Men. Cambridge, MA: MIT Press.
Parnes, Herbert S. and Lawrence Less
   1985   "The volume and pattern of retirements, 1966–1981." Pp. 57–77 in Herbert S. Parnes et al., *Retirement Among American Men*. Lexington, MA: Lexington Books.
Peppers, L. G.
   1976   "Patterns of leisure and adjustment to retirement." The Gerontologist 16:441–446.
Roadburg, A.
   1981   "Perceptions of work and leisure among the elderly." The Gerontologist 21:142–145.
Robinson, John P.
   1977   How Americans Use Time. New York: Praeger.
Simpson, I. H., K. W. Back, and J. C. McKinney
   1966   "Continuity of work and retirement activities and self evaluation." In I. H. Simpson and J. C. McKinney (eds.), Social Aspects of Aging. Durham, NC: Duke University Press.
Weiner, A. I. and S. L. Hunt
   1981   "Retirees' perceptions of work and leisure meanings." The Gerontologist 21:444–446.

DETERMINANTS OF LABOR FORCE PARTICIPATION RATES OF AGED MALES IN DEVELOPED AND DEVELOPING NATIONS, 1965–1975

Fred C. Pampel

ABSTRACT

Explanations of the decline in labor force participation rates of aged males that has occurred in both developed and developing nations have focused on economic development and the needs of industrial economies for a young, recently trained, urban labor force. This paper examines the net influence of three additional groups of variables that may lead to divergence in participation patterns from those expected on the basis of development alone: (1) dependent economic relations in the world systems, (2) political and state characteristics, and (3) pension system provisions. The effects of these variables net of development are estimated using aggregate data for a pooled cross-section of nations over three time points. The results show that dominant effects come from development variables and give primary support to an

Current Perspectives on Aging and the Life Cycle
Volume 1, pages 243-274
Copyright © 1985 by JAI Press Inc.
All rights of reproduction in any form reserved.
ISBN: 0-89232-296-9

industrialism theory which focuses on labor force accommodation to industrial and technological development.

I. INTRODUCTION

In recent decades, nearly all nations have experienced a decline in the labor force participation of aged males (Durand, 1975). The downward trend in participation has been strongest in developed nations where retirement has become fully institutionalized (Friedman and Orbach, 1974), but it also has appeared in developing countries.

This trend has major implications both for society in general and the aged in particular. Societies in which a large proportion of the aged population is out of the labor force must find public or private means of monetary support for them. Developing countries have difficulty obtaining the surplus income necessary to make transfers to nonworking aged persons when resources need to be directed toward industrial investment. Developed countries, having built large, reliable, and liberal pension systems, are having difficulties meeting the monetary commitments they have made to their retired populations (Fisher, 1978). For aged persons, exit from the labor force is seen as a major cause of the declining status that occurs with development (Burgess, 1960; Cowgill and Holmes, 1972). Loss of work can mean lack of a meaningful role in society, segregation from other age groups, and lowered prestige, self-respect, power resources, and income (Dowd, 1981; Rosow, 1974). Thus, declining participation has meant reduced status of aged persons, and attempts to improve their position through transfer programs face increasing difficulties.

A commonly accepted explanation of the declining labor force participation of aged males focuses on economic development and the needs of industrial economies for a young, recently trained, urban labor force (Sheppard, 1976). Theorists argue that the emergence of the retirement role, which is responsible for the decline in labor force participation at the older ages, results from the technological development, urbanization, and shifts in the occupational structure that accompany industrialization (Burgess, 1960; Cowgill, 1974). Thus, labor force participation of the aged is common in preindustrial societies, lower in industrializing societies, and lowest in industrialized or postindustrial societies.

Critics of this industrialism explanation, however, argue that it oversimplifies the relationship between development and position of the aged by focusing on the contrast between ideal types that exist before and after the industrial transition (Achenbaum and Stearns, 1978; Laslett, 1976). In fact, considerable variation in retirement and treatment of the aged exists in both preindustrial and industrial societies (Dowd, 1981; Maddox, 1979). A number of other factors, ignored by the industrialism explanation, may lead to divergence in participation patterns from those expected on the basis of development alone. While critics have not systematically specified alternative explanations, it is possible to identify some of the variables neglected by the industrialism explanation. For example, the level and scope of public expenditures for pension programs may affect participation. Similarly, other characteristics of nations, such as the intervention of the national government in social and economic institutions or the dependency of the economy on core nations in the world economy, may also affect labor force participation of the aged.

Unfortunately, the literature on retirement has not developed theoretically the relationships of such variables to participation or tested empirically the explanatory ability of the variables relative to the effects of traditional economic development variables. Most studies of retirement are based on individual-level cross-sectional analyses that do not examine historical and cross-national variation in the structural factors affecting participation. A few studies focus on the analysis of time series data for participation in the United States over the last several decades, but variations in levels of development, pension expenditures, political structures, and dependency in this data are either small or nonexistent (Pampel, 1981; Bowen and Finegan, 1969). Other studies (Cowgill and Holmes, 1972; Palmore and Manton, 1974) examine participation in a cross-section of nations at one time point but are based on ethnographic descriptions or bivariate correlations: they do not examine participation in a multivariate context or attempt to examine the net influence of the variables discussed above.

The objective of this paper, then, is to test a model of cross-national labor force participation rates of aged males that includes the effects of economic development variables and other variables measuring dependent economic relations in the world system, political and state characteristics, and public pension system provisions. Theoretically, the paper provides a more stringent test of the industrialism explanation than previous studies (e.g., Palmore and Manton, 1974) and subjects to empirical testing for the first time a number of alternative explanations of participation of the aged. Empirically, this study improves on existing studies by testing the explanations with a large sample of nations and time points, thereby increasing both historical and comparative variation in the independent and dependent variables and making multivariate analysis possible. The following sections thus review the components of the industrialism explanation of declining labor force participation, suggest alternative explanations based on the three groups of variables mentioned above, and test all the explanations using aggregate data for a pooled cross-section of nations over three time points.

II. HYPOTHESES

Although industrialization can be broadly defined as the application of scientific technology to economic production and distribution (Cowgill, 1974), it can also be seen as a process involving several more specific components that directly affect the opportunities of older persons to work. Four such changes can be identified from the industrialism explanation.

First, the growth of a nation's economic product (per person in the population) reflects increases in productivity and efficient energy use that come from substitution of machine labor for human labor. While these processes by themselves do not affect participation, they are related to the growth of surplus income needed to support a large retired population. The higher the level of economic development, the more income can be directed to older persons who are not producing in the labor force (Wilensky, 1975). Thus, a sufficiently high level of development and surplus income is a prerequisite for the emergence of a strong institution of retirement (Cutright, 1965) and a negative relationship can be predicted between a nation's economic product and the labor force participation of aged persons.

Second, economic development involves replacement of primary sector and self-employed occupations by secondary and tertiary sector wage and salary occupations. This shift can reduce participation in two ways. One, occupations which employ older persons are more likely to become obsolescent than newer occupations employing younger persons. Older workers are more likely to find themselves in occupations which were stable or growing, decades before, but which may currently face declining demand and obsolescence. Once out of work, older workers may have difficulty finding another job and may retire.[1] Two, shifts in the occupational structure increase the proportion of older workers in large, bureaucratic organizations with mandatory retirement rules based on chronological age. Where older workers had some autonomy in their retirement age in smaller organizations, they have little choice in the more developed sector of the economy (Friedman and Orbach, 1974; Sheppard, 1976). Hence, bureaucratization of the labor force will increase forced retirement and reduce participation.

Third, upgrading of educational demands for workers places older persons at a competitive disadvantage with younger persons. Growth of the educational system during industrial development gives the youngest cohorts an advantage in the labor force because they will have the highest levels of completed education. As the educational system continues to grow, the gap between the training of recently educated and less recently educated cohorts will grow (Cowgill, 1974). Given the demands of industrial organizations for technologically sophisticated workers, older workers are more likely to be pushed out of the labor force through mandatory retirement or unemployment.

A fourth determinant of participation according to the industrialism explanation is the aging of the population. The drop in fertility and mortality that has accompanied industrialization in nearly all nations increases the number of aged persons competing for a limited number of jobs and reduces the proportion of aged persons who can remain working (Graney and Cottam, 1981). Although the drop in fertility and the consequent aging of the population is not a necessary component of industrialization (the timing of the industrial and demographic transitions often do not coincide; Laslett, 1976), all advanced industrial nations have experienced similar changes in their age structure. Thus, theorists have included this concomitant change in the supply of older workers as an important component of the industrialism explanation (Cowgill, 1974; Burgess, 1960).

A further tenet of this explanation is that cultural, political, and social differences across nations—which may lead to variations in participation in preindustrial societies—come to be dominated by the needs of industrializing economies for a young, mobile, recently trained labor force (Kerr et al., 1960). As all industrial economies have similar technological and labor force needs, they eventually develop similar patterns of labor force participation (Durand, 1975). This suggests that because of the homogenizing nature of the process of industrialization, the effects of any other political or social variables on participation will be negligible.

While not denying the importance of industrialism variables, some alternative hypotheses concerning the determinants of participation rates of aged males can be suggested. First, the more dependent a nation is on core nations and the world system for investment and trade, the lower the participation rate of aged males will be controlling for the industrialism variables. Core nations have a diversified production system, a skilled, highly paid labor force, and industries specializing in highly processed goods. Dependent nations have economies based on the export of a limited number of raw materials to a small number of core nations and on the local production of factories owned by foreign corporations (Bornschier et al., 1978). Short-run economic growth may occur, but this type of dependent growth does not result from the diversification of the internal economy or consumer markets that occurred in advanced industrial nations.

There are a number of implications of dependency for retirement and labor force participation of aged males. Dependency leads to uneven development or economic dualism in which privileged enclaves of the population benefit disproportionately from economic growth while most of the population benefits little (Chase-Dunn, 1975). For most of the economy, growth will not lead to the upgrading of job qualifications and bureaucratization of work that increases forced retirement. In those parts of the economy where development of high-skill jobs in large bureaucratic organizations with mandatory retirement rules does occur, employment of foreign workers is common and participation of the indigenous labor force is not affected. Further, dependent economic growth often leads to a shift in economic sectors that is qualitatively different from the shifts that occurred in core nations. In dependent nations, for instance, increases in the service sector typically involve a large number of workers in menial, unskilled positions; in contrast, increases in the service sector in core nations involve jobs with high skill requirements (Evans and Timberlake, 1980). In short, economic sectors and work organizations may differ substantially in core and dependent nations, with the jobs in dependent nations being less appropriate for retirement.

Thus, even when economic growth occurs, it will not lead to lower participation when dependency is high, and dependency will have its own positive effects on participation.

Second, characteristics of the political system and state may directly affect participation net of development. To directly affect participation, political characteristics would have to create confidence among older workers and retirees that current economic policies and retirement programs will not only be maintained, but improved over time. If economic development and public pension expenditures are high, participation may still remain high if older workers question the ability or willingness of the government to continue supporting economic growth and the pension system at current levels. Conversely, when development and pension expenditures are low, participation may still decline if older workers feel the government strongly supports the interests of retirees and will be improving the programs for the retired population. Two characteristics of the political system may be relevant to participation: levels of political democracy and state strength or activism.

Political democracy has been conceptualized to indicate the extent to which the power of an elite is minimized and the power of the nonelite is maximized (Lenski, 1966). In politically democratic nations, elections will be binding, universal, and fair, and liberties for the press and opposition groups will be guaranteed (Bollen, 1980). With these conditions, interest groups will have greater chances to have their views acted on, more say in the political process, and a greater chance to share power with those in office. In democratic nations, aged persons may develop the voting strength to have their interests represented in political office and feel that governments will be more responsive to their needs. Aged persons will therefore have more confidence in the future of the retirement system and in their ability to continue to have pension benefits and policies keep pace with their needs and interests. This will lead to lower participation rates.

Another relevant characteristic of nations which is conceptually independent of democracy is state strength or activism. Strong states mobilize citizens as agents of the state (Ramirez and Weiss, 1979), regulate and control economic activity (Rubinson, 1976), and substitute public for private resources in economic and social affairs (Delacroix and Ragin, 1981). Persons nearing retirement in strong states may feel more confidence in the state's desire and ability to institute appropriate policies for the economic security of the aged. For instance, strong states will have high levels of taxation relative to the level of economic development, which may more easily be increased to improve the situation of retirees compared with nations whose governments have less control over the affairs of the population. Strong states are also more likely to be committed to the reduction of inequality. Confidence in the ability and desire of states to institute improved pension policies and reduce inequality may thus reduce participation. Finally, strong states may more easily institute policies to speed the process of economic development. One policy may be the early retirement of older workers to make room for more skilled younger workers. Thus, even when the economic base is not highly developed, strong states may be able to encourage retirement policies in industries more easily than weaker states, and thereby reduce participation.

Third, public pension program characteristics may affect participation independent of economic development. In developed nations, retirement has become a desired status: persons often retire well before necessary, enjoy the leisure time that results, and perceive their position as an earned right rather than as a stigma (Friedman and Orbach, 1974). It may also be that in developing nations a retirement ethic is emerging as Western life-styles and consumptive desires diffuse through modern channels of communication (Meyer et al., 1975). If persons desire to retire, they will take advantage of public programs that provide the monetary support needed to leave the labor force. Moreover, levels of monetary support from public pension systems may not be a function of economic development. Surplus income from economic growth is necessary to support pension system expenditures, and the larger the surplus, the higher expenditures will be, both in absolute dollars and as a proportion to economic growth (Wilensky, 1975). Yet, because of differences in cultural, political, social, and class structures, nations may vary in the amount of surplus income that goes to retirees even if the level of economic development is the same (Griffin et al., 1978; Horlick, 1970; Aaron, 1967; Heisler and Peters, 1978). Thus, pension policy expenditures and characteristics may have an independent, direct effect on participation even controlling for economic development.

A number of characteristics of public pension programs may affect participation. The level of benefits, or expenditures of the system per person, may be most important (Clark et al., 1978). Other public expenditures for programs supporting health care, food and energy assistance, public housing, disability and unemployment insurance, and public assistance may also make retirement more attractive to older workers and may lower participation by increasing the nonpension monetary benefits that retirees receive. These monetary expenditures may have the strongest effect on participation when they are standardized by increases in consumer prices or the standard of living. Increases in benefits, if they do not keep pace with prices or the standard of living of workers, may not attract persons out of the labor force.

A number of nonexpenditure characteristics of pension systems of nations may likewise affect participation. Pension programs that cover a large proportion of the population, assuming levels of expenditures are constant, will provide the opportunity for retirement to more persons and will lower the participation rate. Programs that provide for early eligibility for benefits will allow a higher proportion of aged persons to leave the labor force than nations with a later age of eligibility. Programs that have a retirement test will encourage retirement and lower the participation rate of aged males. Retirement tests penalize older workers who continue to be paid wages or salaries by reducing the pensions they are entitled to receive. Rather than sacrificing these benefits, workers will often leave the labor force to get full benefits. Finally, programs that have means tests provide benefits only to persons below specified income levels. Because means-tested benefits take the form of welfare payments rather than insurance payments and because specified levels are relatively low compared with income levels of workers, the existence of a means test is likely to limit retirement and increase participation.

One other characteristic of pension systems may affect participation rates—the years of experience a nation has had with the system. Long experience is likely to summarize a number of characteristics of nations that reduce participation of aged males. For instance, the more years of experience with the system, the more confidence workers may have in the reliability and stability of the pension program and the more willing they will be to retire under the system. Further, the more years of experience with the system, the longer the retirement role has had to become institutionalized, norms of leisure have had to become accepted, and services, organizations, and activities catering to the needs of retirees have had to develop (Cutright, 1965; Foner and Schwab, 1981). All these changes make the social context more conducive to retirement. Thus, pension systems can develop an inertia or momentum over the years that leads to reduced participation.

In contrast to these arguments, the industrialism explanation would suggest that while dependency, state, and pension characteristics have bivariate associations with participation rates of the aged, these relationships will be reduced to near zero when controls for development are used.[2] Thus, development can be argued to completely intervene between dependency and participation of aged males: dependency can slow development, which indirectly limits the drop in participation, but otherwise does not directly affect participation. Similarly, strong, politically democratic governments may emerge as a result of economic development, and these governments may act on behalf of the aged (Jackman, 1975); however, the relationship between government characteristics and participation would be the result of having development as a common cause. Finally, public pension system characteristics may be related to participation in that nations with high expenditures for pensions may have low participation of aged persons. Yet the higher level of pension benefits may result from the surplus income brought about by higher economic growth and the desire to use this surplus for the economic security of aged, retired persons (Wilensky, 1975). Because individuals would have been forced by mandatory retirement rules to retire anyway, it is not pension levels but development which leads to both low participation and high pensions.

In summary, the industrialism explanation hypothesizes that the higher the level of bureaucratic wage and salary work, size of the tertiary educational system, economic product, and age of the population, the lower the participation rate of aged males will be. Further, the explanation hypothesizes that other variables will have no effect on participation. Alternative hypotheses predict that low levels of investment and trade dependency, high levels of political democracy, high levels of state strength or activism in the economy, high levels of public pension expenditures, and less restrictive qualification requirements of public pension programs will reduce participation of aged males.

III. METHODOLOGY

Given the macrosociological, comparative nature of the theories and hypotheses, aggregate data on both developing and developed nations are appropriate. Further, it is desirable to have longitudinal data on each nation so that changes within nations as well as differences across nations can be studied. For this study, published figures for many of the specified variables are available for a sample of about 100 nations for three time points: 1965, 1970, and 1975. This provides a large sample size compared with most aggregate analysis and provides both the cross-national and historical variation in the independent and dependent variables needed for the multivariate analysis of the structural determinants of participation. However, for some variables only data for two time points are available; and for other variables, data is available for three time points, but not all nations. This will require the analysis of subsamples of nations and time points depending on the extent of missing data. Yet, in all equations, nations at both low and high levels of economic development are included, and there are sufficient cases for multivariate analysis.

Measures

The variables, their definitions, sources, and time periods are summarized in the Appendix and are described in more detail below. In general, most measures were obtained from source books which have adjusted and standardized figures to make them comparable across nations and which have been published by reliable statistical gathering agencies such as the United Nations, the International Labour Organization (ILO), and the Security Security Administration. Other variables have been collected and published by individuals for use by researchers in cross-national analyses (Taylor and Hudson, 1972; Bornschier and Heintz, 1979). While it is impossible to eliminate all measurement error in aggregate data, use of data from these sources minimizes the unreliability of the measures.

Labor Force Participation. The dependent variable is the labor force participation rate of males ages 65 and over. Labor force participation is defined according to the standard concepts of the ILO to be the percentage of the age- and sex-specific population that is economically active. The economically active population includes employed persons (paid workers and unpaid family workers) and unemployed persons actively seeking work during the enumeration period. The ILO estimates have been adjusted to accord with the standard definition across all nations.[3] Because this variable is measured specific to males, the independent variables will also be measured for males when possible.

Because of the macrosociological focus of the theory, the analysis is confined to aggregate participation rates rather than retirement. At the aggregate level, retirement is difficult to measure because it involves subjective intentions to work, receipt of a pension, and years of service in a particular job (Atchley, 1976). Labor force participation focuses on whether or not persons are currently employed or looking for a job and can more easily be measured as a percentage of the appropriate age–sex group at the aggregate level. However, the patterns of labor force nonparticipation and retirement are nearly identical—the major difference being that some persons will retire to part-time work or a new job and will not leave the labor force. Because the determinants of retirement also affect labor participation, theories of retirement can be tested using participant data.

Economic Development. The components of economic development predicted to affect participation are measured as follows. First, kilogram energy use per capita is used to measure economic production levels. A related measure, gross national product per capita in constant U.S. dollars, is also available, but is not used because it may inflate the level of economic development of oil-exporting nations and is not available for centrally planned economies. Second, percentage of the male labor force employed in agricultural occupations is used to measure shifts in the nature of work and the occupational structure brought about by economic development. Percent male agricultural employment indicates general bureaucratization of the labor force as well as shifts in the sectorial location of employment.[4] Third, the enrollment rates in tertiary schools are used to measure expansion of the educational system. Enrollment rates are defined as the percentage of males ages 20–24 enrolled in tertiary schools or colleges. They are intended to indicate demand for technologically skilled workers and the competitive advantage of younger workers over older workers in the labor market.[5] Finally, the number of males age 65 and over as a ratio to males ages 25–64 (×100) measures the aging of the population structure.

Pension System. A number of characteristics of pension systems may affect participation. The most important may be the level of expenditures or benefits for retirees, but other nonexpenditure characteristics of the system may also be important. Measures for both types of system characteristics are used. The major expenditure variable is computed by dividing public pension expenditures of the government by the number of persons ages 65 and over. This provides a crude index of average benefits. Pension expenditures is measured in constant (1970) U.S. dollars to control for differences across nations in rates of inflation and monetary units. A weakness of this measure is that it is available (for over all three years) for only 59 nations. This number is much smaller than for other variables but is a necessary result of the need to measure monetary levels of public pensions.

Measures of nonexpenditure pension provisions are available from data gathered by the Social Security Administration. The measures relate to the extent, form, and qualifications of pension expenditures. First, coverage of the population by the public pension program is coded into a four-category ordinal scale where 1 indicates that only employees with limited means are covered, 2 that wage and salary workers are covered, 3 that all employees are covered, and 4 that all citizens are covered. Second, age of eligibility for public pension benefits is measured as a dummy variable with 1 indicating eligibility at or before age 65 and 0 indicating eligibility after age 65. Third, if a nation has a retirement test that limits benefits to those whose earnings exceed a specified amount after the age of eligibility, the retirement test dummy variable is coded 1. If persons can receive their full benefits after the age of eligibility regardless of their earnings in the labor force, the retirement test variable is coded 0. Fourth, if benefits are provided to persons whose income is below a specified level, a means test dummy variable is coded 1; if there is no means test, the variable is coded 0. Fifth, the number of years since the first pension program began in used to measure national experience with pension programs and the institutional strength of the system.

Political Characteristics. The arguments in the previous section focused on the potential influence of politically democratic systems and strong, activist governments. Political democracy, measured by a six-indicator scale developed by Bollen (1980), is based on the fairness of elections and the existence of political liberties. The scale, normed to vary between 0 and 100, is shown by Bollen to be undimensional, reliable, and externally valid. A weakness of the measure, however, is that it is available only for nations for two time points: 1960 and 1965. The variable will have to be lagged to keep both time points of data, and even then the number of time points available for analysis will be lower by one than for many other variables to be analyzed in this paper. However, other political measures are similarly limited in time points and nations (Banks, 1971; Taylor and Hudson, 1972).

Several measures of the strength or activism of state governments will be used. Two common measures of state strength are government revenues and government expenditures as a ratio to gross domestic product (Rubinson, 1976; Rubinson and Quinlan, 1977; Ramirez and Weiss, 1979). These variables measure the economic resources available to the state and the strength of its role in public policy.[6] The higher the revenues and expenditures, the greater the role of the state in the affairs of the population and the more likely it is that the state intervenes to support retired, aged persons. Two other measures of state strength focus on the interventions of the state in the nation's economy. First, general state intervention measures the general state role in industry (from restricted state role to state-planned economy) and nationalization policy (from no nationalization provided by law to nationalization without compensation). Second, sectoral state intervention measures the number of economic sectors which are highly influenced by the state. The higher the score on these variables, the greater the intervention of the state in the economy and the more likely it is that the state will act to protect the interests of the aged (details of the construction of these two indices are presented in Bornschier and Heintz, 1979).

Economic Dependency. The measures of dependency are designed to indicate both the magnitude and form of the economic relationship of nations to the world system (Delacroix and Ragin, 1981). The magnitude of dependency is measured by the stock of foreign private direct investments in millions of U.S. dollars. The higher the foreign investment, both in absolute dollars and relative to gross national product, the higher the penetration of the nation by foreign actors and the greater the dependency is. Following the recommendations of Bornschier et al. (1978), this variable can also be measured as the flow of investment in a nation by taking the change in the stock of investment from 1967 to 1973 and dividing by gross national product in 1973. It is possible that the stock and flow variables will be related differently to economic development and will have different effects on participation.

Measures of trade dependency focus on the limitation of production to a few unprocessed commodities that are exported to a small number of nations. One such measure is commodity concentration—the value of a nation's five most important commodity exports as a percentage of total exports. Dependency on the export of a few products, rather than on a diversified production and export process, results in a high score for this variable. A second measure is foreign trade structure, which shows the extent to which a nation exports raw material and imports processed goods (Galtung, 1971). The variable varies from $+1$ (import all raw materials, export all processed goods) to -1 (export only raw material, import only processed goods). A third measure is trade partner concentration, defined as the percentage of a nation's exports exchanged with its most important trading partner. High concentration of exports with one partner limits diversification of the economy and increases dependence of the nation on one other nation.

Estimation. Given the availability of three time points for most variables, the data can be pooled into a combined cross-sectional time series. This approach differs from traditional panel models in which separate variables are measured for each time point and the sample size is equal to the number of cross-sectional units. The pooled cross-sections increase the sample size (equal to the number of units times the number of time points), but assumes that the causal processes are constant across panels. After testing for this assumption and, barring interactions over time, models will be estimated from the pooled data.

Estimation of such models can be made with ordinary least squares (OLS), although there are special issues involved in analysis of pooled time series data that need to be considered. For one, the residuals may be correlated as a result of time series component of the data. Without a lagged dependent variable the estimates are inefficient; with a lagged dependent variable they are also biased. Standard tests for autocorrelation are not strictly appropriate for pooled cross-section time series (especially when the time period is short), making it difficult to identify the level of autocorrelation. To deal with this problem, all equations will be estimated using a form of generalized least squares (GLS) which corrects for serial correlation in the error terms (Kmenta, 1971). The GLS estimation technique, termed random error components, assumes the error term consists of components for cross-sectional units, time period units, and a random error. Estimates of these components are made and then used to adjust the coefficient estimates using the standard GLS matrix and formula (Hannan and Young, 1977). Comparison of the GLS and OLS estimates should provide information on the extent of serial correlations and its effects on the relationships to be tested.

IV. RESULTS

Given the multiple hypotheses and indicators to be examined, it will be necessary to test for the effects of a large number of variables. The strategy of the analysis is to examine first the effects of the causally prior variables, economic development and dependency, and then add measures of political, state, and pension characteristics to a model including significant economic variables. A final model including significant variables from all four groups can then be presented.

A. Economic Development

The components of development predicted to influence participation are the percentage of the male labor force in agricultural occupations, the old age dependency ratio, enrollment rates in tertiary schools, and level of economic product, i.e., energy use per capita.[7] The latter three variables are related nonlinearly to participation and therefore are measured as their natural logs. This indicates that the largest effect on participation occurs at the low and medium levels of these variables, and that at higher levels, the effect on participation is reduced. The correlations between these variables is high—in all cases over .60. Although such levels are not unusual for cross-national aggregate analyses, care must be taken to ensure that the estimates are stable and do not fluctuate greatly as a result of multicollinearity.

In Table 1 the second column presents an equation predicting participation

Table 1. Standardized Coefficients from Regression of Labor Force Participation of Aged Males on Measures of Economic Development

Independent Variables	r	OLS Standardized Coefficients					GLS
		Pooled Data	1965	1970	1975	Pooled
Percent agricultural labor force	.876**	.659**	.743**	.632**	.608**	.896**
ln old age ratio	−.690**	−.282**	−.281**	−.271**	−.300**	−.072*
ln tertiary education	−.684**	−.119*	−.143	−.077	−.109	.022
ln energy	−.804**	.097	.197	.030	.057	.033
R^2		.816	.818	.804	.823	
df		235	75	75	75	
No. of nations		80	80	80	80	80
No. of years		3	1	1	1	3

**p < .01.
* .01 < p < .05.

which includes all four of the economic development variables (the first column shows the bivariate correlation of the variables with participation). In the equation, percent agricultural labor force and the old age ratio are significant at .01 while energy use and tertiary educational enrollment are not. The effects of percent agriculture clearly are dominant in the equation. Although energy use is strongly correlated with participation, the net effect is nonsignificant because energy use is highly correlated with percent agriculture (r = −.90). When percent agriculture is excluded from the equation (column 3), the effects of energy use are strong, negative, and significant. Given the strong correlation between the two, energy use and present agriculture need not be used at the same time. Because percent agriculture has the stronger effect, it will be used in the equations to follow. Whichever variable is used, however, the variance explained in participation is high.[8]

The effects found in the pooled regression equations are much the same when separate equations are estimated for each year. The next three equations in Table 1 show results from cross-sectional analyses done separately for each time period. In each equation, the effects of percent agriculture are strongest. The next largest effects come from the old age ratio, which are also similar to the estimates for the pooled model. Both tertiary enrollment and energy use are nonsignificant for the separate years. Thus, the consistent effects of the determinants across time suggest that the causal processes determining participation have not changed greatly during the period studied and that the data can accurately be pooled in estimating the effects of the industrialism variables.

The last equation in Table 1 estimates the effects of the industrialism variables using GLS and adjusting for the effects of autocorrelation. In this equation, the effects of percent agriculture remain strong, even stronger than in the OLS equation. The effects of the old age ratio are reduced but remain significant. The effects of tertiary enrollment are reduced to nonsignificance while the effects of energy remain nonsignificant. This suggests a simplified industrialism model that includes the effects of occupational structure to measure changes in the demand for older workers and the effects of the age of the population to measure changes in supply of older workers.[9]

A more traditional approach to analyzing panel data is to include a lagged dependent variable in the equation with the independent variables. This makes the model dynamic by changing the focus from level of participation to changes in participation, i.e., with a lagged dependent variable, the independent variables predict participation controlling for participation in the previous period; hence, the focus is on change in participation from one time period to the next. When a lagged dependent variable is added to the pooled equation the effect is large (β = −.941) and increases the variance explained to .987. However, it leaves little variation left over for the more theoretically meaningful variables to affect participation. Only percent agriculture continues to have a significant effect net of participation lagged and its standardized coefficient is reduced to .014. The strong effect of participation lagged indicates stability in participation across time (levels of participation are not identical across years, but the rank ordering of nations has been relatively constant over time). Thus, inclusion of the lagged dependent variable in the model provides little additional information on the determination of participation, other than to show stability of participation, and has the drawbacks of eliminating the 1965 panel and creating the possibility of biased estimates (if there is autocorrelation). For these reasons, the models to follow do not include the lagged dependent variables as a predictor.

In summary, using a variety of models, estimation techniques, variables, lags, and functional forms, the results show stable significant effects of percent agricultural labor force and the old age ratio. In the equations to follow, only these two variables are used to summarize the effects of industrialization.

3. Economic Dependency

The indicators used to measure economic dependency on the world system are presented in Table 2. Of the measures of foreign investment, only the absolute dollar measure is significantly correlated with participation. Yet the level of foreign private investment is negatively related to participation when the hypotheses predict a positive relationship. The measures of trade dependency, however, are all significantly correlated with participation in the predicted direction. Concentration of trade on a few commodities, limitation of trade to a few partners, and reliance on export of raw materials and import of processed goods are associated with high participation rates.

To test for the net effects of industrialization and dependency, the dependency indicators are added one at a time to the baseline industrialization model (Table 2). The variables are added separately because each is available for a different sample of nations; if all the variables were included in the same equation, only nations with data on all six variables for all three time points could be included and the sample size would be small.[10] Also, including only one variable at a time allows for the strongest possible effect from each variable and limits the canceling out of the effects of the many dependency indicators. Thus, the equations with industrialism and dependency indicators are presented in Table 2 [equations (1)–(6)]. Although standardized OLS coefficients are presented for each variable, the GLS coefficients are also presented below the OLS coefficients in parentheses. The results show that while the effects of percent agriculture and the old age ratio are similar to those without controls for dependency, not one of the dependency variables is significant at .01.[11] Only the absolute level of foreign private investment is significant at the .05 level for the GLS estimates. Yet the effect of this variable is negative—the direction opposite of the hypothesis. Given the small size of the coefficient, low level of significance, and negative direction, it is difficult to attribute substantive importance to this variable.

Assuming that dependency causally precedes development, however, suggests

Table 2. Standardized Coefficients from Regression of Labor Force Participation of Aged Males on Measures of Economic Development and Dependency

OLS and GLS Standardized Coefficients[a]

Independent Variables	r	(1)	(2)	(3)	(4)	(5)	(6)
Percent agricultural labor force	.876**	.670**	.679**	.666**	.755**	.702**	.742**
		(.788)**	(.809)**	NA	(.930)**	(.887)**	(.902)**
ln old age ratio	−.690**	−.259**	−.277**	−.287**	−.185*	−.234**	−.176**
		(−.104)**	(−.111)**	NA	(−.086)*	(−.101)**	(−.068)*
Foreign private investment	−.379**	−.022					
		(−.036)*					
Foreign private inv./GNP	−.019		−.012				
			(−.005)				
Δ Foreign private inv./GNP	−.005			−.016			
				NA			
Commodity concentration	.463**				−.001		
					(.023)		
Foreign trade structures	−.582**					−.034	
						(−.023)	
Trade concentration	.303**						.045
							(.009)
R^2		.794	.817	.819	.843	.840	.837
df		208	200	98	134	260	221
No. of nations		106	102	102	46	88	75
No. of years		2	2	1	3	3	3

[a]Standardized coefficients from GLS estimation are presented in parentheses below OLS estimates.
**p < .01.
*.01 < p < .05.

259

that dependency has indirect effects on participation through development, even if the direct effects are small. For example, commodity concentration is correlated .48 with percent agriculture and −.59 with the old age ratio. Its indirect effect on participation through percent agriculture is .36 and through the old age ratio is −.11 Similar calculations can be made for the other indicators of dependency, which also limit the drop in participation by limiting development.

C. Political and State Characteristics

Analysis of the political and state characteristics follows the same strategy used for analysis of the dependency indicators—each indicator is added separately to the baseline industrialism equation (Table 3). The equations are estimated using both OLS and GLS techniques to ensure that the results are not spuriously due to the existence of autocorrelation. Note that all the variables except sectoral intervention are significantly correlated with participation.

With controls for the industrialism variables, the OLS estimates show that three of the variables are significantly related to participation. Yet some of these effects appear to be due to autocorrelation because only government revenues (as a percentage of the gross national product) remains significant in the GLS estimates. And even government revenues remains significant at only the .05 level and has a standardized coefficient of only −.03.[12] Thus, state strength as indicated by high levels of revenues relative to the gross national product has small negative effects on participation, but these effects are largely outweighed by the stronger effects of percent agriculture and the old age ratio.

D. Pension Expenditures and Provisions

Table 4 examines the effects of characteristics of the public pension system in order to determine if pension system mediates the effect of development and are necessary for the drop in participation or if development can reduce participation regardless of the status of the public pension system.

The first equation in Table 4 adds a measure of pension expenditures to the two industrialism variables. Pension expenditures in constant U.S. dollars is divided by the number of persons age 65 and over.[13] The bivariate correlation of pension expenditures with participation is high (−.707), larger than most of the correlations found for the other variables studied thus far. Further, the correlation of pension expenditures with percent agriculture is also high (−.67). In the equation, however, the net effects of pension expenditures with controls for percent agriculture and the old age ratio are reduced considerably. In fact, when adjustments for autocorrelation are made, the effect of pension expenditures becomes insignificant.

Of the other pension provision variables included in Table 4, the existence of a means test, existence of a retirement test, and level of coverage are all insignifi-

Table 3. Standardized Coefficients from Regression of Labor Force Participation of Aged Males on Measures of Economic Development and Political and State Characteristics

Independent Variables	r	OLS and GLS Standardized Coefficients[a]				
		(1)	(2)	(3)	(4)	(5)
Percent agricultural labor force	.876**	.743**	.638**	.635**	.573**	.601**
		(.806)**	(.849)**	(.870)**	(.821)**	(.812)**
ln old age ratio	−.690**	−.203**	−.268**	−.247**	−.363**	−.295**
		(−.121)**	(−.078)**	(−.084)**	(−.073)	(−.078)
Political democracy t − 5	−.407**	.048				
		(.015)				
Government revenues/GNP	−.641**		−.050			
			(−.029)*			
Government expenditures/GNP	−.578**			−.103**		
				(−.017)		
General intervention	.283**				−.063	
					(−.012)	
Sectoral intervention	−.112					−.182**
						(−.016)
R^2		.794	.804	.812	.777	.799
df		212	299	284	116	113
No. of nations		108	101	96	40	39
No. of years		2	3	3	3	3

[a] Standardized coefficients from GLS estimation are presented in parentheses below OLS estimates.
**p < .01.
*.01 < p < .05.

Table 4. Standardized Coefficients from Regression of Labor Force Participation of Aged Males on Measures of Economic Development and Pension System Provisions

OLS and GLS Standardized Coefficients[a]

Independent Variables	r	(1)	(2)	(3)	(4)	(5)	(6)
Percent agricultural labor force	.876**	.679** (.921)**	.711** (.888)**	.707** (.882)**	.681** (.864)**	.767** (.872)**	.739** (.826)**
ln old age ratio	−.690**	−.171** (−.080)*	−.261** (−.090)**	−.244** (−.095)**	−.278** (−.118)**	−.161** (−.069)**	−.121** (−.052)*
Pension expenditures/population 65+	−.730**	−.137** (−.010)					
Age eligibility	.206**		−.081** (−.006)				
Means test	−.386**			.016 (−.001)			
Retirement test	.285**				−.038 (.004)		
Coverage	−.423**					.000 (−.005)	
Year since first law	−.698**						−.080* (−.123)**
R^2		.862	.832	.822	.842	.790	.793
df		167	302	257	212	365	368
No. of nations		57	102	87	72	123	124
No. of years		3	3	3	3	3	3

[a]Standardized coefficients from GLS estimation are presented in parentheses below OLS estimates.
**p < .01.
*.01 < p < .05.

cant. The existence of early retirement provisions has a significant negative effect in the OLS estimates but not in the GLS estimates. Only years since the first pension law was instituted has significant effects for both types of estimates.

E. Summary Models

A number of variables other than percent agriculture and the old age ratio have significant effects. As a final step in the analysis, models that include all of these variables are estimated (Table 5). Included from the political and state variables is government revenues.[14] Included from the pension variables are pension expenditures, early retirement provisions, and years since the first law. Each of these variables was significant in either the OLS or GLS estimates in the previous tables but needs to be tested with controls for the others.

The first equation in Table 5 includes six variables—two industrialism variables and four others. Of all the variables, only pension expenditures is insignificant in both the OLS and GLS estimates. In the next equation, the same sample of nations and time points are used for a model in which pension expenditures is deleted. The effects of the other variables, as would be expected, change little, and the variance explained remains high. Because the pension expenditures measure contains much missing data, equation (2) can be reestimated using a larger sample of nations. This model is shown in equation (3). Even with the larger number of nations, the patterns of effects remain much the same. In the OLS estimates, all the variables except years since first law are significant. In the GLS estimates, years since first law becomes significant along with percent agriculture and the old age ratio; government revenues and early retirement are no longer significant. Because there are inconsistencies between the OLS and GLS estimates, it is difficult to settle on a final model. Until further analyses with other data can be done, it is best to avoid deleting any of these final five variables.

Given this final model in equation (3), some comparisons of the effects of the industrialism and public pension/state variables can be made. In equation (3), the coefficient for percent agriculture is over four times the size of the largest coefficient for the political and pension variables. The second largest coefficient is for the old age ratio. The effects of the other variables have standardized coefficients less than .2 in absolute value. Another indication of the importance of the two groups of variables comes from comparing the explanatory ability of each group of variables separately. In equation (4), the results of an equation with percent agriculture and the old age ratio show that the variance explained is .839—only .017 less than the variance explained by all the variables. In contrast, equation (5) shows that the variance explained by the political and pension variables is .627—well below the variance explained by the industrialism variables alone. Thus, the results show dominant effects from the industrialism variables and suggest that other variables make only minor contribution to the determination of the participation of aged males.

Table 5. Standardized Coefficients from Regression of Labor Force Participation on Selected Determinants[a]

	OLS and GLS Standardized Coefficients[a]							
Independent Variables	(1)	(2)	(3)	(4)	(5)	1965	1970	1975
Percent agricultural labor force	.520**	.529**	.544**	.640**		.569**	.514**	.542**
	(.814)**	(.812)**	(.782)**	(.884)**				
ln old age ratio	−.270**	−.296**	−.316**	−.316**		−.290**	−.327**	−.353**
	(−.065)	(−.065)	(−.076)**	(−.080)**				
Government revenue/GNP	−.181**	−.214**	−.130**		−.394**	−.128	−.143*	−.129*
	(−.023)	(−.021)	(−.023)		(−.024)			
Pension expenditure/population 65+	−.077							
	(.004)							
Age eligibility	−.130**	−.132**	−.113**		−.085	−.101	−.123*	−.120*
	(−.024)	(−.024)	(−.014)		(−.003)			
Years since first law	−.029	−.029	−.058		−.516**	−.053	−.067	−.030
	(−.192)**	(−.188)**	(−.188)**		(−.595)**			
R^2	.891	.889	.856	.839	.627	.842	.856	.868
df	143	144	240	243	242	76	76	76
No. of nations	50	50	82	82	82	82	82	82
No. of years	3	3	3	3	3	1	1	1

[a]Standardized coefficients from GLS estimates are presented in parentheses below OLS coefficients.
**p < .01.
* .01 < p < .05.

As a final check on these models, separate equations were estimated for each time period to determine if pooling the panels is appropriate and if the process of labor force participation determination has changed. The OLS estimates for the model within each time period are presented in the last three equations of Table 5. The results show stability of the coefficients across time. None of the coefficients change by more than .05 unit over the time period. They thus reflect in each year what shows up in the pooled estimates: percent agriculture and the old age ratio have the largest effects followed by government revenues, early retirement, and years since the first law.

V. DISCUSSION

This paper provides a more stringent test of industrialism explanations of retirement and aging than previous studies by examining a variety of both developmental and nondevelopmental determinants of the labor force participation of aged males. The study also uses a larger number of cases and time points than previous studies, thus providing sufficient variation and degrees of freedom to test for the effects of a large number of variables in a multivariate context. The results show clearly that two components of modernization—transformation of the labor force from primarily agricultural to bureaucratic and industrial, and aging of the population—predict participation better than any of the other variables. In fact, the standardized coefficient for percent agriculture is four times the size of any nondevelopmental variables.[15] Three other variables—general government revenues (as a ratio to the gross national product), eligibility for early pension benefits, and years since first law—have small but significant effects on participation. Yet a variety of dependency, political, and pension measures did not significantly affect participation net of development despite sometimes large bivariate correlations with participation.

The results thus reaffirm the industrialism explanations of retirement and aging. Retirement can be seen as an accommodation of the work force to the requirements of a technologically advancing economy (Graebner, 1980). Despite social and cultural differences affecting the contribution of older persons to the economy that may exist in nations before the onset of industrialization, nations converge toward a pattern of low participation of aged males as they advance industrially. Similar methods of production and organization in developed economies lead to similar social structures and patterns of participation. Furthermore, to the extent that retirement or nonparticipation is associated with loss of prestige, power, and income, industrialization can also be seen as the major determinant of the more general status of the aged.

Given the importance of pension benefits found in individual studies of the retirement decision, it is perhaps surprising that pension expenditures did not have a significant effect net of other variables in this study. Yet the results of the analysis do not suggest that pension expenditures are unrelated to retirement (the bivariate correlation is strong); rather, they suggest industrialization and development as responsible for both the increase in pensions and the decline in participation. Thus, it may be that pensions are a consequence of retirement brought by industrialization rather than a determinant of national participation rates. Additional analyses are needed to unravel this question (Pampel and Weiss, 1983). Further, general government revenues, which are closely related to pension expenditures, appear more important in determining participation than pension expenditures. High revenues summarize the effect on participation of nonpension programs such as food, energy, welfare, and health assistance as well as the effect of pension expenditures. General government support for welfare may be more important in determining rates of retirement than specific levels of pension expenditures (although in either case the effects are smaller than for the industrialism variables).

These results suggest that levels of participation may be difficult to manipulate with social policy variables. Industrializing nations, which may desire to make room for younger workers, may have difficulty encouraging retirement while industrialized nations, which may desire to ease the burden on their pension systems, may have difficulty discouraging workers from retirement. The small effects of the policy-manipulable variables suggest that some changes can be made but that the structure of the economy and labor force, which is more difficult to change, is the more important factor.

These conclusions run counter to much of the recent literature on industrialization and aging which has been critical of initial formulations and tests of the explanation. The criticisms have come from case studies which find that some societies deviate from patterns that would be predicted by the industrialism explanation (e.g., Laslett, 1976, on England; Fischer, 1978, and Achenbaum, 1978, on the United States; Smith, 1978, on a colonial Massachusetts; Palmore, 1975, on Japan; Dowd, 1981, on a number of tribal societies; Harlan, 1964, on three Indian villages; and Lipman, 1970, on Portugal).

There may be a number of reasons why the results of these and other studies differ from the results of this paper. First, where most studies—including the original formulations of the industrialism theory—focus on the general status of the aged, this paper looks more specifically at retirement or labor force participation. Status of the aged is a multidimensional concept in which many of the components may differ in their response to industrialization (Williamson et al., 1982). In this case, focusing specifically on labor force participation leads to support of the theory. Other studies of deference or family relationships may lead to different conclusions. Yet by clearly identifying and delimiting the meaning of the status of the aged, researchers can better evaluate the scope of the theory.

Second, the sample used in this study differs from that used in many of the studies listed above. Most of the previous studies have examined preindustrial societies, often very small tribal societies or villages, whereas this paper has examined nation-states, most started to some degree in the process of industrialization. Much of the criticism of the industrialism explanation has been based on the existence of variation in the status of the aged in preindustrial societies. Early formulations which identify preindustrial societies as the Golden Age of the elderly are rightly criticized (Burgess, 1960). However, with a sample of industrializing and industrialized nations in the contemporary world, support for the explanation is strong. This suggests a revision in the industrialism theory that does not predict similarities in preindustrial societies where cultural and historical factors are important determinants of the status of the aged. Rather, it predicts that the variations existing before industrialization decline in the face of the logic of industrialization. Such a revision is consistent with other theories of industrialism (Kerr et al., 1960; Form, 1979) and is more precise in the scope of nations to which it applies.

Third, much of the previous research is based on case studies whereas this paper examines a relatively large sample of nations. Where case studies attempt to note unique characteristics of nations, studies which look at a larger sample of nations attempt to find regularities across nations and how they fit a more general pattern. The latter approach does not claim that there are no unique characteristics of nations that are important in determining status or that development completely determines status of the aged. Rather, the statements are probabilistic, and the existence of deviant cases does not necessarily invalidate the explanation. The advantage of case studies is to suggest factors important in the status of the aged that can be translated into theoretically generalizable statements, operationalized for a larger number of nations, and tested empirically. Thus, the industrialism theory needs to be tested, as in this paper, by developing probabilistic models that apply to a number of societies.

Fourth, there is a tendency in other studies of the industrialism thesis to classify societies into two groups, preindustrial and industrial; when the status of the aged is not identical among all societies in each group, the theory is found lacking. In this paper, a continuous notion of industrialization is used instead of the crude two-group classification. Differences in level of industrialism exist among both industrializing and industrialized nations, making it necessary to distinguish degree of industrialization more carefully than has been done in the past.

In summary, keeping these points in mind leads to the following conclusion from this paper: in a study of labor force participation rates of aged males for a sample of nation-states in recent decades, level of industrialization—as measured by the percentage of the labor force in agricultural occupations—was strongly related to labor force participation of aged males, thus providing support of the industrialism explanation of changes in the status of the aged.

APPENDIX:
MEANS (SEPARATELY BY YEAR), STANDARD DEVIATIONS, NS, DEFINITIONS, AND SOURCES FOR VARIABLES

Variable	$\bar{X}$	S	$\bar{X}_{65}$	$\bar{X}_{70}$	$\bar{X}_{75}$	Definitions
Labor force M65+	52.3 (429)	21.1	55.8 (143)	52.2 (143)	48.9 (143)	Percent of males age 65 and over in the labor force (ILO)
Percent agricultural labor force	51.0 (429)	26.9	54.1 (143)	50.9 (143)	47.9 (143)	Percent of male adults in the labor force employed in agricultural occupations (ILO)
Old age ratio	11.5 (429)	5.1	10.8 (143)	11.6 (143)	12.0 (143)	Males age 65 and over as a ratio to males 25–64 times 100 (ILO)
Tertiary education	9.4 (348)	10.2	7.8 (118)	8.9 (128)	11.8 (102)	Percent of males ages 20–24 enrolled in tertiary schools (UN)
Energy	1386 (357)	2045	1140 (118)	1447 (119)	1567 (120)	Energy consumption in kilograms of coal equivalents per capita (B&H from UN)
GNP	1273 (309)	1719	1072 (103)	1291 (103)	1456 (103)	Gross domestic product per capita in constant 1975 U.S. dollars (B&H)
Foreign private investment	1145 (222)	3103	793 (115)	1523 (107)	— 0	Estimates of stock of private foreign direct investment in millions of U.S. dollars (B&H)
Commodity concentration	40.5 (224)	23.2	43.2 (87)	41.5 (87)	33.8 (50)	Values most five important export commodities as a percentage of total exports (B&H)
Trade structure	−0.36 (304)	0.33	−0.36 (95)	−0.38 (110)	−0.34 (99)	Scale between −1 and 1 measuring the degree to which exports are processed and imports are raw materials (B&H)
Trade concentration	30.3 (278)	13.5	32.5 (92)	30.1 (97)	28.3 (89)	Percentage of total foreign trade exchanged with most important partner (B&H)
Political democracy	59.3 (228)	30.1	62.7 (109)	56.1 (119)	— 0	Scale (between 0 and 100) measuring political liberties and popular sovereignty (Bollen)
Government revenues/ GDP	20.8 (310)	9.7	18.9 (103)	21.5 (104)	21.9 (103)	Current government revenues as a percentage of gross domestic product (B&H from World Bank)

(continued)

APPENDIX (Continued)

Variable	$\bar{X}$	S	$\bar{X}_{65}$	$\bar{X}_{70}$	$\bar{X}_{75}$	Definitions
Government expenditures/ GDP	18.8 (305)	8.7	17.2 (100)	19.4 (104)	19.9 (101)	Current government expenditures as a percentage of gross domestic product (B&H from World Bank)
General intervention	23.4 (148)	8.7	22.0 (49)	22.0 (44)	25.6 (55)	Scale (between 0 and 60) measuring extent of state role in industry and nationalization policy (B&H)
Sectoral intervention	52.4 (147)	19.9	46.1 (49)	51.6 (43)	58.7 (55)	Scale (between 0 and 100) measuring percentage of 10 industrial sectors highly influenced by the state (B&H)
Pension expenditures/ population 65+	.392 (193)	.605	.298 (59)	.330 (72)	.553 (62)	Government expenditures for pensions in thousands of U.S. dollars divided by number of males age 65+ not in labor force (CSS)
Age retirement eligibility	.94 (319)	.23	.93 (102)	.95 (107)	.95 (110)	Eligibility for pensions at or before age 65 = 1, after age 65 = 0 (SSTW)
Means test	.22 (291)	.42	.22 (87)	.20 (95)	.25 (109)	Means-tested benefits = 1, no means test = 0 (SSTW)
Retirement test	.79 (258)	.41	.80 (80)	.77 (82)	.79 (96)	Retirement test = 1, no retirement test = 0 (SSTW)
Coverage	2.1 (371)	1.1	1.9 (123)	2.1 (124)	2.3 (124)	Pension system coverage: (1) some employees; (2) all wage and salary employees; (3) all employees; (4) all citizens (SSTW)
Years since first law	23.4 (372)	22.1	19.3 (124)	23.3 (124)	27.6 (124)	Years since first pension law was instituted

Sources:
B&H Bornschier and Heintz (1979).
Bollen Bollen (1980).
CSS Cost of Social Security, International Labour Organization (1979).
ILO Labor Force Estimates and Projections, International Labour Organization (1977).
UN United Nations Statistical Yearbook (1980 and other various years).
SSTW Social Security Throughout the World, Social Security Administration (1977 and other various years).

ACKNOWLEDGMENTS

I would like to thank Sookja Chung for her competent and energetic assistance in gathering and analyzing the data in this paper, Jane A. Weiss, whose initial collaboration helped make this paper possible, and Kofi Benefo, Charles Mueller, Vijayan Pillai, Halowell Pope, James Price, and Robert Szafran for comments on an earlier draft of the paper. This research was supported by a grant from the National Institute on Aging, No. AG 01568.

NOTES

1. Cohn (1982) argues that the effect of obsolescence of jobs on participation will show up in the effect of change in ecnomic production participation. Levels of economic product will also reduce participation through making surplus income available for retirement. Rather than conceptually separating the effects of surplus income from occupational change, he thus uses a distinction between economic product level and change. Although I will examine different effects of surplus income and occupational change directly, it may still be useful in the analysis to consider the separate effects of levels and change in these variables.

2. The variables can be ordered causally with dependency preceding economic development, and with political and pension characteristics intervening between development and participation. When controls for development are argued to eliminate the effect of dependency on participation, it suggests a model of intervention whereby development completely mediates the effect of dependency. When controls for development are argued to eliminate the effects of political and pension characteristics on participation, it suggests a model of spuriousness whereby development is a common cause of political characteristics, pensions, and participation. Although the theoretical models differ, the empirical result predicted by the industrialism explanation is the same: no variables other than those measuring the components of development will have significant net effects on participation.

3. There are some problems with the data. Dixon (1982) shows that the ILO standardizations, while reducing artificial fluctuations due to changes in definitions, may overestimate participation of males in developing nations. Further, some developing nations have participation rates estimated on the basis of level of economic development and patterns of neighboring countries. These procedures may upwardly bias the size of the relationship between development and participation. However, given that the ILO data remain the best available for a large number of nations and time points, and that attempts to purge the data of all cases with biased estimates would greatly truncate the range of nations studied, the analysis proceeds with the participation figures as given. Many nations with the least reliable participation data have missing values on other variables and will be deleted, thereby reducing the bias. But it is also necessary to examine the stability of the development effect across different sets of nations to determine if bias among the least developed nations greatly affects the results.

4. This measure is intended to tap changes in the general bureaucratization of the labor force and the increase in the size of work organizations as well as the shift of workers from one sector to another. In fact, percent agricultural labor force is closely related to mean size of work organization (Land and Pampel, 1977) and with percent managerial occupations for a subset of nations studied in this paper.

5. The ideal measure would show the ratio of the mean education of older cohorts to younger cohorts, but such age-specific data are not available. Another way to measure the competitive advantage of the young is to examine change in educational levels, assuming that the greater the rate of change, the greater the advantage of the young.

6. Government revenues and expenditures, in addition to measuring state strength, may also indicate the level of nonpension welfare support available to retired persons (as well as the rest of the population). For instance, revenues and expenditures include money for housing, food, energy, disability, unemployment, and welfare assistance which may benefit the aged.

7. Energy use per capita is correlated .98 with real gross national product per capita. Because the two variables behave identically in the results that follow and because energy use is available for a larger sample of nations, the results for gross national product are not reported.

8. It would also be possible to factor analyze the components of industrialization and use a summary scale in the equations to follow. Although this is a strategy worthy of future consideration, it may be more useful in these preliminary analyses to treat each component as a separate measure. By combining the components into one scale, it would be more difficult to determine if controls for

the dependency, scale, and pension variables differentially affect the individual industrialism variables. For instance, percent agriculture is stable with controls for other variables whereas the old age ratio is affected more by controls. Thus, the industrial components are allowed to have separate effects in the equations.

9. The independent variables measured as change scores or lagged one period had effects on participation smaller than those shown for the variables in Table 1. Because use of both lagged independent variables and change scores create missing scores for all nations in the first time point, use of level of the independent variables at time t in Table 1 makes use of the maximum information available.

10. Some of the dependency variables are available for only two time points. Equations with all variables included would eliminate one panel for all the other variables. The sample sizes would be greatly reduced. Adding variables separately maintains the size of the sample but may lead to two other problems. The first problem, one of spuriousness from lack of controls for other dependency variables, turns out to be no problem because none of the indicators has large effects net of development. The second problem, one of suppression, is unlikely because the pattern of correlation coefficients is not consistent with this possibility.

11. The effects of the dependency variables are also insignificant when lagged, measured as change scores, or measured as natural logs.

12. Although most theory and research treats pensions as a determinant of retirement, it may be that participation is causally antecedent to government expenditures or pension expenditures. It is possible that having a large proportion of the aged population out of the labor force requires governments to expend more for social welfare programs and pensions. This is a question, however, that requires a great deal of further analyses to resolve. In this paper, specifications based on previous research, with retirement as a consequence rather than a cause of government programs and pensions, are used.

13. It makes little difference what denominator for pension expenditures is used. The population over age 65, the male population over age 65 not in the labor force, and the total population all provide nearly identical results.

14. When government revenues and sectoral intervention are included in the same equation, only government revenues remains significant. Given the small sample size of sectoral intervention and its small net effects, further analyses will focus only on government revenues.

15. These effects are sufficiently strong that even without bias in the measures of participation the effects of development would dominate. Moreover, the stability of the effects of several measures of development, even when different samples of nations with different amounts of error are used, increases confidence in the findings. In fact, the results in this paper are consistent with other analysis of more developed nations in which measurement error in participation is small (Pampel and Weiss, 1983).

REFERENCES

Aaron, H. J.
    1967   "Social Security: international comparisons." Pp. 13–48 in Otto Eckstein (ed.), Studies in Economics of Income Maintenance. Washington, DC: Brookings Institution.

Achenbaum, W. Andrew
    1978   Old Age in the New Land: The American Experience Since 1790. Baltimore, MD: Johns Hopkins University Press.

Achenbaum, W. A. and P. N. Stearns
    1978   "Old age and modernization." The Gerontologist 18:307–312.

Atchley, Robert C.
    1976   The Sociology of Retirement. Cambridge, MA: Schenkman.
    1982   "Retirement as a social institution." Annual Review of Sociology 8:263–287.

Banks, Arthur S.
 1971   Cross-Polity Time-Series Data. Cambridge, MA: MIT Press.
Bollen, K. A.
 1980   "Issues in the comparative measurement of political democracy." American Sociological Review 45:370–390.
Bornschier, V., C. Chase-Dunn, and R. Rubinson
 1978   "Cross-national evidence of the effects of foreign investment and aid on economic growth and inequality: a survey of findings and a reanalysis." American Journal of Sociology 84:651–683.
Bornschier, Volker and Peter Heintz (eds.)
 1979   Compendium of Data for World-Systems Analysis. Zurich: Sociological Institute, University of Zurich.
Bowen, William G. and T. Aldrich Finegan
 1969   The Economics of Labor Force Participation. Princeton, NJ: Princeton University Press.
Burgess, E. W.
 1960   "Aging in Western culture." Pp. 3–28 in Ernest W. Burgess (ed.), Aging in Western Societies. Chicago: University of Chicago Press.
Chase-Dunn, C.
 1975   "The effects of international economic dependence on development and inequality: a cross-national study." American Sociological Review 40:720–738.
Clark, R., J. Kreps, and J. Spengler
 1978   "Economics of aging: a survey." Journal of Economic Literature 16:919–962.
Cohn, R. M.
 1982   "Economic development and status change of the aged." American Journal of Sociology 87:1150–1161.
Cowgill, D. O.
 1974   "Aging and modernization: a revision of the theory." Pp. 123–146 in Jaber F. Gubrium (ed.), Late Life, Communites and Environmental Policy. Springfield, IL: Charles C. Thomas.
Cowgill, D. O. and Lowell D. Holmes (eds.)
 1972   Aging and Modernization. New York: Appleton-Century-Crofts.
Cutright, Phillips
 1965   "Political structure, economic development and national security programs." American Journal of Sociology 70:537–548.
Delacroix, J. and C. C. Ragin
 1981   "Structural blockage: a cross-national study of economic dependency, state efficacy, and underdevelopment." American Journal of Sociology 86:1311–1347.
Dixon, R. B.
 1982   "Women in agriculture: counting the labor force in developing countries." Population and Development Review 8:539–566.
Dowd, J. J.
 1981   "Industrialization and the decline of the aged." Sociological Focus 14:255–270.
Durand, John D.
 1975   The Labor Force in Economic Development. Princeton, NJ: Princeton University Press.
Evans, P. B. and M. Timberlake
 1980   "Dependence, inequality, and growth in less developed countries." American Sociological Review 45:531–553.
Fischer, D. H.
 1978   Growing Old in America. Expanded ed. New York: Oxford University Press.
Fisher, P.
 1978   "The Social Security crisis: an international dilemma." Aging and Work 1:1–14.

Foner, Anne and Karen Schwab
- 1981 Aging and Retirement. Monterey, CA: Brooks/Cole.

Form, W.
- 1979 "Comparative industrial sociology and the convergence hypothesis." Annual Review of Sociology 5:1–25.

Friedman, E. A. and H. L. Orbach
- 1974 "Adjustment to retirement." Pp. 604–645 in Silvano Arieti (ed.), American Handbook of Psychiatry. New York: Basic Books.

Galtung, J.
- 1971 "A structural theory of imperialism." Journal of Peace Research 8:102–116.

Graebner, William
- 1980 A History of Retirement: The Meaning and Function of an American Institution, 1885–1978. New Haven, CT: Yale University Press.

Graney, M. J. and D. M. Cottam
- 1981 "Labor force nonparticipation of older people: United States, 1890–1970." The Gerontologist 21:138–145.

Griffin, C. J., J. A. Devine, and M. Wallace
- 1981 "Accumulation, legitimation, and politics: the growth of welfare expenditures in the United States since the Second World War." Paper presented at the Annual Meetings of the American Sociological Association, Toronto.

Hannan, M. T. and A. A. Young
- 1977 "Estimation in panel models: results on pooling cross-sections and time series." Pp. 52–83 in D. Heise (ed.), Sociological Methodology. San Francisco, CA: Jossey-Bass.

Harlan, W.
- 1964 "Social status of the aged in three Indian villages." Vita Humana 7:239–252.

Heisler, M. O. and B. G. Peters
- 1978 "Comparing social policy across levels of government, countries, and time: Belgium and Sweden since 1870." Pp. 149–175 in Douglas Ashford (ed.), Comparing Public Policies. Beverly Hills, CA: Sage.

Horlick, M.
- 1970 "The earnings replacement rate of old-age benefits: an international comparison." Social Security Bulletin 33:3–16.

International Labour Organization
- 1977 Labour Force Estimates and Projections. Geneva: International Labour Office.
- 1979 The Cost of Social Security. Geneva: International Labour Office.

Jackman, Robert W.
- 1975 Politics and Social Equality: A Comparative Analysis. New York: John Wiley & Sons.

Kerr, Clark, John T. Dunlop, Frederick H. Harbison, and Charles A. Meyers
- 1960 Industrialism and Industrial Man. Cambridge, MA: Harvard University Press.

Kmenta, Jan
- 1971 Elements of Econometrics. New York: MacMillan.

Land, K. C. and F. C. Pampel
- 1977 "Indicators and models of changes in the American occupational system, 1947–1973: some preliminary analyses." Social Indicators Research 4:1–23.

Laslett, P.
- 1976 "Societal development and aging." Pp. 87–116 in Robert H. Binstock and Ethel Shanas (eds.), Handbook of Aging and the Social Sciences. New York: Van Nostrand Reinhold.

Lenski, Gerhard
- 1966 Power and Privilege: A Theory of Social Stratification. New York: McGraw-Hill.

Lipman, A.
- 1970 "Prestige of the aged in Portugal: realistic appraisal and ritualistic deference." International Journal of Aging and Human Development 1:127–136.

Maddox, G. L.
 1979 "Sociology of later life." Annual Review of Sociology 5:113-135.
Meyer, J. W., J. Boli-Bennett, and C. Chase-Dunn
 1975 "Convergence and divergence in development." Annual Review of Sociology 1:223-246.
Palmore, Erdman
 1975 The Honorable Elders: A Cross-Cultural Analysis of Aging in Japan. Durham, NC: Duke University Press.
Palmore, Erdman and K. Manton
 1974 "Modernization and status of the aged: international correlations." Journal of Gerontology 29:205-210.
Pampel, Fred C.
 1981 Social Change and the Aged: Recent Trends in the U.S. Lexington, MA: Lexington Books.
Pampel, Fred C. and Jane A. Weiss
 1983 "Economic development, pension policies, and the labor force participation of aged males: a cross-national, longitudinal approach." American Journal of Sociology 89:350-72.
Ramirez, F. O. and J. Weiss
 1979 "The political incorporation of women." Pp. 238-252 in John W. Meyer and Michael T. Hannan (eds.), National Development and the World System: Educational, Economic, and Political Change, 1950-1970. Chicago: University of Chicago Press.
Rosow, Irving
 1974 Socialization to Old Age. Berkeley, CA: University of California Press.
Rubinson, R.
 1976 "The world economy and the distribution of income within states: a cross-national study." American Sociological Review 41:638-659.
Rubinson, R. and D. Quinlan
 1977 "Democracy and social inequality: a reanalysis." American Sociological Review 42:611-623.
Sheppard, H. L.
 1976 "Work and retirement." Pp. 286-309 in Robert H. Binstock and Ethel Shanas (eds.), Handbook of Aging and the Social Sciences. New York: Van Nostrand Reinhold.
Smith, D. S.
 1978 "Old age and the great transformation: a New England case study." Pp. 285-302 in S. F. Spicker, K. M. Woodward, and D. Vantassel (eds.), Aging and the Elderly. Atlantic Highlands, NJ: Humanities Press.
Social Security Administration
 1977 Social Security Programs Throughout the World. Washington, DC: U.S. Government Printing Office.
Taylor, Charles C. and Michael C. Hudson
 1972 World Handbook of Political and Social Indicators. New Haven, CT: Yale University Press.
United Nations
 1980 Demographic Year Book. New York: United Nations.
Wilensky, Harold L.
 1975 The Welfare State and Equality. Berkeley, CA: University of California Press.
Williamson, J. B., L. Evans, L. A. Powell, and S. Hesse-Biber
 1982 The Politics of Aging: Power and Policy. Springfield, IL: Charles C. Thomas.

SOCIAL SECURITY–TYPE RETIREMENT POLICIES:
A CROSS-NATIONAL STUDY

Robert C. Atchley

ABSTRACT

Retirement policies are formulated by governments in a context that includes the degree of economic development and the extent of population aging. The current debate about social security in the United States has largely ignored this context. Accordingly, this paper examines U.S. national policies such as extent of coverage, minimum retirement ages, length of service requirements, the retirement test, dependents' benefits, indexing, and replacement rate in comparison with similar policies in 97 other countries having national social insurance retirement systems as of 1979. The results show that many retirement policies are closely tied to economic development or population aging or both. The results also show that if U.S. social security policies were comparable to those of her economic and demographic peers, especially with regard to tax rate, funding from general revenues, and universal coverage, then the current "crisis" would not exist. The results also show that raising the minimum

Current Perspectives on Aging and the Life Cycle
Volume 1, pages 275-293
Copyright © 1985 by JAI Press Inc.
All rights of reproduction in any form reserved.
ISBN: 0-89232-296-9

retirement age is both unnecessary and dangerous in that it would hamper the unemployment-control function of retirement.

I. INTRODUCTION

The current debate over social security in the United States has raised nearly all of the policy questions that national social insurance retirement pension systems must answer. Should everyone be covered? How should the system be funded? What should be the minimum retirement age? What length of service should be required to qualify for benefits? Should men and women be treated equally in terms of age and length of service requirements? What provisions need to be made for persons with occupations for which the retirement age ought to be lower than normal? Should early retirement be available? If so, should benefits be reduced and by what amount? Should withdrawal from the labor force be a requirement in order to receive a pension? If so, should withdrawal be partial or complete? Should benefits be related to earnings? If so, should pensions be tied to peak earnings or to average earnings over the work life? Should benefits increase if retirement is delayed? If so, should this increase be actuarial? Should there be a pension supplement for dependents? If so, what types of dependents should be eligible and how much should the supplement be? Should benefits be indexed to provide protection from inflation? What percentage of earnings prior to retirement should be replaced by pension?

One way to evaluate our current answers to these questions is to compare them with the approaches taken by other nations with social security-type retirement pension systems. We can also look at how economic development and population aging are related to variations in retirement policies cross-nationally in order to provide other points of comparison.

This paper employs data collected in 1979 by the Social Security Administration (1980) on 98 countries with national social insurance-type pension systems to provide a point of comparison for U.S. policies. Data on population and economic development collected by the Population Reference Bureau (1979) together with data collected by the International Labour Office (1980) are then used to examine the correlates of various types of policies. The paper concludes with a brief look at how retirement policies combine with other factors to influence the proportion of the older population in the labor force.

II. BACKGROUND

National social insurance programs to provide disability, retirement and survivor benefits were developed in the late nineteenth century. They were part of an emerging role of national governments in planning, coordinating, and regulating economic activity in complex industrial societies (Donohue et al., 1960). In founding the first social security system, Prince Otto von Bismarck stressed the need for the German government to demonstrate concern for the welfare of labor as well as owners. One way to do this was to provide pensions for the "soldiers of labor." These ideas caught on quickly, and by 1920 ten European countries had social security programs.

Figure 1 shows that in the 1920s social security spread to eastern Europe and the Americas. No particular trend emerged in the 1930s, the interval when the

Figure 1. Historical Development of National Social Insurance Retirement Systems.

Pre-1900	**1901–1920**	**1921–1930**	**1931–1940**
Germany	Austria	Belgium	Barbados
	Czechoslovakia	Brazil	Ecuador
	France	Bulgaria	Finland
	Luxembourg	Chile	Greece
	Netherlands	Hungary	Norway
	Romania	Poland	Peru
	Spain	USSR	United States
	Sweden	Uruguay	
		Yugoslavia	
		United Kingdom	

1941–1950	**1951–1960**	**1961–1970**	**1971–1979**
Albania	Bahamas	Benin	Bahrain
Algeria	Bolivia	Cameroon	Iraq
Argentina	Burudi	Canada	Ireland
Columbia	Cape Verde	Cent. African Rep.	Jordan
Costa Rica	China	Congo	S. Korea
Dominican Rep.	Cyprus	Cuba	Kuwait
Egypt	El Salvador	Denmark	Liberia
Guyana	Guinea	Dominia	Mauritius
Mexico	Honduras	Cabon	Pakistan
Panama	Iran	Guatemala	Senegal
Paraguay	Israel	Haiti	Seychelles
Sudan	Ivory Coast	Lebanon	Trinidad & Tobago
Switzerland	Jamaica	Madagascar	W. Samoa
Turkey	Japan	Mali	
	Libya	Mauritania	
	Malta	Niger	
	Morocco	Saudi Arabia	
	Nicaragua	Togo	
	Phillipines	Venezuela	
	Rwanda	Vietnam	
	Syria		
	Tunisia		
	Upper Volta		
	Zaire		

United States enacted its system. During the war years of the 1940s, social security plans were developed in Latin America and a smattering of other countries. A majority of the plans now in operation were begun after 1950.

Social security systems vary considerably in coverage, funding sources, age and service requirements, benefit formulas, and replacement rates. These variations make it possible for us to look at specific variations first and then at the population and economic correlates of retirement policies.

III. COVERAGE

Coverage is the proportion of employed persons that are included in the social security retirement system. Some nations include all employed persons; some have major exceptions, usually separate systems for particular industries or occupational categories; and some are limited, excluding large categories such as agricultural workers or the self-employed.

The U.S. system covers the overwhelming majority of workers, but with major exclusions. When the system was enacted, state and local governments could maintain their own systems rather than go under the new social security system. Many did so. In addition, federal civil service workers are not covered by the system. However, agricultural workers and self-employed persons are covered. How does this compare with other countries?

Only about one-third of the systems cover all employed persons. Another third has broad coverage with major exceptions, and a third has very limited systems. But this distribution is very strongly affected by both economic and population variables. For example, the United States is in the top 15 percent of the gross national product (GNP) range for the sample. In that category, 75 percent of the systems include all employees. Countries with a large proportion of older people are also likely to include all employees in their systems. For example, 10 percent of the U.S. population is age 65 or over, and in that category more than 75 percent of the countries include all employees in the system. What this means, of course, is that the U.S. policy of allowing major groups of employees to remain outside the system is a minority approach among our economic and demographic peers.

The coverage issue involves two very different types of evaluation. On the one hand, limits and exclusions can mean that major categories of residents do not have access to retirement systems. On the other hand, limits and exclusions may exist because preexisting systems already provided pensions that were generally better than social security pensions, resulting in political pressure to retain these systems outside the social security system. The latter is what happened in the United States. Thus, the fact that the United States has major exclusions is not a defect in terms of availability of retirement pensions.

However, exclusions also affect funding, and this is where the debate has tended to center. It is held that forcing federal civil service workers to enter the system would ease cash flow pressures on the social security system that have resulted from prolonged recession (which lowers income to the system because of unemployment) and high inflation (which increases liabilities of the system because benefits are indexed and rise with inflation). This argument is essentially accurate. However, including federal civil servants would not affect the long-run picture because eventually they would begin drawing full benefits tied to their earnings. It would improve the funding base because civil service workers are generally less likely to become unemployed.

IV. FUNDING

Funds to pay social security benefits in the United States come from a payroll tax of about 10 percent, split evenly between employers and employees. No general government revenues are involved. Self-employed persons pay about 7 percent. (These percentages are for 1979, the year the data for this study were collected. The percentages are higher now.) The system is pay-as-you-go, with the taxes from today's workers being used to pay pensions to those who are retired. Virtually all social insurance systems use this method rather than establishing large trust funds that then have to be managed and that can be seriously eroded by inflation (Ross, 1979).

Contributions from both employed persons and employers are part of the funding for 90 percent of the social insurance plans studied. Such taxes are nearly universal among the countries in the top GNP category. However, the level of taxation varies considerably, as shown in Table 1. Taxes on employers

Table 1. Payroll Tax Rates for Social Insurance Retirement Systems, Selected Countries, 1979

Country	Total	Employer	Employee
Austria	19.50	10.25	9.25
Belgium	14.00	8.00	6.00
Canada	3.60	1.80	1.80
France	12.90	8.20	4.70
Germany (Fed. Rep.)	18.00	9.00	9.00
Italy	23.76	16.61	7.15
Japan	9.10	4.55	4.55
Netherlands	28.20	10.40	17.80
Sweden	20.30	20.30	—
Switzerland	9.40	4.70	4.70
United States	10.16	5.08	5.08

Source: Social Security Administration (1979).

range from 1.8 percent to 20.3 percent of payroll, and taxes on employees range from none to 17.8 percent. The average for the top GNP category is 9 percent from employers and 6.4 percent from employees. In these taxes the United States is not far from the average for similar countries. However, when the total from both employers and employees is taken together, the range is 3.6–28.2 percent, with an average of 15.4 percent. The U.S. total of 10.16 is substantially lower than the average for highly industrialized countries. Thus, the United States has one of the lower payroll tax rates.

The United States is also among the 52 percent of the 98 countries that have no contributions to social security retirement from general tax revenues. However, among the highly industrialized countries, less than 20 percent do not include some general tax revenues as support for their social security systems. Much of the revenue used to provide government support to social security systems in Europe comes from value-added taxes, which are similar to retail sales taxes but are levied on wholesale goods at various stages in manufacture (Ross, 1979; Schulz, 1980). The United States does not use the value-added tax, although using such taxes has been recommended because they encounter less popular resistance than income or sales taxes, which are more obvious to the consumer.

Thus, the overall picture we get is that the United States devotes a relatively small proportion of taxes to social security, especially from government, compared with other countries in the top GNP category. This would seem to imply that the United States has the economic capacity to increase revenues to the system substantially through both taxation and government support.

V. MINIMUM RETIREMENT AGE

Retirement age requirements vary by gender; therefore we will discuss minimum retirement ages for men first. The most common retirement ages for men are 60 (39 percent), 65 (27 percent), and 55 (22 percent). Among the 98 countries, 66 percent allow retirement by age 60. It is also significant that in only four countries must men be 65 or older in order to retire. However, once again policy is related to population aging and economic development.

As Table 2 shows, retirement age for men is very much related to life expectancy. In those countries where life expectancy is low, 91 percent of retirement ages are before 60. But in those countries where life expectancy is 70 or more, only 29 percent are before 60. Likewise, later retirement ages are very much related to high life expectancy.

The pattern in relation to GNP is not as clearcut (see Table 3). Retirement age before 60 is very much related to GNP, but having a retirement age of 65 or older is not. And the direction of the relationship is not what might be anticipated. Early retirement is commonly thought to be a function of wealth, yet the higher the GNP the *lower* the incidence of early retirement. Apparently, the lower the

Table 2. Minimum Retirement Age for Men, by Life Expectancy at Birth, 1979

	Life Expectancy at Birth							
Minimum Retirement Age (Men)	55 or Under		56–69		70 or Over		Total	
	N	%	N	%	N	%	N	%
Under 60	31	91.2	21	63.6	9	14.8	61	62.2
60–64	3	8.8	11	33.3	19	61.3	33	33.7
65 or over	—	—	1	3.0	9	9.7	4	4.1

GNP, the lower the costs of financing early retirement. In addition, the generaly lower life expectancy in less developed countries exerts pressure for earlier retirement.

For women, the most common retirement age is 55 (39 percent), followed by 60 (31 percent), 65 (12 percent), and 50 (10 percent). Retirement ages for women show more dispersion than those for men and the average minimum retirement age is considerably lower. Retirement ages for women are also tied to population aging and economic development, but not nearly as strongly as for men. The association is diminished mainly by the tendency toward early retirement for women regardless of life expectancy or GNP. Eighty percent of retirement ages for women are under 60 regardless of life expectancy or GNP.

In the United States, minimum retirement age for both women and men is 62.

Table 3. Minimum Retirement Age for Men, by Per-Capita GNP, 1979

	GNP per Capita[a]									
Minimum Retirement Age (Men)	Under 1000		1000–3000		3001–5000		Over 5000		Total	
	N	%	N	%	N	%	N	%	N	%
Under 60	38	84.4	13	50.0	6	54.5	4	25.0	61	62.2
60–64	6	13.3	12	46.2	5	45.5	10	62.5	33	33.7
65 or over	1	2.2	1	3.8	—	—	2	12.5	4	4.1

[a] In U.S. Dollars.

This is a very typical figure for men among countries in the same life expectancy and GNP categories, but for women this is a relatively high retirement age.

Recently there have been proposals to raise the minimum retirement age in the United States to 65. The comparative data show that this is an abnormally high retirement age even in countries with very high life expectancy.

A good part of the debate has ignored some important functions of retirement while focusing only on the problem of financing it. As we shall see later, nearly all industrial societies have large retired populations, regardless of economic or political philosophy. Industrial societies do not need large proportions of children or old people in their labor forces. Most of them have difficulty employing all persons 18–64 who want employment. Thus, retirement is a major means of controlling unemployment (Graebner, 1980).

Increasing the flow of funds into social security could be done in a number of ways. As we saw earlier, there is still considerable room for increasing taxes and government subsidies before the United States will even be at the average for highly industrialized countries. This would not affect the unemployment control function of retirement. However, if we raise the retirement age, this will surely keep thousands of older people in the labor force and greatly influence the role of retirement in controlling unemployment.

VI. LENGTH OF SERVICE REQUIREMENTS

All social insurance-type retirement plans have service requirements. The most common are 10 or 15 years, each of which is required by 20 percent of the countries. The next most common requirement is 20 years (13 percent). While retirement ages vary by gender, service requirements seldom do.

Length of service requirements are slightly related to economic development and population aging. For example, 45 percent of countries with high life expectancy require 20 years service or more compared with only 12 percent among countries with low life expectancy.

The service requirement of 10 years for the United States is low compared with other countries in the same GNP and life expectancy category. Thus far, increasing the service requirement has not entered into the debate about social security financing. But this analysis shows that increasing it would be in line with policies of other countries.

Increasing the service requirement would not have the same effect on the unemployment control function of retirement that raising the retirement age would. Those who would be most affected would be persons who had worked at jobs outside the system (and who presumably would be covered by another pension) and women who entered the labor force in midlife. But raising the service requirement to 15 would not affect reentry women in large numbers. Its main effect would be to reduce the number of social security pensions going to people already covered by some other retirement system. This prospect deserves careful consideration.

VII. RETIREMENT AGE AND BENEFIT AMOUNT

Some plans require that retirement at the minimum age be accompanied by a reduction in benefits. For example, in the United States benefits are reduced five-ninths of 1 percent for each month prior to age 65. This reduction is actuarial in the sense that the average worker will receive the same total amount of benefits over his or her total years in retirement regardless of retirement age from 62 to 65.

The United States is unusual in this respect. Only 5 percent of countries with social insurance retirement plans require such reductions. Among the highly developed countries, only the United States requires a reduction for retirement after age 60.

In addition, some countries (40 percent) allow a benefit increase if retirement is delayed. Most of these increases are below actuarial in the sense that even though the monthly pension will be higher, it is not high enough to make up for the benefits lost by delaying retirement. This is the case with the United States, where benefits increase only 1 percent per year if retirement is delayed. Such policies are not significantly related to population aging or economic development.

As a whole, policies that modify benefit amounts in relation to retirement age tend to promote retirement at the minimum retirement age and to discourage delayed retirement. This is in keeping with a strong unemployment control function of retirement.

VIII. RETIREMENT TESTS

Retirement tests require that persons actually be retired in order to receive retirement pensions. The usual notion is that retirement tests keep older workers out of the labor force. Accordingly, we would expect that retirement tests would be most common among the highly developed countries because they presumably have a greater need for the unemployment control function that retirement tests serve. However, the data do not bear out this idea.

Among countries in the lowest GNP category, 78 percent have retirement tests whereas only 50 percent of countries in the highest GNP category do. This same relationship exists for life expectancy. This illustrates another relationship between retirement policy and employment. In developing countries, unemployment tends to be even higher than in industrial countries. In addition, a relatively small proportion of jobs generate retirement pensions in developing countries in comparison with industrial ones. Thus, in developing countries there are two pressures to create retirement tests: high unemployment and the need to circulate as many people as possible through a relatively small number of pension-producing jobs. These countries also tend to have low retirement ages and low service requirements. They are able to finance such systems because their low standards of living mean that the cost of retirement is not very high.

Indeed, the absence of retirement tests increases steadily with GNP, with 50 percent of highly developed countries having no retirement test. This suggests that a retirement test is not the most effective way to increase retirement in industrial societies.

The United States has a retirement test. For every two dollars of earnings over $4,500 (in 1979), benefits were reduced by one dollar. This policy has stirred much debate, and there has been consistent pressure to raise the amount of employment allowed. Given the fact that retirement tests decline in importance with economic development, it could probably be eliminated completely in the United States with little aggregate effect on the proportion of older people in the labor force.

IX. PENSION AMOUNT TIED TO EARNINGS

In 85 percent of the 98 countries, the amount of pension is based on some indicator of earnings. The result of such policies, of course, is to perpetuate income differences into retirement. The 15 countries that do not use earnings to determine pension amounts are proportionately distributed across GNP and life expectancy categories.

The formulas used to determine average earnings for pension purposes vary widely, but they can be roughly categorized into conservative and liberal formulas. The conservative formulas use earnings averaged over the bulk of the working life. This tends to produce a low average, especially for people who enter the labor force in midlife or who have had interrupted or sporadic employment. The liberal formulas use earnings over some peak period, such as the highest five years or the highest three years, which tends to produce much higher averages than lifetime averages do.

Conservative formulas are used in 31 percent of the 83 countries that tie pensions to earnings. But 62 percent of countries in the top GNP category use conservative formulas. On the other hand, using a conservative formula is unrelated to life expectancy. This means that it is economic development and not population aging that influences the use of a conservative formula.

The United States uses a very conservative formula. Average earnings for pension purposes are determined by dividing total covered earnings by 35–45 years. This formula greatly reduces the pensions of women who do not enter the labor force before ages 35–45 because a large number of years they were not in the labor force are counted in averaging their earnings with no credit for the child care tasks they may have been performing during those years.

In effect, the earnings–pension formula can create an unseen service requirement. For although the service requirement in the United States is only 10 years, a person must actually be employed at a covered job for 35–45 years to qualify for a pension that reflects his or her actual level of earnings while employed. However, this aspect of our social security policy has received relatively little attention.

X. SPECIAL PENSIONS FOR THOSE IN UNHEALTHY OCCUPATIONS

In 32 percent of the 98 countries, special provisions are made to take into account the fact that some unhealthy occupations require retirement at earlier ages. Such provisions are slightly more likely in countries with high GNP and life expectancy.

The United States does not make special provisions for unhealthy or hazardous occupations. However, given the rates of disability retirement among construction workers, miners, foundry workers, asbestos workers, and numerous other occupations, a good case could be made for enacting such provisions. It will be especially important to consider early retirement for some occupations if the retirement age is raised.

XI. SUPPLEMENTS FOR DEPENDENTS

Half of the systems studied provide no supplemental benefits for dependents. Of the half that do, most provide supplements for both spouses and children, but some provide supplements only for children (12 percent) or only for spouses (5 percent).

Provision of dependents' supplements is highly related to both population aging and economic development. No dependent benefits are provided in 66 percent of countries with low GNP compared with only 13 percent of those with high GNP. On the other hand, supplements to all dependents are provided in 63 percent of high GNP countries while benefits to both children and spouse are provided in only 16 percent of countries with low GNP. The same relationship exists for life expectancy.

The median supplement for spouses is 15 percent and for children 10 percent. In the United States, the supplement is 50 percent for a spouse and each dependent child or grandchild under age 18. In this respect, the United States has one of the more liberal policies. The 50 percent spouse benefit plays an important role in bringing replacement rates for social security up to a level comparable with other highly developed nations. It is difficult to assess the impact of supplements for children and grandchildren because the statistics compiled by the

Social Security Administration do not differentiate between benefits to children of retired workers and benefits to surviving children of workers who have died.

Cutting spouse benefits is an unlikely source for easing the financial costs of retirement, at least in the United States. But benefits to dependent children is another matter. Despite the fact that putting children through college as a retired person is likely to be very difficult, benefits to college students ages 18–22 were eliminated. However, even with these cuts, the United States still has a liberal policy with respect to supplements for dependents.

XII. INDEXING

Indexing policies provide for an automatic increase in social security retirement pensions when required by inflation. Although the methods used to determine when inflation is enough to require a benefit increase and the amount of increase required vary considerably, 43 percent of the countries studied had some form of indexing.

Indexing is very much related to economic growth, but not in a linear fashion. As Table 4 shows, countries with low GNP are not very likely to index, but the 11 countries in the high intermediate range are the *least* likely to index. Yet 75 percent of the high GNP countries, including the United States, index their social security pensions. This suggests that industrial countries having difficulty with economic growth are less likely to index. (Countries in this high intermediate category include Czechoslovakia, East Germany, Italy, Poland, Spain, the United Kingdom, and the USSR.) Indexing is unrelated to population aging.

As the United States has encountered economic problems, there have been attempts to alter the formula for indexing pensions. Because these formulas tend to be complex and difficult to understand, they may be easier for governments to manipulate than more definite policies, such as retirement age or length of service, because the public is less likely to know how to evaluate proposed changes. Yet in terms of the welfare of the retired population, indexing is one of

Table 4. Prevalence of Indexing, by Per-Capita GNP, 1979

Pensions Indexed?	GNP per Capita[a]								Total	
	Under 1000		1000–3000		3001–5000		Over 5000			
	N	%	N	%	N	%	N	%	N	%
Yes	17	38.6	10	38.5	3	27.3	12	75.0	42	43.3
No	27	61.4	16	61.5	8	72.7	4	25.0	55	56.7

[a]In U.S. Dollars.

the more important policies and one that is common in the economically developed world.

XIII. REPLACEMENT RATE

Replacement rate is the percentage of earnings in the year prior to retirement that is replaced by a social security retirement pension. Intuitively, one might expect replacement rates to be related to economic development on the basis that wealthier nations could afford higher replacement rates. On the other hand, population aging might be expected to reduce replacement rates because the higher the proportion of older people in the population, the greater the pressure on pay-as-you-go systems. The data show that there are no significant differences in replacement rates by per capita GNP. However, replacement rates are positively associated with life expectancy (Table 5).

Replacement rates vary considerably in the United States between couples and single individuals. For couples, social security retirement benefits replace about 58 percent of earnings. However, for single persons the replacement rate is only about 38 percent. Thus the figure for couples is good in relation to other highly industrialized countries, but the figure for single persons is fair to poor. This inequity is a major problem in the system at present, although it has received less attention lately than funding problems.

XIV. COMBINED INFLUENCE OF GNP AND LIFE EXPECTANCY

Throughout the analysis so far we have seen that in most cases both economic development and population aging are related to retirement policy variables in national social insurance retirement systems. Although it is possible to separate

Table 5. Relative Relationship of GNP and Life Expectancy to Selected Policy Variables

	GNP	Life Expectancy
Minimum retirement age (men)	.19[a]	.37
Minimum retirement age (women)	.18	.44
Length of service requirement	.27	.42
Replacement rate	NS[b]	.69

[a]Standardized regression coefficients.
[b]Not statistically significant.

population aging and economic development conceptually, it is more difficult to do so operationally.

Economic development can be indicated in a number of ways. In this study, per capita GNP, percentage of the population living in urban areas, percentage of the labor force engaged in agriculture, and percentage of the labor force engaged in manufacturing were available. Of these, GNP had a substantially higher correlation with the retirement policy variables and was selected for the analysis.

Population aging is indicated by life expectancy at birth, percentage of the population 65 and over, and the aged dependency ratio (the older population divided by the population 18–64). Of these, life expectancy was generally the indicator most highly correlated with retirement policy variables.

The correlation between life expectancy and GNP is .61, a strong correlation but far from perfect. This allows us to treat them as separate concepts and to examine the relative contribution of each in predicting various retirement policy variables. Table 5 shows the results of regression analysis on several continuous policy variables. These results show that while GNP is significant in three of four cases, life expectancy has much greater predictive power. Thus, we can infer that population aging has a greater impact on retirement policy variables than economic development. This is theoretically interesting because it is often assumed that retirement policies are caused by the changing relationship of workers to production or by economic development, but this analysis indicates that population aging is probably a more powerful factor.

XV. EFFECTS OF RETIREMENT POLICIES

We have seen that retirement policies are affected by both population aging and economic development. But what effects do these policies have on the level of retirement across nations? To examine this issue, data on the labor force participation of persons 65 and older were taken as the dependent variable in a regression analysis, with population aging, economic development, and retirement policy variables used as independent variables. In this analysis, the percentage of the labor force employed in agriculture was used to indicate economic development (Pampel and Weiss, 1982) and the percentage of the population 65 or over was used to indicate the level of population aging. The retirement policy variables used were minimum retirement age for men, the percentage of employer contributions to social security financing, the length of service requirement, and the presence of a retirement test. These variables all had the highest raw correlations with labor force participation of older people.

Table 6 shows that between them, population aging and economic development account for 68 percent of the variance in percentage at 65 and over in the labor force. Note that the higher the percentage in agricultural employment (and

Social Security–Type Retirement Policies

Table 6. Predictors of Labor Force Participation of Older People[a], 1979

Independent Variable	R^2	Simple R	Standardized Regression Coefficient
Percent employed in agriculture	.577	.759	.533
Percent of population age 65 or over	.680	−.700	−.358
Percent of employer contributions	.686	−.336	−.073
Length of service requirement	.688	−.296	−.050
Retirement test	.690	−.102	−.044
Minimum retirement age for men	—[b]	—	—

[a]Age 65 and over
[b]Produced no improvement in the regression equation.

therefore the lower the economic development), the higher the proportion of older people in the labor force (and therefore the lower the level of retirement). The greater the percentage of the population over age 64, the lower the labor force participation of older people.

These factors make sense. Agricultural employment is flexible. It can readily accommodate the changing capacities of older people. Agricultural societies also do not have large economic surpluses that can be used to finance retirement for agricultural and self-employed workers. Agricultural societies also do not have large proportions of their population living to old age and having to be accommodated within the labor force.

Industrial societies, on the other hand, have large economic surpluses. Their use of nonhuman energy in production means less need for workers. Industrial societies also tend to have large proportions of old people, and as the age of the older population goes up, so does the variability in capacities and the potential problems associated with accommodating them within the labor force. The elderly are thus a convenient segment to exclude from the labor force, and retirement is a social institution created to accomplish this task.

Retirement is an excellent case where "functional causal imagery" applies (Stinchcomb, 1968). According to Stinchcomb (1968:80), "Whenever we find *uniformity of the consequences* of action but *great variety of the behavior causing those consequences,* a functional explanation in which the consequence serves as the cause is suggested." Industrial societies vary considerably in culture, political philosophy, economic organization, and even retirement policies. Yet they are remarkably consistent in the relations among economic development, population aging, and extent of retirement in the older population. This suggests that retirement policies are caused by an underlying need to justify and support a necessary level of retirement given a particular degree of population aging and economic development.

The relative explanatory weakness of the retirement policy variables can be seen in Table 6. The retirement policy variables, although moderately correlated with the labor force participation of older people, have no explanatory power above that to be gained from knowledge of economic growth and population aging.

One implication of these findings is that we should not expect too much of the retirement policy variables. There seems to be an inevitability to retirement among those countries with high economic development and aging populations.

Indeed, the same set of destabilizing factors tends to be causing problems in social security systems of nearly all highly industrialized countries. There is generally opposition to increasing payroll taxes. Sporadic growth and decline in birth rates have created "humps" in the age structure of populations that cause periodic funding problems in pay-as-you-go systems. Early retirement is popular in all highly industrialized countries in which replacement rates are above 40 percent. Accordingly, most developed countries have entered a "plateau" period in contrast to the expansive growth that most systems experienced in the 1960s (Ross, 1979). As we move to summarize the results of this study and its implications for the current dialogue on social security in the United States, we should not overestimate the impact that any given policy change is apt to have.

XVI. DISCUSSION

Retirement policies represent a complex of rules and procedures that enable retirement but are not its underlying cause. Both the level of retirement and the key policies that enable it are caused by economic development and population aging. Among the 98 countries studied, the relationships can be summarized as follows:

1. As economic development and population aging increase, the proportion of the population covered by national social insurance (social security) retirement systems increases.
2. As economic development and population aging increase, the incidence of government funding of social security from general revenues increases.
3. As population aging increases, minimum retirement age increases. This relationship is stronger for men than for women.
4. As economic development increases, minimum retirement age increases. This influence is much weaker than that of population aging.
5. Few societies (4 percent) require persons to work beyond age 64.

6. As economic development and population aging increase, length of service requirements increase.

7. Adjusting social security retirement benefits to account for age at retirement is unrelated to economic development or population aging.

8. As population aging and economic development increase, the incidence of retirement tests *decreases*.

9. As economic development increases, the use of a conservative formula (lifetime average) for computing average earnings increases in frequency.

10. As economic development and population aging increase, provision of pension supplements for dependents becomes more prevalent.

11. Indexing of benefits to offset inflation is unrelated to population aging.

12. Indexing is most prevalent in highly industrialized societies but *least* prevalent in moderately industrialized societies.

13. As population aging increases, pension replacement rates increase.

14. Replacement rates are unrelated to economic development.

In the context of these general trends, we can make the following points about retirement policies in the United States compared with other countries with a similar degree of economic development and population aging:

1. The United States is in the minority in allowing major exclusions from its national social insurance retirement system. This is not a problem from the standpoint of availability of pensions to excluded workers. It does reduce the funding base available to the system because government workers are generally less likely to become unemployed.

2. Payroll taxes to support social security retirement in the United States are well below average for highly industrialized countries. Although increasing payroll taxes cannot be expected to be popular, the data show that the United States can afford economically to do so.

3. The United States is in a minority in providing no general revenue support for social security. The value-added tax seems to be the best prospect for providing added federal revenues.

4. Given below-average payroll taxes and no general revenue support, the United States should be able to afford economically to handle the funding needs of social security by increased funding alone.

5. The minimum retirement age in the United States is average for men and high for women. Raising it would make the United States retirement age unusually high for countries with large older populations and high economic development. Raising the retirement age would also defeat the unemployment control function of retirement.

6. The 10-year length of service requirement for the United States is low. It could probably be increased to 15 years with little effect on the vast majority of

covered workers. This change would mainly affect workers who already qualify for a pension from government employment. Little study has been made of this option.

7. The United States is alone among high GNP countries in requiring those who retire at 62 to take reduced benefits. The pension increment of 1 percent per year for delayed retirement costs the retiree money to delay retirement. These policies need to be reassessed. The reduction in benefits for early retirement does not discourage retirement. It does increase expenditures for public assistance due to inadequate social security benefits. Improving the increment for delayed retirement might well increase the number who stay in the labor force (and continue to contribute to social security).

8. The United States has a retirement test, but such tests have little effect on the proportion of older people in the labor force, which in turn means that they do not serve to keep unemployment down. Therefore, there is little reason to keep the retirement test.

9. The United States' conservative formula for tying social security pensions to earnings imposes an indirect service requirement of 35–45 years if retirement benefits are to accurately reflect actual earnings during employment. This policy creates special hardships for women and needs to be reconsidered. However, use of conservative formulas is "normal" among highly developed countries.

10. If the retirement age is raised, the United States needs to reconsider its policy against providing younger minimum retirement ages for workers in unhealthy or hazardous occupations.

11. Dependent supplements are common among highly developed countries. Spouse benefits in particular are an important reason that social security is adequate for couples in the United States.

12. The generally adequate replacement rates for couples in the United States mask a serious replacement rate problem for individuals.

13. Indexing is nearly universal among highly developed countries. However, these policies are among the first to be examined during economic slumps. Reducing the level of indexing is equivalent to cutting benefits.

In general, the social security debate has been too limited in the United States, focusing too much on the funding problem and paying too little attention to such issues as control of unemployment and the need for workers. The solutions proposed have thus been misguided.

Retirement is an institution that serves society first and individuals only second (Graebner, 1980; Atchley, 1982), although the debate makes it appear just the opposite. Hence, it is worth recognizing that we need retirement in order to manage unemployment. Yet is it reasonable to expect older people alone to pay the cost for this social good by cutting their level of living? Or is it better to acknowledge that the whole society benefits from retirement and distribute the costs accordingly? If we decide that older people should pay, then we will raise the retirement age, reduce indexing, continue to punish retirement at the minimum age, and keep the retirement test. If we decide that the whole society should pay, then we will increase payroll taxes and provide general revenue funding. What remains to be seen is whether we have the national courage to take the socially equitable course of action or whether we will impose the costs on a convenient scapegoat, the elderly (Binstock, 1982).

REFERENCES

Atchley, Robert C.
   1982 "Retirement as a social institution." Annual Review of Sociology 8:263–287.

Binstock, Robert
   1982 "Reframing the agenda of politics on aging." Pp. 3–20 in the Proceedings of a Symposium on Income Maintenance. Waltham, MA: Brandeis University Policy Center on Aging.

Donohue, Wilma, Harold L. Orbach, and Otto Pollak
   1960 "Retirement: the emerging social pattern." Pp. 330–406 in Clark Tibbitts (ed.), Handbook of Social Gerontology. Chicago: University of Chicago Press.

Graebner, William
   1980 A History of Retirement. New Haven, CT: Yale University Press.

International Labour Office
   1980 Yearbook of Labor Statistics. Geneva: ILO.

Pampel, Fred C. and Jane A. Weiss
   1982 "Economic growth, pension policies, and the labor force participation of aged males: a cross-national, longitudinal approach." Iowa City, Iowa: The University of Iowa Press.

Population Reference Bureau
   1979 1979 World Population Data Sheet. Washington, D.C.: Population Reference Bureau.

Ross, Stanford G.
   1979 "Social Security: a worldwide issue." Social Security Bulletin 42(8):3–10.

Schulz, James H.
   1980 The Economics of Aging. 2nd Ed. Belmont, CA: Wadsworth.

Social Security Administration
   1980 Social Security Programs Throughout the World. Washington, D.C.: U.S. Government Printing Office.

Stinchcomb, Arthur L.
   1968 Constructing Social Theories. New York: Harcourt Brace Jovanovich.

CHINESE RETIREMENT:
POLICY AND PRACTICE

Deborah Davis-Friedmann

ABSTRACT

Since 1951 the Chinese government has had a national pension program. Eligibility, however, is restricted to the 20 percent of the labor force in "state" jobs. Most elderly therefore rely on either employment in marginal jobs or financial contributions by adult children to provide economic security in old age. Continued demand for manual labor guarantees employment of the old and a severe housing shortage necessitates multigeneration households with pooled incomes. Thus despite the limited access to pensions, few elderly become destitute. An assumption that pensions are rewards not entitlements partially rationalizes the elite nature of the pension program. But the most fundamental constraint on expanded coverage is poverty.

I. INTRODUCTION

In 1951, only two years after the establishment of the People's Republic of China, the leaders of the Chinese Communist Party (CCP) introduced a comprehensive pension program. Immediately 16 million citizens employed in industry and government service became eligible for lifetime pensions[1] (Blaustein, 1962; Beijing Review, 1982c). By December 1982, eligibility had been extended to 85 million workers and 11 million retirees were regularly collecting monthly pensions (Beijing Review, 1983b). Nevertheless, despite 30 years of growth, pensions remain the privilege of a minority. In 1982 four times as many workers were excluded from the government pension plan as were included, and among those over the age of 60, the nonpensioned outnumbered the pensioned by a ratio of 10:1.[2]

A related feature of the elite status of Chinese pensioners is the administration of government pensions as rewards. In contrast to programs that distribute pensions as legal "entitlements," Chinese administrators authorize pensions only after a case-by-case review of each individual's work history, current financial needs, and past record of political behavior. As a result of this discretionary process, long-term demographic trends—particularly the increasing number of citizens over age 60—have not produced the same steady increase in the number of pensioners observed in other socialist and nonsocialist countries (Wilensky, 1975). Instead the pattern of expansion in China has been sensitive to ideological shifts, and at least twice, first during the Great Leap Forward (1958/59) and later during the most radical years of the Cultural Revolution decade (1966–1976), the percentage of elderly receiving pensions fell even as the number of those officially eligible increased (Davis-Friedmann, 1983).

In previous studies of pension programs, there has been a divided opinion on the importance of political ideology. Generally, researchers have concluded that the most critical explanatory variables are economic and demographic (Pryor, 1968; Wilensky, 1975; Simanis, 1983; Zeitser, 1983). Only a few have found ideology to be the most decisive (Mitchell, 1983; Ascher, 1976). Nevertheless, despite the highly politicized nature of Chinese society and the apparently direct response of retirement rates to political upheaval, an overview of Chinese retirement programs since 1951 strongly supports an economic explanation, and in particular indicates the power of poverty to force ideological compromise.

In 1949, the leaders of the CCP outlined a program of "socialist transformation" that combined a fundamental commitment to egalitarian redistribution of wealth with an investment and tax policy to spur rapid industrialization. Expecting sustained economic growth in all sectors, CCP leaders assumed that even after major redistribution of income, only the former elite would experience a reduced standard of living.

In less than 10 years it became clear that it would be impossible to shift painlessly and quickly to a higher standard of living for all segments of the population. Labor productivity, particularly in agriculture, was growing too slowly to generate the surpluses to sustain both high investment rates and improved levels of consumption. The CCP leadership entered a protracted debate over economic and political priorities that by 1962 culminated in a de facto agreement to compromise socialist ideals of equality and accept a dual economy. That compromise, still in effect as of 1983, divided the Chinese labor force into "state" and "collective" workers, which for all practical purposes corresponds to the urban–rural dichotomy that divides many Third World economies. In terms of social welfare programs the result is a grossly inequitable two-tier system whereby the national government takes full responsibility for the medical, disability, and pensions needs of state employees and requires workers in the collective sector to observe the principle of "self-reliance," turning to family and local community funds to cover the costs of illness, injury, and old age (Davis-Friedmann, 1984). In 1981, 84 million people worked full time in the state sector, 348 million in the collective (Beijing Review, 1981b, 1982c). It is within this administrative and ideological compromise of the original blueprint for socialist transformation that the world's largest pension system continues to serve only a minority of its elderly population.

II. CHINESE PENSION BENEFITS

From their first draft to their most recent revisions, the Labor Insurance Regulations of the State Council have provided lifetime pensions to all those who were full-time employees in the state sector (Blaustein, 1962; Fujian Province Revolutionary Committee, 1973; Cai Zheng Bu, 1979; Davis-Friedmann, 1983). As originally drafted, state workers were guaranteed a pension that replaced 70 percent of the last wage. Men became eligible after 25 years of work experience at age 60 and women after 20 years experience at age 50. Everyone in a state job that required prolonged exposure to dangerous working conditions became eligible five years earlier than the minimum age.

Subsequent revisions in 1953, 1958, 1964, and 1978 reduced the work requirement (Davis-Friedmann, 1983). According to the most recent revision in 1978, those who meet work criteria at ages 50 (women) and 60 (men) qualify for pensions that replace 75 percent of last wage and those with even 10 years of state employment become eligible for "minimum" pensions that replace 60 percent of last wage. In addition, since 1978, retirees who have performed "revolutionary work" before Liberation or who have been selected as national labor heroes after 1949 qualify for pensions that replace 80 to 100 percent of last wage. For CCP officials pension benefits are even more generous. Those who were active in service of the Party between September 1945 and September 1949 receive 100 percent of last wage; those active between January 1943 and September 1945 receive 108 percent; those active between July 1937 and December 1942 receive 112.5 percent; and those active prior to July 1937 receive 116 percent (Yuan, 1983).

Although in general Chinese pensions replace a higher percentage of preretirement wages than most government programs in the West, the Chinese system does have one important restriction: it provides no survivor benefits. After the death of a pensioner, surviving family members receive a lump sum funeral benefit, and in cases of proven need, nonemployed dependents are eligible for a percentage of the deceased person's pension for up to a maximum of 12 months (Cai Zheng Bu, 1979). After that transition period, nonemployed dependents are expected to find alternate sources of support. In the most common case—that of the nonpensioned widow—adult children assume financial responsibility. Government welfare is provided only in cases of the childless who have no pension themselves and who can no longer work in even marginal jobs (see Sec. IV.C for further discussion of welfare provisions).

A. Moves Toward Mandatory Retirement

Until the 1978 revisions of the Labor Insurance Regulations retirement was not mandatory (Davis-Friedmann, 1983). Most state employees continued to work past the minimum ages of eligibility, and in the first seven years of implementation the government even authorized a cash bonus to those who continued to work after meeting the criteria for retirement. Then in 1958 Chinese economic planners saw retirement as one means to increase job openings in the state sector and the bonuses were eliminated. Retirement, however, did not become mandatory. On the contrary, between 1958 and 1978, the CCP consistently pressed workers in good health to delay retirement, permitting only the very old or disabled to apply for pensions.

During the high tides of political struggle, most notably during the Great Leap Forward and the Cultural Revolution, retirement by those in good health was often viewed as "antisocialist," and most workers who had fulfilled the age and work criteria waited until their supervisors urged them to apply before requesting a pension. As a result, for most of the post-1949 years, ordinary employees have worked several years beyond the minimum age of eligibility and highly placed government officials have stayed at their posts until death.

Since 1978, and particularly since 1980, policy has changed. The 1978 revision of the Labor Insurance Regulations specifically requires that after 10 years of continuous employment in the state sector, male workers and staff retire at age 60 and females at age 50.[3] In 1982 the government announced, and even enforced, retirement ages for government officials (People's Daily, 1982; Zhong Guo Nong Min Bao, 1982; Beijing Xin Hua, 1982; Peng Zhen, 1982; Beijing Review, 1983a). Henceforth, ministerial rank officials would retire at age 65 and those at the rank of vice-minister or department head at age 60 (Beijing Review, 1982a). Consistent with this effort to enforce mandatory retirement were the significant increases noted above for pensions for Party members who had served the nation before 1949.

Interviews conducted by the author and a colleague during field trips to China (Davis-Friedmann, 1979, 1981; Frolic, 1982) indicate that the policy of mandatory retirement has not been immediately implemented. Instead, at least through July 1982, retirement was still occurring at the mandatory ages only when both the employer and the employee found it economically expedient. If a worker has a special technical skill or provides irreplaceable political leadership, the employer often does not require retirement and in some cases even opposes the worker's efforts to obtain a pension. Another situation in which workers routinely stay beyond the minimum age of eligibility is when the worker or staff member performs an ordinary job but has such heavy financial obligations to dependent family members that he or she can not afford any reduction in monthly income. Furthermore, because state enterprises must guarantee a minimum per capita monthly income to households of workers and pensioners, supervisors do not force retirement if the postretirement drop in income will require the enterprise to use their own welfare funds to subsidize the new retiree's household in order to bring them up to the guaranteed minimum standard of living.

B. Paid and Unpaid Postretirement Employment

The Labor Insurance Regulations permit, but do not encourage, paid employment after retirement. Officially the total monthly income from pension and postretirement employment can exceed the preretirement earnings only in the case of labor heroes and former government officials. In practice, it is not unusual for new retirees to earn 120–140 percent of their previous salaries. Generally, however, this phenomenon is limited to the three or four years immediately after retirement and appears to be rationalized primarily as a means to help a family maximize income during the period when their children are marrying and setting up new households. Less explicitly it is justified as a means to persuade older workers who are reluctant to retire to leave the workplace in order to create new openings for unemployed youth or reduce excess labor capacity.

Between 10 and 15 percent of recent retirees have regular paid jobs (Davis-Friedmann, 1981). Another 15 percent hold volunteer posts that employ them outside the home for 20 hours a week. Typical volunteer jobs are part-time attendant to a bedridden neighbor, baby sitter during after-school hours, crossing guard, or guardian of a neighborhood telephone. In general, females hold volunteer jobs and paid positions are reserved for males. Furthermore, because women retire at a younger age than men and because housework continues to be viewed as "women's work," retirement rarely brings female retirees as much leisure time as males. Thus during the summer months, one often sees elderly men gathering in the parks to chat or play chess with friends, while elderly women remain close to home, busy with an endless round of unpaid household tasks.

C. Funding Pensions

When the Labor Insurance Regulations were first drafted in 1951, some large, urban industrial enterprises whose workers were protected by the provisions of the legislation were not owned by the national government. Even by 1953, a significant number remained outside the state sector, surviving as collectives or cooperatives. Thus funds for pensions in the first years after Liberation did not come exclusively from the national government but came also from contributions of enterprises and private owners. As originally legislated, part of the pension would be paid directly by management and part would be paid through the labor insurance fund. The fund was first created by depositing 3 percent of the total payroll into the account of the National Labor Federation at the State Bank. After two months, the deposit was divided so that 30 percent went to the bank account of the National Labor Union and 70 percent to the account of the enterprise level union (Blaustein, 1962).

Since 1956, all workers covered by the Labor Insurance Regulations have worked in the state sector. Therefore there is no longer a need for a special employer's fund. Instead, funding of pensions is now handled primarily as part of the transfer of wages between central government ministries and their subordinate enterprises. According to a personnel officer interviewed by the author in November 1981, state enterprises include pensions in the "wage bill" they submit to the ministry that absorbs their profits and losses, and pensions are taken from the same source as wages. Currently, we do not fully understand the exact financing and accounting procedures. Thus, all that can be said with any certainty is that after 30 years of experience with the Labor Insurance Regulations, state enterprises show little overt concern with the high cost of current pension outlays and one presumes that this lack of concern is the result of a centrally planned economy that does not differentiate clearly between financial procedures for pensions and those for salaries.

As China moves into the 1980s, however, there are signs that the situation is changing. The post-Mao leadership is concerned with state deficits and the high cost of social welfare services to state workers. They have taken concrete steps to decentralize financial accountability and management decisions and have tried to increase enterprise contributions to health and pension funds (Lao Dong Zhu, 1980). One possible scenario, therefore, would be for state sector enterprises to move toward the accounting procedures currently used in the collective sector. Since 1964, large, urban collective enterprises[4] have funded pensions from enterprise profits (Davis-Friedmann, 1983). In the first years, replacement ratios averaged 40–60 percent of last wage, and the pension was not fully guaranteed for the lifetime of the retiree. However, as large collectives matured, benefits improved and one union spokesman told the author in 1979 that in urban areas the greatest difference in terms of pension benefits was no longer that between state and collective employees, but rather that between employees in large and small collectives. Based on the evolution of pension programs in the urban collective sector since 1964, it would seem likely that as the state loosens control over enterprise welfare funds and requires greater accountability for profits and losses, enterprise level management will become increasingly concerned, and explicit, about the sources of their pension funds and seek a favorable ratio between wages and pensions.

D. Additional Perquisites of State Pensioners

Prior to retirement, workers eligible for pensions under the Labor Insurance Regulations qualify for free medical care, full disability coverage, paid maternity leave, and a variety of subsidies on consumer goods and services. In the 1970s these nonwage benefits averaged 80 percent of a state worker's annual salary (Lardy, 1983). After retirement, former state workers not only remain eligible for the medical benefits and consumer subsidies they received as workers, but they also qualify for a cash payment for moving expenses incurred after retirement (Cai Zheng Bu, 1979). The relocation subsidy provides payments of 150 yuan to retirees who move out of enterprise housing to another home within the same city and payments of 300 yuan to those who move from the city to the countryside.

In addition, between July 1978 and September 1983, new state pensioners had an extra—and rather unusual—privilege denied to all other working or retired parents. During these five years, pensioners were guaranteed that one of their children would be given permanent employment in the retiree's former place of work provided the child was between the ages of 16 and 30 and was not already permanently employed in the state sector. In short, the 1978 revisions of the Labor Insurance Regulations provided for inheritance of jobs within the labor elite of the state sector.

The response to this new perquisite was overwhelmingly positive among elderly parents on the verge of retirement. In all the enterprises the author visited in 1979, 80 percent of retirees used this "substitution option" and between 60 and 100 percent of all new jobs in these workplaces had gone to children of post-1978 retirees. Labor Bureau officials and enterprise level managers, however, were not as enthusiastic about the new benefit as new retirees. In 1980 CCP leaders began to express dissatisfaction (Kiu Jiaonong, 1982), and in the summer of 1983 they eliminated the "substitution option," returning to an earlier policy which only permitted preferential hiring among qualified children from families in extreme financial difficulty (Ren Min Ri Bao, 1983).

E. Pattern of Growth

In the first decade after the Labor Insurance Regulations were legislated, few workers qualified for pensions. The state labor force consisted primarily of young adults recently recruited into industrial jobs and government administration. Insurance payments, therefore, were concentrated on job-related injuries, maternity leaves, or acute medical crises. By 1957, out of a total population of 632 million, only 67,000 former state employees were regularly collecting monthly pensions (Davis-Friedmann, 1983). Even in 1967, when the total population had grown to 762 million and more than 40 million worked in the state labor force (Liu, 1982) fewer than 150,000 retirees collected state pensions (Davis-Friedmann, 1983). In terms of growth rates, the numbers of pensioners was increasing faster than the total population, but in terms of absolute numbers, the total remained small.

In the early 1970s the situation should have changed dramatically as those who had entered the state sector during the rapid expansion in the mid-1950s reached retirement age with the requisite 20 years of continuous employment. Based on this demographic "push" one would have predicted a rapid increase in the number of new retirees between 1972 and 1976. Political upheaval and ideological struggle suppressed the expected increases. During the early 1970s the number of retirees remained relatively constant and in the mid-1970s grew at only a modest rate. The primary "depressant" was a "radical" Maoist position that condemned pensions as "capitalist" materialist incentives and a politically motivated attack on the municipal and enterprise level unions that administered pension programs. In response to these attacks, workers and their immediate supervisors often felt that a request for a pension by a healthy older worker would be viewed as 'anti socialist', and only the weakest and most disabled applied to retire.[5]

After the death of Mao and the fall of the most "radical" Maoist leadership in September 1976, the retirement decision became less politically charged. Municipal level unions regained their respectability, and pensions could be routinely granted to healthy as well as disabled elderly workers. Still growth was only moderate. The primary explanation then became economic. Elderly parents were unwilling to retire until all or most of their children had found permanent jobs. During the early and mid-1970s CCP leaders had continued to repeat the official orthodoxy that there was no unemployment under socialism. Elderly and middle-aged parents responsible for their dependent children knew the situation to be quite different. Between 1952 and 1964, urban China experienced the biggest baby boom in its history. By the late 1960s these children were crowding into the urban labor market at the rate of 4–5 million per year and there simply were not enough new job openings. Nevertheless, national leaders refused to confront the problems directly. Instead they launched a massive relocation of urban youth in the countryside as part of an ideological commitment to reduced inequalities between urban and rural living standards. By sending urban high school and junior high school graduates to work in the countryside, the CCP leaders hoped to rapidly upgrade the technical skills in rural areas and simultaneously to "toughen" a generation of urban youth who had never known the hardships of pre-1949 China. Between 1968 and 1976, approximately 20 million urban teenagers were sent to the countryside. Some did settle in successfully and work as teachers, paramedics, and accountants. Most, however, lived marginal lives in "youth teams." They never were able to integrate themselves into village life or succeed as agricultural workers, and they consequently depended on monthly cash stipends from their parents to survive.

In 1978, the national leadership abruptly shifted from the Maoist legacy of the earlier years and launched a massive ideological and structural reform of the Chinese economy. Under the newly consolidated power of Deng Xiao-ping, "moderate" CCP leaders demanded that more attention be given to knowing "the facts." Unemployment among urban youth became a topic of open discussion (Prybla, 1982) and increased retirements were officially advocated as a means to create new jobs (Davis-Friedmann, 1979). The 1978 revisions of the pension plan provided a specific clause for unemployed children to "substitute" for their retired parents and the response by elderly workers was immediate (Gold, 1980). In January 1979, there were approximately 1 million pensioners; one year later there were 2 million. By July 1982 it had risen to 9.5 million and labor union officials were predicting a growth rate of at least 1 million per year through 1985 (Frolic, 1982).

How long the Chinese economy can sustain increasing expenditures for pensions is unclear. If inflation and promotion rates stay at current levels, average pensions will continue to exceed entry level wages by 20 percent for at least a decade. Furthermore, each time a new worker replaces a retiree, the total labor costs to an enterprise, and therefore to the state, rises substantially. And most significantly for predicting long-term patterns of growth, projected expansion of state sector jobs (Ren Tao, 1983c) indicates that an annual retirement rate of 1 million will provide only one-sixth of the new openings needed. Thus it is already clear that increased retirements provide no easy solution to unemployment among youth. Based on the history of past shifts in retirement policy and the enormous discretionary power of the government in allocation of pensions to "qualified" applicants, it seems likely, therefore, that the pattern of growth after 1985 may diverge from that of the preceding five years and that the rate of increase will drastically decline.

III. RETIREMENT FROM AGRICULTURE

Eighty percent of the Chinese population live in rural areas. Most of these rural residents work full time in farm work, and among those over age 50 the percentage who have spent their adult lives as field laborers averages between 80 and 90 percent of the age cohort. For these elderly farm workers, withdrawal from the paid work force occurs under very different conditions than for manual laborers in the cities. For the one out of 80 who work on state farms, there is a small pension; for the majority there is no steady income after they stop work. But in contrast to urban retirement, withdrawal from farm work is gradual. As physical strength declines, agricultural workers move first to less taxing jobs and later concentrate on "unpaid" jobs within the household. These tasks, such as caring for poultry, washing, cooking, and watching grandchildren, are highly valued by the younger generation and in terms of the household economy elderly are usually considered economically active well into their 70s. Only in advanced old age do they become totally financially dependent on their children (Davis-Friedmann, 1983).

Throughout the post-1949 era, rural elderly have looked to their families for support in much the same way as did their parents and grandparents before them. But there also have been some experiments with increased contributions by nonfamily institutions. In the first 30 years of CCP leadership there was a gradual movement toward increased public responsibility for the food grain of the elderly. Since Deng Xiao-ping's new economic reforms, however, policy has become differentiated between rich and poor villages. In rich areas the CCP is advocating pensions whereas in poor areas they are stressing greater reliance on family support. A summary of these shifting and ambiguous trends highlights the continuing need for CCP leaders to compromise socialist ideals in the face of economic exigencies.

A. The Elderly Farm Worker Under Mao

In the first five years after the CCP victory, the household was the basic unit of production in rural China and incomes varied according to the number of working members, the skill of the individual laborers, and the vagaries of local climate and soil conditions. Elderly generally lived with at least one married child (usually the son) and the security of the old depended on the wealth of the family and the quality of the relationship between parents and child (Davis-Friedmann, 1983).

In 1955/56 farmland was collectivized. Farm families were grouped into production teams of between 10 and 20 households and team harvests were divided among workers in proportion to the labor each individual contributed. Under this system elderly men averaged 50–70 percent of the wages of younger men and elderly women 30–50 percent of the wage of elderly men (Davis-Friedmann, 1983). However, although team accountants calculated the value of each worker, income was distributed to the household head and not to each laborer (Davis-Friedmann, 1983). Because the vast majority of elderly lived jointly with a married son, the intergenerational transfers were accomplished rather effortlessly within the boundaries of a single household budget and few elderly were deserted or destitute.

In 1958 Mao launched the Great Leap Forward into communism. For the first six months of the leap, harvests were distributed among rural residents entirely on the basis of need. Inequalities based on differences in work performance disappeared within (but not between) villages. Six months later, the "free supply" system was bankrupt, and within a year the economy had plunged into a deep depression that held most rural residents to starvation rations until Fall 1962. Upon recovery from the disasters of the Great Leap, the CCP turned to a mixed payment system that was to persist without major alterations for the next 20 years.

In the mixed system of income distribution, between 30 and 40 percent of the harvest was distributed according to need and the remainder according to the quantity and quality of labor contributed. In no circumstances, however, was grain distributed free of charge. If in any one year a family failed to work enough to pay for the grain distributed according to need, they incurred a debt against their next year's work effort. Eventually they would earn a surplus and then it would be their responsibility to finance the debts of other, less productive members of the production team.[6] In this way each village partially subsidized those who came from households too poor to provide even a subsistence level diet.

The closest rural residents came to a collectively financed old-age benefit program based on age rather than need was a grain distribution system used in some villages to provide all nonworking elderly 25-50 kilos (or one-eighth to one-quarter of an adult grain ration) of unhusked grain each year without charging the cost against the total earnings of their working spouse or children. Although far inferior to the generous cash pensions of state workers, this "free grain" nonetheless represented a significant gesture in the direction of collective aid to the elderly and laid the foundation for the more generous payments that developed in the richest villages after 1979.

B. Changes After the Death of Mao

In 1979, the CCP leaders fundamentally altered the nature of collective farming. They dismantled the collective management system and turned to a system of production contracts negotiated between the state grain procurement offices and individual families (Domes, 1982). Simultaneously they increased the percentage of land given to "private plots"[7] and relaxed restrictions on private sales of agricultural goods. At first this decentralization of authority and emphasis on private efforts were encouraged only in the poorest areas, but by December 1982 they were the norm throughout rural China.

The impact of the new "privatization" of agricultural production on collective support for the elderly has varied according to the complexity and wealth of village level economies. In periurban areas where small-scale industry, cash crops, and food processing account for 60-80 percent of total income, village leaders have been unwilling or unable to reorganize production on a household basis. In these areas, the collective economy remains strong, there are funds for locally financed social welfare programs, and pensions continue to expand (Xin Min Wan Bao, 1983; Beijing Review, 1982b). This trend is particularly true outside the largest cities. Thus in Shanghai, for example, the number of rural elderly drawing monthly pensions from collective welfare funds trebled between 1979 and 1982 (Yuan, 1981; Frolic, 1982).

In villages beyond the urban periphery where 80-85 percent of rural elderly live, grain crops are the main source of income and technology is preindustrial. In these typical villages few oppose the new contracting system and village leaders stress family obligations. Collective welfare programs have lost financial and political support (Davis-Friedmann, 1984) and elderly appear to depend more completely on private arrangements than they did in the 1960s and 1970s.

IV. A COMPARISON OF PENSIONS AND OTHER INCOME TRANSFERS

Pensions are the financial core of the Chinese retirement program for state workers. They do not, however, represent the government's total effort to provide financial support to the nonworking old. In addition to pensions, there are also disability, medical, and welfare payments that represent significant intergenerational transfers of income from the employed to the unemployed. Therefore a brief summary of these three "supplemental" programs completes the overview of retirement policy and provides one final documentation of the kind of compromises that maintain large differences between the financial security of state pensioners and other nonpensioned elderly.

A. Disability Benefits

The Labor Insurance Regulations that provide pensions to state workers also guarantee lifetime incomes to disabled state workers who must withdraw permanently from the work force prior to the minimum ages of retirement. If a health problem forces a man at age 50, or a woman at age 45, to stop work after 20 years of full-time employment in the state sector, the enterprise can authorize a disability payment that replaces 75 percent of a last wage (Cai Zheng Bu, 1979). If the person worked between 15 and 19 years, he or she receives 70 percent of the last wage and if the person worked between 10 and 14 years, 60 percent. Furthermore, regardless of their wage level at the time of disablement or the exact replacement ratio, all permanently disabled workers with 10 or more years work experience in the state sector are guaranteed a minimum payment of 25 yuan. In addition, if workers or staff have been so disabled by a job-related injury that they need nursing care, the minimum payment is raised to 35 yuan and the former employer pays for a nurse's aide to work full time in the home (Cai Zheng Bu, 1979).

Regardless of length of service or cause of injury, workers outside the state sector have no comparable protection. At best they receive a lump sum payment. More often they are merely reassigned to a less physically demanding job at reduced pay. The most important, long-term compensation for disabled workers in the collective sector, in fact, goes not to the individual but to his or her family. When a worker has been seriously injured on the job, local leaders in charge of job assignments make a special effort to allocate other members in the disabled person's family the best paid jobs for which they are qualified. For example, in rural areas the spouse or children may be given the prized assignment of a day job at a state-financed construction project; a city child might be selected for special technical training. However, should a collective worker be disabled as the result of chronic illness or a non-job–related accident, local supervisors will assume less responsibility for the disabled person and his or her dependents.

Furthermore, even when aid is extended, the context in which compensation is offered is a means-tested assessment of the total household. Thus a disabled father would receive special consideration only if the family was unable to maintain the basic standard of living by their own efforts.

B. Medical Benefits

Government-financed medical coverage similarly favors the elderly in the state sector. After retirement former state employees can either see doctors in their enterprise clinic or go directly to the hospital in their residential neighborhood. Upon submission of the bills, the former employer subsequently will reimburse the pensioners for all physician, hospital, and laboratory fees and partially reimburse the patient for the costs of medicines and transfusions. There is no maximum reimbursement for any one illness and no type of treatment is excluded from coverage. However, it should be noted that it is only since the sudden growth in the number of pensioners since 1979 that the government has actually assumed primary responsibility for the medical care of large numbers of elderly retirees, and even in 1983 the majority of elderly still paid for most of their medical bills.

This is not to say that prior to the upsurge in the number of pensioned former state employees the government made no financial contribution to the health care of the old. As early as 1951, an elderly person who was fully supported by a state worker was eligible for partial coverage as the dependent of a state worker. By 1983, the majority of urban elderly who were not retired state workers were dependents of a state worker and in this capacity qualified for some state aid. It continues to be unclear, however, as to whether elderly who qualify for medical aid as dependents receive the same level of treatment as those who qualify as pensioners. At this point it appears that pensioners who face no financial constraints on medical expenses are referred to hospitals more freely and receive more sophisticated treatment than those whose families pay a substantial portion of medical bills.

When one turns to the medical situation of rural elderly with no ties to the state sector, the financial burden on the individual increases greatly. Nevertheless, here also there have been improvements under CCP leadership. In 1949 rural elderly had virtually no access to modern medicine, and even traditional healers and herbalists charged fees beyond the reach of the weakest and poorest. CCP health policy lowered costs and increased access. They dispatched urban-trained doctors to innoculate the rural population against infectious diseases free of charge. They sent state health workers to improve water supplies and instruct rural residents in the treatment of sewage. In the first years after 1949 they reduced and standardized medical fees, making hospital care more affordable to rural residents. During the Great Leap Forward (1958/59), state subsidies helped build new hospitals in rural areas. During the Cultural Revolution (1966–1969), the national leadership launched a major effort to improve access yet further through the establishment of village health cooperatives, funded through annual membership charges, subsidies from village welfare funds, and registration fees. The primary innovation of the health cooperatives was the establishment of a network of paramedics ("barefoot doctors") who do preventive health work and provide first aid in the villages as well as referring patients to rural hospitals. In addition, the health cooperatives partially reimburse members for costs incurred in purchase of medicines or for extended stays in county hospitals. The richest cooperatives pay as much as 80 percent of the costs; more typically the health cooperative pays 30–50 percent.

The lower rate of reimbursement for medical charges is only one difference between state and collective medical coverage. There are also different patterns of use by the elderly. Because all rural health cooperatives have a finite amount of cash, they must follow criteria that establish referral priorities among patients. The criteria can vary from one year to the next but, in general, priority is given to only-children and to acutely ill adults whose deaths would cause the greatest financial hardship to surviving family members. Under these conditions, rural elderly are unlikely to enter hospitals, but instead remain in their native villages dependent on the barefoot doctor and traditional folk remedies.

The clear-cut advantages of urban health care do not appear in all forms of treatment. In one area in particular, nursing home care, urban and rural elderly are both poorly served. In China, the chronically ill are the responsibility of their adult children, and neither state workers nor pensioners receive any financial aid to provide long-term nursing care. There are some residential facilities for childless, destitute elderly who can no longer manage on their own—8,800 homes for 116,000 rural residents (Ren Min Ri Bao, 1982) and 600 homes for 23,000 urban residents (Liu, 1982)—but these are neither administered nor funded as medical institutions. The rural homes use commune and village welfare funds for support and the urban homes rely on state funds provided by the Bureau of Civil Affairs (Davis-Friedmann, 1983). In either case, services reach only a small percentage of elderly and the level of nursing care is spartan.

C. Welfare Benefits

By law children in China are financially responsible for elderly parents who can no longer support themselves (Beijing Review, 1981a). In practice, this has meant that in rural areas adult sons must care for their parents and in the cities both sons and daughters are held accountable. As a result only those "without responsible kin" turn to the government for support. In the first years after 1949, between 10 and 15 percent of all elderly were eligible for government aid. Over the next 30 years the percentage of childless elderly declined as the majority of middle-aged men and women raised at least one child to maturity (Davis-Friedmann, 1983). Nevertheless welfare programs created for this minority among the elderly form an integral part of CCP efforts to aid nonworking elderly. In addition, they give a good illustration of how in some areas CCP principles have triumphed in the face of extreme poverty.

In urban areas, destitute elderly have received regular monthly stipends through the municipal government since the early 1950s. Each individual applies through the residence committee[8] in their neighborhood, and after a "favorable" review they are guaranteed free housing, fuel, medical care, and a monthly cash stipend that varies according to the standard of living in that city and the nutritional needs of the individual (Davis-Friedmann, 1983).

In rural areas, a comprehensive program for the childless has been in effect since 1956. The review procedure is highly personalized and the standard of aid varies according to the wealth of the village and the social standing of the applicant in the eyes of fellow villagers (Davis-Friedmann, 1978, 1983, 1984). The basic grant consists of the average grain ration for that village, fuel for cooking, two sets of clothing as needed, and a cash stipend of 2–5 yuan per month for purchase of oil, salt, and matches. Medical care within the village by the barefoot doctor is provided free of charge; payments for hospital stays vary from one case to the next. In general, those who are perceived to be "innocent victims" fare better than those who are assumed to be responsible for their childless status, and in some villages former landlords, drug addicts, or 'anti-socialist' elements are given no more than subsistence grain rations. In December 1982, 3 million childless elderly depended on the village welfare program for their daily survival (Ren Min Ri Bao, 1983) and the vast scale of the rural program alone documents one important instance when CCP ideological priorities realized a national commitment to the most impoverished elderly even when per capita income remained low.

V. CONCLUSION: PROGRESS WITHIN COMPROMISE

The original CCP pension program was motivated by the egalitarian ideal of guaranteed financial security for all elderly. Regardless of family circumstances or type of employment, all citizens who had worked full time for 20 years or more were to be guaranteed full support for the rest of their lives. In practice the ideals were compromised by the constraints of severe material shortages. The outcome has been a highly inegalitarian situation whereby after 30 years of socialism the majority of elderly still must depend on filial sons to guarantee their security in old age and only a minority qualify for government pensions.

Current trends in employment and welfare policy promise no significant diminution of these sectoral inequalities. On the contrary, the "privatization" of agricultural production and the failure to increase rural social welfare budgets make it unlikely that the 1980s will see any fundamental change in the restrictive criteria for pensions. On the contrary, current policies suggest that existing inequalities among the old will perpetuate themselves among subsequent generations of retirees.

Persistent inequality is only one characteristic of post-1949 society. Increased family stability is another. In the decade immediately preceding the CCP victory in 1949, 10–15 percent of the population over age 60 had no surviving children to support them. Another 10–15 percent were separated from their families or had only married daughters. Without help from either family or government, these "familyless" elderly struggled to survive on their own resources and it was a meager and marginal life. Even for the majority who had surviving sons, life in old age was precarious and only a wealthy few were protected from the risks of inflation and unemployment.

In the years since 1949, CCP efforts to improve public health, control inflation, provide full employment of adult males, and redistribute the basic necessities has stabilized family life and the oldest generations, in particular, have experienced a significant increase in their standard of living. As death rates fell and birth rates remained high, the percentage of childless adults among the elderly declined and the majority of parents could realistically expect that at least one son would survive, marry, and establish a third generation. For the elderly who defined success in life largely in terms of a stable household in which grandparents could see their grandchildren reach maturity, the gains of the post-1949 years were tangible and substantial. Surrounded by their families, protected against starvation, and optimistic about the continuity of the family line, even elderly without pensions experienced a heightened sense of security and achievement. Thus, even though the original promises of the CCP have been compromised as government pension funds have been unequally distributed between different occupational groups, the subjective criteria used by elderly themselves reveal gains that must be balanced against the inequalities. Therefore when the entire post-1949 period is placed in this perspective it is clear that within a compromise there has been substantial progress.

NOTES

1. In the first draft of the Labor Insurance Regulations men needed 25 years of continuous employment to qualify for a full pension and women needed 20. In 1958 this was reduced to 20 years for both men and women.

2. In 1982, there were 75 million people aged 60 and above (Zeng, 1983). However because we have no age breakdown for retirees we do not know exactly what percentage of the 11 million retirees are 60 and older. A conservative estimate would be 7.5 million, based on the assumption that one-third of the recent retirements were by women who retire at age 50 or 55 and by disabled men. It is on the basis of this figure that the 10:1 ratio was derived. The 4:1 ratio for eligibility among current workers is derived from the ratio of 348 million nonstate to 84 million state workers.

3. Women in white-collar jobs must retire at age 55.

4. In urban China, approximately 20 percent of the work force is employed in collectively owned enterprises outside the state sector. Between 20 and 30 percent of these collectively owned units are large, profit-making enterprises with welfare benefits comparable to those paid state workers. However, the majority, and the growing segment of the collective economy, is composed of small enterprises that pay wages well below state levels and provide no benefits.

5. During these years forced retirements were occasionally used as punishments to workers or staff with political problems, thereby further discouraging ordinary, healthy older workers from applying.

6. In his study of rural poverty, Nicholas Lardy (1983) questioned the viability of this collective welfare system for the 20 percent of the rural population living in chronic poverty. I agree with Lardy that the system does not work for the poorest of the poor, but for the majority it is effective.

7. Between 1960 and 1979, 5 percent of collectively owned arable land was distributed among rural households for them to use as their private vegetable gardens to meet their family food needs. Since 1979 the percentage has been increased to 15 percent and many families use it to raise cash crops as well as their own vegetables.

8. Chinese cities are devided into districts which in turn are divided first into street committees and within street committees into residence committees. Typically, a street committee has financial responsibility for the welfare of all adults not employed in the state sector and the residence committee is responsible for direct service. In cities like Shanghai or Peking cadres in a residence committee would know well 400–500 families and take responsibility for 50–60 individuals.

REFERENCES

Ascher, Isaac
    1976   China's Social Policy. London: Anglo-Chinese Education Institute.

Atchley, Robert
    1976   The Sociology of Retirement. Cambridge: Schenkman.

Beijing Review
    1981a   "China's marriage law." No. 11 (March 10):24–27.
    1981b   "Communique on fulfillment of China's 1980 National Economic Plan." No. 20 (May 18):17–20.
    1982a   "Events and trends." No. 11 (March 15):5–6.
    1982b   "Peasants enjoy pensions." No. 40 (Oct. 4):8.
    1982c   "National economy: major trends." No. 48 (Nov. 29):17–19.
    1983a   "Enterprises reform the cadre system." No. 4 (Jan. 31):5–6.
    1983b   "Events and trends." No. 37 (Sept. 12):6.

Beijing Xin Hua
    1982   (November 13) translated in Foreign Broadcast Information Service (Nov. 16, 1982):K. 3–4.

Blaustein, Albert P.
    1962   Fundamental Legal Documents of Communist China. Hackensack, NJ: Rothman.

Cai Zheng Bu
    1979   Finance Regulations for Those Working in State and Central Units. Peking: Finance Ministry.

Davis-Friedmann, Deborah
    1978   "Welfare practices in rural China." World Development 6:609–619.
    1979   Interviews with labor union officials, Peking, Nanking, and Shijiachuang and 85 retirees.
    1981   Interviews with personnel officers and ten recent retirees from Wuhan University, Wuhan China.

1983 Long Lives: Chinese Elderly and the Communist Revolution. Cambridge, MA: Harvard University Press.
1984 "Essential services in rural China." Pp. 205–223 in Richard Lonsdale (ed.), Rural Public Services. Boulder, CO: Westview Press.

Domes, Jurgen
1982 "New policies in the communes." Journal of Asian Studies 41:253–267.

Frolic, B. Michael
1982 Interviews with union officials in Shanghai and Wuhan, China.

From Youth to Retirement
1982 Beijing Review Publishers.

Fujian Province Revolutionary Committee
1973 Collected Documents on Wages. Fujian, China.

Gold, Thomas
1980 "Back to the city." China Quarterly 84:755–770.

Kiu Jiaonong
1982 "Strive to turn those who passively wait for jobs into active participants." Liao Wang 3:18–19. Trans. in China Report: Political, Social, and Military Affairs No. 316 (July 12):30–31.

Lao Dong Zhu
1980 Zhong Guo Lao Dong Li Fa.

Lardy, Nicholas
1983 Agriculture in China's Economic Development. Cambridge: Cambridge University Press.

Liu, Lillian
1982 "Mandatory retirement and other reforms pose new challenges for China's government." Aging and Work 5:119–130.

Mitchell, Neil J.
1983 "Ideology and the Iron Laws of Industrialism." Comparative Politics 15(Jan.):177–201.

Parish, William and Martin K. Whyte
1978 Village and Family in Contemporary China. Chicago: University of Chicago Press.

Peng Zhen
1982 "Report on the draft of the revised constitution." Beijing Review No. 50 (Dec. 13):9–23.

People's Daily
1982 "Happy to see veteran comrades writing new chapters." April 2. Trans. in Foreign Broadcast Information Service (April 5):6–9.

Prybla, Jan
1982 "Economic problems of communism." Asian Survey 22(Dec.):1206–1221.

Pryor, Frederic
1968 Public Expenditures in Communist and Capitalist Nations. Homewood: R. D. Irwin.

Ren Min Ri Bao
1982 "Nationally there are over 8,800 old-age homes." (Dec. 10):4.
1983 "Editorial." (April 19):2.

Ren Tao
1983a "Why a change in emphasis." Beijing Review No. 1 (Jan. 3):14–18.
1983b "Chinese type modernization." Beijing Review No. 2 (Jan. 10):13–16.
1983c "Population and Employment." Beijing Review No. 13 (March 28):7.

Simanis, Joseph
1983 "Farmer's pensions in the Polish economic crisis." Social Security Bulletin 46:3–22.

Wilensky, Harold
1975 The Welfare State and Equality. Berkeley, CA: University of California Press.

Xin Min Wan Bao
1983 "Editorial." (March 27):2.

Yuan Jihui
   1981 "Living conditions of elderly retirees in Shanghai." Paper presented at conference on Retirement in Cross-Cultural Perspective, Bellagio, Italy.
   1983 Public lecture. For Connecticut Coalition on Aging. July 7, Hamden, CT.

Zeitzer, Ilene
   1983 "Social security trends and developments in industrialized countries." Social Security Bulletin 46:52–62.

Zeng, Shuzhi
   1983 "China's senior citizens." China Reconstructs 31(Jan.):5–8.

Zhong Guo Nong Min Bao
   1982 "Withdrawn but not retired." (June 6):1.

THE VANISHING *BABUSHKA:*
A ROLELESS ROLE FOR OLDER
SOVIET WOMEN?

Stephen Sternheimer

ABSTRACT

The demographic changes associated with modernization in the USSR have left large numbers of Soviet women of pension age (55 years or more) facing many of the same dilemmas as older women in other societies. The "feminization" of the older Soviet population and the large numbers of single older women mean that Soviet female old age pensioners bear a disproportionate share of the burdens of old age, even as satisfactory roles have yet to be institutionalized or diffused. Work roles, as a rule, are not eagerly embraced by women beyond pension age and then only to a lesser extent than by their male counterparts. When such roles are adopted, material need rather than intrinsic gratification from the work itself is the motivating factor. Meanwhile, the traditional role of *babushka* (grandmother, child minder, housekeeper) holds little appeal for many contemporary Soviet female pensioners even as changing family structures and patterns of residence make such a role inaccessible for large numbers of older Soviet women. What will eventually fill the vacuum of a "roleless role" that aging currently presents to older Soviet women still remains unclear. There is no indication that older women themselves will play an active part in framing the policies that shape such roles.

I. INTRODUCTION

Like her North American counterpart, today's older Soviet woman differs radically from her forebearers.[1] As a group, the 30-odd million Soviet women aged 55 and over in 1982 are better educated, have raised fewer children, have longer experience in the labor force, and enjoy a greater life expectancy than any previous generation (Baldwin, 1982). Their levels of political involvement—Communist Party membership, participation in the activities of local government bodies—have risen steadily over the past few decades, and their professional credentials cover a wide range of specialities (Rigby, 1968:359–63, 517; Hough and Fainsod, 1979:312–14).

Mounting evidence suggests as well that today's Soviet female old age pensioner (OAP) has not managed to avoid entirely those burdens of aging that fall on the shoulders of older women in other industrialized societies. Recent commentary on the status of the aged in the United States might apply equally well to the Soviet situation: "Some people grow old gracefully, few gratefully, [for] the average mortal balks at paying the dues of age for the boon years of youth" (*Newsweek,* 1982). More particularly, as Matilda White Riley (1979:7) so eloquently described the position of older American women, it is also true that Soviet women of pension age "have more to offer to society than society is ready to receive, and more to offer themselves than they believe possible."

What Riley observes in the United States may hold as well in the USSR: women of retirement age are doubly disadvantaged "because they are *old* and because they are old *women*" (1979:7). As in the United States, older Soviet females outnumber older Soviet males. Increasingly these women live alone (one-fifth of all older women in cities, one-fourth in the countryside) and frequently they exist on largely inadequate state pensions. Forces for social change—the nuclearization of the family—threaten to deprive these women of the traditionally sanctioned role of *babushka* (or grandmother). These same forces may strip this role of much of its social and economic meaning even for those older women who assume it.

This paper is designed to probe the impact of the socioeconomic change (modernization) that has taken place in the USSR over the past two decades on the function and status of older women in Soviet society. We are concerned first with the extent to which a centrally planned, nonmarket economy and a system professing socialist goals *and* achievements has succeeded (1) in preserving traditional roles for older females, e.g., the *babushka* role, or (2) in developing new roles, e.g., that of the "working pensioner" or WP to take the place of outmoded ones.

Second, we want to ascertain, if only provisionally, why traditional roles may be vanishing and what, if anything, Soviet policymakers are doing about it.

Third, from a theoretical perspective, this paper represents a 'case study' of a larger sociological issue. Is the "roleless role" for the older woman (1) the product of sociodemographic factors linked to modernization that show no respect for national or ideological boundaries or (2) a function of Western industrial capitalist structures? From a public policy perspective, this paper also represents an analysis of some of the reasons why government policy for the aged "in general" fails to speak to the problems confronted by older females—Eastern and Western—"in particular." Even if the lessons that U.S. policymakers can draw are only negative ones, this paper will have served its purpose.

II. THE DEMOGRAPHIC PICTURE

In the aggregate, older Soviet women shoulder whatever burdens or benefits aging confers disproportionately, owing to the "feminization" of the Soviet pension age population (males 60 and over, women 55 and over). Unfortunately, age-specific results from the most recent (1979) national census have yet to be published. Indeed, they may never see the light of day, owing to the gloomy picture they paint of the declines in Soviet male and female life expectancy. Soviet gerontologists, however, with presumed access to what is still officially treated as "secret data" stated authoritatively in 1980 that women in the over-60 age group outnumber their male counterparts by a factor of more than 2:1. Other recent Soviet sources suggest an even larger demographic disproportion, on the order of seven to eight females over 60 for every two to three males in the same group[2] (Chebotarev and Sachuk, 1980:402; *Sovetskoe zdravookhranenie*, 1981:17).

Over time the sex imbalance in the Soviet pension age population has been dwindling slowly. While there were 284 females of retirement age for every 100 males over 60 in 1959, U.S. calculations suggest a decrease to 263 Soviet females per 100 males by 1980. The size of the female majority (19.5 million in 1964) will be less (13.8 million) in 1985 and is scheduled to drop further (to 4.7 million) by the end of the century. Still, a balanced sex ratio probably will not appear before the year 2010 (U.S. Department of Commerce, n.d.:13–15).

The distribution of older women within a total Soviet population that is rapidly aging is skewed in other ways as well. In the rural areas of the Russian republic (RSFSR), the nation's political, economic, and ethnic heartland, a number of aggravating factors are at work. First, the "iron laws" of Soviet demographic processes—the outmigration of rural males, the outmigration of rural females of childbearing age, a low rural birthrate—have produced a situation in which the pension age cohorts rose from one-fifth of the total rural Russian population in 1966 to one-fourth by 1978. One a national basis, however, for urban and rural areas combined, those of pension age comprised but 15.3–15.5 percent of the total population in 1980. By 1975, when the USSR had already become a predominantly urban society (56.3 percent of the population in cities), the elderly constituted a larger share of rural inhabitants (15.2 percent) than of urban dwellers (11.4 percent) (Sternheimer, 1981:6). Meanwhile, the number of rural females over 60 grew by 15.3 percent between the 1959 and 1970 censuses even as the share of males in these age brackets increased at less than half this rate (Novitskii and Mil', 1981:68, 99).

Such evidence suggests to us that older, rural females in the USSR may be increasingly thrown back on their own resources. By 1979, for example, in the Estonian republic over two-fifths of all rural women over 60 were widowed and living alone (*Sovetskoe zdravookhranenie*, 1981:17). In Latvia, the proportion stood at about one-third, and in the Russian republic, the Ukraine, Byelorussia, Lithuania, and Moldavia, older widowed single females accounted for at least one-quarter of rural women of all ages. The national average of older widows in 1979 stood at about 24 percent of all Soviet women.

The roots of this situation go deep and do not represent simply a temporary aberration. Males over 60 are twice as likely to remarry as females in the USSR, and at least a third of the males who do remarry choose a mate aged 50 or less (Valentei, 1979:46–47). Whereas widowed females form less than half of all males and females, age 40 or younger, who are single or widowed in the Soviet rural population, the female segment increases rapidly with each successive age group. Older widowed women comprise over nine-tenths of those individuals who are single or widowed, aged 60 and over and living in villages (Valentei, 1979:44–45).

In urban areas the problem is also widespread but perhaps less chronic. For the USSR as a whole, in 1975 23 percent of all women over 60 in cities lived alone, as did a larger proportion in republics such as Estonia (35.9 percent) (Rumiantsev, 1976:130). Interviews conducted by the author in 1981 revealed that in cities such as Moscow, old age pensioners (OAPs) form fully one-fifth of the city's population. Within this group, the largest single component consists of elderly females, either single or widowed.

Part of the problem, as Soviet gerontologists and demographers are quick to point out, can be attributed to male population losses in World War II. But the passage of time alone possibly may not correct the demographic imbalance for older women. For example, the rise of the number of divorces in the over-40 age group—what one Soviet demographer terms the "postponed" or *otsrochennyi* divorce—promises to create additional numbers of single older women even as the demographic impact of World War II fades into history[3] (Interviews, 1981).

Demographic changes thus set the stage for the altered roles that older Soviet women perform in the social dramas of which Soviet society is composed. As we have seen, certain roles, such as those of spouse and independent homemaker, seem to be increasingly foreclosed. Further, changes in family structure—to be analyzed in Section III.B of this article—mean that the traditional role for the older Soviet woman as a *babushka* or "grandmother-nanny" also is being curtailed. This is paradoxical because state-run child care facilities remain sufficient for but half of those children eligible in the cities and as few as one-fourth in the countryside (Polk, 1976:2). However, many rural women cannot take over the role of child minder and housekeeper simply because their families have left the area. Likewise, in cities, many elderly Soviet females no longer live with their families, which makes the *babushka* role more tenuous. Work roles for female OAPs have yet to take up the slack.

III. ROLES FOR SOVIET PENSION-AGE WOMEN

A. Work

The Soviet social system has been built around Marx's contention that the social identity of the individual is that of *homo farber* ("man who works"). Officially sanctioned values assign work roles the pride of place in the Soviet social structure. Pensions for retirees are justified both as remuneration for past labor performed and as compensation for those who theoretically are no longer able to work. The history of the Soviet retirement system suggests that, as in the United States, the system emerged and has been periodically transformed mostly as a matter of short-term concerns in labor policy rather than out of substantive ideological shifts.

In the mid-1960s, official Soviet policy, which had favored retirement since 1956, reversed itself. A variety of incentives designed to entice OAPs to remain in the labor force were enacted. Whatever their success—and it has been rather mixed—the option of continued employment over retirement has *not* been one that a majority of older Soviet women have eagerly embraced (Sternheimer, 1982a;84–87; also 1979).

Current Soviet estimates concerning the capacity for work of the pension age population maintain that fully four-fifths of all individuals among OAPs are still capable of full- or part-time work for the first year after they reach retirement age. Soviet medical studies suggest that working old age pensioners (WPs) are two times less likely to display signs of organic aging than nonworking pensioners (NWPs) (Sonin, 1981:22). In macroeconomic terms, such findings are probably encouraging to Soviet policymakers. It follows logically that, in theory, able-bodied WPs could serve as a growing labor reserve to partially offset the looming manpower shortage among younger age groups. By 1971, WPs composed 6.8 percent of the RSFSR work force, and 8.2 and 9.0 percent, respectively, of all employed in Leningrad and Moscow (Majkov and Novitskii, 1975:60).

The actual prospects for a growing work force of employed OAPs, however, are not especially encouraging. Secular trends show an *increased* preference for nonwork roles among all OAPs, 1959–1970, and the continued dominance of retirement as a preferred role, 1971–1982.

Among *older women,* the number of WPs declined from 3.0 million to 2.2 million between the 1959 and 1970 censuses, a 27 percent decrease. The number of male WPs declined more dramatically, from 2.6 million to 1.2 million, probably owing to the relatively higher pension benefits they enjoyed. As a proportion of the entire female population of working age, female WPs dropped from 4.6 percent in 1959 to 3.3 percent in 1970. Male WPs, as a share of all working males, diminished from 4.7 to 1.9 percent. For both sexes, the preference for nonwork roles increases with age: whereas four-fifths of all those in the 55–59 age bracket continue to work, the proportion falls to 32 percent for those aged 60–64 and 17.5 percent for those aged 65–69 (Stezhenskaia et al., 1978:21, 27).

The leveling off of retirement rates among older Soviet males and females after 1970 was accompanied by a gradual rise in WPs to roughly one-third of all Soviet citizens of pension age by 1982. Today's older Soviet female, however, still displays only a lukewarm interest in retaining a work role. A study carried out in Moscow in 1973/74 showed that even though Soviet women become pension-eligible at a chronologically younger age (55 years old) than men (60 years old), these youthful "young–old" females are less likely to work *even one year beyond this point in time* than are their older male counterparts. Among individuals whose length of time on an old age pension is four years or more, the proportion of females still working is more than one-third less than that of males (Table 1).

According to another, more recent survey carried out in 1973/74 and 1976/77 and covering the entire RSFSR—the "average" female WP is employed for 4 years 2 months vs. 5 years 5 months for her male counterpart. Breakdowns by branch of the economy and by profession indicate that continued employment rates are highest in the following areas: female junior service personnel working in industry and male white-collar personnel employed in what the Soviets term "the local economy," e.g., repair services, maintenance work, housing construction and repair, sanitation facilities, public services such as cafeterias and theaters (Novitskii and Mil', 1981:206–207). Another study carried out in Taganrog—the USSR's version of Middletown—in 1973/74 found that male WPs remain employed for an average of six to seven years vs. three to five years for female WPs (Bagrova, 1975:18–20).

Analyses of the aspirations of NWPs and the intentions or plans of those of prepension age have also been carried out using the RSFSR survey data described above (1973/74, 1976/77). These highlight the marked preference of

Table 1. Female–Male Differences in Employment Propensity, by Length of Retirement Eligibility[a]

Period of Eligibility	Males WP	Males NWP	Females WP	Females NWP	Percentage Points Difference
3–4 years	65.2	34.8	41.2	58.8	24
2–3 years	61.0	39.0	49.0	51.0	12
1–2 years	77.3	22.7	61.3	38.7	16
0–1 year	100	—	92.5	7.5	7.5

[a] Male N = 464; female N = 631. Coefficients of the difference between dichotomized male–female breakdowns ("under 2" vs. "2–4 yrs.") are Q = −.52 for males in two groups. Q = −.50 for females.
Source: Shapiro, 1979, Vol. II: Tables 15 and 16.

older Soviet women for retirement. Among NWPs in the survey, 32.4 percent of the male contingent expressed a desire to return to the labor force compared with only 28.4 percent of females. Among those individuals of prepension age, 71 percent of the males interviewed planned to continue working vs. 65 percent of the females. Further breakdowns by age-specific categories revealed a lower propensity (33.3 percent) to "reengage" in the workplace among recently retired females (aged 55–59 years) as opposed even to the propensity among *older* males (35.3 percent among those aged 60–64) who had just become pension-eligible. There was an even lower propensity (21.4 percent) among a chronologically identical female cohort, i.e. females aged 60–64 (Novitskii and Mil', 1981:73–74).

The data just cited apply chiefly to urban Soviet females of pension age. The picture for older rural female OAPs is similar, at least with respect to formally sanctioned work roles, i.e. in collective agriculture. The RSFSR survey included rural, prepension age males and females. It showed that although 36 percent of the latter planned to cease work as soon as possible, only 22 percent of Russian males anticipated a similar decision. Moreover, for every type of agricultural worker, a *smaller* percentage of prepension age *females* than *males* said they planned to continue in the labor force. However, this does not include the de facto work roles many older rural women perform in the private plot sector of Soviet agriculture.

A second line of inquiry turned up another interesting finding that divides rural WPs into male and female subgroups. Whereas material motives ("a need for additional income") figured prominently in the decision not to retire among those workers in predominantly female occupations (animal husbandry, field work), "social" motives ("a need for work," "wanting to stay in the collective") characterized the decisions of agricultural specialists, administrators, tractor drivers, and mechanics. These are all predominantly male occupations in rural Russia (Novitskii and Mil', 1981:118, 140). The data, unfortunately, do not allow us to determine whether sex differences, status differences, income differences, or all three together are the motivating factors in these differing assessments of the work role by rural OAPs.

Overall, among rural OAPs in the RSFSR 29.9 percent of females stay on in the work force vs. 35.2 percent for males. For every age cohort in the group of those rural OAPs over 60 years of age, the proportion of females working ranges from 4 to 11 percentage points *lower* than for males. Among those female NWPs who did express a desire to resume employment (a minority of the total), most of those seeking to return to work wanted only part-time employment (83.3 percent). Among those wanting to return to work at a new specialty, about half said they desired piece work "at home" (Novitskii and Mil', 1981:105, 120, 136, 138).

Why do most female WPs choose work over retirement? The answer is complex, and one that Soviet sources have yet to illuminate fully. A 1974 study of urban female WPs during the first five years after they reached pension eligibility showed that most continue in their previous jobs or professions. The decision to postpone retirement until some later date was governed most frequently by material necessity (53 percent of all responses), (Shapiro, 1980:58-60).

The same data suggest that female WPs have a "future orientation" characterized by a certain amount of uncertainty and fear, especially in contrast to the material motivations of males. Presumably this reflects in part what these women perceive as actually having happened to those women, aged 55-59 years, who retired immediately. As such, it may tell us not only about perceptions but about the reality behind them as well (Shapiro, 1980:61).

Research in Moscow and Dnepropetrovsk confirms that material motives figure prominently in the work/retirement decisions of urban female WPs at the level of 46 and 72 percent, respectively (Interview, 1981). An earlier (1971) Leningrad study pegged the frequency of material motivation for urban female WPs at 69 percent of all cases vs. 31 percent who were moved by social considerations (Rumiantsev, 1976:41, 45-46). Males in the 1971 study were two times more likely to mention social factors in their decision to forego retirement than female WPs. The large-scale study of the entire RSFSR mentioned earlier confirms that social incentives play a bigger role in the work decisions of male WPs than female WPs. This still holds true when age, education, *and income* differences between men and women of pension age are entered into the calculations. Sex differences therefore probably qualify as primary variables in any model of the retirement/work decision (Novitskii and Mil', 1981:83-85).

Analysis of other possible inputs into the decision reinforce the conclusion regarding sex differences. When different work features (full time, shortened day, reduced work week, work at home) are examined, the female/male distinction in motives for staying in the work force does not vanish. On the average, female WPs working either full or part time mention material considerations in 10–11 percent more instances than men. The proportion of such replies for at-home workers and for females working a reduced week stood at 14–22 percent of all cases, even as they disappeared from the decisional framework of males in these categories entirely (Novitskii and Mil', 1981:88). Nor did the branch of the economy in which employment occurred make a major difference. Material considerations influenced 53 percent of the work decisions of female WPs in the service sector (vs. 41 percent for males) and 63.2 percent of the decisions of female WPs in industry (vs. 36.1 percent for males) (Novitskii and Mil', 1981:176).

What do the survey data just presented tell us in general about work roles and older Soviet women? First, Soviet female OAPs are more likely than their male counterparts to choose retirement over continued employment—even when age, income, occupational, and other differences are taken into account. Second, the data indicate that when female OAPs do work, they are motivated more by perceived material necessity than by attachment to the work role itself, in contrast to the work motivations of males. Such a situation could be explained either by basic differences in male and female work roles (that are not captured by the occupational/income controls mentioned above) or by basic differences in attitudes toward work between the sexes that persist across time. In any event, the work role in the USSR today appeals to only a minority of Soviet pension age women, and then largely for instrumental purposes.

The data needed to address the issue of material necessity as an objective factor in the decision of older Soviet women not to retire remain incomplete. We suspect, however, that the reported motive of material necessity is not a purely subjective one. Among all OAPs who are working part time, over half in both industry and consumer services come out of a situation in which per capita family income stands at less than 70 rubles a month. Of all NWPs wanting to work, 70 percent received a pension of under 60 rubles a month (Novitskii and Mil', 1981:176). Many in both groups are older women.

The significance of these figures lies in the fact that, as Soviet economists pointed out to the author in private conversations, one can live, though not well, on 70 rubles a month. One cannot subsist even minimally, they maintained, on 50 rubles a month, which is the officially recognized poverty level (*pozhitochnyi minimum*). Meanwhile the average Soviet urban old age pension for males and females, circa 1980, was only 70 rubles a month according to unpublished figures from the State Planning Commission (Sternheimer, 1982a:85–86; 1982b:36–43). It is probable that urban females of retirement age received a lesser amount on the average owing to their lower wage levels overall. How much less we no not know.

Work roles for female OAPs in the USSR do not necessarily confer economic equality with younger women. For example, whereas the average, prepension age female at-home worker (*nadomnitsa*) earns 70–89 rubles a month for piece-work, the average female *nadomnitsa* aged 55 or over earns only 30–49 rubles a month (Novitskii and Mil', 1981:195). Similarly, when we survey the range of occupations in which all OAPs (male as well as female) are currently concentrated in the USSR, we find the largest proportion of pensioners in those low in both prestige and remuneration. Unfortunately, the absence of combined age-specific and sex-specific data on the work force composition of Soviet occupations renders any precise statements impossible. A certain amount of downward mobility, however, seems to be associated with the status of WP for both females and males in the USSR today.

The influence of material considerations in the decision of some older Soviet women not to retire suggests that many female Soviet OAPs, like their American counterparts, still labor under the burden of an inequitable pension system (Ranker, 1981). Pensions in the USSR are tied to past earnings. Despite wage creep in recent years, the pension–wage scale, i.e., pensions as a percentage of past wages, has not been modified since 1956. All OAPs are thereby disadvantaged because the replacement value of even recent pensions does not exceed 50 percent of prepension earnings. Older women, however, suffer more as the income inequalities they faced earlier mount with age and probable widowhood.

Historically, the earnings of Soviet females have been lower than those of Soviet males. A Western economist who specializes in Soviet labor and welfare economics estimates that in the period 1956–1975, the average female worker earned wages equal to three-fifths those of her male counterpart. A 1976 Soviet source points out that Soviet female piece rate workers earn only 86 percent as much as their male colleagues (McAuley, 1981; Rumiantsev, 1976:50). It is likely, therefore, that the working female pensioner in the USSR receives a lower pension and a lower wage than a male WP. She also bears responsibility for a disproportionate share of the household chores—15–20 percent more than the male, according to one noted Soviet economist (Sonin, 1981:22). Riley's assessment (1979) of older women in the United States as doubly disadvantaged appears equally applicable in Soviet society as well.

B. Family

The evidence presented in the preceding section suggests that the attraction of the work role for Soviet women of retirement age and older remains ambiguous at best, a kind of "roleless" role. This holds despite the fact that official calculations by the USSR State Committee on Labor and Social Questions demonstrate that fully four-fifths of all Soviet citizens of retirement age can be classified as able-bodied and that 86 percent of NWPs are also physically capable of some sort of employment in the labor force. (Novitskii and Mil', 1981:50; Rumiantsev, 1975:79). According to Soviet surveys carried out in the 1970s, however, within the latter group (of NWPs) only 25–31 percent indicate any interest in rejoining the work force (Rumiantsev, 1975:13; Kogan, 1973:15). In addition, among NWPs the female contingent is only half as likely as the male contingent to display any inclination to return to the world of work. Similarly, among OAPs still working, we find that women OAPs are twice as likely as men to anticipate eventual retirement (22 percent vs. 10 percent) and are undecided about their future retirement plans in only half as many instances as older males (14 percent vs. 30 percent) (Kogan, 1973:15; Panina, 1979:119, 126).

Can we therefore conclude that a majority of older Soviet women, shunning the continuation of work roles, therefore eagerly embrace the role of the *babushka* as a positive alternative for the retirement years? Other Soviet survey data, as well as aggregate statistics, suggest that the *babushka* role also may be less attractive and less widespread than is commonly believed in the Soviet Union as well as in the United States.

Soviet survey data on perceptions of retirement roles among Soviet female OAPs, and on the relationship of the work/retirement decision to the *babushka* role, shed some additional light on this issue. A 1973/74 survey of youngish Soviet female WPs (aged 55–59 years) revealed that 40 percent did not look forward with any anticipation to an eventual assumption of *babushka* responsibilities when they retired. Another 40 percent in the survey were neutral on the issue and only 20 percent replied affirmatively (Shapiro, 1980:62–63). In response to another question in the survey, one-fifth of the sample displayed a negative attitude toward assumption of the kinds of homemaker chores that traditionally accompany the *babushka* role.

The large-scale 1973/74 and 1976/77 surveys of male and female OAPs in the RSFSR (cited in the preceding section of this paper) indicate that older Soviet women do not list "care of younger children" as a major reason for leaving the work force. Among female NWPs in the sample, seven out of ten cited "poor health" as their chief reason for retiring. A like proportion of female NWPs cited various medical reasons as the main factor in their decision not to seek employment after spending some time as retirees (Novitskii and Mil', 1981:74, 96, 133; Shapiro, II, 1979:Table 88). Even when controls were imposed for level of education of respondents and urban/rural residence, no major differences in the responses of female NWPs surveyed appeared (Novitskii and Mil', 1981:134).

A third set of survey results also suggests ambiguous attitudes toward the *babushka* role among Soviet female OAPs. A 1977/78 study carried out by the USSR Institute of Gerontology among women in Kiev reveals that most female OAPs—and expecially female NWPs—associate retirement with "increased leisure" or "time to look after oneself." Only about one in four linked it to "care of grandchildren" and fewer than one in six to helping with household chores (Panina, 1979:86).

Interviews with Soviet gerontologists confirmed that the *babushka* role and multigenerational living may not be viewed as altogether desirable in the eyes of many Soviet OAPs. According to these specialists (citing as yet unpublished survey results), among females over 55 living with their extended families, 29 percent of those aged 55–59 and 25 percent of those aged 60–64 expressed a desire to live apart from their offspring and run only their own households

(Interview, Kiev, 1981). An unpublished report to the 1976 Soviet gerontological congress went even further, stating that *helf* of all OAPs wished to live apart from their children and 88 percent of the younger generation expressed a similar preference with respect to their parents (Pyzhov, 1980:33). Anecdotal evidence gathered during multiple research expeditions to the USSR points in a similar direction. As one friend complained in 1968, "My mother claims she's still a competent engineer at age 58, and she refuses to stay home and change diapers." On a more recent visit, a female professional in her midsixties told me that she looked forward to the day "when I can stay at home and amuse myself with my grandchildren"—providing she could continue with part-time teaching, research and writing, and consulting! Even *garderobshchiki* (elderly coat check women who need the income to supplement meager pensions) reported that they would "go crazy with boredom" if they had nothing to do but look at the four walls of their apartments or simply stand in line for food all day. The presence of other *garderobshchiki* with whom to gossip and socialize, a warm room in which to spend cold winter days, access to the institution's shopping facilities, and the kind of companionship generated over the ever-bubbling tea kettle seem to be preferable to performing *babushka* duties, even for elderly women workers with low wages and no skills.

Other kinds of evidence suggest that the traditional components of the *babushka* role may be declining in importance in modern Soviet society. A Leningrad study from the mid-1970s reveals that, contrary to popular assumptions in the West, the *babushka* is no longer the chief workhorse of the modern urban household even when a multigeneration family is present. When time spent on domestic chores within the family is disaggregated by Soviet sociologists, in all except food preparation the Soviet husband outranks the *babushka*. Meanwhile, of course, the wife (whether working or not) continues to bear most household chores on her shoulders alone (Pyzhov, 1980:33).

The role of the *babushka*-cum-child minder may also be disappearing in the aggregate picture. This would deprive Soviet female OAPs of the opportunity to fulfill the *babushka* role, even for those who so desired. In 1979 there were an estimated 8–9 million Soviet children—presumably of preschool age—being cared for by *babushki*. Most of these were concentrated in single-parent families headed by females (*Literaturnaia gazeta,* 1979:13). The absence to date of age-specific results from the 1979 Soviet census makes it difficult to gauge exactly what kind of "*babushka* coverage" such a figure represents. However, using the estimates of Soviet population growth and age distributions prepared by the U.S. Bureau of Census, we can estimate that in 1979 the Soviet preschool population included between 22 and 37 million boys and girls. For the total preschool population in that year, this would mean *babushka* coverage at the national level of between 24 and 36 percent (U.S. Department of Commerce, n.d.:9).

We recognize, however, that such a statistical picture of opportunities for the *babushka* role on a national basis can be misleading in several respects. The continued presence of a disproportionate number of multigeneration families in the traditional Muslim cultures of Soviet Central Asia might skew the figure on the high side. Conversely, the rural outmigration of young families, leaving elderly women with no family to look after, might push the level of coverage downward. Therefore, as a check on our calculations, we decided to look as well at the extent of *babushka* coverage in the European, industrialized, urban areas of the USSR as typified by cities such as Leningrad.

In such an urban setting, a 1973/74 survey of families found that in less than half of all cases did either the grandmother—or both grandparents—actively assist in child rearing for the first offspring. By the time the second child had appeared, the level of assistance by the older generation had fallen to about one case in every three (Boiko, 1980:160–61, 205). A recent study based on 1979 census materials for Leningrad confirms these earlier findings. Only about 33 percent of all Leningrad children aged 3 or under live with their maternal grandmother in the same household, and between 13 and 18 percent live with the paternal grandmother in similar circumstances. For the early preschool group, therefore, the level of *babushka* coverage extended to between 46 and 51 percent of very young children. By the time these children had reached school age, however, the level of coverage dropped to 42 percent (Klut, 1981).

Moreover, as retired Soviet women grow older, the *babushka* role may hold fewer and fewer attractions. For example, a 1979 study in the Latvian republic showed that while 56 percent of female NWPs carried out *babushka* functions during the first five years after they retired, the proportion of those so occupied aged 60 or older dropped to 40 percent (*Literaturnaia gazeta*, 1979:13).

There are also structural constraints on the *babushka* role in contemporary Soviet society which are growing irreversibly. By 1970, for example, the number of nuclear families in the Soviet Union exceeded the number of multigeneration families by about one-third. Similarly, the increasing tendency of generations to live apart and at some distance from one another—even when they still reside in the same city—makes child rearing and child minding by older Soviet women increasingly difficult. A 1980 study suggests that *babushka* assistance varies from a high of 64 percent of urban families (where different generations live nearby, i.e., less than 30 minutes travel time) to a low of 25 percent (where travel time separating generations within a city totals one hour or more) (Panina, 1979:90). The significance of such figures ought not to be underestimated. In Moscow, a trip from one end of a subway line to another—or from the center city to a suburb when a bus connection is involved—can easily consume an hour.

Based on all the available data, we conclude the following:

- Caring for grandchildren as part of the *babushka* role is no longer important in the plans older Soviet females make for their retirement years. Nor is it an especially important part of their lives once they stop working.

- However, the reality of the Soviet family situation—high labor force participation rates for women with young children, inadequate child care facilities, little male assistance with domestic chores—means that the *babushka* role is one into which many Soviet female OAPs still are thrust even if they do not particularly relish or plan for such a role.
- Over time, the reality of the *babushka* role seems to be declining and probably will continue in this direction. The nuclearization of the family, population mobility, a lack of enthusiasm for the role on the part of a substantial number of OAPs, and the fact that fewer than half of all urban Soviet children of preschcool age live in families with three generations present may all be contributing factors.

What of the future? Interviews in 1981 with Soviet gerontologists suggest that some are convinced that the *babushka* role is somehow redeemable. Researchers at the Institute of Gerontology in Kiev with whom the author spoke have set themselves the task of "modernizing" the *babushka* role. Arguing that progressively higher levels of education will equip each generation of older Soviet women better than the last to play a positive role in the upbringing of the Soviet child, these researchers have proposed an educational program on child development and child psychology targeted to *babushki* in Kiev. The purpose, as one informant put it, is to "update the convictions, stereotypes and ideas of today's *babushka* and to help her accept the values and convictions of the parents so as to minimize conflict within the family." They also argue that in order to "save the *babushka*," it is important to learn more about the positive functions such an individual actually performs in the contemporary Soviet family from the perspective of each generation involved. A pilot study is underway to see which family functions are viewed positively by all concerned and which might serve as a cause of intrafamilial conflict. Plans are also underway to assess the positive aspects of the role of the *babushka* in the moral, social, emotional, and physical development of the child, using as a control group children cared for in state-run institutions.

These specialists see three structural alternatives for the *babushka* in Soviet society between now and the year 2000. For rural areas, given the (apparently) irreversible outflow of the younger generations, one arrangement would be for the *babushka* to come into the newly urban family during the winter months when life in the village becomes difficult. There she could care for the children, help out with chores, and generally do what *babushki* have always done. In the summer months, she would return to the familiar surroundings of the village—to her house, her friends, and her small private plot, taking the child with her. All would presumably profit by such an arrangement.

In urban areas, two variants are possible. The first is the *prikhodiashchiiasia babushka* or the dayworker *babushka*. This would be an individual living apart from the family but in the same city and region/district who would come daily to

The Vanishing Babushka 329

help with child minding, cleaning, and shopping. The second alternative, the *babushka-nadomnitsa,* is a variant of the at-home worker among Soviet OAPs more generally. Here the grandmother, while living apart, would take the child into her own home and care for him or her, returning the grandchild to parents on the weekend. Each of these is presented as a normative model, as a set of guidelines for policy decisions designed to eliminate normlessness among older, retired Soviet women. Presumably any of the three would fit well with the pronatal policy which the Soviet regime is currently committed to pursuing. While each could eliminate structural sources of loneliness and feelings of uselessness among older Soviet women, it is less clear that even a newly constituted *babushka* role would reflect the preferences of older women themselves.

IV. CONCLUSIONS

The picture painted in previous sections reveals graphically how and why retirement and aging for the older Soviet female involves some of the same dilemmas facing women of retirement age in the West. The "iron laws" of demographic change do not respect either political or ideological boundaries. The "feminization" of the Soviet older population that will persist until at least the end of the century renders the problem of aging especially acute for the older Soviet women.

Older Soviet females bear a disproportionate share of the burdens of aging, especially in the rural areas of the Russian republic. The exodus of younger family members, the hardships associated with the life of the elderly in the Russian village, and the persistent backwardness of Soviet agriculture all conspire to undermine the social, economic, and familial support systems available to today's older rural woman. In cities, too, many older women are widowed and living alone. The net effect is to foreclose willy-nilly many of the traditional roles—including that of *babushka*—performed by older females. At the same time viable alternative roles for older Soviet women have yet to be adopted.

Work roles as a rule are still not eagerly embraced by Soviet women of retirement age. While both official retirement policy and changes in the work/retirement decisions of Soviet OAPs have reversed direction in recent years, older Soviet women remain less inclined than older men to accept work roles beyond retirement age. Even though they become eligible for retirement chronologically five years earlier than Soviet males, older Soviet women are less likely than their male counterparts to work even one year beyond the date at which they start receiving a pension. Even when they do keep working, they will still withdraw from the work force more rapidly than Soviet pension age males. Soviet female NWPs also display lower levels of enthusiasm about returning to work in comparison with males.

For Soviet female pensioners who do still work, material necessity rather than social satisfaction functions as the chief catalyst. Soviet women average lower salary and wage levels during the course of their careers than do male workers. Because pensions remain closely tied to average wage levels, income inequality between the sexes persists across the age boundary.

The classic Western assumption that under Soviet socialism older women fare well in the aging process because they opt for and are needed as *babushki* appears to find little confirmation in fact. Only a minority of female WPs in fact may eagerly anticipate the *babushka* role. Older Soviet women seem to associate retirement from the work force with leisure and self-care rather than with child minding and housework. Some find the *babushka* role assuming more importance than they had intended or desired.

The stereotype of older Soviet single women always living with their children and grandchildren is also misplaced. It appears from data on the Soviet family that most Soviet OAPs—and female OAPs—do not live in a multigeneration family setting. Between one-fifth and one-fourth of all Soviet women of retirement age live entirely alone, with neither spouse nor children.

What this points to is a situation in the USSR in which, as in the United States, the need for new and different role models for older women has taken on a new urgency. The forces of social and economic change to which Soviet gerontologists have just begun to turn their attention are already at work to render the status of the older woman in Soviet society increasingly fragile.

Meanwhile, the forces of modernization seem likely to render the traditional *babushka* of Russian and early Soviet society a vanishing breed. What will replace her is still unclear. For those who still exist, it is hard to generalize. Perhaps, as in Tolstoy's famous description of types of families in the opening pages of his novel *Anna Karenina,* all happy ones are satisfied for the same reasons while those who are discontented each has her own particular tale of woe. In any case, a basic problem in Soviet as in American society for the older woman is that the powers-that-be decide "for her, without her." Indeed, it may be the absence of a meaningful political role, or even the prospects of one, that in the Soviet Union constitutes the most important disadvantage under which older Soviet women labor now and for the foreseeable future.

ACKNOWLEDGMENT

The research on which this paper is based was supported by the National Institute of Aging as part of a larger project, "Retirement and Aging in Cross-Cultural Perspective," grant AG 02160-01. The views expressed in this publication are those of the author and do not necessarily represent the official views of any U.S. government body.

NOTES

1. For purposes of this essay, "older" and "aged" refer to Soviet women aged 55 years and over unless otherwise specified. "Normal" eligibility for an old age pension for Soviet women starts

at age 55. For those working in hazardous occupations or raising large numbers of children, pension age is lower (Soviet Legislation Series, 1967:1-40).

2. By way of contrast, the latest census reports a population ratio of 53.3 percent female to 46.7 percent male, with a preponderance of females by 17.6 million. This is high in comparison with other nations, where a 51.4 percent ratio is the rule. Overall, 15.5 percent of the population was of retirement age in 1970, and the share is scheduled to rise to 17.6 percent by 1990 and 19.2 percent by the end of the century (Radio Free Europe/Radio Liberty, 1979:3; Joint Economic Committee, 1979:15).

3. The issue, of course, is complicated by declining male life expectancy and the historical failure of male life expectancy to rise as fast as that of women in the USSR. Interestingly enough, the first Russian census found an almost equal proportion of males and females over 60 (at 6.9 and 7.0 percent of the population, respectively). By 1979, almost a century later, the share of older males in the population had risen only slightly (to 8.7 percent) whereas that of older females had more than doubled (to 16.7 percent) (Maksudov, 1981:8; Sternheimer, 1982b:46-47). Today, the gap between Soviet male and female life expectancy—almost 12 years—is the largest in the world.

REFERENCES

Bagrova, I. V.
    1975 "K voprosu sovershenstvovaniia uchota pensionerov," in A.M. Rumiantsev (ed.), *Tezisy dokladov uchastnikov Vsesoiuznoi konferentsii "Sotsial'noekonomicheskie aspekty gerontologii."* Moscow: IMEMO. Pp. 18-20.

Baldwin, Godfrey
    1982 Unpublished estimates, U.S. Department of Commerce, Bureau of Census (May).

Boiko, V. V.
    1980 Malodetnaia sem'ia. Moscow: Statistika.

Chebotarev, D. and N. Sachuk
    1980 "Union of Soviet Socialist Republics," in Erdman Palmore (ed.), *International Handbook on Aging.* Westport, CT: Greenwood Press. Pp. 400-415.

Hough, Jerry and Merle Fainsod
    1979 How the Soviet Union is Governed. Cambridge, MA: Harvard University Press.

Interviews, USSR
    1981 Institute of Sociology, Institute of Gerontology, Central Economics-Mathematics Institute, Center for Population Studies at Moscow University, Institute of Economics.

Joint Economic Committee, U.S. Congress
    1979 Soviet Economy in a Time of Change. Washington, DC: U.S. Government Printing Office.

Klut, M. A.
    1981 "Sovershenstvovanie metodov statistiko-demograficheskogo analiza zhizni tsikli cheloveka i sem'ia." Unpublished candidate dissertation, Leningrad, LFEI.

Kogan, V. S.
    1973 Ekonomiko-demograficheskii aspekt zaniatosti naseleniia v pozhilom vozraste. Abstrakt dissertatssi. Moscow, MGU.

Literaturnaia gazeta
    1979 No. 26 (June 27):13.

McAuley, Alastair
    1981 Women's Work and Wages in the Soviet Union. Boston: Allen and Unwin.

Majkov, A. Z. and A. G. Novitskii
    1975 Problemy nepol'nogo rabochego vremeni i zaniatost' naseleniia. Moscow: Sovetskaia Rossiia.

Maksudov
    1981 "Nekotorye prichiny rosta smertnosti v SSSR." Unpublished manuscript, Russian Research Center, Harvard University (October).
Newsweek
    1982 (Nov. 1):56.
Novitskii, A. G. and G. V. Mil'
    1981 Zaniatost' pensionerov. Moscow: Finansy i Statistiki.
Palmore, Erdman (ed.)
    1980 International Handbook on Aging. Westport, CT: Greenwood Press.
Panina, N. V.
    1979 "Problemy sotsial'noi adaptatsii pozhilykh liudei." Unpublished candidate dissertation, Moscow, Institute of Sociology.
Polk, Peggy
    1976 "Soviets prescribe work for the elderly." UPI dispatch, Moscow (May 1).
Pyzhov, N. N.
    1980 "Obshestvenno-politicheskii aktivnost' pensionerov." Unpublished candidate dissertation, Moscow, Institute of Sociology.
Radio Free Europe/Radio Liberty (RFE/RL)
    1979 "First results of the all-Union census." Radio Liberty 141/79 (May 4).
Ranker, Deborah
    1981 "Women, the losers in pensions." The New York Times (Jan. 14):3.
Rigby, T. H.
    1968 Communist Party Membership in the Soviet Union. Princeton, NJ: Princeton University Press.
Riley, Matilda White
    1979 "Old women." Radcliffe Quarterly (June):7–13.
Rumiantsev, A. M. et al.
    1976 Sotsial'no-Ekonomicheskie problemy gerontologii. Tbilisi: Georgian Academy of Sciences.
Rumiantsev, A. M. (ed.)
    1975 Tezisy dokladov "Sotsial'no-ekonomicheskie aspekty gerontologii." Moscow: IMEMO.
Shapiro, V. D.
    1979 "Faktory zaniatosti pensionerov v obshestvennom proizvodstve." Unpublished candidate dissertation, Moscow, Institute of Sociology.
    1980 "Otnoshenie zhenschin-pensionerok k rabote na proizvodstve." Pp. 58–64 in Z. A. Iankova and A. A. Basalai (eds.), Sotsial'noe problemy ratsional'nogo sootnosheniia funktsii zhenshchen. Moscow: Institute of Sociology, AN, SSSR.
Sonin, M.
    1981 "Obraz zhizni-trudovoi." Nauka i Zhizn' 9:21–22.
Sovetskoe zdravookhranenie
    1981 8(August):17.
Soviet Legislation Series
    1967 Pension Laws. Moscow: Progress Publishers.
Sternheimer, Stephen
    1979 "Retirement and aging in the Soviet Union." Paper presented at the AAASS Annual Convention, Philadelphia.
    1981 "Soviet retirement policy and working pensioners: fruitless quest?" Paper presented at XII International Congress of Gerontology, Hamburg, West Germany (July).
    1982a "The graying of the USSR." Problems of Communism (Sept–Oct):83–88.

The Vanishing Babushka

1982b   "The graying of the USSR and quality of life issues." Paper presented at AAASS Annual Convention, Washington, DC (October).

Stezhenskaia, E. I. et al.
1978   Usloviaa zhizni i pozhiloi chelovek. Moscow: Meditsina.

U.S. Department of Commerce, Bureau of the Census
N.D.   Projection of the population of the USSR, By Age and Sex, 1964–1985. Series P-9p, No. 13. Washington, DC: U.S, Government Printing Office.

Valentei, D. I.
1979   Semi'ia segodnia. Moscow: Statistika.

EMPLOYMENT POLICY AND OLDER AMERICANS:
A FRAMEWORK AND ANALYSIS

Steven H. Sandell

ABSTRACT

This paper examines several government policies that influence the retirement decision. After describing the labor market context in which these policies fit, a framework is developed to analyze them. The relationship between the policies and the maximizing behavior with respect to employment decisions of both firms and workers is examined. The policies affecting older Americans discussed in this paper include regulation of employment in the private sector, income security policies, and employment and training programs.

I. INTRODUCTION

Employment problems of older Americans provide a critical focus for national employment policy in the 1980s. Continued employment of the aged is an important ingredient of many proposals to reinforce the financial integrity of the social security trust fund. Also, the aging of the labor force, together with the restructuring of the nation's industrial capacity, will heighten the importance of meeting the labor market problems of the aged. If the nation is to have, by the turn of the century, personnel practices and government policies that properly use the talents of older Americans, their development must begin during this decade. For most purposes in this paper, older Americans are defined to be persons aged 45 and above.

The labor market problems of older Americans will achieve a greater prominence within the context of national employment policy in the next few decades because both the population and the labor force are aging. Although the postwar baby boom cohort will not be in their fifties until the end of this century, the median age of the labor force is already rising. This stems from improved health and longevity as well as the aging of this group.

The employment problems of older people must be considered in the context of a comprehensive framework. This is necessary because policies interact with each other, with employment decisions of individuals, and with the hiring decisions of firms. For example, an analysis of the effects of changes in social security benefits must consider not only their immediate effects on decisions of people to postpone retirement, but their secondary effects on retirement incentives in private pensions, their relation to eligibility rules for employment and training programs, and the potential for increased age discrimination.

Reviewing one policy at a time and ignoring possible changes in institutional arrangements can be misleading. Will a particular firm's normal retirement age remain at 65 if the age of eligibility for social security becomes 68? Will the laws regulating pensions be changed to mandate the accrual of pension benefits after age 65? Will there be a reduction of early (pre-65) retirements and with it a reduction in the number of older Americans seeking part-time jobs? Examining employment and retirement policies requires that these policies be embedded into a framework that can be used to explain institutional features of the labor market affecting older workers and behavorial interactions between workers and firms as well as the apparent immediate effects of policies themselves.

Two basic questions are central to any discussion of government policies affecting the employment of older Americans:

- What levels of participation in the labor market, earnings, and employment for older Americans are appropriate goals for employment and training policy?
- What programs and policies, if any, would be most effective in reaching these goals?

Although it is presumptuous of any one person to unilaterally set these goals, for the purpose of this paper the following will be used: the level of labor force participation desired is that which would exist in the absence of government involvement in the retirement decision. The employment goal is full employment for older Americans. That is, people who want to work at their market wages should be able to obtain jobs. Finally, the earnings goal is the earnings of people in a labor market that achieved the first two goals without age discrimination. The paper will consider the labor market effects of government policies and their effectiveness in achieving these goals.

A. Evaluation Criteria

Evaluation of government employment policies toward the aged presupposes criteria by which these policies can be judged. I use three criteria: efficiency, equity, and civil rights. Efficiency examines the policy by the economist's yardstick of resource allocation. Does the policy lead to distortions (such as too-early retirement, too few or too many hours of work) in firm, or employee behaviors that lower the welfare of society? Equity concerns the "fairness" of the policy as it affects one group in society compared with others. Does the policy inappropriately increase the income of one group compared to another? The civil rights criterion implies that certain opportunities are so basic that they should be open to all as a matter of principle. Although these criteria will often lead to conflicting judgments, using only one would provide too narrow a basis to judge the wide variety of policies that touch the employment of older workers.

In order to design appropriate policy responses, it is necessary to correctly diagnose the sources of the problems. The labor market problems of older workers include some that are specifically related to age, those compounded by the difficulties older workers often have in adjusting to changed employment conditions, and difficulties that may be a continuation and accentuation of past problems. Labor market problems connected with poor health and disability, conditions more likely in advanced years, belong in the first category. Displaced older workers whose unemployment spells are often long and sometimes extend into involuntary early retirement belong in the second group. Finally, elderly women and minority group members and workers with low levels of education have problems that may be compounded by present or past discrimination.

B. The Key Policies

There are several federal programs and policies that influence older Americans' employment. Employment and training programs, including those designed specifically for older persons, such as the Senior Community Service Employment Program and those programs without age restrictions in which older workers participate, e.g., programs authorized by the Comprehensive Employment and Training Act (CETA) and its recent replacement, the Job Training Partnership Act, are a small part of the broader governmental policies affecting this group. The several income security programs, including Social Security and Supplemental Security Income, influence not only the income of older persons but, through their rules and payment levels, the elderly's labor supply decisions as well. Government regulates the labor market directly by the Age Discrimination in Employment ACT (ADEA) and indirectly via the regulation of pensions by the Employee Retirement Income Security Act of 1974 (ERISA). These greatly affect the work and retirement patterns of the elderly. Finally, tax policies, health and safety policies, and the whole gamut of economic and employment-related federal, state, and local policies have an impact on the elderly—sometimes disproportionately.[1]

The rest of this paper is organized as follows: Section II describes the labor market context within which policies that affect the employment of older Americans fit. After presenting some descriptive statistics highlighting the labor market position of the elderly, the implications of maximizing behavior with respect to employment decisions of both firms and workers are examined. The implications of pensions and finite work lives are emphasized. Section III examines employment and training programs for older Americans. Section IV discusses the relationship among several government policies and employment in the private sector. These include prohibitions against age discrimination and pension regulation. Section V describes how income security policy affects the employment of older Americans. The final section emphasizes the relationship of these policies to one another, their effects on the employment of the elderly, and lists some considerations for future reforms.

II. THE LABOR MARKET POSITION OF OLDER AMERICANS

By describing the labor market environment for programs and government policies toward the aged, this section develops a framework for analyzing employment policy affecting older Americans. The position of older workers in the labor market, some considerations that affect either the demand for or their labor supply, and several government programs are examined.

Labor market earnings are a key component of the income of older Americans. These earnings are the largest portion of workers' incomes. Earnings are the basis for contributions to pensions and Social Security and for other savings and asset accumulation, and thus for retirement income. Table 1 shows earnings as a percentage of total income for various age categories. Table 2 shows the effect of full-time, year-round work on the income of older people.

It is readily seen that the average income of full-year workers is substantially higher than for all other persons in the age bracket. Also, whereas the income position of all workers deteriorates dramatically with age, that of full-year workers falls more slowly. While these data imply that those who remain in full-time

Table 1. Earnings as a Percentage of Total Income (1978) by Age for Persons 50 and Over

Age	Male	Female
50–54	91.8	84.4
55–59	85.5	78.2
60–65	73.4	57.0
65 and over	27.3	11.1

Source: Derived from U.S. Department of Commerce, Bureau of the Census, *Current Population Reports,* Series P-60, Number 123, Tables 49 and 51 (Washington, D.C.: U.S. Government Printing Office, June 1980).

employment fare better than persons who relinquish a full-time commitment to the labor force, they provide little information on who chooses or is able to hold full-time, year-round employment.

Table 3 presents labor force participation rates by sex and age. While rates decline with advancing age, the most dramatic declines occur after ages 60 and 65. The extensive literature on retirement behavior attributes the reduction in labor force participation to the push of the increased likelihood of health interfering with work as individuals age and the pull of alternative income sources for the elderly.

Table 4 presents unemployment rates by age for men and women. Women generally have lower unemployment rates than men up to 60 years of age. Notice

Table 2. Income for Total Population Full-time and Year-Round Workers by Age and Sex (in 1979 dollars)

	Male		Female	
Age	Civilian Full-time Year-Round Work	Total Population[a]	Civilian Full-time Year-Round Work	Total Population[a]
50–54	$20,435	$17,827	$10,893	$5,398
55–59	19,967	16,638	10,939	4,870
60–64	18,489	12,502	10,750	3,951
65–69	16,713	7,725	10,944	3,842
70 and over	15,092	5,824	9,906	3,726

[a]Persons 15 and over will include members of the Armed Forces living off-post with members of their families.
Source: U.S. Department of Commerce, Bureau of the Census, *Current Population Reports,* Series P-60, Number 125 (Washington, D.C.: U.S. Government Printing Office, 1981), Table 12.

Table 3. 1980 Civilian Labor Force Participation Rates (in percent)

Age	Male	Female
16 and over	77.4	51.6
45–54	91.2	59.9
55–59	81.9	48.6
60–64	61.0	33.3
65 and over	19.1	8.1

Source: U.S. Department of Labor, Bureau of Labor Statistics, *Employment and Earnings, January 1981,* 28, Number 1 (Washington, D.C.: Bureau of Labor Statistics, 1981), Table 3 and 4.

the slight rise in the unemployment rate between 65 and 69 years of age, after which the rates drop significantly for both sexes.

Difficulties that older Americans have in finding jobs are somewhat hidden in these conventional unemployment rates. In 1980, median duration of unemployment was 7.6 weeks for all men, but 9.6 weeks for men between 45 and 64. Median duration was 5.4 weeks for all women and 7.3 weeks for women between ages 45 and 64. Looked at another way, whereas 28 percent of unemployed men and 20 percent of unemployed women had been jobless for 15 or more weeks, the comparable statistics are 36 and 28 percent for the 45–64 age group.

Because involuntary retirees are not counted as unemployed, both the official

Table 4. 1980 Civilian Labor Force Unemployment Rates (in percent)

Age	Male	Female
16 and over	6.9	7.4
45–49	3.9	4.7
50–54	3.3	4.3
55–59	3.2	3.4
60–64	3.5	3.0
65–69	3.6	3.8
70 and over	2.4	2.0

Source: U.S. Department of Labor, Bureau of Labor Statistics, *Employment and Earnings, January 1981,* 28, Number 1 (Washington, D.C.: Bureau of Labor Statistics, 1981), Tables 3 and 4.

unemployment rates and the duration of unemployment statistics may understate the employment problems of older Americans. Discouraged workers (those persons who withdraw from the labor force or retire because they do not expect continued job search to be successful) are missing from the unemployment statistics. More than one out of four persons over 60 years old who were unemployed in a particular month dropped out of the labor force by the next month. This compares with a statistic of one out of 10 for all unemployed persons. Dropping out of the labor force ends the unemployment spell and thus artificially reduces the measurement of its duration.

The availability of retirement income allows older persons to purchase more leisure, i.e., reduce the number of hours they would be willing to work. Also, the "earnings test," the 50 percent reduction of Social Security retirement benefits after the level of excludable earnings is reached (not offset by an actuarially fair augmentation of benefits in future years), implies that the gain for working and, hence, additional work hours will be reduced. The effects of these and other supply side disincentives must be considered in designing employment policies, including policies that increase job opportunities, for older workers.

The demand for older workers should be viewed in the context of the demand for all labor. This is affected by cyclical and structural changes in the economy. Drops in aggregate demand imply fewer employment opportunities for older workers. Structural changes, such as reduced demand for automobiles, will also have an adverse impact on older workers.

Firm-specific investment and seniority rights help older workers keep their jobs. However, the same institutions make it difficult for those who do lose their jobs to find new ones. Seniority benefits, including higher pay attributed to job tenure, inhibit the mobility of older workers. A new job is often associated with a lower starting wage compared with a job at the same firm. Analyses of compensation policies, especially the effects of induced retirement through pension provisions, should be integrated into the analysis of the demand for older workers.

Employment Decisions and Older Americans

Before examining the policies that affect older workers, it would be useful to look more closely at the employment decision from the perspectives of the firm and the individual. Both institutional factors and government policies should be examined in the context of these decisions. This framework will permit the delineation of causes of employment problems of some older Americans as well as an examination of the labor market behavior of the majority of older Americans, a group whose decisions are strongly influenced by policies and institutions beyond their immediate control.

The standard economic analysis of labor supply decisions, of which the retirement decision is one part, assumes that the individual chooses between the gains from additional leisure and the monetary rewards from additional work. The possibility of older persons receiving private pension income and public retirement benefits (Social Security) can greatly affect the monetary gain for additional work. Receipt of Social Security for persons meeting age and other eligibility criteria is conditional on retirement from the labor force, and receipt of private pension benefits is conditional on retirement from the particular firm.

Thus, it would seem at first blush that a person would compare pension benefits and the current wage in deciding whether to retire. However, because pension benefits and Social Security benefits often increase if their acceptance is deferred and because contributions to the pension fund related to continued work can further increase the value of future retirement benefits, the simplistic comparison may not be appropriate. If the deferral of benefit receipt is actuarially fair, then eligibility for a pension influences retirement in a way similar to possession of other assets, i.e., the income from the assets can be used to purchase more leisure. If the present value of the pension benefits increases (or decreases) with additional work, the change must be added to (or subtracted from) cash earnings in computing the value of additional work.

The firm's (unfettered) decision to employ the older worker is based on a comparison of the cost (wage, fringe benefits, and pension) with the productivity of the worker. As long as the value of the worker's production exceeds his cost, it is profitable to employ the worker. Again, the actuarial fairness of the pension affects the firm's decision. An "unfair" pension plan means that the firm's deferring payment of pension benefits implies a net savings (or expenditure); thus the cost of continuing the worker's employment is less (or more) than the wage.

The following is derived from a detailed empirical analysis of the structure of corporate pension plans (Lazear, 1982): workers receive a bonus for each year (up to four) they retire early and pay a penalty for each year they retire beyond the firm's conventional retirement age. This "fact" combined with the growth of pension coverage may explain a good deal of the trend toward early retirement. Government policies, in turn, can explain the increase in pension coverage.

Discussions of the employment incentive aspects of pensions should begin with an acknowledgment of their primary purpose: to provide income to long-term workers during retirement. Thus the growth of the pension coverage coincides with both the lengthening of the expected life and the reduction of the age of retirement. Pensions provide a tax savings to workers by the firm's payment of some compensation in the form of deferred payments. Workers trade current earnings for future pension income. The combination of inflation and the progressive income tax implies that the tax savings associated with pensions have increased over time.

Although pensions (as currently structured) have the effect of inducing "early" retirement, before suggesting that this institution should be changed it is necessary to examine their structure. The approach taken here is to first acknowledge that if this aspect of the compensation package were not desired by any of the participants, i.e., workers or employers, it would be changed. Thus the "normal" retirement age can be viewed as a subject for collective bargaining in unionized firms and "determined by the market" in other cases. Several writers have noted that the lowering of the retirement age is a natural consequence of increased income, i.e., part of the rise in per capita income is spent on increased leisure at the end of the life cycle. Furthermore, there is little evidence that the trend toward early retirement has reversed. That workers continue to retire early in spite of the sacrifice of earnings (wages plus the increment in the present value of the pension) may imply a preference for early retirement.

From the firm's point of view, the current pension structure could be a response to legal and institutional rigidities in the wage structure. If the gap between workers' pay and their productivity widens as they age, firms may be willing to pay higher pensions as a form of severance pay to workers who retire early (Lazear, 1982). Firms may be precluded from directly lowering the wages of older workers by social convention and legal constraints. One problem with this reasoning, however, is that it would be more efficient for firms to single out individual workers and provide them with severance pay than to use a pension structure that provides the incentive for all workers to retire early.

Finally, a distinction must be made between retirement in the sense of withdrawal from the labor force and leaving the long-duration employer in order to collect a pension. Persons retired in the latter sense may continue to work, perhaps at reduced hours and/or at reduced wages.[2] The addition of the pension income to the wages received from the job at a different firm is the current money income for the worker. His net income, however, is the increase in the asset value of his pension from leaving his long-term employer and the wages received from the new job. Thus, one aspect of the age dimension of employment decisions is its integral relationship to pension and Social Security benefit formulae and thus the costs to employers and return to employees of an additional year of employment.

The finite employment horizon, whether due to physical deterioration, social norms, or incentives embedded in public and private plans, is another age-related aspect of employment decisions, at least for older Americans approaching retirement. A short future work life combined with a desire for part-time work may make costly training uneconomical for either the individual or the firm. Ignoring questions of legality, the reported difficulties of some older Americans in finding jobs and the low participation of older persons in government training programs can be partly attributed to the relationship between the period to reap the benefits from training and the retirement age.

Welfare losses for society occur, i.e., the efficiency criterion is not met, when a discrepancy exists between the true resource costs (as measured by prices that would exist in a perfectly functioning market) and the prices facing private players in the real world. The distortions are caused by taxes, government transfer programs, or market imperfections (externalities, monopolies, or institutional arrangements). Thus, if the age of retirement is influenced by Social Security, then training and hiring decisions that respond to that age may be optimal for the individual but inefficient for society.

In some instances, private institutions (pension rules and wage rigidities) and public programs (Social Security) provide the wedges to cause private optimizing decisions to be different than the social optimum that would occur in an unfettered market. These include distortions in the work/retirement decisions, the part-time/full-time decision, and the hiring choice of firms. Thus, some of the resource distortions are caused by rational actions by firms and individuals. Others are due to decisions based on stereotypes and institutional rigidities.

III. EMPLOYMENT AND TRAINING PROGRAMS

Retraining (improving the quality of labor supplied) is one vehicle for improving the labor market potential of older persons. Examining the incentives for older workers to partake of available training implies examining the costs and benefits of training older workers for the employer, for society, and for the older person.

The benefits for workers from training are primarily increased earnings. The benefits for persons who would not have been employed are total earnings less any income conditional on not working. The benefits for persons who would have had other employment are only the difference between earnings from employment and the earnings received as a result of the training. The benefits therefore depend directly on the length of time in the labor force. Only the information on expected labor force attachment is known at the time the training/investment decisions are made. Thus, statistics on the life expectancy and work life expectancy of older workers are important.

The cost of training involves the direct costs, including tuition, and foregone earnings for the training period. The latter are negligible for the unemployed with limited job prospects.

The two principal employment and training programs for older people are the Senior Community Service Employment Program (SCSEP) authorized by Title V of the Older Americans Act and administered by the U.S. Department of Labor, and the programs authorized under the Job Training Partnership Act which replaced the Comprehensive Employment and Training Act (CETA). The former provides part-time employment for low-income persons aged 55 and over in community services agencies. It is viewed by many as emphasizing income maintenance for the eligible rather than training, job development, and job placement, CETA, after the elimination of funding for the Public Service Employment (PSE) titles, and its replacement provide only training to participants. The program goal is to increase the participants' labor market earnings by successful placement into private sector jobs.

These programs should be examined with several policy decisions in mind.

We can observe past decisions that have been made by legislators, administrators, and older persons themselves. In that vein, we can look at eligibility rules and participation in these programs. After a presentation of these we can consider the programs in the context of the realities of the labor market as well as by the normative criteria developed earlier in this paper.

While both are designed to serve the poor, the explicit eligibility rules for the two programs are different. The family must receive public benefits or its income must be below 125 percent of the Office of Management and Budget (OMB) poverty for SCSEP eligibility level. Eligibility for CETA training (Title IIB) required that the individual be economically disadvantaged *and* unemployed, underemployed, or in school. The CETA regulations define economically disadvantaged as being in a family that receives public assistance or whose income does not exceed the OMB poverty level.[3] The CETA classification of "unemployed" is broader than the conventional Bureau of Labor Statistics definition because it includes institutionalized persons, persons with minimal earnings (under $30 in the last seven days) who were seeking and available for work, and persons whose families receive public assistance. Underemployment includes part-time workers seeking full-time jobs and full-time workers with low earnings (the same as for economically disadvantaged). The details of definitions of "family" and the delineation of items to be included in measuring income have important consequences for the determination of eligibility but are beyond the scope of the current analysis.

Tables 5 and 6 present estimates of 1980 eligibility rates and participation in CETA and SCSEP from a study prepared by Kalman Rupp (1983) for the National Commission for Employment Policy. Three facts stand out from a perusal of the numbers: First, a relatively large number of older persons are eligible for the programs. Approximately 5 million persons aged 55 or over, or almost 11 percent of the population, are eligible for CETA training and more than 11 million persons, about 25 percent of the population, are eligible for SCSEP. Second, only a very small fraction of those eligible are able to participate in these programs. About 23,000 persons (~0.5 percent) of those eligible persons aged 55 and over participated in CETA and 77,000 persons (less than 1 percent) of those eligible participated in the SCSEP in 1980. Third, the percentage of eligible persons participating in these programs usually declined with age.

These numbers reflect both policy decisions made by Congress, the Department of Labor, and program operators, and behavioral decisions made by older Americans. All of the available slots in these programs are generally filled. It is difficult to disentangle the role that program operators play in allocating the limited training positions from the lack of interest that many older persons show in receiving CETA training. Some of the reduced participation in CETA with higher age is probably voluntary and mirrors the decline in labor force participation, the increase in health problems affecting work, and the availability of income from sources other than labor market earnings, i.e., Social Security,

Table 5. Eligibility and Participation by Age for CETA Title IIB in 1980

Age	Eligible as a Percentage of Population in Age Group	Participants as a Percentage of Eligibles in Age Group	Number Eligible in Age Group	Number of Participants in Age Group
14–21	17.6	6.8	5,707,000	387,500
22–44	14.1	4.1	10,777,000	444,300
45–54	9.7	1.8	2,177,000	38,700
55–61	10.8	1.0	1,717,000	16,200
62–64	8.9	0.5	523,000	2,700
65–70	9.6	0.3	984,000	2,700
71+	12.0	0.1	1,727,000	1,300
Total 14+	13.3	3.8	23,612,000	893,400
Total 45+	10.3	0.9	7,128,000	61,600
Total 55+	10.7	0.5	4,951,000	22,900

Source: "Participation of Older Workers in Employment and Training Programs and the Effectiveness of These Programs," by Rupp et al., paper prepared for National Commission for Employment Policy (1983).

pensions, and Supplemental Security Income. Immediate plans for retirement obviates a need or desire for additional training. If physical problems preclude working, a subsidized or unsubsidized job is irrelevant. However, to the extent that planned retirement itself is a product of age discrimination in the labor market, the labor force and program participation choices of older Americans are not free.

The size of these programs is constrained by budgets established by the federal government. That only a small fraction of the technically eligible participate may

Table 6. Eligibility and Participation by Age for Senior Community Service Employment Program in 1980

Age	Eligible as a Percentage of Population in Age Group	Participants as a Percentage of Eligibles in Age Group	Number Eligible in Age Group	Number of Participants in Age Group
55–61	17.4	1.0	2,755,000	27,200
62–64	20.1	1.1	1,180,000	13,200
65–70	24.8	0.9	2,552,000	23,300
71+	34.7	0.3	4,995,000	13,300
Total 55+	24.8	0.7	11,482,000	77,000

Source: "Participation of Older Workers in Employment and Training Programs and the Effectiveness of These Programs," by Rupp et al., paper prepared for National Commission for Employment Policy (1983).

reflect a legislative desire not to unduly restrict the operation of the program. It could be expected that selections of the most appropriate participants could be done by older persons themselves and the local program operators. However, given the magnitude of the statistics presented above, it is doubtful that this *laissez faire* hypothesis is the whole story. The funding is not nearly enough to serve those eligible persons who might like to enroll. Because it is unlikely that funding for these programs will increase 50-fold, tightening of the eligibility requirement, particularly for SCSEP, would permit the services to be received by *only* the most needy.

With respect to goals as well as eligibility, the hope is greater than the possible. The goals of income support for the neediest, training, and private sector placement are diffuse. Those who most need training are usually the most difficult to place; older persons who would be easiest to place are often the least income-needy. All of the goals are laudable, but it would probably be more efficient to have multiple programs for the multiple goals. A subsidized jobs program for the eldest and the poorest as well as training and placement for persons in their fifties without emphasis on immediate income support may be warranted. Unless the funding levels are dramatically increased, it may not be sensible to take a completely age-blind orientation toward the participation of older Americans in employment and training programs. However, if incentives in Social Security are changed, so that it becomes common for people to work until their seventieth birthdays, then training opportunities for people in their sixties should become a reality.

Finally, state and local governments, the job service, and educational institutions—particularly those offering vocational training or college level courses—have to improve their services for potentially employable older Americans. The federal programs discussed above serve only the lower income aged; the majority of older Americans must use other services—public or private. Placing "older worker specialists" in the Job Service could help improve service to the population in this overcommitted government agency.

In conclusion, it seems there are government employment and training programs that respond to the labor market-related problems of older Americans. However, neither the size nor the focus of these programs is sufficient to meet the perceived need for assistance to potential older workers.

IV. FEDERAL REGULATION AND THE PRIVATE SECTOR: AGE DISCRIMINATION IN EMPLOYMENT ACT

If employment opportunities of older workers are to be increased, their jobs for the most part will be in the private sector. Federal employment and training programs serve only a small fraction of the low-income elderly who are eligible and it is not realistic to expect funding for these programs will increase 50-fold, which may be necessary to enable all eligible persons to be served. Therefore, examination of the effects of government policies on employment of older workers in the private sector is essential.

It is important to examine how government regulation of aspects of the labor market of older workers affects employers' demand for older workers' services. While the Age Discrimination in Employment Act (ADEA) and the Employee Retirement Income Security Act of 1974 (ERISA) were passed with the intention of protecting older workers and their pension income, respectively, the implementation of these laws together with employers responses to their provisions may have had unintended consequences. For example, mandating coverage of workers ages 65–69 under their employers health plans in amendments to the Age Discrimination in Employment Act included in the Tax Equity and Fiscal Responsibility Act of 1983 increases the total labor costs for these workers and therefore could reduce their employment opportunities.

The Age Discrimination in Employment Act (ADEA) enacted in 1967 and amended in 1978 attempts to promote the employment of older persons by prohibiting arbitrary age discrimination in hiring, discharge, pay, promotions, fringe benefits, and other aspects of employment for persons aged 40–70. The effectiveness of this act in achieving its purposes must be subjected to thorough investigation. Difficulties in distinguishing between age and functional discrimination make this a perplexing policy problem.

Enforcement of the ADEA was the responsibility of the Department of Labor until 1979 when by executive order it was shifted to the Equal Employment Opportunity Commission (EEOC). The change consolidated all federal enforcement of job-related civil rights actions into one agency. The EEOC received more than 10,000 age discrimination complaints by the end of 1981, a significant (and the fastest growing) portion of their caseload (Special Committee on Aging, 1982:110–111). Slightly less than 40 percent of the charges were brought by women. Complaints about discriminatory denial of promotion, wages, and training were more than proportionally filed by women. Refusal to hire and discriminatory benefits were more likely to be subjects of male complaints. Because "the Commission has apparently not engaged in a careful program of tracking charge filing to determine the nature and extent of age discrimination within various industries or among various age groups" and (Special Committee on Aging, 1982:65), it is difficult to evaluate the enforcement of the law.[4] Much of the litigation in the age discrimination area is filed privately. The threat of administrative enforcement as well as the possibility of private suits influences employers to examine their policies with compliance to the provisions of the law in mind.

Empirical documentation of pervasive age–wage discrimination is virtually nonexistent. That individuals have suffered discrimination is certified by EEOC and court records. However, this fact in concert with the large numbers of older

Americans who have employment problems does not necessarily indicate that age discrimination by employers is rampant. A recent study that examined the age–wage relationship among male workers 45 and older who were involuntarily unemployed and subsequently found new jobs concluded that except for workers over age 65, age–wage discrimination is not evident among displaced older male workers (Shapiro and Sandell, 1983).

Under the ADEA there is no area ["hiring, job retention, compensation, terms, conditions and privileges of employment" (29 U.S.C. 621 et seq., 92 Stat. 189 (1978)] of personnel policy where age alone can be the legal basis for employers' decisions. However, the 1967 law provides a key exception if age is a "bona fide occupational requirement":

> It shall not be unlawful for an employer, employment agency or labor organization to:
> (1) take any action otherwise prohibited . . . where age is a bona fide occupational qualification (BFOQ) reasonably necessary to the normal operation of the particular business, or where the differentiation is based on reasonable factors other than age (RFOA);
> (2) observe the terms of a bona fide seniority system or any bona fide employee benefit plan such as retirement, pension, or insurance plan, which is not a subterfuge to evade the purposes of this act, except that no such employee benefit plan shall excuse the failure to hire any individual, or
> (3) discharge or otherwise discipline an individual for good cause. (29 U.S.C. 624).

The court decisions dealing with the application of these exceptions are ambiguous. However, the burden of proof that the exception is applicable is left to the employer and the regulations provide very strict rules for using the BFOQ defense:

> Respondent must show that age-limit is reasonably necessary to the essence of business, that all or substantially all of the persons within the age group would be unable to perform the duties in question *or* that some members of the group possess a disabling characteristic which could not be detected through individual testing.[5]

There are several aspects of the regulations promulgated to administer the ADEA that merit discussion. Two will be discussed here because they are important in their own right and because they illustrate the dangers of examining policies without a broad framework. They are limits for admission to apprenticeship programs and pension accrual after normal retirement age.

In July 1981, the Equal Employment Opportunity Commission reaffirmed the Labor Department interpretation that age limits for admission into bona fide apprenticeship programs were not intended to be affected by the ADEA. The factor motivating this decision was that lifting the age ban might limit apprenticeship opportunities for minority youth (Special Committee on Aging, 1982:67). Thus, a conflict between the spirit of Title VII of the Civil Rights Act and the

ADEA was brought to the surface. Policymakers should discuss these trade-offs openly and not limit the discussion to platitudes about the rights of the elderly, women, or minorities.

Congressman Claude Pepper, former chairman of the Select Committee on Aging, believes that because "there is no validity to the argument that pension accruals for work after age 65 will cost companies more than pension accruals for workers age 60–64 . . . the exemption should be abolished (Select Committee on Aging, 1982:viii). Under current regulations the practice of nonaccrual of benefits past the normal retirement age, the value of pension benefits decline after that age, providing an incentive for retirement. Of course, the increased cost of accruing post-65 benefits could lead to a decreased demand for the labor market services of the very old. Thus the contradiction between prohibiting mandatory retirement or age discrimination in pay before age 70 but allowing total compensation reductions by age beyond the normal retirement age exists as federal policy. This, of course, lets firms encourage retirement differentially by age. Furthermore, as was discussed earlier, ERISA provisions allow firms to provide higher (actuarially) pension benefits for early (pre-65) retirement thus allowing age–pension discrimination to exist while age–wage discrimination is illegal.

Although the principle has been agreed to by many legislators and the President that the age 70 cap should be removed from mandatory retirement prohibitions, agreement has not been reached to amend the ADEA. One issue responsible for the stalemate on new legislation is whether tenured faculty in universities should be excluded from any extended protection. Another, conceptually more interesting point is whether already employed workers should be protected while allowing age discrimination to occur in hiring decisions for applicants past age 70 (the current upper limit for protection under the act). Some employers feel that training costs incurred on behalf of new workers makes age (in conjunction with expected date of retirement) a consideration for hiring persons past age 70. The civil rights criterion conflicts with this implicit efficiency argument.

In conclusion, while age discrimination is illegal by statute and in principle, some contradictions remain in the regulations. The relationships between pension benefits and retirement as well as competing needs of disadvantaged groups in the labor market must be considered in establishing employment policy toward older Americans.

V. INCOME SECURITY POLICIES

Opportunities for older Americans to receive public or private pensions conditional on the level of their labor market earnings affects their labor force behavior. Although researchers have not reached agreement on the magnitude of these effects, the increased availability and level of these pensions accounts for at least part of the decrease in the labor force participation rates of older men during the past quarter century.

The direction of these effects is consistent with economic theory. Higher earnings defer, while higher pensions and Social Security benefits speed up, retirement, ceteris paribus (Fields and Mitchell, 1982). It is essential, however, to consider how net income, including the change in the present value of pension or Social Security benefits, changes with deferral of retirement for an additional year. Because individuals face different incentives depending on the exact rules of their pensions, their lifetime contributions to Social Security, and their age, it is difficult to prognosticate individual retirement choices without considerable information. However, there is evidence that those persons who have more to gain by retiring later do so.

The policy interest in this behavior relates to the financial problems of Social Security and the labor supply implications of proposals to restructure benefits to solve that problem. Deferral of cost-of-living benefits for six months is in effect a reduction of the real value of Social Security benefits for each retiree by one-half of the average annual inflation rate. This benefit reduction will save the trust fund $40 billion between 1983 and 1989 and 0.27 percent of the expected 1.8 percent of payroll which the National Commission on Social Security Reform declared as the system's actuarial imbalance for the next 75 years. Likewise, taxation of benefits for high-income persons projected to save $30 billion between 1983 and 1989 and 0.60 percent of payroll in the long run is a decrease for the high-income group of real retirement benefits.

Restructuring Social Security benefits could alter retirement behavior. However, several proposals designed to increase the incentives for later retirement may have only a minor effect on behavior (Fields and Mitchell, 1982). The biggest impact (about a third of a year) in delaying retirement is achieved by increasing the early (pre-65) reduction factor but increasing the gain for post-65 retirement would have only a negligible effect on the retirement age (Mitchell and Fields, 1983:29). Changes in Social Security could be offset or magnified by concomitant changes in private pensions.

Health problems are often given as a reason for retirement. According to Herbert Parnes (1983:13), "A large portion of very early retirees (prior to age 62) have substantial health problems. Thus, if the current ages for normal and early retirement are to be increased, provision needs to be made for individuals who should not be expected to work."

Providing disability for persons unable to work presents a verification or moral hazard problem. Benefits contingent on disability make it likely that some individuals who want to retire for other reasons may exaggerate disability to collect the insurance payment. Because it is in the interest of the applicant to claim disability even if it does not exist and the interest of a private insurer to deny the disability even if it is present, the private market provision of disability insurance will be limited. However, a higher ratio of disability payments to labor market earnings opportunity increases the incentive for dropping out of the labor force. The increased generosity of disability payments since the World War II period partially accounts for the decrease in older men's, especially black men's, labor force participation (Parsons, 1980).

Supplemental Security Income, a means-tested transfer payment for persons 65 years of age and older, is the primary noncontributory support for the aged poor. The limitation of real and personal property that can be owned by persons receiving SSI payments and the effective 100 percent tax rate on Social Security payments together imply that this program is effectively targeted at the elderly who cannot work and have severely limited means of support. This in turn implies that it has little effect on the retirement decision and thus falls outside of the purview of this paper. However, the existence of this program should influence discussions concerning minimum levels of Social Security benefits and the attendant labor supply effects.

Thus the various income security programs must be evaluated not on their effectiveness in maintaining the income levels of the elderly, but for their impact on retirement decisions. The specific rules in these programs (benefit structure, earnings test) must be examined with respect to incentive effects even if they are small. The existence of the programs may affect savings and other behavior throughout the life cycle as well as the personnel policies of individual firms.

VI. CONCLUSIONS

Several aspects of government policies that affect the retirement decision have been examined in this paper. Only in a framework that focused on both the demand for labor by firms and the labor supply decisions of individuals did that make sense. The retirement decision is influenced by labor market practices that in some instances, e.g., pensions, are directly influenced by government policies. Changing these policies might have only small immediate effects on labor market behavior because institutions, developed as a consequence of previous policies, change slowly.

Dramatic increases in the proportion of the work force over age 50 will not take place before the turn of the century. However, the development and implementation of policy change takes time. Furthermore, new government policies should be in place about 10 years before retirement ages are due to change to mitigate financial and personal costs necessitated by changed personnel policies and individual decisions. Serious discussion among nonspecialists should begin now to allow policies to be developed before the need is acute.

Policies discussed in this paper were categorized as employment and training programs, regulation of employment in the private sector, and income security programs. Clearly the relationship of each to the others must be kept in mind as reforms of individual policies are considered. Changing the retirement age for Social Security will affect participation in employment and training programs.

Changing the mandatory retirement age under the Age Discrimination in Employment Act will influence the need for income maintenance programs. Expanded training programs for women may change their labor force participation and thereby increase their Social Security and pension incomes when they retire. Most important, policies that change retirement ages will affect the incentives of employers to retrain older workers.

The structure of the U.S. economy implies that employment opportunities for older workers will be in the private sector where 80 percent of all the jobs exist. Ensuring that government policies do not create disincentives for private sector firms to develop personnel practices to deal directly with job requirements of older Americans is important. New government policies, such as reduced Social Security taxes for firms that retrain and provide jobs for disadvantaged older Americans, can be implemented to encourage the private sector to play an expanded role in alleviating the employment problems of the elderly.

Let us reemphasize four points made earlier:

1. There are several interacting policy areas that must be considered part of employment policy for older workers: employment and training programs, income security policy, and government regulations that affect the labor market.
2. Because these policies interact with each other and with firms' hiring decisions and older Americans' employment decisions, they can only be analyzed within a comprehensive framework.
3. Good policy formulation requires the application of evaluative criteria that include the examination of efficiency, equity, and civil rights issues.
4. Relevant and accurate numeric estimates are needed to understand the effects of various policies and thus to formulate appropriate policies.

ACKNOWLEDGMENTS

This paper does not necessarily represent the views of the National Commission for Employment Policy or any other government agency. Comments on earlier drafts by Laura von Behren and Stephen Baldwin, Marc Rosenblum, Sally Coberly, John Menefee, and Carolyn Paul are gratefully adknowledged. Errors are the author's sole responsibility. Some of the material contained in this paper was presented by the author at the conference on National Employment Policy and Older Americans sponsored by the National Commission for Employment Policy in January 1983.

NOTES

1. For example, if these policies make it more costly for firms to hire part-time than full-time employees, employment opportunities for the elderly may be greatly affected. In general, analysis of these policies is beyond the scope of this paper.

2. Gustman and Steinmeier (1982) examined hours constraints in the decisions of older workers to leave their long-term employer as well as the wage structure of these "retired" workers in comparison with those who stayed.

3. Foster children on whose behalf state or local government payments are made and persons who have significant barriers to employment, i.e., handicapped individuals, are also defined as economically disadvantaged.

4. These documents include age and industry but they are not very useful without comparable data on the age/sex/industrial distribution of the labor force.

5. "Final Interpretations," Age Discrimination in Employment Act, 29 CFR Part 1625, September 29, 1981, 46 FR 47724. Summary Section 1625.6.

REFERENCES

Fields, Gary S. and Olivia S. Mitchell
 1982 "Earnings, pensions, Social Security, and retirement." Paper presented at the American Economic Association Meetings. New York: New York (December).
Gustman, Alan L. and Thomas Steinmeier
 1982 "Partial retirement and wage profiles for older workers." Working Paper No. 1000, National Bureau of Economic Research (October).
Lazear, Edward P.
 1982 "Pensions as severance pay." Working Paper No. 944, National Bureau of Economic Research (July).
Mitchell, Olivia S. and Gary S. Fields
 1983 "Restructuring Social Security: how will the labor market respond?" Paper presented at the National Commission for Employment Policy's Conference on National Employment Policy and Older Americans (January).
Parnes, Herbert S.
 1983 "Health, pension policy, and retirement." Paper presented at the National Commission for Employment Policy's Conference on National Employment Policy and Older Americans (January).
Parsons, Donald O.
 1980 "The decline in male labor force participation." Journal of Political Economy 88(February):117–134.
Rupp, Kalman et al.
 1983 "Participation of older workers in employment and training programs and the effectiveness of these programs." Paper presented at the National Commission for Employment Policy's Conference on National Employment Policy and Older Americans (January).
Select Committee on Aging, U.S. House of Representatives
 1982 An Analysis of the Costs of Pension Accrual After Age 65. Washington, DC: U.S. Government Printing Office.
Shapiro, David and Steven H. Sandell
 1983 "Age discrimination and labor market problems of displaced older male workers." Paper presented at the National Commission for Employment Policy's Conference on National Employment Policy and Older Americans (January).
Special Committee on Aging, U.S. Senate
 1982 Equal Employment Opportunity Commission Enforcement of the Age Discrimination in Employment Act: 1979 to 1982. Washington, DC: U.S. Government Printing Office.

INDEX

Aaron, H. J., 249
Abbott, J., 194–197, 201–203, 208, 214–216
Ability
   adult attainment and, 64, 73, 76–77
   measures of, 68
Academic self-concept
   adult attainment and, 65, 74, 76–77
   measures of, 69
Achenbaum, W. A., 244, 266
ADEA (*see* Age Discrimination in Employment Act)
Adolescence, in America, 2–3 (*see also* Early life transitions)
Adult attainments
   ability and, 64, 68, 73, 76–77
   academic self-concept and, 65–66, 69, 74, 76–77
   aspirations and, 69, 74, 77–78
   data source for study of, 67–68
   defining, 3–4
   determinants of, 64–66
   earnings and, 78–79
   family socioeconomic status and, 64

   family support and, 64–65
   findings, 74–79
   measures of, 68–70
   model specification and methodology in measuring, 70–74
   parent support and, 69, 73–74, 76–78
   school achievement and, 66, 69, 74, 76–77
   school influences and, 73–74
   socioeconomic status and, 68, 73
   status attainment process, 66–67
   teacher support, 65, 73–74, 76–77
Age, reported job satisfaction and, 89–107
Age Discrimination in Employment Act (ADEA), 338, 348–350, 353, 354
Aging, industrial explanations of, 265
Albrecht, R., 224
Alexander, K. L., 67
Anderson, B. E., 195, 196, 216
Anna Karenina, 330
Ascher, I., 296

Aspirations
  adult attainment and, 77–78
  measures of, 69
Atchley, R. C., 198–200, 202, 205, 224, 225, 252, 275, 292
Attainments, measures of, 69 (*see also* Adult attainments)

Babushka, definition of, 315, 316
Babushka role, 324–329
Bachman, J. G., 62, 65, 67, 68, 82
Bagrova, 320
Baldwin, G., 316
Banks, A. S., 253
Barfield, R. E., 116, 129, 149, 151, 199
Bayer, A. E., 18
Beck, S. H., 199–201
Bednarzik, R. W., 170
Beijing Review, 296–298, 305, 308
Beijing Zin Hua, 298
Belbin, E., 143
Belbin, R. M., 143
Bell, B. D., 224
Beller, D. J., 178
Bengston, V. L., 7
Binstock, R., 293
Bismarck, Prince O. von, 277
Black, K. D., 7
Black retired elderly, 193–217
  comparing the working, retired, and nonretired, 211–213
  profile of, 213–214
  sources of incomes of retired and nonretired, 206–208
  work histories of retired and nonretired, 208
Black women
  retirement and, 216
  in work force, 195
Blacks
  continuity of work and retirement experiences among, 202–204
  health and, 199
  retirement at early age and, 200
  retirement experiences of, 198–202
  work and economic experiences of, 195–198
Blau, P., 5, 7, 15, 62, 66, 296, 297, 300
Bloom, B. S., 64
Boiko, V. V., 327
Bollen, K. A., 248, 253
Bornschier, V. C., 247, 251, 254
Boskin, M. J., 112
Bossé, R., 224, 226, 227
Bould, S., 200
Bowen, W. G., 112, 245
Bowman, P. J., 194, 205
Bronfenbrenner, U., 82
Brophy, J. E., 65
Bumpass, L. L., 8
Bureau of Census, 117
Bureau of Labor Statistics, 345
Burgess, E. W., 244, 247, 267
Burkhauser, R. V., 120, 143, 147, 151, 152, 159, 166
Butler, N., 143
Byrne, J. J., 170

Cai Zheng Bu, 297, 298, 301, 306
Cain, G. G., 196
Campbell, R. T., 70, 114, 201, 241
Card, J. J., 5
Carter, T. M., 5, 66, 79
CCP (*see* Chinese Communist Party)
Center for Human Resource Research, 240
Chase-Dunn, C., 247
Chatters, L. M., 197, 201, 205
Chebotarev, 317
Cherlin, A. J., 14
Chinese Communist Party (CCP), 295–298, 301–305, 309, 310
Chinese pension benefits
  additional perquisites of state pensioners, 301

Index

funding pensions, 299–300
moves toward mandatory retirement, 298–299
National Labor Federation and, 300
National Labor Union and, 300
paid and unpaid postretirement employment, 299
State Bank and, 300
Chinese retirement, 295–311
Bureau of Civil Affairs and, 308
Cultural Revolution and, 296, 307–308
Deng Xiao-ping and, 302–304
disability benefits and, 306–307
Great Leap Forward and, 296, 304, 307
Labor Insurance Regulations of State Council and, 297–299, 301, 306, 310
MAO and, 302, 304–305
medical benefits and, 307–308
pension benefits and, 297–303
retirement from agriculture, 303–305
"Socialist transformation" and, 296
welfare benefits and, 308–309
Chronological age, in defining adulthood, 3
Civil Rights Act, 249
Clark, V. A., 149, 249
Cohn, R. M., 270
Cohort succession, 2
Coleman, J. S., 2, 64, 82
Comprehensive Employment and Training Act (CETA), 337, 344, 345
Compulsory retirement with pension coverage (CRAPE), 121, 123, 126–133
Comstock, G., 107
"Continuity theory," 224
Coopersmith, S., 65

Corcoran, M., 195–197, 214
Cottam, D. M., 246
Cottingham, D. H., 195, 196, 216
Cowgill, D. O., 244–247
CRAPE (*see* Compulsory retirement with pension coverage)
Cumming, E., 224
Current Population Reports, 195, 196, 216
Cutright, P., 246, 250

D'Andrade, R. G., 65
Danziger, S., 149
Datan, N., 4
Datcher, L., 197
Davey, I. E., 2
Davis, N. J., 8, 178
Davis-Friedmann, D., 295–301, 303–305, 308, 309
Delacroix, J., 248, 254
Demographic statuses, 4, 5
Demographic transitions, 3, 4
Depner, C., 198
Disengagement theory, 224
Dixon, R. B., 270
Domes, J., 305
Donaldson, G., 2
Donohue, W., 276
Dowd, J. J., 244, 266
Duncan, B., 5, 7, 66, 81
Duncan, G. J., 195–197, 214
Duncan, O. P., 5, 7, 15, 62, 63, 66, 73, 197, 214
Duncan's socioeconomic index (SEI), 68, 124, 132–133
Durand, J. D., 244, 247

Early life transitions
analysis results, 22–51
control variables, 44–45
data on, 11–19 (*see also* High School and Beyond Survey)
duration dependence, 22–44
educational achievements and, 8

Early life transitions (*cont.*)
  educational aspirations and, 49–50, 52
  entry into first regular job and, expected rate of, 28–31
  financial achievements and, 8
  first marriage and, expected rate of, 36–39
  having a child and, expected rate of, 40–43
  independent residence and, expected rate of, 32–35
  intergenerational links and, 6–7
  modeling transition expectations, 19–22
  occupational aspirations and, 50–51
  parental education and, 46–48
  parental influences on, 6–7, 16–17, 47–49
  parental occupational aspirations and, 48–49
  parental sex role attitudes and, 46–47
  parental transition expectations and, 48–49
  peer pressure and, 4
  planning process in, 8–11
  racial differences and, 52–53
  rational planning considerations and, 49–51
  school completion and, expected rate of, 24–27
  school grade cohort and, 44–45
  sex roles and, 53–54
  social expectations and, 4–5
  subcultural affiliations and, 45–47
  uncertainties in planning and, 9–10
Educational aspirations, in youth-to-adult transitions, 15
Edwards, A., 117
Ekerdt, D. J., 224, 226, 227
Elder, G. H., Jr., 2, 5
Employee Retirement Income Security Act (ERISA) of 1974, 178–179, 189, 338, 348, 350
Employment policies and older Americans, 335–354 (*see also* Black retired elderly, Older Americans)
  evaluation criteria, 337
  income security policies and, 350–352
  key policies, 337–338
Epstein, L. A., 112
Equal Employment Opportunity Commission (EEOC), 348
ERISA (*see* Employee Retirement Income Security Act of 1974)
Evans, P. B., 247
External locus of control, 10

Fainsod, M., 316
Fallo–Mitchell, L., 4
Family socioeconomic status, and adult attainment, 64
Feather, N. T., 2
Featherman, D. L., 3–7, 15, 62, 66, 67, 74, 79, 81, 83
Ferman, L. A., 197
Fields, G., 149, 351
Finch, M. D., 61, 73, 76, 80, 82, 83
Finegan, T. A., 112, 245
Fischer, D. H., 266
Fisher, P., 244
Foner, A., 2, 224, 250
Ford, K., 7
Form, W., 267
Fox, A., 177, 190
Freeman, R. B., 83
Friedenberg, E. F., 2
Friedman, E., 115, 116, 244, 246, 249
Frolic, B. M., 303, 305

Index

Fuchs, V., 118
Fujian Province Revolutionary Committee, 297
Fullerton, H. N., Jr., 170

Galtung, J., 254
Garn, S. M., 2–4
Garrison, H. H., 6, 54
Gecas, V., 62, 63
General Aptitude Test Battery (GATB), 68
General Social Surveys, 107
Generalized least squares (GLS), 255, 257–265
Gibson, R. C., 193, 194, 195, 200, 201, 202, 208, 212, 213, 215, 216
Glenn, N. D., 9, 89, 90, 98, 101, 104, 107
GLS (*see* Generalized least squares)
Gold, T., 303
Goldscheider, C., 5, 6
Good, T. L., 65
Gordon, C., 62, 65, 195–197, 203, 216
Gorman, L., 143
Goudy, W. J., 150, 189
Graebner, W., 265, 282, 292
Graney, M. J., 246
Green, R. L., 195
Greenberger, E., 6
Griffin, C. J., 249
Gross, A. J., 22
Gustman, A. L., 354

Haber, L. D., 113
Haggstrom, G. W., 6
Hall, A., 149, 150, 159
Hamilton, 90, 107, 196
Hannan, M. T., 20, 22
Hanushek, E. A., 122
Hardy, M. A., 111, 112, 114, 118, 136

Harlan, W., 266
Harris, L., 224, 226
Hatch, S., 166
Hatchett, 205
Hauser, R. M., 5, 7, 15, 62, 68, 70, 73, 77–79, 81, 82
Havighurst, R. J., 224
Heintz, V., 251, 254
Heisler, M. O., 249
Hendricks, J. and D., 226
Henretta, J. C., 114
Henry, W. E., 224
Herrick, N. Q., 107
Herzog, R., 201
High School and Beyond Survey, 11–12
  defining control variables and, 12–13
  defining independent variables and, 13–19
  dependent variables and, 18–19
  information collected, 12
  rational planning considerations and, 18–19
Hill, M. S., 195
Hill, R. B., 195, 196
Hofferth, S. L., 5
Hoffman, M. L., 2
Hogan, D. P., 1, 4–10, 14, 15, 18, 21
Hollingshead, A., 6
Holmes, L. D., 244, 245
Horlick, M., 249
Horn, J. L., 2
Hough, J., 316
Hudson, C. C., 251, 253
Hulin, C. L., 107
Hunt, S. L., 224

ILO (*see* International Labour Organization)
Ingersoll, B., 198
International Labour Office, 276

International Labour Organization (ILO), 251, 252, 270
Irelan, L. M., 152, 189

Jackman, R. W., 250
Jackson, J. E., 122
Jackson, J. S., 193, 194, 197, 205
Jacobson, D., 116
Janson, P., 107
Jencks, C., 63, 73, 83
Job satisfaction (*see* Reported job satisfaction)
Job Service, 347
Job Training Partnership Act, 337
Johnson, D. W., 65
Johnson, T., 149, 150, 159
Joint Economic Committee, 331
Jones, L. Y., 90, 103, 105
Joreskog, K. G., 70

Kaestle, C. F., 2
Kalleberg, A. L., 107
Kantner, J. F., 14
Kaplan, M., 226
Kart, C. S., 224
Katz, M. B., 2
Kerckhoff, A. C., 65, 73
Kerr, C., 247, 267
Kertzer, D. I., 2
Kett, J. F., 2
Kifer, E., 63, 74, 83
Kimmel, D. C., 199–200
Kinney, J. A., 107
Kitagawa, E. M., 6, 14, 51
Kiu Jiaonong, 301
Kleemeier, R. W., 224, 226
Klein, D. P., 170
Klut, M. A., 327
Kmenta, J., 167, 255
Kobrin, F. E., 5, 6
Kogan, V. S., 325
Kolodrubetz, W., 112, 113, 129, 132

Komarovsky, M., 65
Kraut, R. E., 80
Kronus, S., 195

Labor force participation rates of aged males, 243–271
  appendix: means, standard deviations, NS, definitions, and sources for variables, 268–269
  definition of, 251–252
  economic dependency and, 254, 258–260
  economic development and, 252, 255–258
  estimation and, 254–255
  GLS and, 255, 257–265
  hypotheses, 245–251
  measures of, 251
  methodology, 251–255
  OLS and, 255, 257–265
  pension expenditures and provisions and, 260–263
  pension programs and, 249–250
  pension system and, 252
  political and state characteristics and, 260
  political characteristics and, 253–254
  results, 255–265
  summary models, 263–265
Lambing, M. L. B., 202, 213
Land, K. C., 270
Lao Dong Zhu, 300
Lardy, N., 301, 311
Laslett, P., 244, 247, 266
Lazear, E. P., 151, 153, 155, 157, 342, 343
Leisure activity in elderly males, 223–241
  data set and, 225–227
  definition of, 226
  life satisfaction and, 238–239

Index

mandatory retirement and, 240
multiple classification analyses (MCAs), 230–239
principal variables in, 225–227
variations in, 227–237
Lenski, G., 248
Less, L., 223
Lewis, R., 82
Liebert, R. M., 107
Life satisfaction
  leisure activities and, 238–239
  measuring, 226–227
Liker, J. K., 5
Lingg, B. A., 170
Lippman, A., 266
Literaturnaia gazeta, 326, 327
Liu, L., 301, 308
Long, J. S., 68
Longino, C. F., Jr., 224
Looker, E. D., 63
Lorence, J., 73, 80
Loscocco, K. A., 107
Lowenthal, M. D., 197

McAuley, A., 324
McCarthy, J., 22
McEaddy, B. J., 177
McFadden, D., 143
McGarvey, B., 68, 70, 82
Maddox, G. L., 244
Majkov, A. Z., 320
Maksudov, 331
Mallan, L. B., 190
Mandatory retirement, 240
Manton, K., 245
Mare, R. D., 5
Marini, M. M., 5–7, 18
Martin, J. K., 107
Maruyama, G., 61, 62, 68, 70, 82, 83
Maymi, C. R., 170, 176, 177
Menken, J., 22
Meyer, J. W., 249

Mil', G. V., 318, 320–325
Miller, J., 54
Miller, P. Y., 6
Minkler, M., 199
Mitchell, N. J., 296
Mitchell, O. S., 149, 351
Modeling transition expectations, 19–22
  censored data in, 20–21
  continuous-time semi-Markov models, 19–20
  duration dependence in, 21
  interpreting results, 22
  survival table analysis, 22
Modell, J., 4, 6, 9, 18
Moen, P., 5, 8
Montagna, P. D., 196
Moore, K. A., 5
Morgan, J. N., 116, 129, 149, 151, 198, 200
Mortimer, J. T., 61, 62, 65, 73, 74, 76, 80
Mullan, C., 143
Munnell, A. H., 195, 196
Murray, J., 112, 198
Mutran, E., 63, 199

National Center for Educational Statistics (NCES), 11
National Commission on Social Security Reform, 351
National longitudinal studies, 200
National Longitudinal Survey, 113, 195
National Longitudinal Surveys
  of Labor Market Experience, 223
  on leisure activity, 227–237
  of Older Men, 118
National social insurance retirement systems, historical development of, 277
National Survey of Black Americans (NSBA), 202

NSBA (cont.)
  analysis of data from, 204–214
  sample design of, 204–205
Neighbors, H. W., 201
Nestel, G., 194, 198, 200, 201, 213, 214
Neugarten, B. L., 4
Neulinger, J., 231–232
Newsweek, 316
Nonmarried women approaching retirement, 169–190
  data and sample on, 171–172
  employment characteristics of, 172–179
  family characteristics of, 172
  financial characteristics of, 179–181
  occupational differences between men and, 175–176
  pension characteristics of, 172–179
  PIA and, 177–178
  preretirement characteristics of, 172–181
  reasons for retirement of, 182–188
  retirement age of, 181–182
Novitskii, A. G., 318, 320–325

Office of Management and Budget (OMB), 345
Older Americans
  age discrimination in employment and, 347–350
  employment and training programs for, 344–347
  employment decisions and, 341–344
  labor market position of, 338–344
Older American Act, 344
OLS (*see* Ordinary least squares)
O'Malley, P. M., 68, 82
Orbach, H. L., 115, 224, 244, 246, 249

Ordinary least squares (OLS), 255, 257–265
Otto, L. B., 6, 7

Palmore, E. B., 199, 213, 224, 240, 245, 266
Pampel, F. C., 245, 266, 270, 288
Panel Study of Income Dynamics (PSID), 197, 200, 216
Panina, N. V., 325, 327
Parent support
  adult attainment and, 73–74, 76–78
  measures of, 69
Parnes, H. S., 113, 114, 194, 198, 200, 201, 213, 214, 223, 240, 351
Parsons, D. O., 352
Pearlin, L. I., 63, 74, 77
Peer pressure, 23
Peng Zhen, 298
Pension coverage without compulsory retirement (PENCR), 121, 123–125, 128
Pensions, 155–157
People's Daily, 298
People's Republic of China, 295
Pepper, C., 350
Peppers, L. G., 224, 227
Peters, B. G., 249
Petersen, A. C., 2, 3
PIA (*see* Social Security primary insurance amount)
Pindyck, R. S., 122
Pineo, P. C., 63
Political democracy, measuring, 253
Polk, P., 319
Population Reference Bureau, 276
Portes, A., 67
Potter, R. G., 22
Prybla, J., 303
Pryor, F., 296
Public Service Employment (PSE), 344

Index 363

Purkey, W. W., 80
Pyzhov, N. N., 326

QUAIL, 143
Quinlan, D., 253
Quinn, J. F., 107, 112, 116, 118, 136, 147, 151, 152, 159, 162, 166

Racial differentials
  in early life transitions, 45–46
  in youth-to-adult transitions, 14–15
Radio Free Europe/Radio Liberty, 331
Ragin, C. C., 248, 254
Ramirez, F. O., 248, 253
Ranker, D., 324
Reitzes, D. C., 63, 200
Ren Min Ri Bao, 301, 308, 309
Ren Tao, 303
Reno, V., 112, 113
Reported job satisfaction, 89–107
  compositional effects, 91–104
  implications for future, 106–107
  possible sources of cohort effects, 104–106
  television and, 105
Retirement (*see also* Black retired elderly, Chinese retirement, Women approaching retirement)
  age of, 181–182 (*see also* Retirement, at early age)
  blue-collar versus white-collar, 126–128, 134–135
  defining, 119, 171, 198, 205–206, 343
  at early age, 148, 342–343
  health and, 119–120, 150, 199
  industrial explanations of, 265
  job and worker characteristics and, 120–122
  job tenure and, 126, 133, 136
  likelihood ratio statistic and, 124
  mandatory retirement rules and, 151–152
  policies of, 120
  reasons for, 182–188
  replacement rate concept as predictor of, 151
  self-employment and, 118, 150
  wages and, 121
Retirement and occupational structure
  age variables and, 135–136
  comparisons among eight occupational categories, 128–134
  likelihood ratio statistic and, 144
  method of study, 118–124
  previous studies and speculations, 113–117
  purpose of study, 117–118
  results of analysis, 124–133
  t-test framework and, 144
Retirement History Study (*see* Social Security Administration, Retirement History Study (RHS) of)
Retirement of Blacks, lack of attention to, 194–195 (*see also* Black retired elderly)
Retirement plans
  accuracy of, 152–155
  correlates of accuracy and, 155–162
  definitions of variables and mean values for logit equations, 165–166
  at early age, 166
  empirical analysis of, 162–164
  health and, 157–159
  job tenure and length, 153–154
  mandatory retirement and, 155–157, 164
  pensions and, 155–157

Retirement plans (*cont.*)
  planning horizon and, 154
  regression analysis and, 167
  retirement determinants, 149–152
RHS (*see* Social Security Administration, Retirement History Study (RHS) of)
Rigby, T. H., 316
Riley, M. W., 2, 5, 316, 324
Rix, S. E., 216
Roadburg, A., 224, 226
Robinson, J. P., 226
Rockwell, R. W., 5
Rodgers, W. L., 101
Rogers, G. T., 16, 169, 178, 182
Rosen, B. C., 65
Rosenberg, M., 63, 65, 74, 77, 80
Rosenshine, B. V., 65
Rosow, I., 244
Ross, S. G., 279, 280
Rubin, L., 114
Rubinfeld, D. L., 122
Rubinson, R., 248, 253
Rumiantsev, A. M., 318, 322, 324
Rupp, K., 345
Ryder, N. B., 2, 5
Ryff, C. D., 4

Sachuk, 317
St. John, N., 82
Sandefur, G. D., 20
Sandell, S. H., 335, 349
Scheck, D. C., 65
Scheirer, M. A., 80
School achievements
  adult attainment and, 66, 74, 76–77
  measures of, 69
Schooler, C., 62
Schulz, J. H., 280
Schwab, K., 113, 115, 116, 224, 250
Schwalbe, M. L., 63

Schwartzberg, N. S., 107
Scott, W. J., 20
Second pensions, definition of, 189
SEI (*see* Duncan's socioeconomic index)
Select Committee on Aging, 350
Self-employment, retirement and, 118, 123–124
Senior Community Service Employment Program (SCSEP), 337, 344, 347
Sewell, W. H., 64–67, 70, 73, 77–82
Sex roles, in youth-to-adult transitions, 8, 15–16
Shah, V. P., 6, 7
Shapiro, D., 349
Shapiro, V. D., 325
Sheppard, H. L., 107, 115, 116, 190, 216, 244, 246
Simanis, J., 296
Simon, W., 6
Simpson, I. H., 224
Slavick, F., 115
Smith, D. S., 266
Smith, S. J., 170
Social class
  in early life transitions, 46
  in youth-to-adult transitions, 15
Social Security, 120, 148, 151, 159–162, 164–167, 170, 171, 181, 183, 188–190, 206, 214, 216, 217, 338, 342, 344, 351, 395
  earnings test, 185, 341
  funding, 279–280
  length of service requirements, 282–283
  minimum retirement age, 281–282
  pension amount tied to earnings, 284–285
  policy questions regarding, 276
  retirement test, 284

Index 365

special pensions for those in unhealthy occupations, 285
supplements for dependents, 285–286
in United States, compared with other countries, 291–292
Social Security Administration (SSA), 112, 149, 251, 253
  Longitudinal Retirement History Study of, 150, 171
  Retirement History Study (RHS) of, 113, 116, 152, 166, 173, 189, 190, 198, 200, 201
Social Security primary insurance amount (PIA), 177, 178, 182, 183, 190
Social Security Survey of Disabled, 113
Social Security-type retirement policies, 275–293
  background, 276–278
  combined influence of GNP and life expectancy, 287–288
  coverage, 278–279
  effects of retirement policies, 288–290
  funding, 279–280
  indexing, 286
  length of service requirements, 282–283
  minimum retirement age, 280–282
  payroll taxes for selected countries, 279
  pension amount tied to earnings, 284–285
  replacement rate, 287
  retirement age and benefit amount, 283
  retirement tests, 283–284
  special pensions for those in unhealthy occupations, 285
  supplements for dependents, 285–286

Socioeconomic status
  adult attainment and, 73
  measures of, 68
Sonin, M., 319, 324
Sorbom, D., 70
Sørenson, A. B., 19, 20
Sovetskoe zdravookhranenie, 317, 318
Soviet pension-age women, 315–331
  demographic picture, 317–319
  family and, 324–329
  roles for, 319–329
  State Planning Commission and, 323
  work and, 319–324
Spaeth, J. L., 66
Special Committee on Aging, 348, 349
Spenner, K. I., 5, 74
SSI (*see* Supplemental Security Income)
Stack, C., 6, 14, 45
Status attainment process, 66–67
Stearns, P. N., 244
Stecker, M., 112
Steinmeier, T., 354
Stephenson, C. B., 107
Sternheimer, S., 315, 319, 323, 331
Stezhenskaia, E. I., 320
Stinchcomb, A. L., 289
Strasser, A., 178
Supplemental Security Income (SSI), 216, 217, 252, 338, 346
Sweet, J. A., 8
Szinovacz, M. E., 194

Tanner, N., 14
Tax Equity and Fiscal Responsibility Act of 1983, 348
Taylor, B., 2, 3
Taylor, C. C., 251, 253
Taylor, M. C., 65

Teacher support
  adult attainment and, 65, 73–74, 76–77
  measures of, 69
Teachman, J. D., 22-
Thomas, D. L., 65
Timberlake, M., 247
Tittle, C. K., 6
Tolstoy, L., 330
Tucker, B., 194
Tuma, N. B., 18, 20, 21
Turner, J., 151, 166

United Automobile Workers, retirement plans of, 116
United Nations, 251
United States, retirement policies compared with other countries, 291–292
University of Michigan's Institute for Social Research, Survey Research Center of, 205
U.S. Bureau of Census, 225
U.S. Commission on Civil Rights, 195
U.S. Department of Commerce, 317, 326
U.S. Department of Labor, 113, 345
USSR Institute of Gerontology, 325, 328
USSR State Committee on Labor and Social Questions, 324

Valentei, D. I., 318
Vesting, as term, 189–190
Vinovskis, M. A., 2
Vollmer, M. H., 107

Waldman, E., 177
Weaver, C., 89, 90, 104
Weiner, A. I., 224
Weiss, J., 248, 253
Weiss, J. A., 288
Wentworth, E., 112
Wheaton, B., 79, 83
White, K. R., 64
Wilensky, H. L., 246, 249, 250, 296
Wiley, R. C., 63, 74, 83
Williamson, J. B., 266
Wills, H., 143
Wilson, K. L., 67
Wise, L. L., 5
Wohlwill, J. F., 2, 3, 4
Wolfbein, S. L., 115
Wright, E. O., 135
Wright, J. D., 90, 107

Xin Min Wan Bao, 305

Yuan, Jihui, 297, 305

Zeitzer, I., 296
Zelnik, M., 7, 14, 18
Zeng, S., 310
Zhong Guo Nong Min Bạo, 298

Research Annuals and Monographs in Series in
SOCIOLOGY

Research Annuals

Advances in Group Processes
Edited by Edward J. Lawler, *Department of Sociology, University of Iowa*

Advances in Health Economics and Health Services Research
Edited by Richard M. Scheffler, *School of Public Health, University of California, Berkeley.*
Associate Editor: Louis F. Rossiter, *Department of Health Administration, Medical College of Virginia, Virginia Commonwealth University*

Comparative Social Research
Edited by Richard F. Tomasson, *Department of Sociology, The University of New Mexico*

Current Perspectives in Social Theory
Edited by Scott G. McNall, *Department of Sociology, The University of Kansas*

Current Perspectives on Aging and the Life Cycle
Edited by Zena Smith Blau, *Department of Sociology, University of Houston*

Knowledge and Society
Edited by Henrika Kuklick, *Department of History, University of Pennsylvania* and Elizabeth Long, *Department of Sociology, Rice University*

Political Power and Social Theory
Edited by Maurice Zeitlin, *Department of Sociology, University of California, Los Angeles*

Research in Community and Mental Health
Edited by James R. Greenley, *Department of Psychiatry, University of Wisconsin Medical School*

Research in Economic Anthropology
Edited by Barry Isaac, *Department of Anthropology, University of Cincinnati*

Research in Human Capital and Development
Edited by Ismail Sirageldin, *Departments of Population Dynamics and Political Economy, The Johns Hopkins University*

Research in Law and Policy Studies
Edited by Stuart S. Nagel, *Department of Political Science, University of Illinois*

Research in Law, Deviance and Social Control
Edited by Steven Spitzer, *Department of Sociology, Suffolk University* and Andrew T. Scull, *Department of Sociology, University of California*

Research in Micropolitics
Edited by Samuel Long, *Psychology Department, Pace University, Pleasantville*

Research in Philosophy and Technology
Edited by Paul T. Durbin, *Philosophy Department and Center for Science and Culture, University of Delaware.* Review and Bibliography Editor: Carl Mitcham, *New York Polytechnic Institute*

Research in Politics and Society
Edited by Gwen Moore, *Department of Sociology and Anthropology, Russell Sage College*

Research in Political Sociology
Edited by Richard G. Braungart, *Department of Sociology, Syracuse University*

Research in Population Economics
Edited by T. Paul Schultz, *Department of Economics, Yale University* and Kenneth I Wolpin, *Department of Econmics, Ohio State University*

Research in Race and Ethnic Relations
Edited by Cora Bagley Marrett, *University Wisconsin-Madison* and Cheryl B. Leggon, *University of Chicago*

Research in Rural Sociology and Development
Edited by Harry K. Schwarzweller, *Department of Sociology, Michigan State University*

Research in Social Movements, Conflicts and Change
Edited by Louis Kriesberg, *Department of Sociology, Syracuse University*

Research in Social Policy: Critical, Historical and Contemporary Issues
Edited by John H. Stanfield, *Department of Sociology, Yale University*

Research in Social Problems and Public Policy
Edited by Michael Lewis, *Department of Sociology, University of Massachusettes* and JoAnn L. Miller, *Department of Sociology, Purdue University*

Research in Social Stratification and Mobility
Edited by Robert V. Robinson, *Department of Sociology, Indiana University*

Research in Sociology of Education and Socialization
Edited by Alan C. Kerckhoff, *Department of Sociology, Duke University*

Research in the Interweave of Social Roles
Edited by Helena Z. Lopata, *Center for Comparative Study of Social Roles, Loyola University, Chicago*

Research in the Sociology of Health Care
Edited by Julius Roth, *Department of Sociology, University of California, Davis*

Research in the Sociology of Organizations
Edited by Samuel B. Bacharach, *Department of Organizational Behavior, New York State School of Industrial and Labor Relations, Cornell Universitiy*

Research in the Sociology of Work
Edited by Ida Harper Simpson, *Department of Sociology, Duke University* and Richard L. Simpson, *Department of Sociology, University of North Carolina, Chapel Hill*

Research in Urban Policy
Edited by Terry Nichols Clark, *Comparative Study of Community Decision Making, University of Chicago*

Sociological Studies of Child Development
Edited by Peter and Patricia Adler, *Department of Sociology, University of Tulsa*

Studies in Communications
Edited by Thelma McCormack, *Department of Sociology, York University*

Studies in Symbolic Interaction
Edited by Norman K. Denzin, *Department of Sociology, University of Illinois*

Monographs in Series and Treatises

Contemporary Studies in Applied Behavioral Science
Series Editor: Louis A. Zurcher, *School of Social Work, University of Texas at Austin*

Contemporary Studies in Sociology
Editor in Chief: John Clark, *Department of Sociology, University of Minnesota*. Series Editors: Robert Althauser, *Department of Sociology, Indiana University*, John Kasarda, *Department of Sociology, University of North Carolina* and Clark McPhail, *Department of Sociology, University of Illinois*

Public Policy Studies - A Multi-Volume Treatise
General Editor: Stuart Nagel, *Department of Political Science, University of Illinois*

Monographs in Organizational Behavior and Industrial Relations
Edited by Samuel B. Bacharach, *Department of Organizational Behavior, New York State School of Industrial and Labor Relations, Cornell University*

Please inquire for detailed brochure on each series

JAI PRESS INC., 36 Sherwood Place, P.O. Box 1678
Greenwich, Connecticut 06836
Telephone: 203-661-7602   Cable Address: JAIPUBL